The Information Revolution in

This provocative new history of early modern Europe argues that changes in the generation, preservation and circulation of information, chiefly on newly available and affordable paper, constituted an 'information revolution'. In commerce, finance, statecraft, scholarly life, science, and communication, early modern Europeans were compelled to place a new premium on information management. These developments had a profound and transformative impact on European life. The huge expansion in paper records and the accompanying efforts to store, share, organize and taxonomize them are intertwined with many of the essential developments in the early modern period, including the rise of the state, the Print Revolution, the Scientific Revolution, and the Republic of Letters. Engaging with historical questions across many fields of human activity, Paul M. Dover interprets the historical significance of this "information revolution" for the present day, and suggests thought-provoking parallels with the informational challenges of the digital age.

Professor Paul M. Dover is Professor of History at Kennesaw State University. He has published widely in the political, diplomatic, and cultural history of late medieval and early modern Europe, and in the history of information. He is the author of *The Changing Face of the Past: An Introduction to Western Historiography*, and editor of *Secretaries and Statecraft in the Early Modern World*.

NEW APPROACHES TO EUROPEAN HISTORY

New Approaches to European History is an important textbook series, which provides concise but authoritative surveys of major themes and problems in European history since the Renaissance. Written at a level and length accessible to advanced school students and undergraduates, each book in the series addresses topics or themes that students of European history encounter daily: the series embraces both some of the more 'traditional' subjects of study and those cultural and social issues to which increasing numbers of school and college courses are devoted. A particular effort is made to consider the wider international implications of the subject under scrutiny.

To aid the student reader, scholarly apparatus and annotation is light, but each work has full supplementary bibliographies and notes for further reading: where appropriate, chronologies, maps, diagrams, and other illustrative material are also provided.

For a complete list of titles published in the series, please see: www.cambridge.org/newapproaches

The Information Revolution in Early Modern Europe

Paul M. Dover
Kennesaw State University

CAMBRIDGE
UNIVERSITY PRESS

CAMBRIDGE
UNIVERSITY PRESS

University Printing House, Cambridge CB2 8BS, United Kingdom

One Liberty Plaza, 20th Floor, New York, NY 10006, USA

477 Williamstown Road, Port Melbourne, VIC 3207, Australia

314–321, 3rd Floor, Plot 3, Splendor Forum, Jasola District Centre, New Delhi – 110025, India

103 Penang Road, #05–06/07, Visioncrest Commercial, Singapore 238467

Cambridge University Press is part of the University of Cambridge.

It furthers the University's mission by disseminating knowledge in the pursuit of education, learning, and research at the highest international levels of excellence.

www.cambridge.org
Information on this title: www.cambridge.org/9781107147539
DOI: 10.1017/9781316556177

© Paul M. Dover 2021

This publication is in copyright. Subject to statutory exception and to the provisions of relevant collective licensing agreements, no reproduction of any part may take place without the written permission of Cambridge University Press.

First published 2021

Printed in the United Kingdom by TJ Books Limited, Padstow Cornwall

A catalogue record for this publication is available from the British Library.

Library of Congress Cataloging-in-Publication Data
Names: Dover, Paul M., author.
Title: The information revolution in early modern Europe / Paul M. Dover, Kennesaw State University, Georgia.
Description: Cambridge, United Kingdom ; New York, NY : Cambridge University Press, 2021. | Series: New approaches to European history | Includes bibliographical references and index.
Identifiers: LCCN 2021024748 (print) | LCCN 2021024749 (ebook) | ISBN 9781107147539 (hardback) | ISBN 9781316556177 (ebook)
Subjects: LCSH: Information science – Europe – History. | Papermaking – Europe – History. | Information organization – Europe – History. | Information resources management – Europe – History. | Written communication – Europe – History. | Printing – Europe – History. | Europe – Intellectual life. | BISAC: HISTORY / Europe / General | HISTORY / Europe / General
Classification: LCC Z665.2.E85 D68 2021 (print) | LCC Z665.2.E85 (ebook) | DDC 020.94–dc23
LC record available at https://lccn.loc.gov/2021024748
LC ebook record available at https://lccn.loc.gov/2021024749

ISBN 978-1-107-14753-9 Hardback
ISBN 978-1-316-60203-4 Paperback

Cambridge University Press has no responsibility for the persistence or accuracy of URLs for external or third-party internet websites referred to in this publication and does not guarantee that any content on such websites is, or will remain, accurate or appropriate.

To my parents

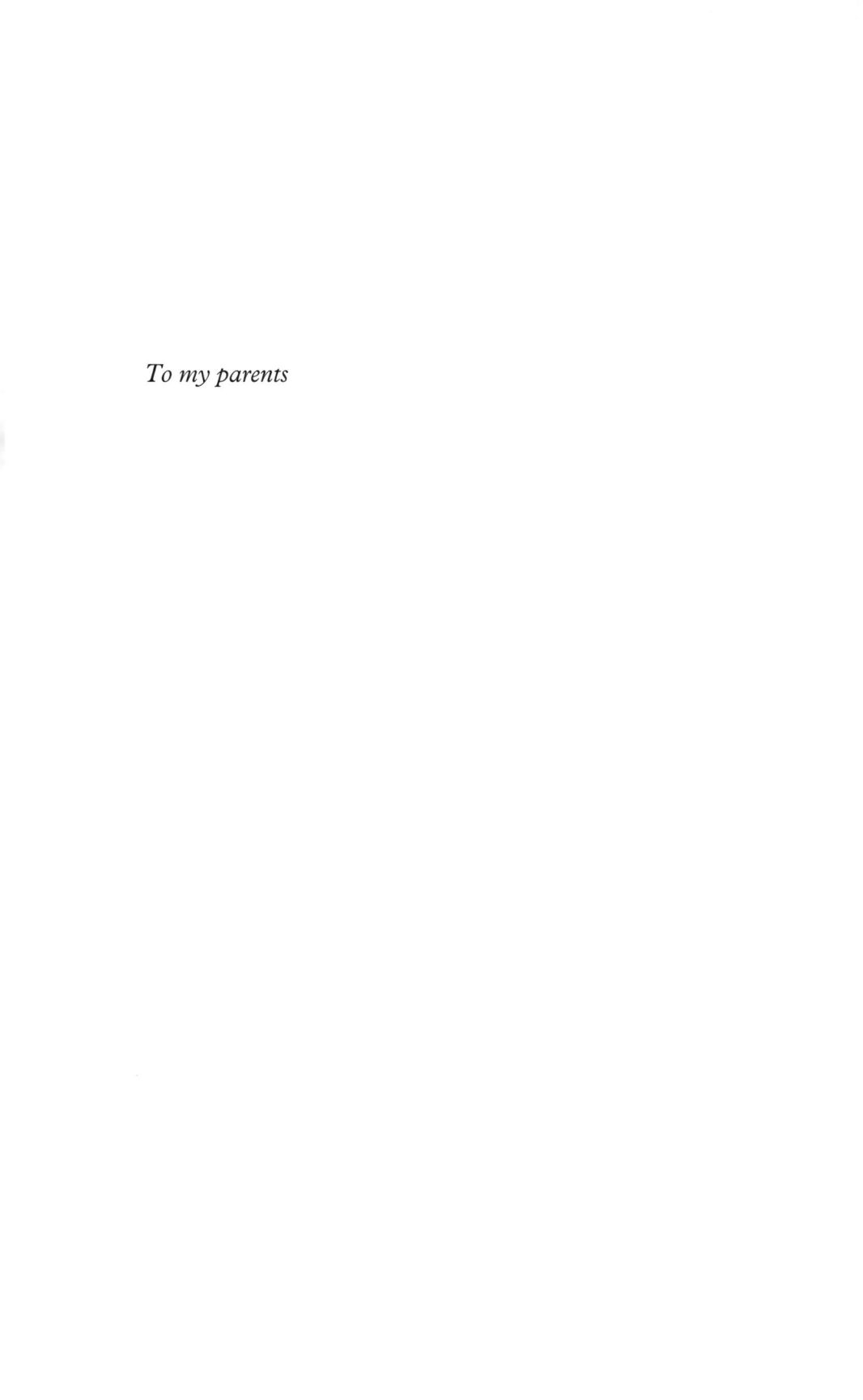

Contents

	List of Figures	*page* viii
	Acknowledgments	x
1	Introduction: Worlds of Paper	1
2	European Paper	38
3	"Ink-Stained Fingers": The Information of Commerce and Finance	56
4	The Paper of Politics and the Politics of Paper	91
5	Revolutionary Print	149
6	The Book of Nature and the Books of Man	191
7	Writing Others and the Self	227
8	Conclusion: Information Revolutions, Past and Present	262
	Bibliography	284
	Index	331

Figures

2.1 From the very beginning of indigenous European manufacture, paper was made of rags. *Stamping Mill for Pulverising Rags* – Georg Andreas Boeckler, Theatrum Macinarum novum etc., (Cologne, 1662) Schlosser Collection of Paper Making, New York Public Library (Getty Images). *page* 47

3.1 In the seventeenth century, Amsterdam became one of Europe's most important centers for the exchange of financial and commercial information. Emmanuel de Witte, *Courtyard of the Exchange in Amsterdam* (1653), Museum Boijmans van Beuningen, Rotterdam (Getty Images). 73

4.1 Early modern archives filled up with registers of copied outgoing letters, such as this one from the chancery of the Marquis of Mantua in December 1479. Archivio di Stato di Mantova, Archivio Gonzaga, *Copialettere*, B.2896, L.95, 30v (reproduced with permission of the Archive). 113

4.2 Instruction for the *Relaciones geograficas* (1577) ordered by Philip II to gather information about New Spain. Benson Latin American Collection, Library of the University of Texas-Austin (reproduced with permission of the Library). 125

4.3 Colbert, looking pleased with his papers. Claude Lefèbvre, *Jean Baptiste Colbert* (1666). Museum of the History of France, Versailles (Getty Images). 143

5.1 Much of the work of the earliest printing presses was dedicated to the production of cheap, high-volume items. Especially lucrative was the printing of indulgences, like this one printed by Johannes Gutenberg in 1455 (Getty Images). 155

5.2 Much early printed material was designed to be written on, like this papal election ballot. *Caeremoniale continens ritus electionis Romani Pontificis* (Rome, 1667). Folger Shakespeare Library, Washington, DC, 176214.2 (reproduced with permission of the Folger). 184

List of Figures

5.3 Almanacs were printed in vast numbers, but rarely survive. Daniel Browne, *A new almanacke and prognostication, for the yeare of our Lord God 1628* (London, 1628). Folger Shakespeare Library, Washington, DC, STC 421 (reproduced with permission of the Folger). 186
6.1 Observation, description, depiction. Ulisse Aldrovandi epitomized the new zeal to capture the expansiveness of the natural world, here in his section on beetles in *De animalibus insectis libri septem* (Bologna, 1605). (Alamy). 206
6.2 The accumulation of particulars. *Ferrante Imperato and his son Francesco showing visitors their cabinet of curiosities*. Engraving from the *Dell'historia naturale* (Naples, 1599). (Getty Images). 207
6.3 Commonplacing politics. The page on "tyranny" from John Milton's commonplace book, begun 1608, British Library Add MS 36353 (Getty Images). 216
7.1 All the news that's fit to write: the Fugger banking family in Augsburg systematically amalgamated the latest news. A *Fuggerzeitung* from August 1568. National Library of Austria (reproduced with permission of the Library). 251
7.2 The emerging early modern culture of news depended on the literate reading to the illiterate and semi-literate. Adriaen van Ostade, *Reading the News at the Weavers' Cottage* (1673). Metropolitan Museum of Art, New York City (Getty Images). 258
8.1 Heinrich Bullinger (1504–75) generated multiple paper flows in his roles as pastor, theologian, author, news aggregator, and international advocate for Reformed Christianity. Jacob Verheiden, *Imagines et elogia praestantium aliquot theologorum* ... (The Hague, 1725) (Getty Images). 273
8.2 Riverby Bookstore, Fredericksburg, Virginia. 282

Acknowledgments

One of the themes of this book is the reality of information overload, and, recognizing my incapacity to master it all, I am acutely aware of how I have benefitted from the assistance and insights of others. Jacob Soll, Hamish Scott, Isabella Lazzarini, Brian Maxson, Ann Blair, Tamara Livingston, Gerrit Voogt, and Randy Patton all read and commented on drafts of chapters. I am also grateful to the anonymous reader at Cambridge University Press. Ann Blair, who perhaps knows more about early modern information than anyone else, has been a repeated source of knowledge and encouragement. I also wish to thank Geoffrey Parker, Anthony Grafton, Michael Levin, Randolph Head, Filippo De Vivo, Meghan Williams, and Suzanne Sutherland, for conversations and advice that have helped shape the book. I have appreciated the opportunities afforded to me over the last several years to present ideas and research related to the book at the University of Glasgow, the University of Toronto, Catholic University in Washington, the University of Groningen, and the Clark Library at UCLA.

Much of the initial research for this book took place at the Folger Shakespeare Library in Washington, DC, where I was a long-term National Endowment for the Humanities Fellow. The Folger was, for a year, my personal Shangri-La, replete with rich scholarly resources and fascinating people. At the Folger, I am indebted to Michael Whitmore, Kathleen Lynch, Caroline Duroselle-Melish, and especially to the late Betsy Walsh and her wonderful staff in the reading room. The scholarly community at the Folger was a merry band of brothers and sisters, who enriched my time in Washington with their learning, advice, and camaraderie. I am thinking particularly of Christopher Highley, Newton Key, Emma Depledge, Claire Bowditch, Elaine Hobby, John Hunt, Alex Walsham, and Lucy Nicholas. "[W]here there is true friendship, there needs none." (*Timon of Athens* I.2). Further support for the book was provided by my home institution, Kennesaw State University, in the form of summer stipends and a semester-long sabbatical from the Center for Excellence in Teaching and Learning in 2018. I also wish to thank Liz

Friend-Smith and Melissa Ward at Cambridge University Press for their guidance, their encouragement, and (especially) their patience in shepherding this project, including during the particularly challenging environment created by the Covid-19 pandemic.

Finally, my biggest source of encouragement during the years I was working on this book has been my parents, Carol and Phil. Academics themselves, but in other fields, they were able to appreciate the project but also ask the questions that might not occur to me within my disciplinary bubble, and reminded me to express my ideas in a fashion accessible to the non-specialist. I hope I have succeeded in doing that. I am incredibly lucky that they provided for their son a life full of books, debate, and love. I dedicate this book to them, as a meager parcel of the gratitude I feel for their many decades of affection, support, and abiding belief. Thanks, Mum and Dad.

1 Introduction
Worlds of Paper

"The fear of obliteration obsessed the societies of early modern Europe," Roger Chartier writes in *Inscription and Erasure*. "To quell their anxiety, they preserved in writing traces of the past, remembrances of the dead, the glory of the living, and texts of all kinds that were not supposed to disappear."[1] The efforts they made to confront this anxiety, however, paradoxically generated a new, related anxiety: the urge to preserve, record, and ward off obliteration frequently led to an unmanageable accumulation of texts, records, and ephemera of wildly varying utility and quality. Most of this was paper, which was not a new technology in early modern Europe but one whose use proliferated and diversified in these centuries. Paper, as never before, became the transactional medium; the repository of personal, communal, and institutional memory; the avenue of communication; the lifeblood of bureaucracies; and the foundation and residue of learning. Early modern Europeans, whether or not they sought to, and whether or not they were pleased with or trusted the new reality, put paper inscribed with text at the center of their lives.

Information might not be knowledge, nor is it wisdom, yet its acquisition and preservation are essential because it might yield *some* knowledge, and perhaps *some* wisdom. Early modern Europe was the locus of informational transition and adjustment, and, as we shall see, the associated disruptions to European society were significant. Lorraine Daston and Katherine Park have made the suggestion that if early modern Europeans had been asked to name their era, they would have labeled it *nova aetas*, with the appearance of a "gusher of novelty."[2] Perhaps because the period is widely regarded as liminal, historians have located a number of revolutions in early modern Europe. A partial list would include the "Military

---

[1] Roger Chartier, *Inscription and Erasure: Literature and Written Culture from the Eleventh to the Eighteenth Century*. Trans. by Arthur Goldhammer (Philadelphia: University of Pennsylvania Press, 2007), vii.
[2] Katherine Park and Lorraine Daston, "Introduction: the Age of the New." In Park and Daston, eds., *The Cambridge History of Science*, Vol. 3: *Early Modern Science* (Cambridge: Cambridge University Press, 2006), 6.

Revolution," the "Print Revolution," the "Correspondence Revolution," the "Scientific Revolution," and the "Communications Revolution."[3] Historians of early modern Europe have pointed to at least three main areas of disruption in European knowledge: the opening up of new worlds in the voyages of reconnaissance and discovery, the rediscovery and embrace of ancient texts, and the upheavals associated with the printing press. Others have pointed to "Knowledge Revolutions," emphasizing, again, the printing press and paradigm shifts in medicine and astronomy wrought by empirical observation and new techniques of observation.[4] There is a lot going on here.

In this book, I argue that information is a central concern in all these various transformations. In particular, there was a new emphasis on information management. Europeans were faced with what, for them, were untamable amounts of data, without the benefits of complex machines, digital files, and Boolean searches. New efforts had to be devised and undertaken to store and categorize both the information itself and the paper that contained it. More and more time was dedicated to what we would call "paperwork," which moved to the center of European life: in the everyday rhythms of commerce, in the working of the state, in the lives of scholars and virtuoso naturalists, in distance-busting communication services, even in the quotidian rhythms of burghers and artisans.

Information begat more information and paper more paper. Ann Blair has undertaken groundbreaking work showing how early modern scholars exhibited what she calls "info-lust," forcing them to develop a range of publications, attitudes, and reading and research practices to cope with the resulting heaps of data.[5] They were faced with a number of recurring questions regarding the information they accumulated: how to store it? How to categorize it? How to distill it? How to make it retrievable? I believe that many of Blair's insights into the history of the book and scholarly life can be extended to European society as a whole. The pressures incidental to the new abundance of books have analogs elsewhere: in the growth of the state and the attendant paperwork, in the

---

[3] Of course, the label of revolution was given to these episodes only much later by historians. Unlike the political American and French Revolutions, contemporaries did not use this terminology. It was only in 1949, for example, that Herbert Butterfield, clearly influenced by the dizzying changes in science and technology in his own day (and despite his famous resistance to Whiggish teleologies), started to use the expression "Scientific Revolution." The "Information Revolution" that is the subject of this book is likewise a reading of the past that is refracted through a particular contemporary moment.
[4] Anja-Silvia Goeing, *Storing, Archiving, Organizing. The Changing Dynamics of Scholarly Information Management in Post-Reformation Zurich* (Leiden: Brill, 2017), 3.
[5] Ann Blair and Peter Stallybrass, "Mediating information 1450–1800." In Clifford Siskin and William Warner, eds., *This is Enlightenment* (Chicago: University of Chicago Press, 2010), 139–163.

proliferation of empirical observation in natural philosophy, in the unprecedented circulation of news and correspondence, and in the general commitment to record-keeping and documentary preservation embraced by all sorts of early modern institutions. In all of these cases, practitioners were compelled to develop and adapt new means of information management.

Many of the emerging habits and practices of the early modern period that have been explored in contexts such as humanism, New World exploration, diplomacy, state-building, accounting, and the new science, can be regarded as features of broader, universal transformations related to the management of information. A non-exhaustive list might include an empirical sensibility; attention to particulars; quantification; the sharing of timely news and data across distances; the commitment to recording ideas, observations, and events in writing on paper (and then preserving them); a zeal for organizing and taxonomizing these records; and the creation of tools to navigate it all. At the core of these practical and epistemological concerns, and linking them all together, was the management of unprecedented amounts of information. A bundle of knowledge practices, technologies, and sensibilities emerged in order to face these challenges, deployed along with many reams of paper, in early modern scholarly life, natural philosophy, astronomy, medicine, law, diplomacy, business and finance, and in private lives.

The responses to the accumulation of information on paper were chiefly processes on paper. As Markus Friedrich has put it: "in early modern Europe, control of knowledge not only meant control of paper, but also control by paper."[6] In general, what early modern Europeans found themselves in need of, and in many areas of European society sought to construct, was a filter, an effective strainer for the data that they generated. It is a challenge familiar to us in an age when a great premium is placed on search engines, social media applications and other information-winnowing technologies. In comparison to ours, of course, this was an information-poor age, and the production of information remained comparatively slow. Nonetheless, early modern Europeans committed unprecedented time, money, and personnel to sorting through the information before them.

The chief focus of this book, therefore, is information management, most of which involved the handling of paper. This was not a new concern, but early modern Europe was an information society in a way that

---

[6] Markus Friedrich, "How to make an archival inventory in early modern Europe: carrying documents, gluing paper and transforming archival chaos into well-ordered knowledge." *Manuscript Cultures*, 10.10 (2017), 160–173 (here 165).

the Middle Ages never were. Europe's long acquaintance and flirtation with paper now became a love match. Like many such attachments, it occasioned pain, frustration, confusion, and boredom, as well as joys and fulfilment. Among other things, the underlying story of the pages that follow is the deepening and diversifying relationship of Europeans with their paper, along with the opportunities, challenges, and vexation this marriage incurred. The nature of early modern political, social, and cultural practices shaped the sorts of paper instrument produced, but the widespread use of paper shaped those practices as well. It changed the exercise of political power, the way in which the pursuit of knowledge was conducted, and the vectors by which Europeans kept in touch with one another. I find it useful to think of the informational transformations of early modern Europe as examples of what evolutionary biologists describe as "coevolution." The changing contours of European society determined the uses to which paper was directed, but paper as a technology actively shaped that society as well. So while Europe domesticated paper, as in other instances of domestication by humankind, as when the wolf became the dog and Einkorn became domesticated wheat, humans and the non-human actor evolved in conjunction with each other.[7] Thus, Europeans deployed paper to address existing political, social, and cultural demands, using it for an expanding array of purposes, but at the same time the availability and wider use of paper created new assumptions and corresponding practices. We are accustomed to speaking of paper as a blank sheet, an empty receptacle of ink and ideas, and, indeed, the bare receptiveness of paper was a common trope in early modern Europe. The history of this period, however, is deeply suggestive that paper was in fact not a passive substance, but a motive participant in the changes that it brought about. Helen Smith has highlighted the comments of the English Baptist minister Christopher Blackwood, who in 1654 compared writing on blank paper with God writing on the will of a Christian convert: "We will when we will, but God makes us for to will . . . As my paper whereon I write, receives the ink passively, and brings

---

[7] The concept of species evolving in tandem can be seen as early as Charles Darwin's *Fertilisation of Orchids*, published in 1862. A good treatment of coevolution in nature is John Thompson, *The Coevolutionary Process* (Chicago: University of Chicago Press, 1994). For a brief discussion of coevolution between dogs and humans as a process of "mutual domestication," see Carl Safina, *Beyond Words. What Animals Think and Feel* (New York: Henry Holt, 2015), 229–239.

Coevolution has been recently located in the study of cosmology and computer technology (where hardware and software are seen to develop synchronically), and its application to social processes seems to me tenable. Particularly suggestive in this regard is Geerat Vermeij, *The Evolutionary World: How Adaptation Explains Everything from Seashells to Civilization* (New York: Thomas Dunne, 2010).

nothing of its own to the writing." But Blackwood complicates matters with a subsequent statement: "being written upon, it becomes an instrument with my writing: and as I write more and more, so it still cooperates with me, though in itself there be no natural beginning of the writing."[8] In this sense, then, paper collaborates and cooperates with the writer.

It is not that paper itself has any power – it only wields effective power when it acts in conjunction with a constellation of social relations.[9] Paper is a material substrate, but as Christopher Hall pithily puts it: "Materials are materials because inventive people find ingenious things to do with them."[10] In many ways, we witness, in the early modern period, the advent of the "age of paper" in the West, one which, we are told, is currently coming to an end amid sequences of ones and zeroes. If there was an early modern Information Revolution, paper was its material embodiment, its essential item of hardware.

1.1 Early Modern Information

Where did the "information age" begin? With the digital processor? With the computer? With television? With the telegraph and telephone? The best answer is that the information age neither began, nor will it end, because every age is an age of information. Information is, as Daniel Headrick has put it, "as old as humankind."[11] It has always been present in human communities. Martyn Lyons insists that every society since ancient Egypt has been an "information society ... in the sense that those who control and restrict access to knowledge in any society thereby control a key component of power."[12]

Nonetheless, important ruptures and departures in information have occurred. Michael Hobart and Zachary Schiffman, for example, have demarcated three ages of information in the history of Western society. The first of these is the classical information age. The authors believe one can only speak of information with the advent of literacy, for written language supplied the degree of abstraction necessary to create mental objects separate from experience. The alphabet allowed greater degrees of

---

[8] Quoted in Helen Smith, "A unique instance of art": the proliferating surfaces of early modern paper." *Journal of the Northern Renaissance*, 8 (2017) n.p.
[9] Especially germane on this point is Arndt Brendecke, *The Empirical Empire. Spanish Colonial Rule and the Politics of Knowledge* (Berlin: De Gruyter Oldenbourg, 2016).
[10] Christopher Hall, *Materials. A Very Short Introduction* (Oxford: Oxford University Press, 2014), xiii.
[11] Daniel Headrick, *When Information Came of Age. Technologies of Knowledge in the Age of Reason and Revolution, 1700–1850* (Oxford: Oxford University Press, 2000), 8.
[12] Martyn Lyons, *A History of Reading and Writing in the Western World* (Basingstoke: Palgrave Macmillan, 2010), 1.

abstraction and abetted a classifying mindset resulting in new taxonomies of knowledge. This age extended roughly until the arrival of the printing press, and the abundance of printed books, which led to a surfeit of information and to what the authors call a "rupture of classification," which overwhelmed existing categories. The most important responses were Cartesian analysis and frames of reference. Numeracy and quantification were hallmarks of the early modern adaptation to a world replete with unprecedented volumes of data. Finally, there is the contemporary age of information, which has seen the attenuation of the connections between digital symbols and the world they represented. Literacy, numeracy, and digitization demarcate three ages, which demonstrate an increasing propensity to draw further away from the world in encoding reality, to the point now that much of what we experience has been reduced to a vast sequence of ones and zeroes. Hobart and Schiffman suggest that the three ages now overlap with one another, as the digital age has not lessened the importance of literacy and numeracy.[13]

Alex Wright has undertaken similar segmentation of human history into information ages. Wright, a former librarian and now a self-described "information architect" (if ever there was a job description suited for our age, that is it), places his focus on the repeated episodes across the millennia when humankind has struggled with information overload.[14] Wright's emphasis is on the cataloging and categorization of information such as we see in the "memory theater" of Giulio Camillo (1480–1544), the *Encyclopédie* of Denis Diderot (1713–1784), and the nineteenth-century Dewey Decimal System for organizing library holdings. Unlike Hobart and Schiffman, Wright believes that writing and the alphabet were not necessary to have information: "the building blocks of complex information systems were in place long before the first scribe set stylus to clay."[15] He even identifies an "ice age information explosion," which he believes brought humankind in its hunting-gathering stage to the brink of literacy. Wright sees the struggle to stay on top of the information we produce as a distinctive feature of human society. Describing the transformations of the early modern period, Wright, following the work of Frances Yates, emphasizes the abandonment of the medieval *ars memoria* amid the abundance of printed books. The hero of the piece for Wright is the English polymath Francis Bacon (1561–1626), who abandoned the art of memory in which he had been trained in favor of an empiricism that

---

[13] Michael Hobart and Zachary Schiffman, *Information Ages: Literacy, Numeracy and the Computer Revolution* (Baltimore, MD: Johns Hopkins University Press, 1998).
[14] Alex Wright, *Glut: Mastering Information through the Ages* (Washington, DC: Joseph Henry Press, 2007).
[15] Wright, *Glut*, 48.

rested on observation and inductive reasoning. Bacon recognized the continued importance of memory, but also emphasized practical tools, such as commonplacing, for the retrieval of particulars gleaned through systematic study and observation. These observed phenomena and "facts" were the essential building blocks of knowledge, rather than the forms and categories inherited from the Middle Ages and largely shaped by Aristotle's speciation.

Every society, Robert Darnton stresses, develops its own means and methods of hunting for and gathering information.[16] He identifies four essential changes in information processing in the history of humankind since it gained the ability to speak. Darnton points first to the development of early forms of writing in about 4000 BCE, and the emergence of alphabets about 3,000 years later. Then came the invention of the codex in late antiquity, which transformed the practice of reading and greatly simplified cross-referencing. The third break came with printing, with its impact on the availability of texts and the size of the reading public. Finally, we come to the ongoing Digital Revolution and emergence of electronic communication. One cannot help but notice the accelerating pace of change: several thousand years between the first writing and the codex; a little less than a millennium between the codex and movable type; half a millennium between Gutenberg and the World Wide Web; and then less than half a decade between the Internet and the algorithmic search engines of Google.

Amid this change, however, Darnton chooses to focus on continuity across the millennia of information processing. Each epoch was an age of information, and a unifying feature of all of them was the inherent instability of information. As each transformation introduced more information to digest and categorize, it also produced greater volumes of uncertain information and downright misinformation. Thus, in an age where we find ourselves lamenting internet hoaxes, fake news, gossipy blogs, and essays cut and pasted from termpaper.com, we might do well to realize that information has never really been stable. Perhaps textual stability is a chimera – writing, the codex, the printed book, and the Internet: all of these means of presenting information have been shifting, unreliable, and unstable.

All three of these efforts to periodize the history of information identify the early modern period, and especially the printing press, as transformative. The changes wrought by print were profound, greatly expanding the

---

[16] Robert Darnton, 1999 presidential address to the American Historical Association, January 5, 2000: "An Early Information Society: News and the Media in Eighteenth-Century Paris" (www.historians.org/about-aha-and-membership/aha-history-and-archives/presidential-addresses/robert-darnton).

volume and range of learning and information available to an unprecedented array of people, but this focus on books and typography is unduly narrow. Most of the fundamental transitions related to information generation, exchange, and management were only tangentially related to print. Even without Gutenberg's invention, there would have been an early modern Information Revolution. We must not reduce the period to an "age of print," a label that both exaggerates the role of print and serves to exclude the non-printed forms that most information continued to assume. Acknowledging the pervasive (and steadily broadening) impact of print need not mean totalizing its influence.

Today, we are accustomed to speaking of "information" in a detached, antiseptic fashion, treating it as a bland, featureless substance. It is quantifiable, transferable, and shorn of any of the subjective specificities of its content. We speak of information in the abstract, as a "thing" that can be disassociated from the social and cultural circumstances of its creation. At the same time, we speak of "pieces" of information, discrete packets that can exist independent of the undifferentiated mass. The Web, for example, is a fathomless reservoir of information, but we also wade into it "looking for information," specific items consonant with our needs and required for the establishment of knowledge.

In early modern language, the term "information" rarely had this double connotation – while it might be employed to describe discrete packets of information, it did not describe information in the abstract. While the story of early modern information involved progressive levels of abstraction, as we shall see, information remained associated with tangible things: books, letters, notebooks, files, registers, accounts, as well as speeches, sermons, and pronouncements.

The word *informatio* was typically employed to describe a process of shaping or forming, and often carried didactic connotations, in the sense that it involved "in-forming" (or teaching) someone something that they did not already know. It was something gathered, collated, and then "informed" for the recipient: the delivery of information served to help knowledge take "form" within the recipient.[17] We still capture some of this connotation when we declare that we share something, "for your

---

[17] One recurring version of this in early modern parlance was the work that the Holy Spirit did in the "information" of a Christian believer, which we see in titles such as William Shewen, *The true Christian's faith and experience briefly declared ... written for the confirmation, and consolation of the one, and for the information in order to the restoration and salvation of the other* (London, 1675) and John Alcock, *Plains truths of divinity. Collected out of the sacred Scriptures, & set forth by way of question and answer the best way conceived for the information of the judgment of the Christian reader* (London, 1647).

information," with a specific communicative intent to impart on the recipient or listener.

In the late Middle Ages, legal and inquisitorial bodies referred to *informatio* in relation to the discovery and collection of information for their cases. The word was employed to characterize the empirical facts discovered and introduced in the proceedings, which could then be processed, stored, and referenced subsequently, regardless of the outcome of the case. In late medieval parlance, it was frequently used to describe a charge placed with a magistrate's court. In the church, *informatio* appeared in relation to the data gathered during the examination of candidates for ordination or higher ecclesiastical office – again in the sense of empirical information gathered with particular ends in mind. Already implicit in these various uses are features of the empirical process that we now associate with information. There are facts to be sought out and gathered for specific ends, although they may not end up being used for those purposes. These facts were also, importantly, subject to recording, nearly always through documentation, to memorialize their discovery and make them available for consequent consultation.

Late medieval and early modern Europeans also regularly spoke and wrote in the abstract about "being informed." It often meant being in receipt of the empirically gathered facts. Thus in romance languages, *informarse* and *s'informer* mean to become aware of knowledge of this kind. One "informed oneself" of the relevant news by reading or speaking with others. An early modern diplomat who delivered novel facts was an "informant." Being "informed" might be among the reasons for taking a legal or political action – it was a form of legitimization, the obverse of ignorance. A decision might be delayed until one could become "well informed" or "fully informed" of the requisite facts. One became "informed" by the acquisition of intelligence, often supplied by others in the know. Information was not recognized as knowledge until a figure or body of authority recognized it as such – it had to receive that *imprimatur*. In April 1535, King Charles I issued to a viceroy in New Spain royal instructions which illustrate how informing oneself might mean gathering the available facts:

First of all, and above all else, inform yourself, as soon as you have arrived and are beginning to understand something of the affairs of the country ... I, after seeing your information and opinion, can decree what is appropriate ... Take care that Mexico City and all other cities and settlements in the entire province are visited ... Inform yourself ... inform yourself ... inform yourself.[18]

---

[18] Arndt Brendecke, *The Empirical Empire*, 144.

"Informations" were pieces of news, or particular facts, distinct extracts from books or letters, or experimental data.[19] They were gathered as part of the overall procedure. The Anglo-Irish naturalist Robert Boyle (1627–1691), for example, spoke of "the ways of information" in the study of nature, but information did not exist in inchoate reservoirs that could be consulted at any time. Its meaning derived from the specific contours of its content and the identity of its source.

Early modern Europeans did, however, regularly describe and complain about the accumulation of huge amounts of news, particulars, and numbers, almost always rendered on paper. The great expansion of the role of paper-borne text, both manuscript and print, is the chief informational transformation of the early modern period. The accumulation of information as particulars, which Europeans struggled to store, sort, categorize, and differentiate, over time caused Europeans to think of "information" as an abstract concept.

I am aware of the dangers implicit in writing a book about an "Information Revolution" in early modern Europe when contemporaries never described their circumstances in those terms. No one spoke of being witness to an "Information Revolution" during these centuries. The terms "information" and "revolution" were rarely used in isolation, let alone in conjunction with one another. But it is also the case that natural philosophers of the age did not speak of a Scientific Revolution – it was Herbert Butterfield who first employed the term in the 1950s. No one spoke of the French Revolution or the American Revolution while in the midst of them, either, although few historians would shy away from describing those events as such. It is my purpose to achieve an understanding of this period *in* our present, while remaining faithful to those who lived through it.

The temptation to engage in anachronism is always there when locating referents in the past that track with current concerns. Comparisons of early printshops with 1980s dot-com start-ups and early medieval Irish monastic scribes working in isolation with bloggers in their pyjamas, or indeed televisions with the Elizabethan theater and Habsburg address bureaus with Google (all of which are analogs that I have encountered), are provocative but problematic history. Many early modern Europeans experienced their version of information overload, but they simply could not have conceived of something akin to the World Wide Web.

But there is also nothing wrong with reading the past in light of current concerns. As Benedetto Croce once remarked: "every true history is

---

[19] Unlike Romance languages and German, English does not use "information" in the plural.

contemporary history ... The past does not live otherwise than in the present, resolved and transformed in the present."[20] The historian must always mediate between the past and present, employing the language of the present that serves to make the past legible, even when it is not technically the language of the past. Humanist scholars of the Renaissance contended that, in order to gain an understanding of the past, it was necessary to acknowledge the effective distance between themselves and the past they sought to fathom. There are degrees of anachronism, and the vigilant use of terminology that was largely absent among the time and subjects in question does not to me seem to come close to crippling the case we wish to make.[21]

Thus, we can speak of information, and an "Information Revolution," in the early modern period with a careful confidence, and without embarrassment that our historical vision is unduly shaped by present concerns. Perhaps we now need to speak of an "informational turn" in early modern studies, one made in the awareness of our own current informational challenges. It is inescapable really, and in many cases the resonances between past and present can be enlightening. Historians are always having to navigate the Scylla and Charybdis of similarity and difference, and should recognize that pointing out echoes and resonances does not invariably mean we end up dashed on the rocks. History does not repeat itself, but, as Mark Twain may or may not have said, it does rhyme.[22] Or at least paraphrase itself.

1.2   Learning to Trust the Written

The Middle Ages betrayed a widely held and profound mistrust of information that arrived in written form. There was a long-standing association, centuries old, between the veracity of information and the reputation of the person uttering it. Written information was necessarily

---

[20] Benedetto Croce, *History, its Theory and Practice*. Trans. by Douglas Ainslie (New York: Harcourt Brace, 1921), 12, 91.
[21] An interesting consideration of anachronism in one area of study that is especially vulnerable to it, the history of science, is Nick Jardine, "Uses and abuses of anachronism in the history of the sciences." *History of Science*, 38 (2000), 251–270.
[22] Though this expression is often attributed to Twain (and it sounds like something he would say), there is no direct evidence that he ever uttered the words. The closest I have found to it in the published works of Twain is "It is not worthwhile to try to keep history from repeating itself, for man's character will always make the preventing of the repetitions impossible," the spirit of which is somewhat different. Elsewhere, he wrote that "history repeats itself; whatever has been the rule in history may be depended upon to remain the rule," which offers a considerably more deterministic view of history. Both of these are in Bernard DeVoto, ed., *Mark Twain in Eruption. Hitherto Unpublished Pages about Men and Events* (New York: Harper, 1940), 2, 66–67.

abstracted from its creator, and the physical connection with the teller was placed in jeopardy. This calculus shifted in the early modern period, as Europeans largely followed a "trajectory of distrust to trust in written records." Written records gradually came to be regarded as both effecting an act in the present and then confirming in the future that the transaction had indeed occurred. Trust in written records in this period was rooted in a twin assessment of reliability and authenticity. Were they what they purported to be, and did they tell the truth?[23]

Mary Carruthers, in her seminal book on the arts of memory in medieval Europe, argued that medieval culture was "fundamentally memorial, to the same profound degree that modern culture in the West is documentary."[24] This emphasis on memory was rooted in the largely oral intellectual culture of the Middle Ages, one in which books were relatively rare and did not circulate widely. This stark bifurcation is reminiscent of the one drawn by Walter Ong between a medieval image-based *ars memoria* rooted in a fundamentally oral culture and a new system of knowledge that depended on words written or (especially for Ong) printed on a page. In his work on Ramus and rhetoric, Ong described the sixteenth century as one of transition, from one "cognitive style" to another. The Middle Ages, according to Ong, were aurally attuned and marginally literate, as opposed to the modern outlook, which was visual and text-centered.[25] Ong identified the printing press as the chief reason for a shift away from memory systems rooted in images, to one that was dependent on inscriptions on the printed page, which itself became the spatialized locus of memory. Ong's outlook helped shape that of Marshall McLuhan, whose notion of a "typographic man" is even more dependent on the printing press. There is no doubt that the availability of printed books and their circulation outside of the narrow confines of medieval repositories meant that book knowledge was more readily at hand, and there was less urgency to commit it to memory. But the visions of Ong and McLuhan are too tightly focused on the novelty of the printing press. Lucien Febvre perceives a broader transformation, located in the early modern centuries, from an "age of the ear" to an "age of the eye," indicating a new emphasis on textual transmission in information exchange.[26]

---

[23] Heather MacNeil, *Trusting Records: Legal, Historical and Diplomatic Perspectives* (Dordrecht: Kluwer Academic Publishers, 2000), 1.
[24] Mary Carruthers, *The Book of Memory: a Study of Memory in Medieval Culture*, 2nd ed. (Cambridge: Cambridge University Press, 2008), 9.
[25] Walter Ong, *Ramus, Method and the Decay of Dialogue* (Chicago: University of Chicago Press, 1958).
[26] Lucien Febvre, *The Problem of Unbelief in the Sixteenth Century* (Cambridge, MA: Harvard University Press, 1982).

We should be careful not to take the stark outlines of this transition from medieval to early modern too far. European societies before the fifteenth century did privilege written instruments. There was an alliance between orality and writing, one in which writing replicated, but rarely replaced, oral expression and information. Recent work on the written culture of the early and high Middle Ages has convincingly shown that there was much greater circulation of written material and that much more of this documentation was produced by, and circulated among, the laity than previously assumed.[27] The participation of the laity has been obscured by at least two features of the surviving documentary record. First, nearly all of the lay documents have disappeared, without the continuity in institutions and repositories that might have ensured their survival. Second, many of the records that testify to lay use actually survive in ecclesiastical and monastic libraries, their survival mediated by the interests of those institutions. Ecclesiastical archives were regarded as secure depositories for the secular records of landowners, plaintiffs, or other laypeople dealing in documents. A great many family documents, for example, ended up in monastic archives.[28] Michael Clanchy, in a highly influential book, has identified the eleventh and twelfth centuries as a period that saw essential shifts in England toward a society that externalized memory in the written record, a movement from orality to literacy.[29] English monarchical government post-Norman conquest was one that made the production of written documents a regular, if not daily, operation and a marker of the uniform and impersonal authority of the state. Brian Stock has identified similar, contemporary, shifts on the continent, where the rise of secular documentation effected the emergence of government rooted in writing, what Stock labels "the document nation."[30] Writing was the mechanism by which political and religious institutions sought to impose their will – the ambitious, lettered men who

---

[27] Prominent recent works that have suggested greater than assumed use of writing by the laity in the early and high Middle Ages include Rosamond McKitterick, *The Carolingians and the Written Word* (Cambridge: Cambridge University Press, 1989); Alice Rio, *Legal Practice and the Written Word in the Early Middle Ages: Frankish Formulae, c. 500–1000* (Cambridge: Cambridge University Press, 2009); François Bougard, Laurent Feller, and Régine Le Jan, eds., *Dots et douaires dans le haut Moyen Âge* (Rome: École française de Rome, 2002); François Bougard, Cristina LaRocca, and Régine LeJan, eds., *Sauver son âme et se perpétuer: La transmission du patrimoine au haut Moyen Âge* (Rome: École française de Rome, 2005).
[28] See "Introduction." In Warren Brown, Marios Costambeys, Matthew Innes, and Adam Kosto, eds., *Documentary Culture and the Laity in the Early Middle Ages* (Cambridge: Cambridge University Press, 2013), 1–16 (here 4).
[29] Michael Clanchy, *From Memory to Written Record. England, 1066–1307*, 3rd ed. (Oxford: Blackwell, 2012, c1979).
[30] Brian Stock, *The Implication of Literacy: Written Language and Models of Interpretation in the Eleventh and Twelfth Centuries* (Princeton, NJ: Princeton University Press, 1983).

carried out these efforts were essential agents in what Robert Moore has called "Europe's first revolution."[31] Rosamond McKitterick sees traces of these trends even earlier, in Carolingian Francia as early as the end of the eighth century.[32]

From the twelfth century, inhabitants of the Italian communes relied on writing for a range of needs, and, increasingly, written instruments (such as contracts, deeds, and birth certificates) were essential for full participation in the life of the commune.[33] Italian merchants and financiers produced copious written records in tracking their sales, debts, and deals. Mercantile ledgers, letters, and journals accumulated, especially once the widespread availability of paper provided a ready-made surface for this record-keeping. Before 1300, therefore, there was a thriving documentary culture, one that embraced not only the world of the church but sizable components of the laity as well. After 1300, however, the signs of a genuine sea change are increasingly evident, as written instruments began to proliferate and insinuate themselves into European life in heretofore unseen ways. These transformations were fueled, above all, by a hardware that was not new, but was newly available and affordable: paper.

Still, the volume and variety of things that were written down in the early modern world simply dwarfed those of the Middle Ages. This reality in part reflected the greatly expanded number and variety of early modern people and institutions who were participants in the culture of writing, even if levels of literacy remained low by modern standards. Measuring the fraction of the population that displayed clear signs of literacy only gets us so far, however. As Filippo de Vivo has reminded us, "[t]he salient feature of literacy is not its extent, but its incidence, or relative availability, and in urban society there would have been at least one literate person in most communities."[34] Those exposed to the influence of written and printed material were far more numerous that the literate alone.

The increased authority of the written word and of written instruments during the early modern period rested on multiple proficiencies. Writing had the capacity to present words that might not have ever passed through human lips or existed in oral form, and its use did not mandate any direct contact between speaker and listener. In this way, writing is evidently

---

[31] Robert Moore, *The First European Revolution, c. 970–1215* (Oxford: Blackwell, 2000), esp. 192–197.
[32] McKitterick, *The Carolingians*.
[33] Thomas Behrmann, "Einleitung: Ein neuer Zugang zum Schriftgut der oberitalienischen Kommunen." In Hagen Keller and Behrmann, eds., *Kommunales Schriftgut in Oberitalien: Formen, Funktionen, Überlieferung* (Munich: W. Fink, 1995), 1–16.
[34] Filippo de Vivo, *Information and Communication in Venice. Rethinking Early Modern Politics* (Oxford: Oxford University Press, 2007), 122.

more than visual, transcribed speech. There was also an increasingly shared conviction that writing was more permanent than speech, which was intrinsically ephemeral. This outlook is captured in a popular proverb that had circulated since the Roman Republic: *verba volant, scripta manent*.

The vitality of orally transmitted news and information (such as the witnessing of travelers, soldiers, and other observers) persisted throughout the period. Daniel Woolf has pointed to the enduring, even increased, emphasis on oral modes of expression in the Renaissance, especially with humanists refocusing attention on the importance of rhetoric, which was a fundamentally oral art. The Dutch humanist Desiderius Erasmus (-1466–1536) embodies this liminal state, with one foot in the world of orality and one in that of writing. While he regularly lauded the daily speech of the ancients, he was also keenly aware that spoken and written discourse in his own day were mediated through the written word. "At one time common usage had a great deal of authority," he wrote in his manual on good speech, *De copia verborum*, "but nowadays we acquire our way of speaking not from the community at large but from the writings of learned men, so usage does not have the same predictive power."[35] Throughout the period, we continue to see expressions of concern regarding the credibility of written data, reports, and news, and doubts about the capacity of that which was written to capture reality faithfully. Much of political life continued to revolve around direct encounters, oral exchanges, and performative ritual that were only rarely represented in print or manuscript. A great deal of early modern political information, for example in diplomatic exchanges, was never inscribed on paper (and thus largely lost to us as historians) but nonetheless remained essential to political discourse and to the exercise of political power. Similarly, a great deal of financial and economic transactions were conducted without leaving a written trace; the world of scholarship and learning, despite the great proliferation of books and avenues for writing, continued to depend on patterns of non-scriptural pedagogy, erudition, and socialization; and, of course, the bulk of all human day-to-day interactions took place without recourse to any writing whatsoever. Much, and perhaps most, information in early modern Europe was spoken and heard only by those within earshot, and we will never be privy to it.

The pulpit also remained an important source of oral information, and it is likely that its importance only increased with the Protestant focus on preaching. Preachers often worried that much could be lost from their

---

[35] Daniel Woolf, "Speech, text and time: the sense of hearing and the sense of the past in Renaissance England." *Albion*, 18.2 (1986), 159–193.

sermons when they were rendered in writing – "I know well that the same sermon, as to the life of it, is scarcely the same in the hearing, and in the reading," the English pastor John Ward declared in 1645.[36] A Dutch political pamphlet from 1650 conceded that "one sermon from the pulpit can do more evil than a hundred blue books (i.e. pamphlets)."[37] The printing process was generally too slow to be the conduit of first-time news, and the town crier remained a staple across Europe through most of this period; the office of town crier at the Palais de Justice in Paris was eliminated only in 1667.

In the fifteenth and sixteenth centuries, we see many examples where written and oral information possessed a hybrid, and often mutually reinforcing, authority. At the end of the fifteenth century in the High Court of the German city of Lüneberg, for example, we see increased elaboration of oath formulas preserved in writing, reinforcing what had previously been an exclusively oral exercise. Oaths were written down according to a prescribed formula, then uttered, and recorded word for word in the protocol book of the Court. The Court became an environment in which all stages of any case were recorded in writing, and sometimes copied multiple times. In court, the assumption became that social status and nationality were associated with the possession of certain documents. Even the very "facts of one's birth," so important in premodern societies, could not be confirmed without a written instrument. "Writing permits people to 'call each other names.'" Andrea Litschel describes a court case from 1596 in Lüneberg, where a plaintiff claimed that his letter of birth had been stolen and he could not therefore prove his German, rather than Wendish, birth. The plaintiff had by that time been a master of the guild of smiths for some sixteen years, but still felt he needed this written affirmation to be preserved in the city archive.[38] Ultimately, the resolution of the social status of the plaintiff came only with affirmation of the town council *and* its confirmation in writing through an entry into the court book. In the legal profession

---

[36] Donald Francis Mackenzie, "Speech-manuscript-print." In Dave Oliphant and Robin Bradford, eds., *New Directions in Textual Studies* (Austin, TX: Harry Ransom Humanities Research Center, 1990), 86–109 (here 91).

[37] Craig Harline, *Pamphlets, Printing and Political Culture in the Early Dutch Republic* (Dordrecht: Martinus Nijhoff Publishers, 1987), 66.

[38] Andrea Litschel, "Writing and social evidence 'before the archives': revealing and concealing the written in Late Medieval Lüneberg." In Marco Mostert and Anna Adamska, eds., *Writing and the Administration of Medieval Towns* (Turnhout: Brepols, 2014), 185–208.

more generally, the oral and argumentative nature of the law was increasingly undergirded by growing reservoirs of written precedent and case law with which lawyers were compelled to be familiar.

Script and print were poised in a "reciprocal interaction" with oral communication in early modern Europe. Text was nearly always a spur to further oral communication. Typography did not foreclose avenues of oral exchange, but instead was often grist for conversation, led by those who were able to read. Discussion of a popular pamphlet or newssheet, public debate about a posted royal proclamation, the reading of diplomatic reports in council, deliberations over the proper interpretation of newly available Scripture, and university students engaging in *disputatio* after their communal *lectio*. What Keith Thomas has written about early modern England can be applied to early modern Europe more broadly: "[it] was not an oral society. But neither was it a fully literate one. Although many people could read and write, many others could not ... Indeed it is the interaction between contrasting forms of culture, literate and illiterate, oral and written, which gives this period its particular fascination."[39] This was a society "in which the three media of speech, script, and print infused and interacted with each other in myriad ways."[40] Writing did not replace orality; it became a fundamental (and often compulsory) complement to it. More and more oral interactions and communications were committed to writing. Information moved within, across and between oral and written formats. Nonetheless, Europeans became increasingly accustomed to consuming and sharing information in paper form.

The waxing authority of the written and printed made it increasingly acceptable and commonplace for individuals to privilege the inscribed over the oral, and even to exclude oral forms of information and communication. King Philip II of Spain, for example, famously preferred to receive written petitions over oral audiences. He felt that it afforded him more control and allowed him to delay, block, and expedite the business of governing according to his particular discretion. Protestant reformers

---

[39] Keith Thomas, "The meaning of literacy in early modern England." In Gerd Baumann, ed., *The Written Word: Literacy in Transition* (Oxford: Clarendon, 1986), 97–131 (here 98). Making much the same argument with a wider purview, see Jack Goody, *The Interface between the Written and the Oral* (Cambridge: Cambridge University Press, 1988) and Ruth Finnegan, *Literacy and Orality* (Oxford: Blackwell, 1988). For Italy, see the essays in Luca degl'Innocenti, Brian Richardson, and Chiara Sbordoni, eds., *Interactions between Orality and Writing in Early Modern Italian Culture* (London: Routledge, 2016).

[40] Adam Fox, *Oral and Literate Culture in England 1500–1700* (Oxford: Clarendon, 2000), 5.

emphasized the authority of God's (written) word above all else, and religious life, like never before in Europe, revolved around, and was shaped by, that which was written.

Just as we should not construct stark divisions between an age of manuscript and an age of print, nor should we draw similarly bright lines between an oral culture and a succeeding culture of inscription. McLuhan's "typographic man" did not now stalk the land, throwing all that was not printed into shadow. Nor did Ong's new paradigm prevail. The reality was that more information of every variety, written and non-written, was in circulation. One of the reasons why early modern Europeans faced a revolution in information was that new forms and habits of writing duplicated pre-existing media and systems of representation.

So, while we should acknowledge the enduring importance of the oral and the visual, the history of information in the early modern period can be seen as an extended testimony to the importance of writing inscribed on paper. The multiplication of writing practices and protocols and the general increase in written instruments in circulation were the result of multiple causes. What Bruno Latour and Steve Woolgar identified as central to the scientific outlook can be, I believe, applied to early modern Europeans in general: they had a "strange mania for inscription."[41]

1.3   The Secular Scriptorium

Writing, therefore, became an everyday activity for many in early modern Europe. There were numerous stimuli for the production of documents: the availability of printing; the competing confessions of the new churches; new means of self-expression and self-definition; the emergence of capitalist economic models; the rise of the state and its bureaucracies; urbanization and rising levels of full and partial literacy; and new attitudes toward history, education, and scholarship wrought by the Renaissance. At the most basic level, however, the systematic creation of written information was a self-reinforcing process, as writing begat more writing. Specifically, inscription begat transcription. Once thoughts, opinions, observations, and data were inscribed, they were

---

[41] Bruno Latour and Steve Woolgar, *Laboratory Life: the Construction of Scientific Facts*, 2nd ed. (Princeton: Princeton University Press, 1986), 48. This is cited in reference to early modern practices by Nicholas Popper, "Archives and the boundaries of early modern science." *Isis*, 107.1 (March 2016), 86–94 (here 90).

then routinely subjected to multiple instances of organization, categorization, and recombination. This meant transcribing copies of what had already been written and then classifying and filing the resulting paper. In diplomatic and political chanceries, secretaries copied letters, proclamations, and instructions, in order to store them in files and archives. Scholars and natural philosophers transcribed documents, notes, and occasionally entire works (both manuscript and print), sharing them with colleagues or making them part of one's "papers." Merchants copied the entries in their chronological *adversaria* into double-entry registers. Students copied passages of texts and composed commonplace books based on their reading of print and manuscript works. Once information was on paper, it frequently remained mobile, moving from paper to paper with the actions of scribes. Once on paper, it was uniquely available for replication, for extraction, and for segmentation. This was not yet the cut-and-paste universe of cyberspace, but the availability of paper and the *habitus* of writing created a "culture of transcription" that fed the overall volume of paper and forced efforts to store and organize.[42]

Whereas a commitment to regular writing had previously been the preserve of a narrow few, it now was undertaken by, and expected of, an unprecedentedly broad segment of the population. The early modern period saw the emergence of what I call the "secular scriptorium," whereby writing as a daily activity was uncloistered and embraced across European society. The islands of writing that had characterized medieval society were now linked by a society-wide shared commitment to writing in personal and institutional communication, transactions, and record-keeping. Keller, Grubmüller, and Staubach (in writing of the Middle Ages) have labeled these activities collectively *pragmatische Schriftlichkeit*. The early modern period witnessed a great expansion of this "pragmatic writing" and of the protocols that governed it, accompanying a vast range of regular activities.[43]

This growth in scribal production was a river with many tributaries feeding into it. As we shall see, across Western Europe, models provided by merchants and financiers proved highly influential, especially their epistolary and accounting practices. Writing letters and keeping their

---

[42] Harold Love has spoken, for example, of a "culture of transcription" in early modern England. See his *The Culture and Commerce of Texts. Scribal Publication in Seventeenth-Century England* (Amherst, MA: University of Massachusetts Press, 1998).

[43] Hagen Keller, Klaus Grubmüller, und Nikolaus Staubach, eds., *Pragmatische Schriftlichkeit im Mittelalter: Erscheinungsformen und Entwicklungsstufen* (Munich: Fink, 1992).

books were both near-daily disciplines for merchants and, as I will emphasize repeatedly throughout the book, similar techniques of information exchange and management became prevalent in multiple sectors of early modern society.

The state also became "archival," as administrations at all levels of government preserved their records, and were staffed by professionals tasked with inscribing, transcribing, and locating documents. Non-state institutions such as the Church, religious orders, trading companies, and scientific societies, came to share this preoccupation with generating paper. The creation and custodianship of paper instruments required new forms of expertise, expertise that was shared by new professionals of writing who worked in various walks of life. We know these individuals by different names depending on their arena of everyday writing. Secretaries, chancellors, clerks, notaries, scriveners, archivists – these were the worker bees of *pragmatische Schriftlichkeit*.

Institutional "hives" were not the only locales for pragmatic literacy. Individuals also increasingly engaged in regular writing, generating accounts of their finances, lineage, family, and selves. The widespread recourse to "family books" (known in Italy as *ricordanze*, in Germany as *Familienbücher*, and as *livres de famille* in France), with their origins in the accounts of mercantile family firms, reflected a new desire and readiness to record in writing, on paper, the details of family affairs, and to preserve them (essentially, to archive them) for generations yet to come. These "ego-documents," which I will discuss in detail in Chapter 7, focused to varying degrees on the personal and self-reflective as well as the financial and transactional. They were archives of the self.

This was a great age of letter writing, both between representatives of the state and other institutions and private citizens. The letters of merchants were vital to the conduct of their affairs: for communicating with partners, customers, and suppliers; for checking up on local conditions and prices; and for reconnoitering new markets. Scholars used letters to reduce the distance between themselves and other thinkers, seeking out books, exchanging ideas, and cultivating virtual ties of sociability. Letters were arguably the most important conduits of international news, and (as we shall see) the origin of news services. This routine letter writing, facilitated by paper, created what I describe in the book as a "letterocracy." These letters were often then preserved by individuals, and this correspondence often made up a sizable chunk, along with a variety of other paper instruments, of what the early modern period christened as one's "papers," the documents that you deliberately kept.

The early modern period also invented paperwork. Some groups of people, as today, felt the millstone of paperwork around their necks more heavily than others did. Diplomats, lawyers, notaries, secretaries, and merchants were among those most burdened by paperwork. Paperwork, of course, is something that we are quite accustomed to complaining about. Our associations with it are rarely happy ones: drudgery, long hours, numbing bureaucracy. It is confusing, time-consuming, and intellectually unsatisfying. But paperwork took root and remains with us (the demise of the actual paper notwithstanding) because it offers distinct advantages. Bruno Latour, in his speculative yet provocative work on the rise of the scientific outlook, has enumerated the benefits to embracing paperwork.[44] The systematic representation of one's activities on paper bestows to the information that it recorded mobility, immutability, and scalability, all of which facilitates the reshuffling and recombination of information. Paperwork presents a flat surface that can be dominated and manipulated by the user, and reproduced and disseminated at little cost. Paper information can be superimposed, despite different scales and origins. It can also be incorporated into other written texts. And while paper has a two-dimensional character, it can nonetheless manipulate objects that exist in three-dimensional space: it is a representative mechanism. One might quibble with any (or all) of these points. My study reveals Europeans seeking to exploit the advantages of paperwork, with varying degrees of both success and frustration.

A society that engaged in routine writing and embraced paperwork as a utilitarian necessity saw the transformation of the "scriptural economy," to borrow a phrase coined by Michel de Certeau. Writing, per Certeau, was a means of structuring and "mythologizing" Western society, a process by which existing came to be equated with being written.[45] Even if one does not accept the totalizing implications of Certeau's idea (and I do not), the widespread use of paper had significant repercussions for the scriptural economy of early modern Europe. Documents exist not only to store information, but also to show it – the word itself is derived from the Latin *docere*, "to show" or "to instruct." They are fundamentally representations, designed to demonstrate something to the viewer, for use in the present or for consultation at a later date.

What might have heretofore been committed to memory was now subject to inscription on paper, as reading notes, shopping lists, transaction records, minutes of meetings, recipes, and fleeting ideas one did not wish to forget. Francis Bacon declared that "If a Man Write little, he had need have a Great Memory." Michel de Montaigne (1533–1592)

---

[44] Bruno Latour, "Drawing things together." In Michael Lynch and Steve Woolgar, eds., *Representation in Scientific Practice* (Cambridge, MA: MIT Press, 1990), 19–68.
[45] Michel de Certeau, *The Practices of Everyday Life* (Berkeley, CA: University of California Press, 1984), 137–156.

recognized his own limitations when he wrote in his essay "On Experience": "lacking a natural memory I forge one in paper." The methods of pen and paper that early modern scribblers employed helped them not only to remember particulars but, just as importantly, to store and categorize these particulars in a way that facilitated retrieval and analysis. The traditional mnemonic devices of the Middle Ages, which had mixed reason with hierarchy, were now augmented by a host of writing practices – compilation, cataloging, note-taking, indexing, commonplacing, and many others that will be described in this book.[46]

Writing on paper serves not merely as a substitute for memory but also as a tool that activates further memory: it conserves but also renews old thoughts and actions. Writing is, in the words of Aleida Assmann, "conserved energy."[47] This conservation of energy was yet another of the benefits of paperwork.

One symptom of all this paperwork is that it presented decisions as to what to do with all the paper that it created. The early modern period also invented bureaucracy (literally, "rule by the desk"). Bureaucracies emerge when institutions make the dual commitment to generating written instruments and then keeping them in profusion. The mediation and management of this material are among a bureaucracy's chief tasks, and essential to the functioning of the organization of which it is a part. A preservative instinct came to prevail across the early modern period, manifested in a commitment to record-keeping and archiving. It is captured in its essence in the decree of Pope Paul IV in 1565 that the Vatican archive should collect "everything pertaining to the Holy See."[48] The practices of medieval merchants and certain political bodies (including the Holy See), which had emphasized the importance of maintaining comprehensive written records of their operations, proved influential and proliferated in the early modern period, with a far greater range of individuals and institutions committing themselves to systematic record-keeping. Hence the great proliferation of archives, accounts, and

---

[46] Eric Garberson, "Libraries, Memory and the Space of Knowledge." *Journal of the History of Collections*, 18 (2006), 105–136; Claire Richter Sherman, *Writing on Hands: Memory and Knowledge in Early Modern Europe* (Seattle: University of Washington Press, 2001). On medieval practices, see Kimberly Rivers, "Memory, Division, and the Organisation of Knowledge in the Middle Ages." In Peter Binkley, ed., *Pre-modern Encyclopaedic Texts. Proceedings of the Second Comers Congress, Groningen 1–4 July 1996* (Leiden: Brill, 1997), 147–158.

[47] Aleida Assmann, *Erinnerungsräume: Formen und Wandlungen des kulturellen Gedächtnisses* (Munich: C.H. Beck, 2007), 179.

[48] Olivier Poncet, "Les Archives de la papauté (XVIe–milieu XVIIe siècle), la genèse d'un instrument de pouvoir." In Armand Jamme and Poncet, eds., *Offices, écrit et papauté (XIIIe–XVIIe siècle)* (Rome: École française de Rome, 2007), 737–762.

Introduction 23

"papers," and of personnel who were capable of shepherding the documentary hoard.

In one of many treatises that appeared in the sixteenth and seventeenth centuries on the work of the "secretary," Angelo Ingegneri in 1592 stressed that the holder of such an office must not only be able to compose letters of many varieties in order to meet the manifold needs of his prince, but he must also be committed to the preservation of documents. He gives detailed instructions on keeping a register of letters, storing the letters themselves in drawers, and constructing alphabetical indices to search through the accumulated records. He also writes: "I consider it better to preserve every piece of writing, no matter how useless, than to throw away anything about which one has a shred of doubt, which might at one time appear a trifle, rather than a necessity."[49] Ingegneri's sentiments were widely shared across early modern Europe. The result was an extraordinary accumulation of documents.

That a secretary, responsible for the oversight of an institution's documents, would err on the side of preserving written records, is predictable enough, but officials and private individuals of all stripes committed themselves to maintaining detailed records of their actions. Ottavio Codogno, writing in the early seventeenth century, compares the vigilance of the chancellor of the post, the official of the postal service who oversees the levying of excises, to that of a soldier: "every day, every hour, every moment, day and night, they have to attend to their tasks ... such that, if one considers the most tiresome and continuous jobs there are, that of the chancellors of the Post undoubtedly holds the first place."[50] This office, therefore, was largely preoccupied with creating and overseeing a paper trail.

The benefit of having these records on hand, of course, was balanced by a whole new coterie of challenges revolving around the central question of how exactly to employ records once they had accumulated. The information in these repositories might be referenced for decision-making and the pursuit of knowledge; it could be manipulated, altered, or selectively extracted for particular ends; and, in a great many cases, it was simply ignored, allowed to gather dust. Never was it recorded and gathered with

---

[49] *Del Buon Segretario Libri Tre di Angelo Ingegneri* (Rome: Guglielmo Faciotto, 1594), 106: "io stimerò sempre meglio il serbar tutte le scritture, quantunque inutile, ch'el gettarne alcuna; della quale s'habbia punt di dubbio, che à qualche tempo ne possa venir capriccio, non che necessità."

[50] Ottavio Codogno, *Nuovo itinerario delle Poste per tutto il mondo di Ottavio Codogno. Aggiountovi il modo di scrivere à tutte le parti. Utilissimo non solo Segretarij, ma à Religiosi, & à Mercanti. Con licenza de' Superiori, & Privilegio* (Venice: Lucio Spineda, 1620), 36, 42–43.

us in mind, let alone a scholar writing about something called "information."

1.4 The New Age of Manuscript

The trends that I have been discussing above all involved a great deal of writing. Almost none of them required the intervention of a printing press. When I have described this project to fellow historians, I am often met with some version of the following response: "Oh you mean the impact of the printing press?" This is an indication of how the early modern period has come to be associated with Gutenberg's invention, and how even historians apply Marshall MacLuhan's narrow conception of typographic man to early modern information. A core conviction of this book is that we need to move away from thinking of post-Gutenberg society solely in terms of books or, indeed, as an "age of print" that superseded a preceding "age of manuscript." Handwritten texts only became "manuscript" when there were printed books and paper from which to distinguish them. The word "manuscript," in its various forms, only came into regular use in the second half of the sixteenth century once print had become commonplace.

In fact, Gutenberg's invention in no way can be said to have ushered out a supposed medieval "age of manuscript," or, for that matter, to have precipitated an "age of print" or created "print culture." Yes, the production and availability of printed materials had wide-ranging cultural impacts, many of which will be addressed in Chapter 5 of this book. The historiographical construct of "print culture," invented in opposition to a medieval "scribal culture" or "manuscript culture," exaggerates the degree of displacement of one textual form by another. It is an invention of the past few decades, with origins stretching back to the typographical caesura identified by Ong and McLuhan and then elaborated upon by Elizabeth Eisenstein.[51] Seen from an informational perspective, however, the advent of print appears less the replacement of one "culture" by

[51] This is an observation made by Joseph Dane in *The Myth of Print Culture. Essays on Evidence, Textuality, and Bibliographical Method* (Toronto: University of Toronto Press, 2003). Dane's argument against the use of the terminology of "print culture" is predicated on a conviction that individual books must be examined and understood as individual material items, rather than as "cultural" elements. There is much to recommend such a particularist approach, but Dane's overwrought and occasionally waspish rhetoric in criticizing those he sees as the partisans of "print culture" detracts from the book's overall effectiveness.
Eisenstein's classic treatment is *The Printing Press as an Agent of Change: Communications and Cultural Transformations in Early Modern Europe* (Cambridge: Cambridge University Press, 1979). A revised and abridged version is *The Printing Revolution in Early Modern Europe* (Cambridge: Cambridge University Press, 2005).

another, and instead the introduction of a new means of circulating information on a surface for inscription that was already widely in use. In my view, while there may have been a "scribal culture," "print culture" is a historiographical unicorn, because it is impossible to disassociate print from the manuscript practices that inform and surround it.

The advent of "documentary" modernity would have taken place with or without the historical accident of Gutenberg's invention. The amount of text inscribed by hand dwarfed the text inscribed by type in this period. With widely available paper and broadly shared practices that demanded the filling of that paper with ink, this was an "age of manuscript" without precedent. The only possible previous analog is a non-European one, the Abbasid Empire, which was genuinely "ruled by paper" and produced millions of books and countless more government instruments on paper.[52] If by "manuscript" we mean a text written onto animal skin, the production of these gradually diminished (but not as quickly or completely as one might expect) and those remaining from the Middle Ages were subject to wastage, to isolation through storage, to repurposing as palimpsests and other secondary uses, as well as to systematic destruction (in the case of the dissolution of the monasteries). If, however, we take manuscript to mean a handwritten text, document, diary, notebook, or loose sheet, invariably made of paper, Europeans were eagerly embracing a booming new age of manuscript. Long-standing practices of writing expanded and novel ones were introduced, almost all of them rendered on abundant paper.

For all of the wonders of print, it could not perform many of the functions that were tasked to manuscript. Printing was costly, cumbersome, and slow, and could not be deployed for a great range of useful purposes. For most administrative, record-keeping, and personal purposes, manuscript remained vastly more important than print. Of England, D. F. Mackenzie has written:

> Just as some social functions could still only be performed orally, so too society could only be administered effectively at a distance by manuscript. Acts and proclamations might be printed and widely dispersed (though many orders and resolutions of Parliament were not – some were merely proclaimed) but most of the executive actions taken to implement them were initiated in writing. All government agencies, the church, law, education, and commerce were more dependent upon written records than printed ones.[53]

[52] On Islamic paper, see Jonathan Bloom, *Paper Before Print. The History and Impact of Paper in the Islamic World* (New Haven: Yale University Press, 2001).
[53] D.F. Mackenzie, "Speech-manuscript-print," in Dave Oliphant and Robin Bradford, eds., *New Directions in Textual Studies* (Austin, TX: Harry Ransom Humanities Research Center, 1990), 86–109 (here 93–94).

Only a miniscule percentage of manuscript writing ended up printed at any point in its lifetime. Many of the uses of writing that had predominated when the available surface had been parchment or vellum only expanded when paper was on hand: contracts, deeds and indentures, statutes, and (in great volumes) letters. New ones also emerged: notebooks, account books, diaries and other ego-documents, memoranda, scribbled notes, and a variety of printed forms that invited the addition of handwritten information. Writing about writing constituted a good portion of the manuscript that was produced. Writing was needed, among other things, to keep tabs on all the writing being done.

Ironically, we now understand this chiefly because of efforts of scholars engaged in the field of the "history of the book," which emerged in the wake of Elizabeth Eisenstein's paradigm-shifting work on the printing press and its impact on European culture. The new focus in their work on the material aspects of book composition and presentation has extended into the study of manuscript culture as well, and revealed that cultural transmission and documentation remained overwhelmingly in script rather than in print. There is little doubt that loss as well as the incomplete nature of European manuscript inventories belie the true volume of manuscript production. Printing's "most radical effect," argues Peter Stallybrass, "was its incitement to writing by hand."[54] The great flood of printed books that inundated Europe was accompanied by immeasurable quantities of manuscript notes and codices that contained extracts, commentaries, and even entire copies of printed books. In addition, numerous items that were not books were printed to be written on: forms, indulgence certificates, almanacs, grammars, writing primers, questionnaires, and censuses.

Nor is the story of the printing press the story of the book. As Chapter 5 will emphasize, none of what came off Europe's presses were "books" in the strictest sense of the word. Instead they were sheets of paper with text and images impressed on them. This is an important distinction, and Peter Stallybrass (again) has pointed out that "printing did indeed produce a revolutionary transformation in communications, but not primarily through books."[55] Much of what printshops produced was not destined to be parts of books at all, but rather in the form of pamphlets,

---

[54] Peter Stallybrass, "Printing and the manuscript revolution." In Barbie Zelizer, ed., *Explorations in Communication and History* (New York: Routledge, 2008), 111–118 (here 111).
[55] Stallybrass, "Printing and the manuscript revolution," 111.

newssheets, indulgence certificates, cheap images, and countless other printed devices. It was all this printed material, as much as books, that was responsible for the genuinely revolutionary impact of the printing press: the manifold increase of information in circulation.

1.5 The Culture of Collection and *Copia*

In his satirical *Anatomy of Melancholy*, which was first published in 1621, Robert Burton spoke at some length about the great surfeit of books and other paper instruments that he saw produced in his day. Burton looked at the output of the presses and found himself overwhelmed. "New books every day, pamphlets, corrantoes, stories, whole catalogues of volumes of all sorts, new paradoxes, opinions, schisms, heresies, controversies in philosophy, religion etc ... What a catalogue of new books all this year, all this age (I say), have our Frankfort marts, our domestic marts brought out!" With so many writing in order to keep the printers occupied, he described his own time as a "scribbling age." The printing industry, he felt, provided an irresistible impetus for those seeking fame through their writing, even if it was mostly "trifles, trash, nonsense."[56] His main lament was how all of this would confuse and muddle the pursuit of knowledge. His chief worry, however, was the ambitions of a certain category of "scribblers" among his contemporaries, rather than the printing press.

In the period 1500–1700, information overwhelmed any efforts to contain it.[57] Every age has expressed some version of the complaint that there is "too much to know." And each age has responded with the creation of discourses tailored to the novel circumstances and with taxonomies constructed to organize and categorize the new information at its disposal. Aristotle's speciation of knowledge, formulated a millennium and a half earlier, for example, was a response to an ancient version of "too much to know." As early as the 1120s, the theologian Peter Abelard (1079–1142) remarked, in *Sic et Non*, on the overwhelming mass of books with which his students had to cope. The numerous high medieval compendia and florilegia were attempts to address concerns over overabundance, early

---

[56] *Anatomy of Melancholy* (London: E.P. Dutton,1961 ed.), Vol. 1, 21–23; quoted in C. John Somerville, *The News Revolution in England: Cultural Dynamics of Daily Information* (Oxford: Oxford University Press, 1996), 28.
[57] Brendan Dooley, "The public sphere and the organization of knowledge." In John Martin, ed., *Early Modern Italy, 1550–1776* (Oxford: Oxford University Press, 2002), 209–228.

examples of mnemotechnics. So too were alphabetic biblical concordances and library catalogs compiled by mendicant orders.[58]

The accumulation of information in early modern Europe was unprecedented, was both inadvertent and deliberate, and it took place in many locales. The gathering and preservation of records were symptomatic of a broader "culture of collection" that prevailed in early modern Europe. The expansion of political, institutional, and scientific archives; the growth of libraries fed by the abundance of printed books; the accumulation of large and varied personal "papers"; the advent and stocking of museums; the proliferation of cabinets of curiosities and *Wunderkammern*; the creation of botanical gardens reflecting the expanded knowledge of the world's flora; and even the early modern encyclopedias that sought to embrace in full the new learning: all of these reflect a commitment to gathering particulars into one place. These various efforts to collect and keep documents and other items created what we today might call databases. Merchants, secretaries, statesmen, scholars, and scientists were all concerned with drawing upon this information as evidence of past events, transactions, and experiments.

Guilds, universities, confraternities, trading companies, and individuals who maintained collections of their "papers" all created archives. Such efforts at collection required subsequent efforts at sorting, labeling, and categorizing. Once any collection becomes large enough, it requires finding aids, and early modern Europeans experimented with many strategies for making their collections navigable and searchable – we will encounter many of these in the course of this book.

Archives were the sum of choices to include and exclude, and reflected the priorities of their prevailing ideology and personnel, as numerous recent studies in early modern archival culture have demonstrated. Politicians, diplomats, and secretaries were always anxious about how posterity might regard the documentary record that they were leaving, and would selectively and strategically destroy papers. Bibliophiles made conscious, directed decisions about what to keep in their collections, dispensing with or neglecting texts that they regarded as irrelevant, irreverent, or outdated. Jennifer Summit, in *Memory's Library*, has shown how the choices made by early modern English keepers of libraries, specifically

---

[58] See Ann Blair, *Too Much to Know: Managing Scholarly Information before the Modern Age* (New Haven, CT: Yale University Press, 2010), 36–38; Ivan Illich, *In the Vineyard of the Text. A Commentary to Hugh's Didascalicon* (Chicago: University of Chicago Press, 1993); and Michael Clanchy, "Parchment and paper: manuscript culture, 1100–1500." In Simon Eliot and Jonathan Rose, eds., *A Companion to the History of the Book* (Oxford: Blackwell, 2003), 194–206 (here 201).

to dispense with medieval manuscripts, shaped our image and understanding of the Middle Ages.[59] Finally, the confessional conflicts associated with the Reformations led to the interdiction and destruction of papers and books deemed unorthodox, dangerous, or heretical. These countervailing trends aside, however, there was an unmistakable move toward preservation of documents, paper, and books, as well as specimens, exhibits, and *exempla*, all components of a culture of collection.

When looked at together, these various projects of collection come to resemble each other closely. In the chapters that follow, we will see that political figures gathering the letters of their diplomats or the reports of their *intendants* and storing in them in state archives were engaged in collecting just as much as botanists gathering specimens for their personal collections were. One provided a simulacrum of the body politic, the other a simulacrum of nature. The ends in mind might have varied, but often included a desire to have a repository of precedence readily at hand, as well as data to make informed decisions about policy or the state of nature. The accumulation of material in archives, libraries, and collections meant that information primarily concerned with past actions was growing in volume, at the same time as was the paper mediating the present; this was a combination that made information management more imperative than ever.

One of the more popular printed texts of the sixteenth century from one of that century's most popular authors was Erasmus's *De copia verborum*, which I cited above. There were more than 150 editions of the text published in the six decades after its first publication in 1512. A guidebook to effective rhetoric and composition, the treatise follows closely the approach of Quintilian in offering a twofold picture of *copia*, relating it both to the variety of words and turns of phrase desirable for effective expression, and to their abundance, which resulted from the piling up of arguments, *exempla*, and parallels. Here and elsewhere, Erasmus offered guidelines for *loci communes* by which to organize knowledge, given the enormous volume of literary examples now readily available to scholars and students with the advent of print. He was presenting an early example of what would become known as commonplacing.

Variety and abundance, the facets of *copia* in rhetorical and humanistic learning highlighted by Erasmus, were in fact recurring features of early modern society and a regular source both of celebration and of organizational, epistemological, and taxonomic anxiety. The idea of *copia* recurred across a great many fields and disciplines in early modern Europe. It appears in the titles of all sorts of print publications, advertising

---

[59] Jennifer Summit, *Memory's Library: Medieval Books in Early Modern England* (Chicago: University of Chicago Press, 2011).

the scope of coverage of human and natural histories, or the range of knowledge and books epitomized within. Readers wanted abundance but wanted it encapsulated and processed inside the covers of a book.

"Coping with *copia*," it turns out, was a concern for many in early modern Europe, from scholars to natural philosophers to royal secretaries. *Copia* might be regarded as a blessing, opening up new opportunities for knowledge, wonder, and political or social control, but it had to be managed, requiring physical and cognitive tools to navigate. The secular scriptorium and the rise of regular paperwork, the impulse to preserve and archive, the emergence of bureaucracy, waxing empiricism, and the culture of collection, all added to the *copia*. Much of this book concerns the mechanisms by which this *copia* of information came into being; the repercussions of the creation of an information-rich society; and the steps taken to pursue profits, knowledge, power, and personal fulfilment amid this new reality.

One of the ironies of early modern information overload was that those who proclaimed to be suffering from it were also the ones who created it in the first place. They created spaces for the efficient accumulation of data and encouraged epistemic shifts and patterns that depended on the collection of that material. The mental and material technologies that they then introduced to contain the information, many of which I will discuss in the chapters that follow, often served only to generate yet further information. As we shall see, such efforts only occasionally succeeded in relieving the informational burden, and sometimes exacerbated the symptoms rather than providing a cure.

1.6 A Taxonomic Age

A good case can be made that the early modern period invented the modern fact: the discrete, descriptive, and often mundane particular. When these facts accumulated in large numbers, as they inevitably did, in ledgers, commonplace books, chanceries, and naturalists' notebooks, they became what we would call "data," although contemporaries did not use the term in the same way.[60] As the facts accumulated, there were accompanying pressures concerning how to organize, classify, and categorize them. Early modern Europeans, faced with a deluge of particulars, were then compelled to figure out where they all fit in their longstanding epistemological schemata. Over time, the sheer volume of facts overwhelmed the previous methods of organizing knowledge: a "crisis of

---

[60] Daniel Rosenberg, "Data before the fact." In Lisa Getelman, ed., *"Raw Data" is an Oxymoron* (Cambridge, MA: MIT Press, 2013), 15–40.

classification," Henri-Jean Martin has called it.[61] For Michael Hobart and Zachary Schiffman, it was a "rupture of classification."[62]

There is, at the center of this story, a fundamental tension, that between the desire to acquire information and the concomitant desire to organize and then use it effectively. Francis Bacon perceived the quandary brought about by the waxing commitment to observation and data gathering in early modern science (in his *Novum Organum*, first published in 1620) : "Natural and Experimental History is so various and scattered that it confounds and disturbs the understanding; unless it be limited and placed in the right order; therefore we must form some tables and ranks of instances in such a manner and order, that the understanding may work upon them."[63] Early modern Europeans, like us, struggled to achieve an effective reconciliation between these two contradictory desires. Compilation ends up compelling taxonomy; once sufficient information accumulates, categorization becomes necessary in order to make its constituent parts legible and usable. We see the apotheosis of this dynamic in what is perhaps the most famous taxonomical project in European history: the speciation of the natural world by the Swedish naturalist Carl Linnaeus (1707–1778). At the start of his career, in 1735, Linnaeus published his *Systema naturae*, in which each kingdom of the natural world was contained within a single table that spanned a double-page spread. The whole thing was some twelve pages long. The last edition of this work was published in three volumes over the course of three years (1766–1768) and ran to 2,400 pages.[64] Even the most rigorous efforts to make the troves of information generated in the early modern world legible and usable might result in similar *copiae*. Even coping with *copia* could produce new abundances.

Information taxonomies have a lengthy history in human communities; it seems that we are predisposed to think in terms of categories. Two basic cognitive capabilities are involved in this tendency: our ability to discriminate between one thing and another, and the tendency of the brain to lateralize, to string things and thoughts together. We are better able to discern packets of data if we have placed them in identifiable categories;

---

[61] Henri-Jean Martin, "Classements et conjonctures." In Roger Chartier and Martin, eds., *Histoire de l'édition française*, Tome I: *Le livre conquérant. Du moyen age au milieu du XVII siècle* (Paris: Fayard, 1989), 429–457.
[62] Hobart and Schiffman, *Information Ages*, 87–111.
[63] Quoted in Staffan Müller-Wille and Isabelle Charmantier, "Natural history and information overload: the case of Linnaeus." *Studies in History and Philosophy of Biological and Biomedical Sciences*, 43 (2012), 4–15 (here 4).
[64] Isabelle Charmantier and Staffan Müller-Wille, "Worlds of paper: an introduction." *Early Science and Medicine*, 19 (2014), 379–397 (here 396).

32   The Information Revolution in Early Modern Europe

we engage in classification because it has a biological basis – it is literally easier on our brains.[65]

The early modern Information Revolution forced people and institutions to generate new taxonomies in which to slot the abundance of information. This impulse was evident across a broad range of activities: certainly in the natural sciences, where the yen for observation required new categories in which to place newly discovered or described plants, animals, and phenomena. But it could also be seen in bureaucratic circles, where institutions and the secretaries who staffed them introduced filing systems and documentary groupings to facilitate storage, finding, and access. Merchants gathered the paper trail of their business in multiple notebooks, organizing it not only by inflows and outflows, but by the various components and concerns of their operations. Scholars, simultaneously blessed and cursed by the abundance of resources made available by print, needed tools to navigate the forest of books. This was, as we will see, an age of catalogs, concordances, and reference books of great variety. Within books, as well, there emerged a new attitude toward the categorization of information. In 1450, less than 10 percent of manuscript books carried folio or page numbers. By the middle of the sixteenth century, the great majority of printed books were foliated or paginated. The codex had been a boon for non-continuous reading; in the age of print, with more books available than ever, tools to facilitate such reading were particularly desirable.[66]

Exemplary of these changes is the emerging organization of the Bible. Holy Scripture, given its length and the need to consult it regularly, especially cried out for organization to facilitate its use, which nearly always took the form of non-continuous reading. Medieval friars applied numbering to its books and chapters but, tellingly, it was not until the sixteenth century that a broadly accepted scheme of book, chapter, and verse emerged.[67] The first printed Bible to number its verses was the Latin translation by Santi Pagnini, published in 1528.[68] The French printer-scholar Robert Estienne (1503–1559) published a concordance in 1555

[65] This tendency is a constituent of Edward O. Wilson's theory of gene-culture evolution, also known as dual inheritance theory, which offers epigenetic rules that dispose us toward thinking in categories. See especially his seminal work with Charles Lumsden, *Genes, Mind and Culture: the Coevolutionary Process* (Cambridge, MA: Harvard University Press, 1981). More recently, see Robert Boyd and Peter Richerson, *Not by Genes Alone: How Culture Transformed Human Evolution* (Chicago: University of Chicago Press, 2005).
[66] Peter Stallybrass, "Books and scrolls: navigating the Bible." In Jennifer Andersen and Elizabeth Sauer, eds., *Books and Readers in Early Modern England: Material Studies* (Philadelphia: University of Pennsylvania Press, 2002), 42–79 (here 44).
[67] Michael Clanchy, "Parchment and paper," 201.
[68] See Paul Grendler, "Italian biblical humanism and the Papacy, 1515–1535." In Erika Rummell, ed., *Biblical Humanism and Scholasticism in the Age of Erasmus* (Leiden: Brill, 2008), 227–276 (here 245).

that introduced the current numbering system. Soon after, Jean Trebon in Lyons printed the Bible in paragraphs. The first English Bible with verse numbers was the Geneva Bible of 1560. The first mention of the term "chapter and verse" was in Matthew Foxe's *Book of the Martyrs*, published in 1563. Publishers also began to present the most popular works of antiquity *in capitula* – Robert Estienne's son, Henri (1528–1598), assigned the works of Plato and Plutarch pagination and numbering schemes that remain in use today.

Publishers increasingly included paratextual material, the purpose of which was to provide navigation within books. These indices and tables generally employed one of the tools for organizing information more familiar to us, alphabetization. In 1549, Conrad Gessner (1515–1565), in his massive *Bibliotheca universalis*, claimed that the "divine invention" of indexing was second only to printing as an aid to scholars. He declared: "it seems to me that, life being so short, indexes to books should be considered as absolutely necessary by those who are engaged in a variety of studies."[69] By the mid-seventeenth century, the English churchman and historian Thomas Fuller (1608–1661) was emphasizing the essential nature of indexes for navigating the contents of big books: "An Index is a necessary implement, and no impediment of a book, except in the same sense wherein the carriages of an army are termed *Impedimenta*. Without this, a large author is but a labyrinth without a clue to direct the reader therein."[70]

Alphabetization took a long time to catch on for a straightforward reason: it requires a great deal of work. In addition, despite some counterexamples, for example in monastic indices and library catalogs, there was in the Middle Ages a shared resistance to alphabetical order, as it appeared to violate the natural moral and spiritual order ordained by God, and was regarded as encouraging forgetfulness rather than burgeoning memory.[71]

Such resistance gradually broke down in the early modern period. Compiling alphabetical lists distilled from a large body of information only made sufficient sense after the advent of paper and then of printing, which allowed their rapid reproduction. Printers often advertised their alphabetical indices and tables of content in their frontispieces: they were marketing devices as well as finding aids. By the sixteenth century, it was customary for indices and tables in printed books to be reasonably carefully compiled and usually roughly alphabetical, although rarely past the second letter. Ermolao Barbaro's Latin translation of Dioscorides' *Materia medica*

---

[69] Quoted in Hans Wellisch, "How to make an index – 16th century style: Conrad Gessner on indexes and catalogs." *International Classification*, 8.1 (1981), 10–15 (here 10).
[70] Quoted in Henry B. Wheatley, *How to Make an Index* (London: Eliot Stock, 1902), 4.
[71] Alberto Cevolini, *De Arte Excerpendi. Imparare a dimenticare nella modernità* (Florence: Olschki, 2006), 29–30.

(1529) included two strictly alphabetical indices, one of plant names that ran to eight pages in two columns, another a subject index of six pages in three columns.[72]

The embrace of alphabetization in paratexts was mirrored elsewhere. Merchants and financiers often used alphabetization in their record-keeping. Early modern scholars frequently organized their commonplace books alphabetically. The Italian naturalist Ulisse Aldrovandi (1522–1605), for example, ordered his notes alphabetically in imitation of the many merchants whom he knew.[73] In the many encyclopedias and other reference works published to distill and summarize the masses of information now available in print, alphabetization became the standard paradigm by which to present material.[74] Printed dictionaries and word lists also now reflected alphabetical organization. For an encyclopedia, perhaps especially ones that aimed for universality, the use of alphabetization necessarily rejected hierarchies of knowledge, replacing them with an order that was morally arbitrary. This tension – between a rationalized and integrated knowledge structure and efficient means of information retrieval – remains with us today.[75]

1.7 The Shape of the Book

The themes I have discussed in this introduction will recur in multiple contexts in the chapters that follow. In Chapter 2, I trace the rise of paper as the material substrate for the information order in late medieval Europe. The chapter describes how paper made its way west and came to be "domesticated" in Europe; it highlights the intrinsic qualities, including its relative affordability, that allowed it to insinuate itself into everyday life.

Among the most eager early adopters of paper were merchants and financiers, who had long had well-defined needs for record-keeping and information management. Chapter 3 examines the manifold ways that practitioners of business from the late Middle Ages onward sought to represent their activities on paper, and experimented with new ways of understanding their reality through numbers, including accounting conventions such as double-entry. Merchants were also among the keenest consumers of timely news and information and, as a matter of course,

---

[72] Hazel Bell, ed., *Indexers and Indexes in Fact & Fiction* (Toronto: University of Toronto Press, 2001), 18.
[73] Fabian Kraemer, "Ulisse Aldrovandi's *Pandechion Epistemonicon* and the use of paper technology in Renaisance natural history." *Early Science and Medicine*, 19 (2014), 398–423.
[74] Ann Blair, "Organizations of knowledge." In James Hankins, ed., *The Cambridge Companion to Renaissance Philosophy* (Cambridge: Cambridge University Press, 2007), 287–305.
[75] A point also made in Headrick, *When Information Came of Age*, 165.

major commercial centers became important informational nodes in the emerging early modern information economy. The chapter also explores the broad influence of mercantile record-keeping, accounting techniques, and commercial attitudes across early modern society.

Chapter 4 examines what I call the "politics of paper," examining how the political landscape of Europe changed as more and more of statecraft was mediated by writing. It is guided by the question "what does early modern politics look like when we approach it from the standpoint of writing, information and information management?" I suggest that the need for the management of state papers effected a shift from a medieval notarial culture to an early modern secretarial one that required the intervention of a great number of writing professionals in the service of the state. Much of this writing was in the form of letters, and I characterize the theater of European politics as a "letterocracy." Early modern princes and states generated unprecedented amounts of information about their realms and subjects. This was the first age of state archives, and every manner of document found its way into these repositories. Along with the expanding chanceries, archives were the state institutions deployed to manage information from past and present and mobilize it for use in the future.

In Chapter 5, I address the printing press as an agent of informational change. I argue that there was a printing revolution, but that Gutenberg's invention was revolutionary chiefly because of the sheer quantity of information that it injected into early modern society. Only part of this information explosion came in the form of books – pamphlets, newssheets, posters, gazettes, journals, and countless other medial forms streamed off Europe's presses. In the realm of books, access and abundance characterized the new landscape – books were available to new populations and individuals accumulated large private libraries for the first time. Printed material also served as a spur to a great deal of manuscript writing. In this way, print combined with existing technologies and practices to reinforce some means of communication, modify others, and create altogether new ones.

Chapter 6 looks at how an explosion of information transformed early modern scholarship and natural philosophy, driven both by the great number of books now in circulation and by the embrace of observation. Early modern scholars, especially those seeking knowledge of nature, dedicated a great deal of time, effort, and creativity to the management of the resulting particulars. I argue that the most important feature of the Scientific Revolution was the sheer increase in the amount of available information about nature. Information management thus became an essential component of learning, and scholars and scientists employed a variety of note-taking schemes, commonplacing conventions, and taxonomies of knowledge to make sense of this cornucopia. These were the tools that led to the demolition of the heretofore-bounded Aristotelian universe.

In Chapter 7, I turn to other examples of Europeans' compulsion to generate information in writing. With ready recourse to pen and paper, they composed huge numbers of letters, creating communicative communities across distance. The early modern "Republic of Letters" consisted of multiple, overlapping, and intersecting networks of information exchange. Europeans also penned a great variety of "writings of the private sphere," written for the self, the family, or posterity. Again, the availability of paper facilitated this regular writing, recorded in journals, memoirs, and family books that often spanned generations. The chapter also examines how information about people and events spread in the emerging early modern news culture, through correspondence, newsletters, gazettes, and (ultimately) newspapers. All of this material added to the information in circulation in European society – including news from faraway places, leading to a more developed sense of a broader world that operated within a shared, simultaneous present.

Finally, in a concluding chapter, I discuss the echoes and resonances between this early modern period of transition and our own age of the Digital Information Revolution. In our digital milieu, we are faced with our own oceans of particulars and, to some degree, are all compelled to be information managers. We are told that we are seeing the end of the age of paper. This may or may not be the case, but I believe that reflecting on the early modern story of informational change can offer novel ways of thinking about where we find ourselves today, and where we may be going.

* * *

In the historian's craft, there are sins of commission and sins of omission. I have no doubt that readers will uncover sins I have committed in the course of this book – I take full responsibility for these. But I am also aware that in a book on a topic this sprawling, centered on a concept that is as inchoate as information, the sins of omission are likely to be more numerous. To seek to avoid all sins of omission, however, would be to submit to the far greater literary transgressions of unwieldiness and unreadability. I confess, therefore, that there is a great deal that I could have included, but have left out. Like so many of the early modern Europeans whom I write about in the pages that followed, I was forced to choose to direct and interdict the flows of information. There is much more I could have said, many more topics I could have introduced, and plenty that would have contradicted my claims. That being said, an important component of writing history is, to paraphrase Kenny Rogers' country music standard, *The Gambler*, choosing what to leave in and what to leave out. I choose to embrace a maxim that Ragnhild Hatton used to share with her students: "A good book is about the material that you leave out rather than what you put in."[76]

Much of what I have decided to leave in is, I am quick to admit, originally the ideas of others. As I reflect on the process of writing this book, I find myself thinking of a remark made by Michel de Montaigne in his essay "On educating children," citing the *Life of Chrysippus* by Diogenes Laertius: "Apollodorus said that if you cut out his borrowings, his paper would remain blank. Epicurus on the other hand left three hundred tomes behind him: not one quotation from anyone else was planted in any of them."[77] I am acutely aware how dependent this book is on the work of countless other authors; I freely admit that this project rests largely upon the growing body of work by scholars of the period who have taken information as the chief subject of their study. This is a work of synthesis, but it is one that seeks to draw out original connections between the insights of others. The approach of my project echoes the words of the great nineteenth-century American naturalist George Perkins Marsh to a friend as he was writing his seminal work on American ecology, *Man and Nature*, first published in 1864: "I shall steal pretty much, but I know some things myself."

Addressing a topic like information in the early modern world, a subject around which it is essentially impossible to put up fences, the information management that became imperative to so many in early modern Europe was also essential for me. I came to realize that the tools that I employed in seeking to make sense of so much information from and about the past resembled, in important ways, those employed by the early modern individuals and institutions appearing in the pages of this book. I used my own search engines, composed a great array of notes, created my own summaries, stored information in files and folders, employed common-placing techniques, repurposed particulars outside of their original contexts, and created paratextual devices such as page numbers, indices, and footnotes to navigate the final product – all of these versions of practices developed and experimented with in the early modern period. They were necessary to cope with my own *copia*. Whether they were effective in making this book convincing and readable, I will leave to the reader to decide.

---

[76] I thank Hamish Scott for sharing this little pearl of wisdom with me.
[77] Michel de Montaigne, *The Essays: A Selection*. Trans. and ed by Michael Screech (London: Penguin, 1991), 39.

2 European Paper

In 1638, the Genoese merchant Giovanni Domenico Peri (1590–1666), in *Il Negotiante*, his treatise on his profession, remarked on the importance of the material that consumed most of his day:

> It has been said that the invention of paper, because it is a material so thin and light, has allowed one to express the concepts of one's mind, and entrust them to a small sheet, enclosed and well-sealed, so that they can securely go to every corner of the world, until, arrived in the hands of whoever it was sent to, and opened by him, it fulfills the task assigned to it; and in this manner friends who are separated by great distances can negotiate with one another, truly a great consolation to those people who love one another, but especially convenient for business.[1]

When Peri wrote this paean to paper, Italian merchants had regularly been employing paper for more than three hundred years. In this work, Peri describes at length the various habits and practices that the good merchant has to pursue in order to ensure the profitability of his business. A great many of these have to do with record-keeping, the mundane and routine tasks of recording transactions with pen and paper, deemed essential for effective commerce. But Peri also wished to point out another, almost magical, feature: how it allows one to project oneself virtually across vast distances. For a merchant such as Peri, as for so many early modern statesmen, scholars, and natural philosophers, paper served both to root the writer to his desk in the drudgery of record-keeping and note-taking and to unmoor him from his current locale, connecting him with people and places many miles away.

---

[1] *Il negotiante di Giovanni Domenico Peri Genovese* (Genoa: Pier Giovanni Calenzano, 1638), 32: "È stata accertata l'inventione della carta, perche in materia si sottile, e di così poco peso si possono commodamente spiegare i concetti d'animo, quali fidati à picciol foglio in se ristretto, e ben sigillato possono sicuramente caminare in ogni parte del Mondo, sinche gionto quello alle mani di che è indirizzato, apertole il seno, compisca l'offitio commessoli; & in questa maniera ancorche allontanati da longhissimo spatio di cammino possono gli Amici trattar insieme, consolatione veramente grande delle persone, che s'amano, ma commodità grandissima della Mercatura."

Mundane, yet magical, paper was thus simultaneously confining and liberating. Peri spoke about paper's flexibility, lightweight nature, and portability; but also about its tendency to accumulate in unmanageable piles, rendering it anything but flexible, light, and portable.[2] Paradoxes such as these abound in the history of early modern paper and the information that it carried: how something celebrated for being so light could become so heavy as it accumulated (as it inevitably did); how something that facilitated communication could end up wreaking confusion because it bore so much contradictory information; how the demand for documents for the purposes of commercial, governmental, and scholarly decision-making could have a constipating effect because information could not easily be turned into actionable knowledge; how something so fragile, pliable, and flammable could be so particularly well suited to preserving information in an unaltered state. As Pierre-Marc de Biasi has written of the oxymora of paper: "it is ephemera and permanence, meaning and insignificance, the precious and the disposable, memory and forgetfulness."[3]

Paper has served as an unmatched conduit for law, tradition, literature, and other forms of memorializing culture. But it is also the ideal medium for recording ephemera, things that might be remembered in short order, but then discarded, both physically and from one's memory. Information was inscribed on paper with the intention to share and circulate, but also to sequester and isolate. Paper thus simultaneously occupied two polarities of a spectrum of information storage – its material qualities made it suitable for circulating small parcels of information of short-term, or even fleeting, duration (think "burn after reading") while also being an excellent vehicle for amassing great quantities of data into files and folios that could weigh tons, intended for storage without end. Such are the paradoxes of paper.

Writing on paper spans every level of formality, from solemn proclamations to notes scribbled on scraps. This spectrum represents the many functions of the same material. Hence the different qualities of paper for different uses: board for diplomas and certificates, fine bond paper for job

---

[2] A welcome focus on the material aspects of the administrative embrace of paper can be seen in a pair of recent articles by Megan Williams: "Unfolding diplomatic paper and paper practices in early modern chancery archives." In Arndt Brendecke, ed., *Praktiken der Frühen Neuzeit. Akteure, Handlungen, Artefakte* (Cologne: Böhlau Verlag, 2015), 496–508; and "'Zu Notdurff der Scheiberey.' Die Einrichtung der frühneuzeitlichen Kanzlei." In Dagmar Freist, ed., *Diskurse – Körper – Artefakte. Historische Praxeologie in der Frühneuzeitforschung.* (Bielefeld: Transcript Verlag, 2015), 335–372.
[3] Pierre Marc de Biasi, "Le papier, fragile support de l'essentiel." *Les cahiers de médiologie*, 2 (1997), 7–17 (here 9–10). "Il est l'éphémère et la permanence, le sens et l'insignifance, le précieux et le jetable, la mémoire et l'oubli."

applications, rough crayon paper for children's drawings. In early modern Europe, too, as paper assumed its great many informational functions, sellers offered paper of many different types and qualities. A variegated market demanded variegated product.

This book is not chiefly a material history; its concerns instead are cultural, communicational, and institutional, tracing shifting attitudes toward information. But its material dimensions are important. In today's terms, it is hardware. Paper is a "material" because it is useful matter, and "it is from the particularities of substances that uses arise."[4] Put simply, paper has proven to be the most convenient and flexible means by which to record human thoughts in writing, long before it was married to the technology of printing. It has demonstrated an appeal and utility that have proven remarkably durable in the face of technologies that might displace it. It was largely the material advantages of paper that led to its widespread use and its insinuation into so many facets of early modern European society. When these were married to availability and affordability, paper became an indispensable hardware.

In essence, early modern Europe became a culture of paper. In ways subtle and obvious, this change in medium effected a change in content. Although paper did, in many cases, simply become a new conduit for brands of information that existed in the Middle Ages, paper also introduced new forms of producing, presenting, and storing information, and encouraged new practices and habits. It is not simply that, as Marshall McLuhan might have it, "the medium is the message," but the medium did help shape the form and content of the messages it contained, and in time, the lives of its messengers.

Perceptive contemporaries were cognizant of the changes that had been wrought by the new medium. The English polymath Francis Bacon, always keenly alert to the utility of knowledge and of human ingenuity, wrote in the *Novum Organum* (1620) that paper, as a human invention, was "a singular instance of art, and a common enough thing." As opposed to the brittleness of many artificial substances,

paper is a tough material and can be cut and torn, so that it imitates and almost rivals any animal hide or membrane or the leaf of any plant and such works of Nature. For it is neither brittle, like glass, nor woven, like cloth; it has fibres, certainly, but not separate threads, being in every way similar to natural materials, so that among artificial materials almost nothing is found like it, and it is obviously

---

[4] The definition supplied in Christopher Hall, *Materials: A Very Short Introduction* (Oxford: Oxford University Press, 2014), xiii, 1.

singular. And certainly we prefer in artificial materials those that most closely copy nature, or, on the other hand, those that powerfully overrule and overturn her.[5]

A virtuosic creation yet exceedingly common, tough yet pliable, made of natural materials and yet a facilitator of artifice and the domination of nature, paper fulfilled many functions for someone like Bacon. It was a means of recording the observations, garnered from nature and from reading, that were essential to knowledge – Bacon believed letters inscribed on paper were of far greater value to memory than images.[6] It was paper that filled the rooms and made up the universal archive in Bacon's "Solomon's House" described in *New Atlantis*. Paper correspondence connected Bacon with others as an essential component in the networked communication that made the pursuit of knowledge possible. For Bacon, paper could also constitute "waste," blank leaves that could be filled with summaries, notes, and reminders. Like merchants, he would keep a "waste-book" of notes, observations, and miscellanea, which would then be organized into his version of a ledger, a commonplace book with headings that allowed for relatively quick reference.[7] Some of the lists that he created in these notebooks were reproduced in his published works, most notably in the *Sylva Sylvarum* (1627). Paper was thus the means for persistent record-keeping in large volumes, but also a medium receptive to organization and distillation. Bacon was a keen participant in what Harold Love has called a "culture of transcription" in seventeenth-century England.[8] In this sense, Bacon's declared commitment to the "total reconstruction of all knowledge" was unthinkable without the use, accumulation, and movement of huge volumes of paper.

Tommaso Garzoni (1549–1589) in his late sixteenth-century treatise on the professions, *La Piazza Universale di Tutte le Professioni del Mondo, e Nobili et Ignobili* (1586), wrote that "it is a certain thing that in the earliest days men did not have paper, in which our own age greatly abounds in many parts of the world as perfection incarnate."[9] Paper was essential for

---

[5] *Novum Organon*. Trans. and ed. by Peter Urbach and John Gibson (Chicago: Open Court, 1994), 200–201.
[6] Aleida Assmann, *Cultural Memory and Western Civilization. Functions, Media, Archives* (Cambridge: Cambridge University Press, 2011), 182.
[7] See Angus Vine, "Commercial commonplacing: Francis Bacon, the waste-book, and the ledger." In Richard Beadle, Peter Beal, and Colin Burrow, eds., *Manuscript Miscellanies, c. 1450–1700* (London: British Library, 2011), 197–218.
[8] Harold Love, *The Culture and Commerce of Texts. Scribal Publication in Seventeenth-Century England* (Oxford: Clarendon Press, 1993), 200.
[9] Tomaso Garzoni, *La Piazza Universale di Tutte le Professioni del Mondo, e Nobili et Ignobili* (Venice: Giovan Battista Somascho, 1586), 242: "E chiara cosa certo, che in quei primi tempi gli'huomini mancavano della carta, della quale abonda sommamente l'età nostra in diverse parti del mondo e perfettione ridotta, ma in vece di carta adoperavano le foglie di palme, & perciò dura fino al giorno d'oggi chiamarsi fogli quelli de'libri."

a wide range of professional practices, and its availability one of the features that separated his own age from those past.

In his treatise on note-taking and excerpting, first published in 1638, Jeremias Drexel (1581–1638) celebrated the availability and ease of use of paper in his present day, compared with what was available to the ancients: "they wrote on all kinds of things: they used wax, wood, cloth, bark, tree leaves, lead, skins and palimpsests. We most conveniently use paper and rejoice in the printers: this way of writing is so easy that leisure is not more pleasant than work."[10] In fact, the ease that Drexel praised was one of the chief reasons that paper accumulated in such heaps, a powerful aid to memory to be sure (as Drexel insisted) but also generating a great deal of additional work that never would have vexed the ancients.

Paper, therefore, was a participant, a collaborator, in the various writing processes that its availability abetted. The use of paper encouraged new habits of mind, or "investigative pathways" (a term coined by Frederic Holmes), which capitalized on paper's material amenableness.[11] Paper encouraged the "writing-up" of experiences, observations, thought processes, and insights in manifold formats: scribbles written on to scraps of paper, notebooks, ledgers, drafts, tables, letters, filled-out printed forms, sketches, doodles, lists, and marginal notes. Writing onto paper was a process both of "abstraction" and of "materialization." To understand the history of early modern information and information management, therefore, it is essential to tell the story of the material.

2.1 The Pre-history of European Paper

Most learned Europeans of this age knew that paper had not originated in Europe. That its genesis was in the East was widely acknowledged, even if the details of its origins, and the important role of the Islamic world in introducing it to Europe, remained obscured or deliberately downplayed. The world had seen genuine cultures of paper prior to the appearance of the first Western one in the Renaissance. Paper was invented in the second century BCE, and by the fourth century CE, its use was widespread in China.[12]

---

[10] Jeremias Drexel, *Aurifodina artium et scientiarum omnium: Excerpendi sollertia, omnibus litterarum amantibus monstrata* (Antwerp: Ioannis Cnobbari, 1638), quoted in Ann Blair, "Note taking as an art of transmission." *Critical Inquiry*, 31.3 (2004), 85–107 (here 91–92).

[11] Frederic Lawrence Holmes, *Investigative Pathways: Patterns and Stages in the Careers of Experimental Scientists* (New Haven, CT: Yale University Press, 2004).

[12] Lucien Polastron, *Le Papier. 2000 ans d'histoire et de savoir-faire* (Paris: Imprimerie Nationale, 1999), 17–18.

By the time of the Tang Dynasty (seventh century), paper appears to have been fully integrated into life in China, both as a writing surface (produced in many colors), but also as a raw material for kites, wrapping, and toilet paper. The Tang's political stability, wealth, and official sponsorship of scholarship created great demand for paper documents. Anyone who wished to advance in the ranks of the imperial bureaucracy had to demonstrate skill in maintaining and organizing paper records. Paper scrolls, including huge numbers of Buddhist texts, were copied in profusion. During the late sixth century, the civil service of the Sui Dynasty provided one emperor with 300,000 paper copies of an edict condemning an imperial rival.[13]

Evidence of the extent and diversity of paper use in China during this period can be seen in the Dunhuang hoard, a vast collection of more than 30,000 paper rolls dating from the fourth through tenth centuries, discovered in a cave in 1907 and including Buddhist sutras, Confucian texts, government documents, business contracts, calendars, anthologies, dictionaries, glossaries, and guides to composition and letter writing, intended for use by children.[14]

The Abbasid Caliphate relied on paper almost from its inception in the eighth century. The precise mechanism of the transmission of paper into the Near East from China remains uncertain, but it is likely that paper made its way down the Silk Road east to west to reach the heartlands of Islam. From a technical standpoint, the chief achievement of Arab papermakers was their advancement of the manufacture of rag paper, the form that would predominate in Europe until the advent of wood pulp paper in the nineteenth century. Arab paper, made from repurposed linen and hemp, was strong, durable, and thick relative to modern papers. In the Abbasid Caliphate, it was produced and purchased in large orders, often prefolded in measures of hands, five hands being a *rizma*, a word that would be adopted in English as "ream." Abbasid society was deeply committed to the use of paper in its institutions of learning and bureaucratic administration. Paper was evidently adopted as a cost-effective alternative to parchment, of which there was an inadequate supply in Mesopotamia in any case.

The Abbasid caliph Harun al Rashid (r. 786–809) mandated the use of paper in all of his government administration. Writing several centuries

---

[13] Alexander Monro, *The Paper Trail. The Unexpected History of the World's Greatest Invention* (London: Allen Lane, 2014), 127.
[14] Tsien Tsuen-Hsuin, "Paper and printing." In Joseph Needham, ed., *Science and Civilization in China*. Vol. 5, Part 2 (Cambridge: Cambridge University Press, 1985), 45.

later, the great Arab historian Ibn Khaldûn (1332–1406) remarked upon the shift to paper in his *Muqaddimah*. He noted that parchment was no longer sufficient to meet the demand for writing surfaces: "Thus, paper was used for government documents and diplomas. Afterwards, people used paper in sheets for government and scholarly writings, and the manufacture reached a considerable degree of excellence."[15] According to Ibn Khaldûn, this step was encouraged by paper's absorptive properties; writing could not be erased (scratched away) as it could be on parchment. The effective functioning of the Abbasid state was bound up in record-keeping with pen and paper, and secretaries assumed prominent roles in public life, tasked with the upkeep of tax records, military registers, the official correspondence of state officials, legal records, and the archives of the state. Numerous treatises on paperwork and secretaries in bureaucracy began to appear as early as the tenth century. There is ample evidence that the use of paper extended beyond the elite levels: Baghdad had a thriving stationers' market, said to be lined with more than a hundred shops selling paper products.

There can be little doubt that the availability and exploitation of paper as a writing and reading surface, inscribed in a common language and shared over the vast distances of the House of Islam, contributed to the remarkable cultural flowering of the Abbasid "Golden Age." Paper became, as it would in early modern Europe, the storage receptacle of learning, and, as material memory, a stepping stone for further learning – as it often has, paper served as a catalyst. Bloom has said of the role of paper in Islamic society: "much in the history of Islamic civilization in the MA, between 600 and 1500, can be seen in terms of conflicting claims of memory and the written record; the triumph of notation – whether written or drawn – came with paper."[16] This movement from memory to inscription echoes the transition that takes place in the "paper culture" of early modern Europe.

Book repositories of the medieval Islamic world could contain tens of thousands of books, including the "House of Knowledge" in Baghdad burned by the Seljuks in 1056; the library of the Ummayad caliph al-Hakam in Córdoba in the tenth century (burned and dispersed by his successors); and the collection of the Fatimid caliph in Egypt, said to number in the hundreds of thousands (if not the 1.6 million claimed by the historian Ibn Abi Tayyi), dispersed by Saladin following his conquest of Egypt.[17] Very few of these books remain extant today.

---

[15] Quoted in Jonathan Bloom, *Paper Before Print. The History and Impact of Paper in the Islamic World* (New Haven: Yale University Press, 2001), 49.
[16] Bloom, *Paper before Print*, ix.   [17] Bloom, *Paper Before Print*, 122.

The famed Geniza documents found in Cairo's Old Synagogue, more than 300,000 documents created by the Jewish community there and datable chiefly to the period 1002–1266, demonstrate that paper had supplanted papyrus in Egypt as the writing surface of choice by the eleventh century.[18] Abundant use of paper and more or less constant writing remained features of Egypt under the Mamluks, as seen in the kaleidoscopic survey of medieval Arab learning by the Mamluk secretary Shihab al-Din al-Nuwayri, who emphasized the central roles of writing (*kitāba*) to the functioning of the chancery, to financial management, to the conduct of law, to the preservation of learning through the copying of manuscripts, and to pedagogy.[19] This Mamluk culture of writing, of course, was only possible with ready access to paper.

Islamic merchants in the Middle Ages were early adopters of paper as a facilitator in their transactions and record-keeping, even if they were not, as is often suggested, the originators of double-entry bookkeeping. Paper was essential to Islamic commerce: "Financial procedure in the medieval Islamic lands was complex and sophisticated and the whole complicated edifice depended on the availability of paper."[20] Muslim merchants across the Middle Ages used paper instruments to record contracts, letters of accounts, bills of credit, and promissory notes. The medieval Islamic world was thus both an incubator for the potential of paper and a conduit for its transmission. The paper cultures of the Near East did not last, however. Papermaking in the Levant went into gradual decline, especially after the cataclysm of the Mongol sack of Baghdad in 1258. Chronicles of the event tell of the mass burning of stacks of paper records, and the dumping of thousands of books into the Tigris, such that the river ran black with ink. By the fourteenth century, most of the paper consumed in Baghdad was imported, much of it from Italy; a manuscript of the Koran produced in Baghdad around the year 1340 was written on paper bearing Italian watermarks. Come the sixteenth century, papermaking had disappeared almost entirely from the Islamic world.

2.2 The Domestication of Paper

That paper did not diffuse throughout European culture at an earlier date is not due to a lack of access or exposure. Like most technologies, paper

---

[18] On the Geniza documents, see Shelomo Dov Goitein, *A Mediterranean Society: An Abridgement in One Volume* (Berkeley: University of California Press, 1999).
[19] Shihab al-Din al-Nuwayri, *The Ultimate Ambition in the Arts of Erudition. A Compendium of Knowledge from the Classical Islamic World*. Trans. and ed. by Elias Muhanna (New York: Penguin, 2016), 105–106.
[20] Bloom, *Paper Before Print*, 154.

emerged within a culture as a response to perceived need. It is important to remember that the story of paper in Europe is one of adoption, rather than invention. Paper as a technology was adopted, improved, and infused into European society only when its existing structures and practices made it fitting to do so. The age of paper in Europe could begin only when supply and demand coincided.

The oldest paper document in Europe, the codex Orient 298 in Leiden's university library, is from a Persian-Arab producer and dates from sometime in the ninth century, several centuries before its use became widespread[21] The use of paper in the Norman chanceries of Sicily may have dated back to the Muslim occupation of the island in the late eleventh century. The indigenous European paper industry began to develop chiefly in Spain, where the Ummayad dynasty had used paper extensively in administration and learning and where there was a correspondingly high volume of paper manufacture. When Christian forces conquered Toledo in 1085, they found a rag-paper mill in operation there. By the second half of the twelfth century, quires of Spanish paper, especially from the mills of Xátiva, were being exported into southern Italy, and imported into Germany by the third decade of the thirteenth century.

European paper was, from its beginning, made from rags. In an interesting confluence of the history of fashion and the history of information, the clothing trends of the 1200s saw a significant uptick in the demand for linen clothing, especially for use as undergarments. This resulting waste was literally grist for the paper mill; there never would have been enough raw material for large-scale paper manufacture without this supply. The basic process by which paper was made varied very little across the five centuries from the first European paper mills to the advent of machine milling. Rags would remain the primary raw material for paper until the nineteenth century, when a shortage of linens was one of the factors that pushed papermakers toward the adoption of wood pulp.

In Italy, where the merchants and municipal administrators of the peninsula's many city-states began to employ paper in their everyday activities, paper was being imported from producers in the Middle East and North Africa by the middle of the twelfth century.[22] Some of the earliest documents copied onto paper in Italy can be found in the Genoese

---

[21] D. A. Felix, "What is the oldest dated paper in Europe?" *Papiergeschichte*, 2.6 (1952), 73–75.
[22] Harold Innis, "The coming of paper." In William Buxton, Michael Cheney, and Paul Heyer, eds., *Harold Innis' History of Communications: Paper and Printing* (Lanham: Rowman and Littlefield, 2015), 15–56 (here 28).

European Paper 47

2.1 From the very beginning of indigenous European manufacture, paper was made of rags. *Stamping Mill for Pulverising Rags* – Georg Andreas Boeckler, Theatrum Macinarum novum etc., (Cologne, 1662) Schlosser Collection of Paper Making, New York Public Library (Getty Images).

archives, dating from the mid-twelfth century; Genoese scribes used paper to transcribe minutes of their acts. The paper used in Genoa was supplied from both Spain and North Africa. In 1145, so many government documents were being recorded on paper in his kingdom that King Roger II of Sicily (r. 1130–1154) ordered the important ones to be copied from paper onto parchment. Over time, cost and convenience overcame any organized resistance to the use of paper. City administrations in Venice and Tuscany were using paper by the 1220s, paper most likely manufactured in Spain.[23] The largest consumers of paper at this early stage were governments and their chanceries. Merchants, by the thirteenth century, were employing paper for their own sums and record-keeping. They were also writing their letters on paper, a practice that was soon customary for state officials as well.

Italy was well positioned to assume the manufacture of paper for reasons having to do with both supply and demand. The mountainous terrain provided fast-moving streams that could be exploited for the power they provided. Raw materials were abundant and cheap – cultivated hemp and flax and ample rags from the textile industry were available locally. Italy's urbanized demography, fractured political landscape, and commercial orientation all encouraged the use of paper. Small-scale production in Italy began by the 1230s and the first major Italian paper mills sprang up in 1276 around Fabriano in the Marches, a region with an ample supply of fast-moving water, allowing the use of paddled wheels with geared camshafts. The manufacturers in Fabriano used hobnailed mallets instead of grindstones to macerate fabrics and exceedingly fine brass wires in their matrices. Fabriano also seems to have been among the first manufacturing centers where gelatin sizing was used for paper – this had the advantage of producing a turgid surface that would stand up to quill pens. These are all features that would come to characterize European paper and give it superior suppleness and durability to the paper produced in the Arab world.[24] By the early fourteenth century, demand for paper in Italy was chiefly met by Italian papermakers. By 1400, there were at least thirty active paper mills in Italy, aligned chiefly along the wool-trade routes, with Fabriano remaining the predominant center of production well into the sixteenth century.[25]

Italian producers soon proved successful in exporting their product to other markets. The earliest attested use of paper in Germany, in the Dean's register at Passau cathedral in 1246–7, was written on Italian paper.[26] By 1300, we see evidence of widespread adoption of paper, generally from Italy, by city governments in northern Europe as well. The municipal account books of several towns in the Low Countries were recorded on paper around the this time: Mons (1285), Bruges (1307), and Mechelen

---

[23] Jean Irigoin, "Les origines de la fabrication du papier en Italie." *Papiergeschichte*, 13.5–6 (1963), 62–67.
[24] Conor Fahy, "Paper making in seventeenth-century Genoa: the account of Giovanni Domenico Peri (1651)." *Studies in Bibliography*, 56 (2003/4), 243–259.
[25] Polastron, *Le Papier*.
[26] Bernhard Bischoff, *Latin Paleography: Antiquity and the Middle Ages* (Cambridge: Cambridge University Press, 1990), 12.

(1311).[27] Some aristocratic courts also adopted paper for their record-keeping: paper registers and notebooks associated with revenue collection exist for several courts from the Low Countries.[28] Italian paper was available for purchase across much of western Europe by the early fourteenth century, even in Spain.[29] Until 1430, paper of Italian origin was predominant in Germany and the Low Countries, but after that, providers became primarily local, as paper production moved in a generally south to north direction.[30] The first French paper mills were in Languedoc, dating from the first decades of the fourteenth century. A Spanish miller known as Jean l'Espagnol was at work in Flanders by 1405. The first paper mill in the German lands was in all likelihood established just outside Nuremberg by the merchant Ulman Stromer (1329–1407). Stromer had seen paper mills during his business travels to Italy, and he relied on the expertise of Lombard specialists in establishing his own operation, which became active for the first time in 1390.[31] By 1392, Stromer was providing paper for the use of the Nuremberg City Council.[32] His mill can be seen in the foreground of the view of Nuremberg included in the *Liber chronicarum* (1493) of Hartmann Schedel (1440–1514).[33]

England had paper mills by 1495, with the founding of a mill by John Tate, and there are records of a number of them (many short-lived) in the

---

[27] Christiane Piérard, "Le papier dans les documents comptables de la ville de Mons aux XIVe et XVe siècles." In Georges Despy, et al., eds., *Hommage au Professeur Paul Bonenfant (1899–1965): Études d'histoire médiévale dédiées à sa mémoire par les anciens élèves de son séminaire à l'Université Libre de Bruxelles* (Brussels, sp. ed., 1965), 341–363; Louis Gilliodts-Van Severen, *Inventaire des archives de la ville de Bruges: Introduction* (Bruges: Gaillard, 1878); Willy Godenne, "Le Papier des comptes communaux de Malines datant du moyen âge." *Handelingen van de Koninklijke Kring voor Oudheidkunde, Letteren en Kunst van Mechelen*, 64 (1960), 36–53.

[28] Erik Kwakkel, "A new type of book for a new type of reader: the emergence of paper in vernacular book production." *Library*, 7.4 (2003), 219–248 (here 221).

[29] Albert d'Haensens, "Un exemple d'utilisation du papier à Tournai peu avant 1350." *Scriptorium*, 16 (1962), 89–92.

[30] Rosella Graziaplena, "Paper trade and diffusion in late medieval Europe." In Graziaplena and Mark Livesey, eds., *Paper as a Medium of Cultural Heritage. Archaeology and Conservation. 26th Congress – International Association of Paper Historians* (Rome-Verona, August 30 – September 6, 2002) (Rome: Istituto centrale per la patologia del libro, 2004).

[31] Wolfgang von Stromer, "Das Handelshaus der Stromer von Nürnberg und die Geschichte der ersten deutschen Papiermühle." *Vierteljahrschrift für Sozial- und Wirtschaftsgeschichte*, 47 (1960), 81–104.

[32] Wolfgang von Stromer and Lore Sporhan-Krempel, "Die Papierwirtschaft der Nürnberger Kanzlei und die Geschichte der Papiermacherei im Gebiet der Reichsstadt bis zum Beginn des 30jährigen Krieges." *Archiv für Geschichte des Buchwesens*, 2 (1958), 161–169.

[33] The woodcut, with Stromer's mill at bottom right, appears on 99v–100r. The digital reproduction by the Bayerische Staatsbibliothek can be viewed at http://daten.digitale-sammlungen.de/~db/0003/bsb00034024/images.

sixteenth century. Alfred Shorter has found evidence of thirty-eight paper mills in operation in England in the first half of the seventeenth century.[34] Despite these establishments, most paper used in England would be imported until that century's end.[35] In the course of the sixteenth and seventeenth centuries, in response to great demand, virtually every corner of Europe had access to ample supplies of paper, either from local mills or via import.

Whatever the local supply or demand, paper was always cheaper than parchment or vellum. Already at the end of the fourteenth century Europe was supplying its own paper, and paper was available at a cost six to eight times less than vellum.[36] By about 1500, however, the price differential between parchment and paper had become a chasm. In 1471, the Innsbruck imperial court obtained forty-eight sheets of common paper and thirty-eight of fine Venetian paper for the price of a single piece of parchment. At Linz in 1531, the *Hofkanzlei* secured ninety-six sheets of common paper for the price of a single parchment skin.[37] It was commonplace by the early sixteenth century for paper to be produced without sizing, reducing its cost even more.

By the early years of the fourteenth century, at the latest, there was a self-reinforcing loop in operation, by which the convenience and availability of a relatively cheap writing surface abetted more and more varied writing, which itself in turn increased the demand for paper. Paper was well on its way to supplanting parchment and vellum as the writing surface of choice for everyday writing. The displacement of parchment occurred first in areas of activity where price pressures were felt most keenly. Price-conscious merchants were among the most zealous early users of paper. They used paper as a convenient storage device, in the keeping of their accounts, but also employed it for the large volume of letters that their day-to-day business demanded.

---

[34] Alfred Shorter, *Paper Mills and Paper Makers in England, 1495–1800* (Hilversum: Paper Publications Society, 1957), 29.
[35] Mark Bland, "Italian paper in early seventeenth-century England." In Rosella Graziaplena, ed., *Paper as a Medium of Cultural Heritage: Archaeology and Conservation* (Milan: Istituto centrale per la patologia del libro, 2004).
[36] Roderick Lyall, "Materials: the paper revolution." In Jeremy Griffiths and Derek Pearsall, eds., *Book Publishing in Britain 1375–1475* (Cambridge: Cambridge University Press, 1989), 11–30 (here 11); Carla Bozzolo and Etio Ornato, *Pour une histoire du livre manuscrit au Moyen Âge: trois essais de codicologie quantitative* (Paris: Éditions du Centre national de la recherche scientifique, 1983), 31–33. On paper production and the explosion of paper mills: Kwakkel, "A new type of book"; Wisso Weiss, *Zeittafel zur Papiergeschichte* (Leipzig: Fachbuchverlag, 1983); Christopher de Hamel, *Scribes and Illuminators. Medieval Craftsmen* (Toronto: University of Toronto Press, 1993).
[37] Williams, "Unfolding diplomatic paper," 499.

But where merchants led, others followed. Paper was, for example, a godsend for the *pecia* system of copying required texts that prevailed in Italian universities by the thirteenth century. Thrifty students could now spend far less for works copied onto paper, rather than vellum. Paper's appeal to governments, as I have already detailed, was self-evident. Importantly, paper did more than simply assume the roles previously occupied by other writing surfaces. It also created and facilitated novel written routines related to note-taking, the girding of memory, regular communication, and record-keeping. Notaries, for example, found it considerably easier to use in the recording of official acts. The copious documentation of late medieval commerce would have been unthinkable had merchants relied on parchment. The volume of record-keeping by municipal governments spiked once they had recourse to paper as their primary writing surface. When presented with a medium that made writing easier, Europeans unsurprisingly filled the new blank spaces available to them. New "necessities" emerged as a matter of course.

In none of this is there a necessary connection between paper and print, although the advent of print in the mid-fifteenth century did create a new, and ample, source of demand. Maria Zaar-Görgens has written of a paper boom in the early fifteenth century (before the appearance of the printing press) driven especially by demand from chanceries and bureaucracies.[38] All of the related tasks were carried out on the medium of paper long before the appearance of print. The paper of print represented only a small portion of the great plenty of paper that flowed through European society. This remains the case today.

The gradual adoption of paper, unsurprisingly, encountered resistance in some quarters. Emperor Frederick II (r. 1220–1250), *stupor mundi*, in 1231 forbade the use of paper in the production of official documents, just as it was beginning to take root in Italy. His contemporary, Alfonso the Wise of Castile (r. 1252–1284), was willing to use paper in his government, but only for records deemed of lesser importance. The chancellor of the University of Paris in 1415 dissuaded his charges from copying texts onto paper, a material that was perishable and undignified. Such examples of late medieval reluctance, however, were exceptional, rather than exemplary. By 1340, King Philippe VI of France (r. 1328–1350) was exempting paper from all tolls, as an "object that is indispensable for all studies."[39]

Even once paper had supplanted parchment and vellum as the surface of choice for regular writing, the use of paper remained rare in manuscript

---

[38] Maria Zaar-Görgens, *Champagne, Bar, Lothringen. Papierproduktion und Papierabsatz vom 14. bis zum Ende des 16. Jahrhunderts* (Trier: Porta Alba, 2004).
[39] Polastron, *Le Papier*, 112.

books before 1400. Paper books tended to be vernacular works or utilitarian works in Latin, intended for a lay audience and written in cursive (which was faster to write and thus to copy) by lay scribes. Devotional books in the vernacular could often be found on paper, being cheaper and more broadly transmitted than parchment works, which remained luxury items. Such books were intended for personal use; religious houses and other institutions resisted paper copies, chiefly, it seems, because they believed parchment would last longer.[40] It was only with the advent of the printing press that paper, which withstood the imprint of metal type well, became the material of choice in book manufacture. Printers routinely bargained and bartered with paper manufacturers to secure a regular and relatively inexpensive supply. The best estimates are that paper made up between one-third and one-half of a printer's total costs.[41] Léon Voet has estimated that purchases of paper accounted for one-third of total expenditures for the Plantin press in Antwerp in the year 1566.[42]

In practice, parchment and paper existed side by side well into the early modern period. Lothar Müller has suggested that the continued dual use of paper and parchment in the late Middle Ages was in part a function of a distinction between "documents" and "records." The so-called documents called for a material that was durable and long-lasting, while records in a register were representative of the everyday transactional nature of governing and business: they operated as a sort of limited-term working memory. Such sentiments persisted until very recently: the British House of Lords decided to abandon its practice of printing laws on vellum only in April 2016, centuries after paper was adopted as the medium of choice for recording every other type of business.

Müller's suggestion has much to recommend it, but the more important trend in this period, related to this division, would prove to be the swamping of "documents" by "records," the latter of which accumulated in files as they were created day after day, act after act, transaction after transaction, letter after letter. There were of course many reasons why record-keeping by institutions expanded geometrically in this period, but the suitability of paper precisely for this task must be considered as foremost among them. Paper's availability changed assumptions about when writing should take place and how often it should be employed to

---

[40] Susan Thompson, "Paper manufacturing and early books." In Madeleine Pelner Cosman and Bruce Chandler, eds., *Machaut's World: Science and Art in the Fourteenth Century*. Annals of the New York Academy of Sciences, 314 (New York: New York Academy of Sciences, 1978), 167–174.

[41] Allan Stevenson, "Briquet and the future of paper studies." In E. J. Labarre, ed., *Briquet's Opuscula* (Hilversum, Netherlands: Paper Publications Society, 1955), xv–l.

[42] Léon Voet, *The Golden Compasses: A History and Evaluation of the Printing and Publishing Activities of the Officina Plantiniana at Antwerp*, Vol. 1 (Amsterdam: Van Gendt, 1969).

record reality. It greatly facilitated the growth of administrative documentation and the institutions and edifices that emerged to house it. The individuals and institutions that adopted paper came to see it as an essential means of representing state, self, events, and circumstances. Systematic record-keeping, for many, became de rigueur. And the paper accumulated as a result.

This expansion of the realm of regularized writing, the creation of the "secular scriptorium," saw the job of inscription cease to be the preserve of ecclesiastical specialists and become part and parcel of many areas of European life. The expense of parchment had precluded many of the ways in which the pen was put to paper – one simply did not want to waste parchment, given its cost. The relative affordability of paper meant that there was less hesitation in writing things down: paper could replace parchment in many of its uses, such as government correspondence and statutes and legal decrees, but also in a number of usages that parchment had in some cases precluded: private correspondence, systematic note-taking, daily commercial accounting, writing for pleasure and self-discovery, impromptu scribbling. The practice of writing abetted more writing, and the use of paper abetted more paper, the production of which exploded.

Paper thus became a familiar and indispensable feature in European society; a constant material presence, ubiquitous yet unnoticed as a conduit of information. An infrastructure for the distribution and sale of paper products gradually took shape. The paper available soon diversified: variegations in the type and quality of paper emerged to meet market demand. Different applications required different sorts of paper and market segmentation emerged to reflect this fact. Paper was generally sold by the quire, which consists of twenty-four or twenty-five sheets of paper; twenty quires make a ream. The general rule of thumb was that the smaller the piece of paper, the easier it was to produce, the lower the quality, and the less it cost. Sheet size and quality were often indicators of paper's social function. Fine, large paper was predictably reserved for important documents and formal communication by and with social superiors. The amount of blank space between lines, and especially between the salutation and the first line of the letter proper, increased with the rank of the recipient.

One of the oldest records we have of the range of papers in production comes from 1389 in Bologna. Here four sizes of paper are mentioned: *reçute* (32 × 45 cm), *meçane* (35 × 52 cm), *realle* (45 × 62 cm), and *imperialle* (50 × 74 cm).[43] The names of the larger formats are a clear indication

---

[43] Paul Needham, "Res papirea: sizes and formats of the Late Medieval book." In Peter Rück and Martin Boghardt, eds., *Rationalisierung der Buchherstellung im Mittelalter und in der frühen Neuzeit* (Marburg: Philipps-Universität Marburg/Institut für Historische Hilfswissenschaften, 1994), 123–145.

of their finer quality. More than two centuries later in England, similar demarcations were still in operation, with pot paper (40 × 31 cm), used for most letter writing between familiars, at the bottom of the scale, through foolscap (42 × 32 cm), crown (45 × 35 cm), demy (50 × 35 cm), and finally royal paper (57 × 60 cm).[44] Watermarks, impressed onto sheets of paper by the copper wire on the molds, were an indication of origins, but also of the relative quality of the paper. Costs across the spectrum varied widely, but the cheaper end was accessible enough that a great many households had paper on hand; writing on paper was not the preserve of those at the top of the social spectrum.

In northern Europe, at least, it appears that apothecaries played an important role in the provision of paper products, as well as other writing necessities, such as ink and wax. Papermakers and apothecaries even belonged to the same guilds. The local apothecary would provide a wide range of papers: from cheap paper with which to wrap small purchases to the writing paper needed in bureaucratic work. Bureaucracies sought to standardize the size and quality of paper that they employed in their everyday activities: this facilitated archiving and subsequent retrieval. In many locales, records were eventually bound into registers, and consistent paper dimensions were thus essential. The Society of Jesus, the Catholic order founded by Ignatius Loyola in 1540, for example, repeatedly reminded their regulars to use the standard size of paper for their correspondence, in order to facilitate recordkeeping.[45] Outfits like print shops and state chancelleries tended to get their paper in bulk, in bales, directly via medium- and long-distance trade from papermakers. But when small quantities were needed in a hurry, these highvolume consumers could go to apothecary shops for their needs. Paper was not as expensive as one might have expected. Paper was a sizable cost of business for merchants, printers, and chancellors, but there is little evidence that cost was a significant barrier to the acquisition of paper, presumably due to its abundant use and the resulting economies of scale.[46] Periodic local shortages of rags and linens might result in price spikes, but we should not extrapolate into the past the shortages of the nineteenth century that drove the development of wood-pulp paper.

---

[44] James Daybell, *The Material Letter in Early Modern England: Manuscript Letters and the Culture and Practices of Letter-Writing, 1512–1635* (Basingstoke, UK: Palgrave Macmillan, 2012), 34.

[45] Markus Friedrich, *Der lange Arm Roms? Globale Verwaltung und Kommunikation im Jesuitenorden 1540–1773* (Frankfurt: Campus Verlag, 2011), 92–93.

[46] A point made in Megan K. Williams, "The Apothecary, the Secretary, and the Diplomat: Apothecaries as Purveyors of Paper, Ink, and Information." Paper delivered as part of the panel, "Paper as a Material Artifact of Governance and Trade, 1500–1800," Renaissance Society of America Annual Convention, Berlin, March 26–28, 2015.

It has been suggested that one index of modernity in a society is its manufacture and use of paper. When paper mills began to appear in North America in the 1750s, with paper employed for packing material, writing documents, and printed texts, its manufacture and use were a measure of the waxing modernity of American society.[47] In Europe, the triumph of paper a few centuries earlier was material, cognitive, financial, and practical. Paper insinuated itself into the everyday life of Europe in the late Middle Ages not as an all-conquering technological novelty, but as a long-familiar tool that now fulfilled manifold applications. These applications grew apace in the early modern period, as the occasions that called for writing multiplied. In many cases, the practice of writing abetted yet more writing, creating further occasions and niches for paper instruments, which, after the mid-fifteenth century, included printed ones. As I described in the introduction, one of the signifiers of paper's triumph was the embrace by Europeans of "paperwork." One's written output was now known as one's "papers." Paper and writing became essential features of early modern life. Europeans developed a love–hate relationship with their paper, as the results of their efforts to exploit its capacities were changed institutions, practices, and *mentalités*, as well as the appearance of a host of familiar complaints about the toils of paperwork. Among the earliest and most enthusiastic users of paper instruments were merchants and financiers. And it is with them that we begin in the next chapter.

---

[47] Konstantin Dierks, "Letter writing, stationery supplies, and consumer modernity in the eighteenth-century Atlantic world." *Early American Literature*, 41.3 (2006), 473–494.

3 "Ink-Stained Fingers"
The Information of Commerce and Finance

A bold, recent thesis contends that capitalism is defined not by flows of capital but instead by the flow of information, in what the author calls an "information nexus." Capitalism, he argues, is possible only when there is a sufficient circulation of information between the system's various stakeholders, along with institutions that abet it, governments that permit it, and practices that encourage it. "The only characteristic that is exclusive to capitalism," the argument goes, "is the enhanced ability to marshal information."[1] The author of this thesis, the historian of modern Russia Steven Marks, accords particular importance in the development of capitalism to early modern Europe. It was there and then that the collection and conveyance of information became sufficiently free and voluminous to make possible the subsequent financial, consumer, and industrial revolutions. It was thus the locus of the very "invention" of capitalism. The broadening commitment of early modern merchants to keeping records; the exchange of price and commodity information at commercial exchanges and in the business press, and the traffic of information over long distances, all served to reduce the "stickiness" of information in the capitalist economy. The resulting diminution in transaction costs was an essential advantage to the capitalist West, and, Marks's argument goes, the real root of the "great divergence" between the West and Asia.[2]

This is not the space in which to evaluate this broad-sweeping recasting of the nature and origins of capitalism, but there can be no dispute that European merchants and financiers, beginning in the late Middle Ages, sought out, recorded, shared, and reused unprecedented amounts of information. During this period, men and women of business employed pen and paper to create records of their activity, in account books,

---

[1] Steven Marks, *The Information Nexus. Global Capitalism from the Renaissance to the Present* (Cambridge: Cambridge University Press, 2016), 78.
[2] Marks is reflecting on the original argument offered in Kenneth Pomeranz, *The Great Divergence: China, Europe and the Making of the Modern Economy* (Princeton: Princeton University Press, 2000).

contracts, and assorted financial instruments; to compose regular correspondence, increasingly across long distances, to drum up business, instruct agents, and check on local business conditions; and to compile and circulate timely news and prices. Marks's focus is chiefly on the commercial environment of northwest Europe in the seventeenth and eighteenth centuries (the same locale as for Pomeranz's great divergence), where he sees Dutch and English merchants, with the tacit (and sometimes open) support of their governments, succeeding in commodifying information. But long before then, European merchants, especially those in the Mediterranean, had made account books, correspondence networks, and business news services important components of commercial life. Merchants were early enthusiasts for habitual inscription on paper, and their routinized writing compelled them to be information managers, developing methods of record-keeping and information recombination that rendered their writing more usable.

Among the more famous examples of such mercantile commitment to writing was Francesco Datini (1335–1410), a textile merchant from Prato with sprawling international business connections, who left an astonishing 126,000 commercial letters sent to him from nearly 300 locales, as well as 11,000 written to his wife, most of which concern their business ventures.[3] Correspondence was only one component of Datini's ocean of paper. His partnership with Toro di Berto in Avignon generated credit notes that altogether added up to more than 10,000 pages, along with some 100,000 entries gathered in more than thirty account books covering five years. Datini instructed his branch managers to take notes constantly and maintain notebooks, to serve as reminders of transactions past, present, and future. He described the work of one of his partners in Avignon, Boninsegna di Mateo, as nothing but reading and writing; his firm essentially existed in duplicate on paper – this was the only way to run effectively a large-sale enterprise such as his.[4] As would happen in many other areas of early modern life, men of commerce like Datini early on adopted an ethic of information storage and management. There is little reason to think that Datini was an outlier in generating all of this paper.

The Datini archive was made possible by paper. As a material tool, paper was custom-made for commerce. It allowed a new brand of communication and reinforced both memory and trust. Paper facilitated the

---

[3] Bruno Dini, "L'archivio Datini." In Simonetta Cavaciocchi, ed., *L'impresa, industria, commercio, banca secc. XIII XVIII* (Florence: Le Monnier, 1991), 45–58; Elena Cecchi, *Le lettere di Francesco Datini alla moglie Margherita (1385–1410)* (Prato: Società Pratese di Storia Patria, 1992).
[4] Jacob Soll, *The Reckoning. Financial Accountability and the Rise and Fall of Nations* (New York: Basic Books, 2014), 19–20.

move away from purely mental mathematics. In a fundamentally transactional milieu, the steps undertaken could be recorded on paper with indelible ink (and thus be subject to preservation and verification). The portability and pliability of paper were conducive to record-keeping while on the move, affording significant advantages to peripatetic early modern merchants.

Medieval merchants were practitioners of "pragmatic literacy" – writing was essential to their craft and the merchant surrounded by his papers became proverbial in the later Middle Ages. Commerce increasingly depended on the abstracting power of inscription: merchants consequently were at the forefront of the efforts to represent oneself and one's actions in writing. The day-to-day use of numbers in commerce and the need to consult the details of past transactions inclined merchants to draw upon the preservative power of pen and paper. Assigning values and prices to items was an act of abstraction and allowed the comparison of fundamentally dissimilar objects. It made the incommensurable commensurable.[5]

3.1 The Compulsion to Write and Record

Giovanni Domenico Peri, whose reflections on the importance of paper I have already discussed, remarked that work as a scribe served as a good preparation for a career in business.[6] Peri's perspective on paper is not that of a scholar, librarian, or diplomat, but of a man of commerce; his outlook was deeply practical. Peri repeatedly emphasized the indispensable role of writing in the conduct of the merchant: he identified three essential qualities for the successful merchant: a proficiency in math, a facility in writing, and a knowledge of good grammar. A merchant's sums should be carried out on spare pieces of paper (*pezzo di carta*) or in a notebook (*scartafaccia d'abbaco*). He must be able to write clearly and quickly in the *cancelleresca* (chancery) style, which he labels the "queen of them all," in order to stay in touch with those who are far away, to put on paper what you would say to them viva voce were they present. The letters sent and received should be recorded in a register, to ensure that letters have been responded to and to serve as a repository of past thoughts that

---

[5] Paper money was, of course, the ultimate paper abstraction, but there was as yet, in early modern Europe, little use of paper currency.
[6] *Il negotiante di Giovanni Domenico Peri Genovese* (Genoa: Pier Giovanni Calenzano, 1638), 85: "E per conclusione di questo discorso dico, che non m'è nascosto essere commun desiderio di tutti gli huomini, che alle cure de traffichi mondani s'impiegano d'avanzarsi, così ne' gradi, come nell'Hazenda; che perciò all'hora, che uno si ritrova d'aver servitor lungamente al carico della Scrittura, acquistate qualche sostanze, vorrebbe attendere a'Negotij per conto proprio."

may have subsequently slipped one's mind. Before responding to a letter, the merchant should jot down on a small scrap of paper all of the particulars that he must include in his response. Paper thus serves an essential role in all the stages of producing correspondence.

Writing accompanied virtually every aspect of medieval and early modern mercantile activity. Checks, bills of exchange, book keeping (if not double-entry), the contracts of maritime insurance – these were among the written instruments that had become standard among medieval merchants. In the 1570s, the agent in Spain of the Fugger firm described merchants in Genoa as living under a "reign of paper," whereby the proliferation of letters, bills of exchange, and promissory notes had undermined the old importance of face to face negotiation. That same agent described Genoese merchants as "having more paper than hard cash."[7]

The practice of accounting in early modern Europe originated in the *habitus* of regular writing. In his *Libro del pregio*, a survey of the various professions of his age, Dino Compagni (1260–1324) wrote: "if one wants to make a profession of being a merchant, it is always worthwhile for him to be writing."[8] A fourteenth-century manuscript in the Biblioteca Nazionale in Florence proffers the advice that a merchant "must know how to keep his books and writings ... it is of the utmost utility to know how to keep one's writings in the correct order; it is one of the most important things for a merchant to know how to do."[9] Gianozzo in Leon Batista Alberti's treatise *Della famiglia* (ca. 1434), remarked that good merchants always had "ink-stained fingers."[10]

The paper of commerce that gathered on the desks and in the satchels of early modern merchants was a product of two inclinations above all: the tendency, greatly facilitated by the accessibility of paper, to manage business through correspondence; and the increasingly broadly shared conventions of accounting and record-keeping. Regular correspondence addressed multiple needs for the merchant. It was a means to explore and

---

[7] Fernand Braudel, *Civilization and Capitalism, 15th–18th Century*, Vol. II: *The Wheels of Commerce*, Trans. by Sian Reynolds (Berkeley, CA: University of California Press, 1982), 360.

[8] Isidoro del Lungo, ed., *La cronica delle cose occorrenti ne' tempi suoi; e la canzone morale del pregio* (Florence: Successori Le Monnier, 1908), 223: "S'agrada pregio aver a Mercatante,/Dritura sempre usare a lui convene."

[9] Gino Corti, "Consiglio sulla mercatura di un anonimo trecentista." *Archivio storico italiano*, 110 (1952), 114–119 (here 116): "la cartta costa pocho, e spesso ne recha buono profitto"; "E vuolsi sapere tenere 'l libro e le scritture ... Utilissima cosa è asapere tenere le scritture come s'apartiene: ed è delle principali che bisogni sapere al mercante."

[10] Leon Battista Alberti, in *I tre libri della famiglia*, (1434) ed. F. C. Pellegrini (Florence: Sansoni, 1911), 321, described a relative named Giannozzo who succeeded in business by "having his fingers at all times stained with ink."

negotiate potential deals, it kept the center connected to agents in the field, it helped manage principal–agent disputes and imperfect information scenarios, and it was the primary means by which to keep informed of the latest news and of the fluctuation of prices.[11] The manifold reasons for merchants to engage in scribal communication meant that their letters accumulated in very large volumes. The Castilian merchant and international financier, Simon Ruiz of Medina del Campo (1525–1597), received more than 50,000 letters in the thirty years after 1558, a rate of nearly five a day.[12] His archive in Valladolid, one of richest commercial archives of the period, shows that he kept nearly all of the letters that he received. Merchants like Ruiz preserved their letters for multiple reasons. In one of the more popular treatises on business of the seventeenth century, translated into seven different languages, Jacques Savary (1622–1690) urged all merchants to keep copies of the letters that they received and sent in a copy book, both to have a record of their activities and to protect themselves in the event of a lawsuit.[13]

By the fifteenth century, account books were common among Italian merchants, who now regularly used Arabic numerals, as opposed to Roman ones, in their sums. The intricacies of trade, especially international trade, demanded the recording of a great deal and variety of information: tariffs and exchange rates, price lists, transport costs and schedules, route maps, the rates and terms of maritime insurance, customs and toll costs and procedures, the content of catalogs – these are the bits of information that one finds in the surviving merchant journals and account books.[14] In 1509, Giovanni di Francesco Morelli, a Florentine merchant recently arrived in Lisbon, wrote home: "one spends all day and half the night writing in the writing room, so much work is required ... I am buried in work, yet I shall go on doing the best I can."[15]

Merchants kept paper records of their activities in an extremely diverse array of formats and types of book. The most basic, and most commonly kept, were the *ricordanze* and *memoriale*. The former was generally a straightforward chronological list of transactions, while the latter,

---

[11] Cited in Anthony Mohlo, ed., *Social and Economic Foundations of the Italian Renaissance* (New York: Wiley, 1969), 55, 57.
[12] Henri Lapeyre, *Une famille de marchands: Les Ruiz* (Paris: Librairie Armand Colin, 1955); Felipe Ruiz Martin, *Pequeño capitalismo, gran capitalismo: Simón Ruiz y sus negocios en Florencia* (Barcelona: Critica, 1990).
[13] Jacques Savary, *Le parfait négociant* (1675). Ed. by Édouard Richard (Geneva: Droz, 2011).
[14] Ugo Tucci, "Manuali di mercatura e pratica degli affari del Medioevo." In Carlo Cipolla and Roberto López, eds., *Fatti e idee di storia economica nei secoli XII–XX* (Bologna: Mulino, 1977), 215–231.
[15] Quoted in Marco Spallanzani, *Mercanti fiorentini nell'Asia portoghese (1500–1525)* (Florence, Edizioni SPES, 1997), 42–43.

which often took the form of a ledger, was divided between credits and debits. Credit transactions were more likely to be faithfully recorded than were cash ones, which suggests that account books were less often intended for recording profit and loss than they were employed as an aid to memory; a data bank that was accessible for subsequent reference; a means of recalling past transactions, calling in debts, and planning for future activity. Merchants, however, often maintained more than just these two basic books. Many kept a cashbook (*libro di entrata e uscita*), a record of long-distance trades (*libro di balle mandate*), a secret book (*libro secreto*) to track business contracts and the profits of associates, and ledgers that assumed a variety of different names.

Numerous printed financial manuals repeated the admonition that one must maintain a full accounting of one's business. By 1588, we read in John Melis's *A Briefe Instruction and Maner How to Keepe Bookes of Accompts after the Order of Debitor and Creditor* that a merchant should systematically keep records in a three-part system: (1) a list of inventory; (2) a memorial, or chronicle, of daily transactions; and (3) a ledger of inflows and outflows.[16] In his *Parfait Negociant*, Jacques Savary repeatedly insists on keeping one's books in good order and conducting regular inventories. He actually counsels that the merchant keep nine different books to represent his business in writing, "in order to have always one's affairs before one's eyes."[17] The aim, suggested Savary, was to achieve "a perfect knowledge of all things," an aim that demanded an immense quantity of paperwork.[18] There are moral and practical imperatives at play here: keeping order, Savary insists, is the "soul of a business,"[19] securing reliable information in order to navigate the dangers and opportunities of the world of business. The tendency among merchants, therefore, like so many dealing with information in early modern Europe, was to keep more records rather than fewer, resulting in multiple simultaneous notebooks and bulging folders of loose paper. Erring on the side of greater volumes of paper was expressly recommended by Peri: "one does not want to be too brief in one's entries, it being better to add a few extra

---

[16] Mary Poovey, *A History of the Modern Fact, Problems of Knowledge in the Sciences of Wealth and Society* (Chicago: University of Chicago Press, 1998), 39.
[17] Savary, *Le parfait négociant*, 297: "pour avoir toujours leurs affaires devant les yeux."
[18] Savary, *Le parfait négociant*, 452.
[19] Savary, *Le parfait négociant*, 452: "L'ordre est l'âme d'une manufacture, sans quoi il est impossible qu'elle puisse subsister: c'est par-là que les négocians qui en entreprendront, auront une connaissance parfaite de toutes choses. Cet ordre consiste premièrement à tenir des livres très exacts, et sans confusion, soit pour les matières que l'on fait venir, et que l'on achète dans les pays où elles croissent, soit pour celles que l'on donne aux ouvriers pour les manufactures; des livres de réception d'ouvrages, de teinture, d'envoi, journaux de vente, de caisse, d'extrait et autres livres nécessaires servant aux manufactures."

words than to omit every necessary thing, and it appears to me that one can adapt for the scribe that which they say about notaries: *Notarius verbosus non est reprehendendus.*"[20] It was a maxim that found general application across early modern Europe and this "verbose" record-keeping meant that merchants, like so many others in this age, found themselves engaged in vast record-keeping operations, forcing them to be information managers, among their other tasks.

Commercial bookkeeping generated paper records that met at least three categories of need. First, they assumed legal and moral functions, to assure the security of the firm, its clients, and associates. Account books over time were accepted as evidence in courts of law, almost on a par with notarial documents. Francesco Datini deployed the account books from his Avignon branch as evidence in a legal dispute at the Court of the Guild in 1400. Account books were also a means of demonstrating the trustworthiness and moral probity of the merchant, in the face of widespread suspicion of his profession (plus distrust among partners could be extremely destabilizing). Both closely kept personal records and accurate, trustworthy public information served to temper the risks associated with interpersonal ties. That many transactions were done on credit made it doubly important to have them recorded in writing.

Second, business records served fiscal purposes, promising to provide a sense of control over the intake and outtake of funds. This included the function that we most associate with accounting today: offering a snapshot of profit and loss and of the amount of cash on hand. They offered a picture of where a merchant stood not only vis-à-vis his creditors and debtors, but also his employees and clients; a well-ordered cashbook was a means of protecting against embezzlement.

Third, records acted as artificial memory, a repository of past transactions and practices that could guide future planning and investment. This memorial function was vital because of the common practice of selling on credit; one needed a reliable record of one's debts and debtors. The myriad details of transactions were invariably subject to reordering to ensure that the information it contained was clear, accessible, and useful. The accounting processes that came to predominate in early modern Europe, foremost among them double-entry bookkeeping, required reprocessing masses of data that accumulated in the course of the merchant's affairs. Merchants engaged in rigorous copying and restructuring of the material they recorded, in order to establish a usable foundation of information. An accurate picture of profit and loss was something that could not be discerned from the unprocessed records of day-to-day

---

[20] Peri, *Il negotiante*, 79.

business activity. Accounting was another example of second-order repurposing of information that became commonplace in early modern European society, as paper records gathered in great volumes and required reorganization and distillation in order to generate actionable knowledge.

Commercial bookkeeping also had external audiences in view. It was a means of proclaiming honesty, achieved through the public visibility of the ledger book and the utilization of rule- and convention-based practices. Double-entry bookkeeping, especially, by reducing transactions to simple debits and credits, turned them into numbers that were transparent and disinterested. Such practical mathematics, practiced alongside everyday pragmatic writing and increasingly deemed an essential skill for the merchant, was a process of abstraction with ends that were both public and private.

For all of this, the important transformations in accounting and information management of late medieval and early modern Europe unfolded haphazardly, the result of expediency and pragmatic volition. The increasingly pervasive *habitus* of everyday writing was of central importance to the development and proliferation of improved bookkeeping methods. Daily documentation of assets, communications, and transactions, and the associated accumulation of paper, heightened the need for arranging this information into formats that combined comprehensiveness, accessibility, and intelligibility. Early modern bookkeeping emerged at the intersection between the great volume of writing that commerce demanded and the necessity to revise and reorder this writing to yield practical information. This discrepancy prompted experimentation in mercantile writing practices and the emergence of new forms of paper technologies and accounting techniques.

In medieval and early modern notarial practice, it was customary to write on unbound paper in quires; these quires might then be brought together, bound in a volume, and given a title on the spine or pages' edge. In merchant practice, by contrast, it became commonplace to work in prebound books of blank paper. These became widely available for purchase by the fifteenth century, a market response to the needs of daily writing.[21] This meant that the unit of space that the merchant encountered in his writing was the page, and it was in terms of the individual page that merchants began to think. The ledger, where debits and credits were tabulated and compared, depended on an open-page format based upon thinking about writing space in increments of the page. Some merchant

[21] Justin Steinberg, *Accounting for Dante: Urban Readers and Writers in Late Medieval Italy* (South Bend, IN: University of Notre Dame Press, 2007).

companies chose to number their account books by open page format rather than by leaf (recto/verso), an indication that they understood their books to be a continuity of individual pages, rather than a collection of bound quires.

These material realities of mercantile and financial record-keeping had important practical implications. The blank notebook became a convenient receptacle for regular and pragmatic writing, and facilitated the keeping of records in sequence. In addition, the simultaneous maintenance of multiple blank notebooks allowed for targeted recording of different sorts of information, as well as the copying and recycling of that information in different formats in separate notebooks. In late medieval Italy, merchants used notebooks to assemble *zibaldoni*, collections of practical information gathered from various places, often from the notebooks of merchants who had preceded them. In some cases, merchants, presumably early on in their careers, copied existing notebooks and arithmetic manuals in large chunks or even in their entirety. Raymond de Roover has suggested that there was a standard manuscript manual available for regular copying by the 1420s. One such manual was incorporated into Luca Pacioli's *Summa de arithmetica* (1494). By the end of the fifteenth century, there were standard texts in circulation, obviating the need for merchants to copy them.[22]

The prebound, blank notebook was a paper technology ideal for the observing, collecting, accounting, and organizing that were essential to the pursuit of profit, and thus a valuable companion for early modern merchants. Its virtues as a container and vehicle for information would be recognized by many who were not merchants, as it became an important tool for travelers, readers, scholars, and students as well, providing for them, as it did for merchants, a medium for recording and organizing thoughts and observations.

The most consequential of the new approaches, of course, was double-entry bookkeeping, a practice refined by practitioners in the merchant republics of Italy by the fourteenth century. The first widely accepted employment of the double-entry system was the communal account books of the city of Genoa in 1340, although there were certainly prior examples. It was in 1381 that Francesco Datini adopted the practice for the various *fondaci* of his sprawling business. A law of 1427 in Florence stipulated that every merchant and landholder in the republic had to maintain double-entry records so that they could respond accurately to

---

[22] Peter Spufford, "Late medieval merchants' notebooks: a project; their potential for the history of banking." In Markus Denzel, Jean Claude Hicquet, and Harald Witthöft, eds., *Kaufmannsbücher und Handelspraktiken vom Spätmittelalter bis zum beginnenden 20. Jahrhundert* (Stuttgart: Franz Steiner, 2002), 47–62.

the inquiries of the *catasto*.[23] The merchant houses of Kreß and Mendel in Nuremberg adopted the outlines of the practice by the fourteenth century, but it was not widespread among northern European practitioners until the sixteenth century. The Welsers in Augsburg were using it by the end of the fifteenth century and each of the branch offices of the Fugger bank, founded in 1486, was expected to submit to the central office in Augsburg annual accounts based on the double-entry method.[24]

The first systematic description of the double-entry approach was in a manuscript treatise of 1459 entitled *Il libro dell'arte di mercatura* by Benedetto Cotrugli.[25] Cotrugli's description of the practice was relatively barebones, and his work would not be published in print until 1573. Far more influential was Luca Pacioli's *Summa de arithmetica, geometria, proportioni et proportionalita* (1494), which offered the first detailed description of double-entry bookkeeping in print. It was chiefly the association with Pacioli (1447–1517) that gave double-entry the sobriquet of the "Italian method." Pacioli declared that the objective of the accounting principles that he laid out was "to give the trader without delay the information as to his assets and liabilities." Set against the theoretical mathematics of the rest of the treatise, Pacioli's chapter on accounting was highly practical, providing advice on how to open new accounts and for setting up ledgers for recording debit cash and credit capital.[26]

Pacioli spawned a great many imitators in numerous languages. The Flemish cloth trader Yan Ympyn de Christoffels, who had resided in Venice for twelve years, published *Nieuwe Instructie ende bewwijs der looffelijcker consten des rekenboeks* in 1543, reproducing much of Pacioli's content and including examples of account books and exchange bills.[27] The first such treatise in English was the *Profitable Treatyse* (1543) by Hugh Oldcastle, of which no copies have survived, but which is acknowledged by John Melis in *A Briefe Instruction and Maner How to Keepe Bookes of*

---

[23] David Herlihy and Christiane Klapisch-Zuber, *Tuscans and Their Families: A Study of the Florentine Catasto of 1427* (New Haven, CT: Yale University Press, 1985).

[24] Tom Scott, *Society and Economy in Germany, 1300–1600* (Basingstoke: Palgrave, 2002), 128–129.

[25] Vera Ribaudo, ed., *Il libro dell'arte di mercatura* (Venice: Edizioni Ca' Foscari, 2016).

[26] John B. Geijsbeek, *Ancient Double-Entry Bookkeeping* (Houston: Scholars Book, 1974), 33–35.

[27] Jacob Soll, "Accounting and accountability in Dutch civic life." In Margaret Jacob and Catherine Secretan, eds., *In Praise of Ordinary People. Early Modern Britain and the Dutch Republic* (New York: Palgrave Macmillan, 2013), 123–137 (here 125); Raymond De Roover, "Aux origines d'une technique intellectuelle: la formation et l'expansion de la comptabilité a partie double." *Annales d'histoire économique et sociale*, 9 (1937), 171–193 and 270–293; Rafael Donoso Anes, *Una contribución a la historia de la contabilidad: análisis de la prácticas contables desarrolladas por la tesorería de la Casa de la Contratación de las Indias de Sevilla (1503–1717)* (Seville: Universidad de Sevilla, 1996), 133–136.

Accompts After the Order of Debitor and Creditor (1588).[28] Melis followed Pacioli slavishly. He recommended the keeping of three books in addition to an inventory of one's merchandise: a memorial, a journal, and a ledger. The memorial recorded the daily business in a sequential fashion, indicating the details of transactions. The journal summarized the entries in the memorial, divided between debit and credit. Melis identified the journal as being specifically for the merchant's "information": "the Inventory or Memorial as hereafter you shal by divers examples have *information*." The ledger was then constructed from the entries in the journal and memorial and organized according to the principles of double-entry accounting. The merchant also needed to maintain a register of his letters, which should be kept and organized into bundles by year and locale, and then stored in a chest. All this writing was essential to the success of a merchant, he insisted: "without a due order of writing, his minde coulde not be quieted, but ever wavering in his businesse." He invoked what he identified as a common Latin saying: *ubi non est ordo, ibi est confuso*.

The adoption of double-entry bookkeeping was far from universal. Many merchants were able to run successful small-scale businesses using simple, single-entry bookkeeping methodology, relying on their memory for their accounting. Ympyn lamented that the accounts of merchants in his day were "grosly, obscurely and lewdely kept."[29] There is scarce evidence in the account books that survive from the fifteenth century that the double-entry method was used to reconcile figures and find and correct mistakes. Merchants continued to regard accounting chiefly as a means of safeguarding their rights (in both commercial transactions and in court proceedings); reinforcing their memory; and keeping track of debtors, partners, and inventories, rather than for the regular calculation of profit and loss.[30] Nor did states eagerly embrace the practice, even though many of them had become gargantuan fiscal operations by the sixteenth century. Monarchs, with their noble lineages and chivalric pretensions, generally disdained accounting as the sullied art of merchants. It would take until the eighteenth century before double-entry would be embraced as a tool of financial management for the ledgers of

---

[28] Basil Yamey, "Oldcastle, Peele and Melis: a case of plagiarism in the sixteenth century." *Accounting and Business Research*, 9.35 (1963), 209–216.
[29] Peter Ramsay, "Some Tudor merchant accounts." In Ananias Charles Littleton and Basil Yamey, eds., *Studies in the History of Accounting* (London: Sweet and Maxwell, 1956), 185–201 (here 186).
[30] James O. Wijnum, *The Role of Accounting in the Economic Development of England, 1500–1750* (Urbana, IL: Center for International Education and Research in Accounting, 1972), 156.

a central state. To some, the considerable demands of keeping such ledgers were just too ponderous, the paperwork just too great.

Bookkeeping as a skill was not routinely taught in schools.[31] Proper practice was something learned only through accumulated experience. Peri suggested that, after a basic training in math, writing, and grammar (presumably at school), apprentices be taught how to record their accounts in their books, employing what he called *scrittura mercantile*. Six separate features of a transaction needed to be recorded: the time, the debtor, the creditor, the amount, the type of transaction, and its cause. They were to learn to separate debits (on the left of the ledger) from credits (on the right) when they transferred records of transactions from the *giornale* to the account book. This was learning that was to take place on the job: the apprentice youth was best off being trained at the feet of his father in the *piazza del negotio*. The *scagno*, the bench, was the ideal school of business.

One of the more remarkable examples of resistance to double-entry was the Dutch East India Company (VOC). The VOC shipmasters maintained an account book on board, the details of which, upon return to port, were incorporated into the books of the Company. The sprawling international corporation was fastidious about record-keeping and information management in the form of routine internal audits and regular calculation of profit and loss. But despite this commitment to accounting, despite widespread awareness and adoption of the practice in the Low Countries, and despite the availability of many individuals who could have done the job, the VOC never adopted double-entry methods.

3.2 Commercial Information

Although much of commercial information created, stored, and shared by merchants came to reside on paper, particular geographic locales retained their importance for face-to-face interactions and transactions between merchants. In early modern Europe, these towns served as nodes in a dense network of information exchange, with a formalization of specific sites and spaces as venues for the circulation of news and ideas. Their role in gathering, storing, and circulating information helped create what Derek Keene has called a "new urban scenography."[32]

---

[31] Franz Josef Arlinghaus, "Account books." In Arlinghaus, ed., *Transforming the Medieval World: Uses of Pragmatic Literacy in the Middle Ages* (Turnhout: Brepols, 2006), 43–69.
[32] Derek Keene, "Cities and cultural exchange." In Donatella Calabi and Stephen Turk Christensen, eds., *Cities and Cultural Exchange in Europe, 1400–1700*, Vol. 2 of *Cultural Exchange in Early Modern Europe*, General ed. Robert Muchembled (Cambridge: Cambridge University Press, 2006), 3–27 (here 16).

Access to a wide array of information was both the product and the cause of the rise of major commercial cities. In such business centers, an informational economy of scale was in operation, whereby the achievement of a certain density of information exchange reduced the cost of access. The gathering and exchange of information are fundamentally transactions, and business profitability often benefits from a reduction in transaction costs.[33] This calculus helps explain why certain well-situated European cities became major centers simultaneously for trade in goods and in information. It also explains why printing houses invariably sprang up in major trading cities, as printers soon recognized how they could employ their machines to meet the informational needs of local merchants.[34]

Early modern merchants increasingly relied on publicly available sources of information, which became essential points of reference in the early modern economy. There was no information economy akin to today's deeply networked market economy. The bulk of transactions were local and required the acquisition and exchange of very small quantities of information. We have seen, however, that in adopting increasingly sophisticated accounting systems, early modern merchants and financiers recognized the benefits of maintaining, and having access to, information about their transactions. For merchants operating complex or geographically expansive businesses, this need for ready information on the micro-level was matched by an appetite for macro-information about market conditions, political circumstances, and commodity prices. There was a Janus-faced approach to information management: a twin recognition of the importance of an accurate *internal* picture of one's affairs, supplied by effective recording and accounting techniques, as well as an *external* one of conditions, threats, and opportunities. Information,

---

[33] Often, but not always. Some businesses undoubtedly thrived in arbitraging disequilibria in information flows. Reducing transaction costs likely improved efficiency overall in the market, but for some enterprises, an improvement in the flow of information likely cut into their profits. In purely theoretical terms, the entirely free flow of information would lead to perfectly competitive markets, which would result in virtually no profit; better, freer information would thus, theoretically, make it possible for a larger number of players to enter the market, resulting in squeezed profits. From an informational perspective, it is the existence of asymmetries that is the key to profits. I thank Randy Patton for pointing out this distinction to me.

[34] The development of the business press and the centrality of information exchange in early modern Europe are covered in essays by the economic historian John McCusker: "Information and transaction costs in early modern Europe." In Rainer Gömmel and Markus A. Denzel, eds., *Weltwirtschaft und Wirtschaftsordnung: Festschrift für Jürgen Schneider zum 65. Geburtstag.* Vierteljahrschrift für Sozial- und Wirtschaftsgeschichte, Beihefte, no. 159 (Stuttgart: Steiner, 2002), 69–83; and "The demise of distance: the business press and the origins of the information revolution in the early modern Atlantic world." *American Historical Review*, 110.2 (2005), 295–321. See also Dirk Couvée, "The first Coranteers – the flow of the news in the 1620s." *Gazette: International Journal of the Science of the Press*, 8.2 (1962), 22–36.

as businesses of today know all too well, is a transaction cost that affects the ability of firms to manage the risks of doing business. Access to relevant and timely information is essential to assessing the probability of success for actions and investments. Information management is thus closely related to risk management, and hence, to profits.

The expansion and interconnection of trading networks in the fourteenth and fifteenth centuries – for example in Italian trading consortia, which established their presence in commercially important locales across Europe and the Mediterranean – greatly facilitated the circulation of international news, and the sensitivity of merchants to events far from home. Over the course of the early modern period, an informational infrastructure emerged that provided merchants with news and data important to the day-to-day functioning of their trades. Business people sought out, and received, this information via face-to-face interactions, rumor, correspondence, and, increasingly, manuscript and then printed news subscription services. By around 1500, information regularly came to be compared to a commodity, as something that had a cost and was destined to circulate.[35] This was a time of considerable innovation and experimentation in the provision of news to merchants, whose operations were particularly sensitive to change in political and economic conditions. It was important to be first with the news, but only if the news proved to be true – a calculus that also applied the world of diplomacy, which, in the same period, also came to see timely information as a political commodity.

Medieval merchants had long gathered information important to their operations via private business correspondence. It was in letters with well-placed individuals that one learned of commodity prices, exchange rates, reports on the quality of locally sourced products, and other strictly commercial concerns. Letters often included details on political, military, and meteorological events that had commercial repercussions. These categories of information were general, and of interest to many, and thus could be separated into a common format of intelligence that could be supplied to all. It was widely believed that merchants had access to the most reliable news; they did have access to dedicated merchant postal services. Italy in the late Middle Ages had numerous postal services carrying the correspondence of merchants between the principal cities. In 1357, seventeen Florentine merchant companies pooled their resources

---

[35] Philippe Contamine, "Conclusion." In Claire Boudreau, Kouky Fianu, Claude Gauvard, and Michel Hébert, eds., *Information et societé en Occident à la fin du Moyen Âge. Actes du colloque international tenu à l'Université du Québec à Montréal et à l'Université d'Ottawa* (9–11 mai 2002) (Paris: Publications de la Sorbonne, 2004), 440; Andrew Pettegree, *The Invention of News. How the World Came to Know About Itself* (New Haven, CT: Yale University Press, 2014), 2.

to create a shared courier service that ran on a set timetable. Regular courier services also emerged in the Low Countries and Germany, heavily urbanized areas with active merchant communities. Nuremberg, a city that Luther called in the sixteenth century "the eyes and ears of Germany," had a dedicated courier service to Augsburg, 150 km to the north. Nuremberg was paying couriers as early as 1377 and, by the next century, had messengers on the town payroll.

These established German postal services, with their weekly courier services, would both augment and compete with the imperial post that took shape in the sixteenth century. In the emergence of such services, as well as interregional ones that connected Italy with southern Germany and the Low Countries and France, we find the origins of the periodical business press. Probably the best-known example of the link between business activity and the provision of news from the sixteenth century is the Fugger family of Augsburg. They took advantage of the city's extensive connections to aggregate newsletters emanating from major commercial cities such as Venice, Cologne, and Antwerp. These compilations became known as *Fuggerzeitungen*. There are 27,000 volumes of them, each containing several thousand letters, in the Austrian National Library in Vienna alone, a testament to the importance that this international house of trading and finance placed on access to reliable information.[36] The Fuggers began to catalog these newsletters in the 1560s.[37] These were news sources that focused not on sensational or grotesque events, like much of the emergent pamphlet press, but instead on relatively mundane economic and political news, precisely the matters that might impinge on the Fuggers' varied financial interests. Their news aggregation service was a private resource, a component of one multinational organization, but it was something of a model for commercial news agencies that began to appear in prominent European commercial centers.

The publication of business news and information soon proved to be a profitable enterprise, and numerous cities became centers of business publication. "Table books" were first commercially produced for the use of merchants around the year 1500. These printed sheets would include important data such as the dates of fairs, useful conversion tables, and

---

[36] Zsuzsa Barbarics and Renate Pieper, "Handwritten newsletters as means of communication in early modern Europe." In Francisco Bethencourt and Florike Egmond, eds., *Correspondence and Cultural Exchange in Europe 1400–1700*, Vol. 3 of *Cultural Exchange in Early Modern Europe*, General ed. Robert Muchembled (Cambridge: Cambridge University Press, 2006), 53–79.
[37] Wolfgang Behringer, "Communications revolutions: a historiographical concept." *German History*, 24.3 (2006), 333–374 (here 340).

blank pages for taking notes and making calculations.[38] It was initially in Italy that such publications were chiefly produced – the origins of the commodity price current were Italian. Large Italian firms sought to formalize the reporting of local prices, stationing agents in the most important trading centers. When newssheets intended for merchants began to appear in Antwerp, they were influenced by preexisting Italian models. The sixteenth century saw more and more locales in central and northern Europe regularly producing business information, reflecting the shift in the center of gravity of European commerce from the Mediterranean to the North Atlantic littoral.

One of the hurdles that had to be surmounted in the creation of a business press was establishing trust in it as a source of information. Trustworthiness had long been a concern of merchants when exchanging news, even in person. What to make of news arriving from a distance and of uncertain or unverified authorship? Over time, as business information had to be consistently reliable for it to garner demand, the news of the business press might in some cases be deemed more valuable than information gathered from face-to-face exchanges. The availability of such public information about prices, availability, local political conditions, and the like, meant that the conduct of trade rested on an unprecedented amount of data.

The handwritten compilations of news, known in Italy as *avisi*, and printed newssheets, both of which were commercially produced items by the seventeenth century, focused chiefly on political and military developments. As news became an acknowledged commodity, however, the prosaic concerns of the business community prompted the emergence of a more specialized variety of periodicals. Especially important in this vein were printed lists of commodity prices and currency exchange rates. Printed lists of commodity prices appeared in Venice and Antwerp as early as the mid-sixteenth century. These were single-page items and closely resembled their handwritten precursors that had circulated for decades. At first, only the headings on these lists were printed, with blank spaces left for the most recent data. Over time, this combination of print and manuscript information gave way to serially printed price currents.

Price currents, commodity lists, and business newssheets were, by the mid-seventeenth century, essential informational resources of the commercial infrastructure. Then, as now, there was a recognition that quicker access to more reliable information served to reduce risk. It allowed for better planning for current and future investment and lowered transaction costs.

---

[38] Ann Blair and Peter Stallybrass, "Mediating information 1450–1800." In Clifford Siskin and William Warner, eds., *This is Enlightenment* (Chicago: University of Chicago Press, 2010), 139–163 (here 146).

The latest, or, as it was often described, the "freshest" news, became a chief concern.[39] The emergence of a business press with the intention of circulating, rather than guarding, prices, exchange rates, and other commercial data is an indication of how pan-European commerce had come to rely on the circulation of information, and that businesses were willing to pay for it, like they would any commodity. What was once sought from business associates through correspondence and conversations could now be accessed via regular and reliable format and delivery. Commercial publishing became a business in its own right and could reinforce the role of towns as pivotal business locales.[40] Daniel Defoe (1660–1731), writing in 1697, expressed how access to news shrank the world of the businessman: "By the help of a strange and Universal Intelligence, a Merchant sitting at home in his Counting-house, at once converses with all Parts of the known World."[41]

Venice is perhaps the most obvious example of a commercial entrepot whose connections made it an information center.[42] Venice had a considerable number of public spaces where political news was regularly discussed among Venetian politicians, foreign ambassadors, and international merchants. Juan Antonio de Vera (1583–1658), who had served as the ambassador of Spain in Venice in the 1630s, observed that "sometimes one can learn more about French business in Spain by means of the ambassador based in Venice, or Rome, than by the means of the ambassador in Paris."[43] Venice was the "nerve center for the arrival and exchange of European political information."[44] Venice was also a major center for the publication of *reporti*, the Venetian equivalent of *avisi*. The *reportisti* responsible for assembling these newssheets drew upon the many networks of correspondence converging on Venice, and the corresponding connections across the Mediterranean. That Venice was also a major center for printing only thickened the ganglia of information exchange in the Republic.

---

[39] John McCusker, "Information and transaction costs," 69–73.
[40] John McCusker, "The demise of distance."
[41] From Defoe's *Essay upon Projects* (1697), quoted in Henry Roseveare, "Merchant organization and maritime trade in the North Atlantic, 1660-1815. Some reflections." In Olaf Uwe Janzen, ed., *Merchant Organization and Maritime Trade in the North Atlantic, 1660–1815* (St. John's, Canada: International Maritime Economic History Association, 1998), 259–268 (here 259).
[42] See Johan Petitjean, *L'intelligence des choses: une histoire de l'information entre l'Italie et Mediterranée (XVIe–XVIIe siècle)* (Rome: École française de Rome, 2013).
[43] Juan Antonio de Vera, *El Anbaxador* (Seville: Francisco de Lyra, 1620), 307.
[44] Alessandra Contini, "L'informazione politica sugli stati italiani non spagnoli nelle relazioni veneziane a metà cinquecento (1558–1566)." In Elena Fasano Guarini and Maria Rosa, eds., *L'informazione politica in Italia (secoli xvi–xviii)* (Pisa: Scuola Normale Superiore, 2001), 1–57 (here 22): "Venezia è il centro nevralgico di arrivo e di raccordo dell'informazione politica europea."

In northern Europe, a similar marriage of trade and information could be seen in Antwerp. By 1460, the bourse in Antwerp accommodated and facilitated trade in commodities and financial instruments. Initially, it was located inside the courtyard of a house.[45] By 1531, the city had dedicated a new permanent facility, committing an astonishing 300,000 golden crowns to its construction. It was based around a large central square, with loggias and galleries looking down from above. The lingua franca of the bourse was Italian, as it was for the Antwerp commodity price list that was printed regularly and could be found posted publicly, by the 1540s. With merchants

3.1 In the seventeenth century, Amsterdam became one of Europe's most important centers for the exchange of financial and commercial information. Emmanuel de Witte, *Courtyard of the Exchange in Amsterdam* (1653), Museum Boijmans van Beuningen, Rotterdam (Getty Images)

[45] Donatella Calabi and Derek Keene, "Exchanges and cultural transfer in European cities." In Calabi and Stephen Turk Christensen, eds., *Cities*, 286–314 (here 290).

of geographically disparate origin present and passing through, it served as an important exchange for international news. It was in the Antwerp bourse that Thomas More (1478–1535) set the conversations with the traveler Raphael Hythlodaeus, from whom we learn about the land of *Utopia* (1516):

In the following century, Amsterdam, the engine room of the Dutch economic machine, became a thriving information exchange. Amsterdam was "the great Staple of News," a term coined by the English historian James Howell in 1645.[46] Reliable postal routes connected it with other major northern European towns, such as Paris and Frankfurt, making personal correspondence an important and effective tool of commerce. The Amsterdam bourse publicly posted prices for more than 400 different commodities. This information was consolidated into weekly price bulletins, which were then distributed across Europe. They were produced under official supervision to assure quality and accuracy. These items were available for individual purchase and by yearly subscription.

Advertisements for services and important commercial information were posted in prominent places in the loggias and arcades (as can be seen in Job Adriaensz's 1670 painting of the Amsterdam bourse). Much of the information exchange continued to take place in face-to-face exchanges and via short-distance correspondence. But Amsterdam is also a very good example of how institutions dedicated in large part to the processing and exchange of information emerged in early modern Europe. The Exchange Bank, known as the Wisselbank (founded in 1609), the Amsterdam bourse, the Dutch East India Company (VOC), and other trading companies were headquartered there. These, as well as the city's thriving business press, were all establishments whose operations depended on information flows. The growth of the VOC bureaucracy was accompanied by the strategic use of the Company's resources to gather information from wide-ranging sources across the globe, for the purposes of planning and marketing. In 1641, the VOC published a guide to the practice of note-taking aboard its vessels' officers. Information gathering, therefore, was a business for sea as well as land. News of the details of the resulting reports compiled by the VOC soon circulated around Amsterdam. Many merchants had their post delivered to the exchange, where they bartered for information from near and far.[47] By the middle of the seventeenth century, specialized information brokers were in operation in Amsterdam. The Dutch diplomat and spy Lieuwe van Aitzema (1600–1669), for example, collected sensitive news by

---

[46] Cited in Sven Dupré and Christoph Lüthy, "Introduction." In Dupré and Lüthy, eds., *Silent Messengers: The Circulation of Material Knowledge in the Early Modern Low Countries* (Münster: LIT Verlag, 2011), 1–12 (here 4).
[47] Calabi and Keene, "Exchanges and cultural transfer in European cities."

bribing local government officials and maintaining contacts within all of the main mercantile institutions of the city. He collated both hard news and gossip and sold it to willing buyers.[48]

In locales such as Amsterdam, therefore, there was a widely shared sentiment that the free circulation of information was essential for improving the flow of wares, people, and capital essential to the profit of merchants and to the thriving of the state. Largely open and public access to information on prices, shares, and exchange rates became an expected commonplace of the international economy. This, of course, remains one of the vital features of the contemporary capitalist system.

It is partly for this reason that Jan de Vries and Ad van der Woude have located the "first modern economy" in the Netherlands of the Golden Age, identifying information flows as essential to the economy's modern character. This information flowed into the Dutch Republic by many different routes: merchant ships, letters from the overseas offices of Dutch trading companies and banks, the correspondence of the India Companies, and news coming in from representatives of the city government abroad. As a result, "Amsterdam and all of Holland overflowed with information." The Netherlands' identity as a central locale into which arrived the latest news from many locations, near and distant, was a source of Dutch advantage over its main competitors: "The natural geographical advantage of the Republic was reinforced by intelligence networks of merchants, further strengthened by the commercial institutions and, finally, solidified by the Republic's toleration of religious minorities (with their intelligence networks) and uncensored publishing."[49]

By the end of the seventeenth century, London had assumed a similar role. In 1700, Thomas Brown remarked on the dizzying array of news and rumor that circulated at London's Royal Exchange:

One would think that all the World was converted into News-Mongers and Intelligencers, for that's the first Salutation among all mankind that frequent that place. What News from *Scanderoon* and *Aleppo*? Says the *Turkey* merchant? What price bears Currants at *Zant*? Apes at *Tunis*? Religion at *Rome*? Cutting a Throat at *Naples*? Whores at *Venice*? And the Cure of a Clap at *Padua*?[50]

---

[48] Woodruff Smith, "The function of commercial centers in the modernization of European capitalism: Amsterdam as an information exchange in the seventeenth century." *The Journal of Economic History*, 44.4 (1984), 985–1005.

[49] Jan de Vries and Ad van der Woude, *The First Modern Economy: Success, Failure, and Perseverance of the Dutch Economy, 1500–1815* (Cambridge: Cambridge University Press, 1997), 149.

[50] Quoted in John-Paul Ghobrial, *The Whispers of Cities: Information Flows in Istanbul, London and Paris in the Age of William Trumbull* (Oxford: Oxford University Press, 2013), 42.

It was in London that stock price lists were printed regularly for the first time. Price currents for commodities had circulated in London since the 1630s, but in the early 1680s James Whitson began to print the prices in *The Merchant's Remembrancer*, published biweekly, supplementing the many ways in which information was already exchanged in London: among merchants, dealers, and brokers; in the streets, in the coffeehouses, and across the tables at Exchange Alley; shouted information by the crier; and correspondence from associates near and far.[51]

The appetite for short-term information, such as prices, exchange rates, and the latest news, over time generated records, which accumulated in files in the offices of merchants and the archives of companies and trading houses. These could be consulted subsequently to provide a snapshot of the past and a road map for the future. The extensive records of the VOC and the systematic records of staple goods prices kept by the municipal government in Amsterdam were now subject to consultation and analysis, revealing patterns, cycles, and precedent in the records. "Checking the files," so emblematic of bureaucracies everywhere, became a feature of commercial life. Long-term information became, for the businessmen, traders, bureaucrats, stockholders, and directors who consulted it, essential for planning and prediction. The gaze of early modern business, therefore, was trained in two directions: all about them, for news and data about current conditions; and into their notebooks and files, for guidance from the past. For Woodruff Smith, this marks an important change in economic consciousness, one related to the systematic analysis of long-term information characteristic of modern business organizations and of capitalism more broadly.[52]

Commercial information gathered on paper thus lived two lives, first in real time and then gathered in files and past accounts. The twin commitment to acquisition and preservation expanded the information available for planning and problem-solving, while also magnifying the requirements of information management. As we shall see, early modern Europe was witness to a greatly expanded proliferation of institutional

---

[51] The emergence of these commercial informational centers bears resemblance to the development of industrial districts, where numerous enterprises in similar lines of production were established in close proximity. Certain locales emerged with agglomerations of specialized economic activity, much in the same way certain towns became associated with the purveyance of information. Pioneering in the study of such districts was the work of Alfred Marshall at the end of the nineteenth century – see Fiorenza Belussi and Katia Caldari, "At the origin of the industrial district: Alfred Marshall and the Cambridge School." *Cambridge Journal of Economics*, 33.2 (2009), 335–355. See also Paul Krugman, *Geography and Trade* (Cambridge, MA: MIT Press, 1991).

[52] Smith, "The function of commercial centers," 1004–1005.

and personal archives, a function of the enormous production of written instruments, but also the widespread commitment to keeping them. There was a broadening recognition that information inscribed on paper could have both present and future applications. Thus, in February 1688, the VOC commissioned a report on the sales level of pepper under past conditions in order to formulate a strategy for the marketing of pepper moving forward. Long-term information became the basis for future business strategy.

3.3 The Influence of Merchant Attitudes to Information

The influence of mercantile and commercial attitudes and practices in the early modern period was profound, if not always direct. The default impulse to record in writing even the most incidental of information; the abstraction of one's activities in systematic patterns of inscription; the assigning of comparative value to items of widely different character; the development of a formal, yet familiar, *mercantesca* form of writing for regular correspondence; a broadly empirical approach that emphasized that which was before one's eyes. This multipronged commitment to pragmatic literacy furnished a variety of models for record-keeping and information management.

The concerns relevant to merchants frequently overlapped with those of diplomats, missionaries, scholars, and travelers of all sorts, as did the skills and practices that they required. Among the first to accumulate large quantities of paper records as a consequence of their daily activities, merchants and financiers were also pioneers when it came to systematic patterns of information management. They often served as official or unofficial diplomatic agents. Merchants were, of course, heavily involved in the European expansion into the Indian Ocean and the New World, and brought with them an empirical eye in their pursuit of potential profit. While it is true that early modern Europe did not entirely lose its longstanding discomfort with profit, nor dispense with the association of merchants with money-grubbing, many, especially those who also had to process quantities of information, looked to mercantile examples for inspiration.

For some time, a prevailing historiographical truism was that the world of commerce and business had inherited a brand of "scientific economics" and empirical approach to facts from the Cartesian deduction and abstraction and Baconian observation and induction that gradually came to prevail in seventeenth-century natural philosophy.[53] Recently,

---

[53] Exemplars of this thrust of thought, which have been applied especially to the case of England, include William Letwin, *The Origins of Scientific Economics: English Economic*

however, a number of convincing studies have suggested this causal relationship should be reversed. They see the empirical outlook and thirst for information that characterized merchants instead bleeding into the practice of natural philosophy. Ways of knowing about commerce rooted in observation and information acquisition ended up reflected in ways of knowing about the natural world.

For example, in *The Merchants Mappe of Commerce* (1638), by the Levant Company merchant Lewes Roberts (1596–1641), the world of the merchant is presented as one full of information that must be negotiated by its inhabitants. Drawing from his own experience in international trade, Roberts insists that the merchant must organize and discern the details of geography, weights and measures, commodity prices, currency values, and exchange rates. Observation and personal experience were essential to navigating this mass of information. It was to be gathered through personal toil and industry.[54] The best merchant "inscribed" the commercial landscape in which he lived and operated, seeking to achieve mastery over it in his paper records.

The activity and mentality of merchants, trading companies, and entrepreneurs contributed in important ways to the development of natural history and astronomy, helping to transform the practices and claims of these emerging disciplines. The words and lives of some prominent naturalists made the connection between commerce and natural science explicit. Galileo Galilei (1564–1642), perhaps the greatest scientific mind of the seventeenth century, taught bookkeeping after leaving university and before securing an appointment as a professor. The Italian naturalist Ulisse Aldrovandi (1522–1605) was a bookkeeper for a company of merchants in Bologna and Brescia; in his autobiography he makes much of his talent at balancing the books. The great Anglo-Irish experimental scientist Robert Boyle (1627–1691), in an essay entitled *That the Goods of Mankind May Be Much Increased by the Naturalist's Insight into the Trades* (1671), wrote that "an insight into trades may improve the Naturalist's knowledge and ... the Naturalist as well by the skill thus obtained, as by the other parts of his knowledge,

---

Thought 1660–1776 (London: Methuen, 1963); Lars Magnusson, *Mercantilism: The Shaping of an Economic Language* (London: Routledge, 1994); Terrence Hutchinson, *Before Adam Smith: The Emergence of Political Economy, 1662–1776* (Oxford: Blackwell, 1988); Carl Wennerlind, *Casualties of Credit: the English Financial Revolution, 1620–1720* (Cambridge, MA: Harvard University Press, 2011).

[54] Thomas Leng, "Epistemology: expertise and knowledge in the world of commerce." In Philip Stern and Carl Wennerlind, eds., *Mercantilism Reimagined: Political Economy in Early Modern Britain and Its Empire* (Cambridge: Cambridge University Press, 2014), 97–116.

may be enabled to improve trades."[55] Boyle was also a director at the East India Company and there was a great deal of overlap between his maritime and scientific endeavors.[56] Isaac Newton (1643–1727) was one of the Company's proprietors and owned more than £10,000 of its stock.

The assignation of measurable values using identical metrics to radically different objects offered a model for measuring the universe. Pacioli's famous and influential treatise on accounting, *Summa de arithmetica, geometria, proportioni et proportionalita*, first published in 1494, was, notably, also about proportion, geometry, and mathematics, all means of rendering nature in abstract terms. Pacioli himself places the importance of double-entry bookkeeping on par with the mathematical system of Euclid and links business arithmetic with Pythagorean harmonies.[57] Pacioli was close friends with Leonardo da Vinci (1452–1519) and there has been speculation that Leonardo's 1487 drawing of Vitruvian Man was informed by his reading of Pacioli's *Summa de arithmetica*.[58] It was the economic historian Werner Sombart who made the connection between the spirits of accounting and early modern science explicit nearly one hundred years ago: "Double-entry bookkeeping is born of the same spirit as the system of Galileo and Newton ... [it] discloses to us the cosmos of the economic world by the same method as, later, the cosmos of the stellar universe was unveiled by the great investigation of natural philosophy."[59]

Merchants may have relied on systematic abstraction for the keeping of their essential records, but in their day-to-day activities they were compelled to focus on facts, images, and material objects. The early modern expansion of long-distance trade facilitated the exchange of exotic plants, animals, minerals, and other curiosities. Commerce in goods and wares from afar opened up new spaces and opportunities for conversation and the sharing of information about these merchandises and their places of origin, as well as for discussion about new natural and technical

---

[55] Michael Hunter and Robert Davis, eds., *The Works of Robert Boyle*, Vol. III (London: Pickering and Chatto, 1999), 444.
[56] Sarah Irving, *Natural Science and the Origins of the British Empire* (London: Routledge, 2015), 69–92.
[57] A point made by Elizabeth Eisenstein, *The Printing Press as an Agent of Change: Communications and Cultural Transformations in Early Modern Europe*. (Cambridge: Cambridge University Press, 1979), 547.
[58] See Yuri Ihri, "The beauty of double-entry bookkeeping and its impact on the nature of accounting information." *Economic Notes*, 22.2 (1993), 265–285. See also the blog post of Doc Searls, "The second coming of double-entry bookkeeping," at https://blogs.harvard.edu/vrm/2014/09/30/why-bookkeeping-is-actually-cool/.
[59] Werner Sombart, *Der moderne Kapitalismus*, Vol. II, Part I (Leipzig: Duncker & Humblot, 1916), 118–199, quoted in Ihri, "The beauty," 266.

information. It also abetted a culture of collecting and an emphasis on experience that offer significant parallels with the practices of early modern natural philosophy.[60] International trading houses had to come to grips with the logistical, technological, and administrative challenges incumbent in extending their familiar practical and cognitive habits beyond the local setting. Steven Harris has called this the creation of "virtual spaces," which allowed vicarious movement of people and objects across large distances, by virtue of cycles of travel and communication, the deployment of agents deemed reliable, and normative means of observation and description.[61]

Dániel Margócsy has shown that, in the case of the Dutch, the spirit of entrepreneurship that characterized the activity of merchants also seeped into the practice of natural history and anatomy: scientific knowledge and many of the items that underlay early modern science were themselves turned into commodities. The circulation of objects supplied by trading companies and entrepreneurs impacted the practices and claims of botanists, anatomists, and natural historians. As commodities, these items were described and taxonomized for sale, mirroring the move to classification evident in early modern science.[62]

The emphasis among traders on local knowledge gathered first-hand, on inventory investment and management, on technologies of storage, and on rigorous classification of both information and goods, all resemble the efforts of contemporary naturalists to accumulate knowledge in gardens, museums, pharmacies, and libraries. Harold Cook argues that there was a convergence of the values of merchants with those of natural philosophers: an appreciation for travel, the importance of seeing things afresh, the exchange of goods and ideas, commensurability, trustworthiness, and an emphasis on plain and precise language. "Above all," Cook writes, "among the values shared by science and commerce were a certain kind of interested engagement with objective knowledge and an attentive appreciation for collective generalizations based on exacting information about the objects with which they dealt."[63] Mercantile approaches to information about the world encouraged the emergence of empirical attitudes toward the natural world. Illustrative of this point is the career

---

[60] William Eamon, "Markets, piazzas and villages." In Katherine Park and Lorraine Daston, eds., *The Cambridge History of Science*, Vol. 3 (Cambridge: Cambridge University Press, 2006), 206–223.

[61] Steven Harris, "Networks of travel, correspondence and exchange." In Park and Daston, eds., *The Cambridge History of Science*, Vol. 3, 341–362 (here 356).

[62] Dániel Margócsy, *Commercial Visions. Science, Trade and Visual Culture in the Dutch Golden Age* (Chicago: University of Chicago Press, 2014).

[63] Harold Cook, *Matters of Exchange: Commerce, Medicine and Science in the Dutch Golden Age* (New Haven, CT: Yale University Press, 2007), 57.

in the Dutch East India Company of Jan Hendrick Adriaan van Rheede (1636–1691), who was the governor of Malabar in India between 1671 and 1677. Amid his administration, he also undertook an "accounting" of Indian plant life. He employed a crew of people and secured the aid of Indian princes in his naturalist endeavors, which resulted in his *Hortus Indicus Malabaricus*, the first edition of which appeared in 1678, to be followed by many more, some extensively illustrated.[64]

The link between the recording and accounting practices of merchants and approaches to documenting information about the natural world is made explicit in the person of Francis Bacon (1561–1626). For Bacon, genuine knowledge of nature came only through direct experience and familiarity with the "stuff" of the world. But raw data garnered from observation was not enough by itself; the fruits of experience had to be subjected to discipline, ordering, and restraint. He saw the practices of merchants, which rendered transactions as numbers, stripped from their contexts, as models for naturalists and scholars, as they similarly sought to bring order to large quantities of data emanating from their day-to-day work. Specifically, Bacon's advice for keeping notes and papers had its origins in mercantile waste-books and ledgers. The former was a rough account book into which records of daily notes and transactions would be transcribed more or less chronologically. The ledger, of course, then effected a division of these records into credits and debits. Bacon borrowed this model in recommendations he sketched out for organizing his own copious and disordered notes. His recommendations for creating commonplace books, in which information gleaned in one's studies would be subject to classification by topic, bore considerable similarity to the merchant's ledger book, in which transactions were distilled down to profit and loss. Such digestion and reduction were intended to make large quantities of information legible and useful – Bacon himself repeatedly employed apian metaphors, whereby the "material from the flowers of the field and garden" was converted into accessible knowledge.[65] Bacon's approach to countering the great volumes of paperwork that accumulated in his scholarly and professional affairs, inspired by his familiarity with financial and mercantile protocols, proved to have a wide reach. In an age with "too much to read," this process, long employed by merchants, became essential to the advancement of learning. Merchants and the likes of Francis Bacon both insisted on purposeful

---

[64] Dirk Struik, *The Land of Stevin and Huygens. A Sketch of Science and Technology in the Dutch Republic during the Golden Century* (Dordrecht: D. Reidel, 1981), 128.
[65] Angus Vine, "Commercial commonplacing: Francis Bacon, the waste-book, and the ledger." In Richard Beadle, Peter Beal, and Colin Burrow, eds., *Manuscript Miscellanies, c. 1450–1700* (London: British Library, 2011), 197–218.

observation and information gathering that would result in fundamentally "useful" knowledge. In both commercial and scientific discourse in early modern Europe, a chief epistemological concern was how to engage in the pursuit of reliable knowledge about the world without that knowledge becoming adulterated by personal concerns. There was a significant convergence of approach and expertise in the interpretation of the data and observation of nature and commerce.

Merchants also played an important role in establishing practical geometry and methods of mensuration in public life, offering models for abstraction for scientists and statesmen alike. The routinization of commodity price lists, exchange rates, and accounting practices meant that numerical information circulated publicly with regularity. In 1582, Simon Stevin (1548–1620) published his *Tafelen van Interest*, a compendium of interest tables for bankers and lenders. In it, he promoted a new form of decimal arithmetic that he promised would be of use not only to merchants and financiers, but to astrologers, land surveyors, and all those who regularly needed to engage in measurement.[66]

Mary Poovey, in *A History of the Modern Fact*, has argued that the increasingly widespread application of accounting techniques in early modern Europe helped to confer cultural authority on numbers. Double-entry bookkeeping, in particular, served to make numeracy an essential skill in the management of commercial information. Numbers did not yet replace words, as there was still suspicion of numbers alone, but numbers did come to connote accuracy and serve as a means of producing truth and virtue. Reflecting on the economic developments of the period as a whole, Karl Appuhn has observed: "If there is one element that ties together all the components of the Renaissance economy – rural and urban, agrarian, carrying and manufacturing – it is numeracy."[67]

This outlook became increasingly evident in statecraft as well. As Erik Thomson has shown, the principles of double-entry bookkeeping, mediated through the writings of Stevin and others, were also deemed useful for the management of state information and data. Stevin's *Livre de compte de prince à la manière d'Italie* (1608) sought to circulate the accounting practices of Italian merchants among statesmen. Stevin served as the principal advisor of the Stadtholder Maurice of Nassau, where he advocated "princely bookkeeping," as a tool for effective political control. Maurice trained in double-entry bookkeeping and then used it both for

---

[66] Simon Stevin, *Disme: The Art of Tenths, or Decimall Arithmetike*. Trans. by Richard Norton (London, 1608), 3–4.
[67] Karl Appuhn, "Tools for the development of the European economy." In Guido Ruggiero, ed., *A Companion to the Worlds of the Renaissance* (London: Blackwell, 2002), 259–278 (here 275).

his personal finances and for those of his administration.[68] Swedish statesmen in the first half of the seventeenth century, most notably the Chancellor Axel Oxenstierna (1583–1654), consciously imitated Dutch commercial practices to aid in the governance of their own state.[69] Government officials in Sweden were inspired by the curious combination of ancient examples and the widespread practices of mercantile accounting to pursue statecraft in a "strikingly quantitative manner." The same was true, on a much larger scale, of Jean-Baptiste Colbert (1619–1683) in France, who sought to incorporate accounting techniques into his stewardship of Louis XIV's administrative project. In his attempts to achieve control of the sprawling royal finances, he employed techniques (although not double-entry bookkeeping) garnered from his Jesuit training.[70] By the seventeenth century, English statesmen came to rely on what William Petty (1623–1687) called "political artithmetick," whereby all of public life might be expressed in terms of "number, weight and measure" with reference to state records.[71] It was this accumulated information that yielded what would become known in the eighteenth century as statistics, used by merchants and bureaucrats as units of abstraction and quantity to measure their realities.[72]

The praxis of commercial information management, therefore, found application in the arena of statecraft. Both merchants and statesmen recognized the benefits of abstraction in seeking to achieve functional control over, variably, profits and subjects. Account books and price lists found analogs in early modern state archives and censuses. Early modern statesmen, of course, retained a suspicion of accounting as the stuff of lowly merchants, even while they demanded accurate pictures of the state of their own finances.[73] And, strikingly, it would be some six hundred years from the first attested use of double-entry bookkeeping by Italian merchants before a major central fisc would employ it as a tool for managing state finances.

As early as 1934, Franz Borkenau, in tracing the transition from feudal to bourgeois worldviews, argued that the exchange of commodities in

---

[68] M. F. Bywater and Basil Yamey, *Historic Accounting Literature: A Companion Guide* (London: Scholars Press, 1982), 120.
[69] Erik Thomson, "Swedish variations on Dutch commercial institutions, practices and discourse, 1605–1655." *Scandinavian Studies*, 77.3 (2005), 331–346.
[70] Jacob Soll, *The Information Master: Jean Baptiste-Colbert Secret State Intelligence System* (Ann Arbor, MI: University of Michigan Press, 2009).
[71] William Petty, *Five Essays in Political Arithmetick* (London: Henry Mortlock, 1672).
[72] The first use of the word "statistics" was by Gottfried Achenwall, who used it to describe the study of the state. The first recorded use in English came in 1770 and it achieved widespread use following the publication of the twenty-one-volume *Statistical Account of Scotland* in the 1790s.
[73] Soll, *The Reckoning*, 60.

early modern Europe provided a model for a "mathematical-mechanistic world-picture."[74] More recently, Simon Shaffer has declared that "long-range systems of accumulation of facts and commodities were decisive aspects of the early modern information order."[75] Merchants dealt in physical wares, but kept records of them in a fashion that rendered all of them as letters and numbers in an account book. Commodities that were fundamentally dissimilar could be profitably compared by calculating their value in units of measurement.

Accounting as a means of representing and organizing the varied objects of commerce found echoes in some of the solutions put forward by scholars to encompass and classify knowledge. The classificatory schemes devised by the French humanist and educational theorist Petrus Ramus (1512–1572) to speciate knowledge into networked categories, essentially rendering all of it related and comparable, bear much in common with the outlook of commercial accounting. Ramus himself had training in mathematics, under the tutelage of Johannes Sturm (1507–1589). Just as a young merchant trained in the principles of accounting could expect to be able to configure and quantify any type of wares he might be trading, a young scholar versed in Ramist taxonomies should be able to achieve control of any trove of knowledge, distilling it into information that could be sorted into patterns and flows.[76] The most sundry of products in account books with little or nothing in common apart from their assessed value intermingle with each other, subject to comparison, addition, and subtraction. Ramus proposed classifications that subjected knowledge to the same sort of leveling. The "methods" and "systems" adopted by Ramists, humanists, and encyclopedists seeking to bound and categorize the vastly expanding pool of knowledge provide yet more evidence of the pervasive fingerprints of accounting.

3.4 Information Management in International Organizations

Record-keeping and the incumbent accounting techniques were both causes of, and responses to, the need for information management in the economic sphere. They were methods that sought to make the sum of one's activities and transactions accessible and legible once it reached a volume that was beyond the capacity of human dead-reckoning. Such

---

[74] Franz Borkenau, *Der Übergang von feudalen zum bürglerichen Weltbild* (Darmstadt: Wissenschaftliche Buchgesellschaft, 1971, c1934).
[75] Simon Schaffer, "Newton on the beach: the information order of *Principia Mathematica.*" *History of Science*, 47 (2009), 243–276 (here 245).
[76] Walter Ong, "Ramist method and the commercial mind." *Studies in the Renaissance*, 8 (1961), 155–172 (here 169–170).

practices could also be employed to provide snapshots of things going on far away. They thus offered a shorthand with which to confront the twin challenges of complexity and distance. The early modern international organizations created in the wake of European expansion into Asia and the Americas had little choice but to rely on paper records and communication. Two such entities were the Society of Jesus and the East India Company, both of which were run from a European metropole, but whose operations spanned the globe. For each of them, assiduous record-keeping, the circulation of paper, and endowment of authority in writing were the means of command and control over vast expanses of time and space. These were, among other things, international paper organizations.

The Society of Jesus was one of early modern Europe's most dynamic, innovative and multifaceted religious organizations, and the way it operated as it sent missions across the globe furnishes ample evidence of the influence of mercantile approaches to the collection, management and deployment of information. Jesuit schools offered a special curriculum that was designed for merchants, one that downplayed the traditional emphases on theology and classical learning and instead accentuated disciplines that depended on observation such as geography and branches of natural philosophy. Across their educational spectra, the Jesuits recognized the importance of managing information, as they routinely offered instruction in reading comprehension, the keeping of files, as well as the systematic taking, ordering and categorizing of notes, comments and observations into notebooks, where they would accessible for consultation.

Similarly, the Society placed especial importance in its curricula and institutions on mathematics, and Jesuit mathematicians were attached to many of their missions. When the Jesuit polymath Athanasius Kircher (1602–1680) undertook to create a global map of magnetic declination, he sought to take advantage of the global distribution of fellow Society members trained in mathematics. At a 1639 meeting of the Congregation of Procurators in Rome, he provided the delegates departing for various parts of the world with instructions for the observation of magnetic declination, to be passed on to the resident Jesuit mathematicians. Although he never completed the project, he did include the initial data he received in his treatise on magnetism.[77] Similarly, Christoph Clavius (1538–1612), the Jesuit mathematician at the Roman College, drew upon

---

[77] Daniel Stolzenberg, "A spanner and his works: books, letters, and scholarly communications networks in early modern Europe." In Ann Blair and Anja-Silvia Goeing, eds., *For the Sake of Learning. Essays in Honor of Anthony Grafton*, Vol. I (Leiden: Brill, 2016), 157–172 (here 166).

the knowledge of a wealth of fellow Jesuit correspondents to compose his many works on mathematics.[78] The Jesuit recourse to mathematics sought to bring order and control to the complex and layered realms in which they operated.

The practice and rhetoric of financial accounting proved to have early modern spiritual applications. In an age of competing confessions, it is perhaps unsurprising that the spiritual well-being of adherents would be measured according to the principles of profit and loss. Analogies with accounting regularly appeared in the writing of churchmen and theologians and in personal diaries. Thomas Watson (1620–1686), a Puritan preacher, made the parallel explicit: "many Christians are like tradesmen that are sinking; they are loth to look over their Books, or cast up their accounts, lest they should find their estates low."[79] As with the financial health of a business, a ledger could reveal the state of one's soul. The Jesuit Order implemented their own system of "spiritual accounting" that bore much in common with the efforts undertaken by international trading houses and banks. The Procurator of the Province of Sicily, Ludovico Flori (1579–1647), composed a treatise on double-entry bookkeeping entitled *Trattato del modo di tenere il libro doppio domestico col suo essemplare*, first published in 1636.[80] It provided a systematic and analytic approach to keeping records, with many practical examples from Flori's experience with the Sicilian colleges and numerous reproductions of journals and ledgers representing accounts from Jesuit institutions. The Society found the lessons of business information management highly applicable to its religious mission and its unitary and hierarchical structure, which sought to govern and control from the center in Rome. Ignatius Loyola's *Spiritual Exercises* had insisted that one undertake a "moral inventory" of one's life and an honest accounting of one's sins. Financial and spiritual accountability went hand in hand in Jesuit missions, with regular auditing of both of the books and of souls of the Society's individual members.[81] The so-called *Catologi triennales*, sent to

---

[78] Luce Giard and Antonella Romano, "L'usage jésuite de la correspondance. Sa mise en pratique par le mathématicien Christoph Clavius (1570–1611)." In Romano, ed., *Rome et la science moderne: entre Renaissance et Lumières* (Rome: École française de Rome, 2009), 65–119.

[79] Thomas Watson, *The Christian Soldier: Or, Heaven Taken by Storm* (London: Thomas Parkhurst, 1669), 56.

[80] Ludovico Flori, *Trattato del modo di tenere il libro doppio domestico col suo essemplare* (Palermo: Per Decio Cirillo, 1636).

[81] The notion of accounting as a blueprint for self-assay has proven enduring. John D. Rockefeller compelled his children and grandchildren to maintain personal account books. In the past few decades, the evangelical Christian finance guru Dave Ramsey has sold millions of books counseling personal financial accounting as a brand of self-assessment and improvement.

Rome every three years, included two books that provided details on each member of each college, ranking them according to eight spiritual and behavioral metrics, the results of which were recorded in rubrics that resembled spreadsheets. A third book provided details of the college's financial situation. Together, they offered a comprehensive balance sheet of the college's spiritual and financial health. Representing the provinces in this manner allowed the Governor General of the Order, ensconced many miles away in Rome, to "see" them. The systematic collection of information, both financial and human, became an obsession for the Society of Jesus, and its management and use essential for effective control from the center.[82] Accountability, for the Jesuits, was not merely about financial accounts, but also about keeping tabs on individuals in accordance with the preoccupations of Counter-Reformation theology and polity. In his 1678 treatise *Idea de un príncipe político christiano en cien empresas*, Diego de Saavedra Fajardo celebrated the Jesuit approach to information management – their system of correspondence and record-keeping meant that the Superior General was informed about the skills and career development of every member of the Order in every province. Were princes able to install a similar system in their approach to the art of governing, Fajardo insisted, they would not have to depend on the plague of unreliable ministers.[83]

Similar dynamics were at play in another international organization of the period, this one committed solely to commercial pursuits. The British East India Company (EIC) produced mountains of paper records authorizing, initiating, describing, tracking, and replicating its activities across the globe. This "Indian Ink" has been the subject of an exhaustive study by Miles Ogborn.[84] The Company's solution to the challenges of its members interacting across vast distances was to construct a social organization mediated by the movement of paper. The relationships essential to the Company, spanning the great distances over which it operated, were worked out through inscription on paper in interlaced networks of correspondence. By the *Lawes or Standing Orders of the East India Company*, composed in 1621, it was decreed that an action could be construed as an act of the Company only when carried out in conjunction with a piece of paper. Thus, as Matthew Hull has put it, "A cash payment made without

---

[82] Paolo Quattrone, "Accounting for God: accounting and accountability practices in the Society of Jesus (Italy, XVI–XVII centuries)." *Accounting, Organizations and Society*, 29 (2004), 647–683.

[83] Arndt Brendecke, *The Empirical Empire. Spanish Colonial Rule and the Politics of Knowledge* (Berlin. De Gruyter Oldenbourg, 2016), 47.

[84] Miles Ogborn, *Indian Ink. Script and Print in the Making of the East India Company* (Chicago: University of Chicago Press, 2007).

a warrant was not a Company transaction, and an individual who made it was required to reimburse the Company. Goods transferred without a receipt were still considered to be in Company possession. Even cooks on Company ships had to produce accounts and receipts for the bursar or repay the funds extended to them. The *Lawes* expressed a thorough-going rejection of trust in people ... .Vouching was done by artifacts, not be people. The *Lawes* specified a kind of documentary buddy system in which every document was to "be vouched" by another, produced by a different person."[85] Paper trumped people.

The dynamics of authority, trustworthiness and civility were thus negotiated and navigated through constant writing, as were the challenges of geographical and temporal distance. At the same time, the Company relied on the drafting and possession of written contracts, charters and royal letters from the Privy Council to confer authority and privileges on its merchants. As a joint-stock company, the EIC was a corporate body whose existence relied on written instruments that bound individuals to the Company through a combination of mandated powers. Important too was access to accurate information regarding the cost of commodities and stock prices. A panoply of modes of writing, manuscript and print, undertaken in London, the East Indies, and everywhere in-between, was the lifeblood of this international organization, one that existed on paper as much as it did in offices, ports, and markets of Britain and Asia. These documents were the "palpable sedimentation of the real."[86]

The Company's very existence, therefore, rested on a lattice of written instruments. So too did its everyday operations. Ogborn makes clear just how much writing and record-keeping were expected of the agents of the Company, even when they were in transit. Captains, masters, merchants and pursers were all required to maintain journals, to allow for systematic consultation, comparison, and assessment. Even the ship was a space for writing and accounting – the purser was to keep a book in which he would record all that was carried on and off the ship, such that an accurate picture of the voyage could be provided to customs agents. In this way, Ogborn suggests, the vessel could be rendered a "calculable space."[87] Company ships traveling to and from England carried boxes of documents in their cargoes: letters and their replies, copies of accounts, price lists, letter-books, and diaries detailing the operations of stations.

The writing continued in country: among the tasks of the Station Master was to oversee the writing and accounting. He maintained diaries that

---

[85] Matthew Hull, *Government of Paper. The Materiality of Bureaucracy in Urban Pakistan* (Berkeley: University of California Press, 2012).
[86] Hull, *Government of Paper*, 8.   [87] Ogborn, *Indian Ink*, 52.

recorded details of the day-to-day operations of his station (or "factory," in the parlance of the Company). He also kept the accounts, and oversaw the correspondence between the directors and their servants in India. Letters to and from London were expected to indicate not only where and when they were sent, but also what letters had recently arrived and been dispatched, and which letters were being answered. The Master's review of accounting procedures was intended to make the pursuit of profit more transparent: there was a moral as well as financial component to it. By the second half of the seventeenth century, Masters were responsible for the production of Books of Consultation, generated at each factory and then forwarded to London, where they would be examined to inform future practice. The Master's "writing office" was described by one observer as "a Roome in the Factory house [where] all Bookes, Letters, Paper, etc are orderly disposed ... And the Accomptants and writers required to attend dayly and dispatch their worke therein." The Court of Directors in 1678 called the writing office a place where "all our bookes and papers may be orderly kept and that none be carried out to any private house or lodging, but that all business may be dispatched there."[88]

At every level, then, the EIC regarded writing as essential in creating a unitary written system that bound together London, the far-flung factories and the ships crisscrossing the seas. As Bhavani Raman has written of the EIC: "From its very inception in the seventeenth century, The British East India Company's political dominance was forged by the sword, built on the spine of the accountant's ledger, and held together by written correspondence."[89] Like the Jesuits, therefore, the EIC regarded the circulation of paper as a means of reinforcing the order and hierarchy of their organization, facilitating its operation across vast geographical space, securing fiscal probity and accountability, and maintaining moral and social order. It has also been suggested that the constipating rule by paper that has prevailed in post-independence India, known as the "Document Raj," has its roots in the practices of the East India Company.[90] Neither the Society of Jesus nor the East India Company would have been conceivable without the paper technologies that propelled the early modern information revolution.

※ ※ ※

The ink-stained fingers of Europe's merchants handled millions of quires of paper on to which they inscribed the information of commerce, which

---

[88] Ogborn, *Indian Ink*, 102.
[89] Bhavani Raman, *Document Raj. Writing and Scribes in Early Colonial South India* (Chicago: University of Chicago Press, 2012), 8–9.
[90] Bhavani Raman, *Document Raj*.

became currency as much as were ducats, florins and guilders. Merchants were among the first in Europe to recognize the potential benefits (and bear the burdens) of pen and paper's capacity to provide a snapshot of past transactions, an ongoing distillation of one's current actions and concerns, and grist for the mill of one's aspirations moving forward. For them, managing large quantities of information became an essential constituent part of the pursuit of profit. For others, many of whom looked upon the accounting practices and record-keeping methods of merchants with interest, information management became indispensable as well. Among those were statesmen, for whom the tasks of governing increasingly transpired with pen in hand. In early modern Europe, the pursuit of political control, like the pursuit of profit, generated an unprecedented paper trail that demanded attention, interpretation and management. It is to the politics of paper that we now turn.

4   The Paper of Politics and the Politics of Paper

Peter Burke has suggested that the "paper state" was an invention of early modern Europe.[1] It was a function chiefly of the desire of early modern sovereigns for information, about the people they ruled, the competitors they faced, and the events they lived through. With the widespread adoption of paper as a container for that information, the institutions of state in Europe were increasingly mediated through the circulation of paper instruments, chiefly the correspondence of the agents of state power: diplomats, governors, *intendants*, and other officials who embodied and projected state authority. One of the most evident measurables of the much-talked-about "rise of the modern state" was the state's consumption of paper. Ben Kafka puts it this way: "modern political thought was founded and confounded by its encounters with paperwork."[2] Perhaps it is worth reconfiguring Charles Tilly's tautology about war and the state: the state produced paper, and paper produced the state.[3]

This chapter is guided by the question: "what does early modern politics look like when we approach it from the standpoint of writing, information, and information management?" It explores both how the widespread employment of paper shaped the practice of politics, and how the incumbent documentation, in its volume, diversity, and ubiquity, became a central preoccupation of Europe's princes. Looking at early modern political life in this way reveals that the preoccupations of political life shaped the sorts of paper that were produced, but also that the widespread adoption of paper shaped politics itself, by endowing new offices and institutions with authority related to writing, by transforming the nature of political communications, and by providing a medium that

---

[1] Peter Burke, "Communication." In Ulinka Rublack, ed., *A Concise Companion to History* (Oxford: Oxford University Press, 2011), 157–176 (here 165).
[2] Ben Kafka, *The Demon of Writing. Powers and Failures of Paperwork* (New York: Zone Books, 2012), 10.
[3] See, especially, Charles Tilly, *Coercion, Capital and European States, AD 990–1992* (Cambridge, MA: Blackwell, 1992).

could translate information and knowledge into power. In sum, it is my intention to illuminate the ways in which the paper of politics and politics of paper interact, in their intertwined historical dance, and how the newfound need for managing paper transformed the nature of early modern political life.

Up until the sixteenth century, European states can be said to have exerted a chiefly jurisdictional authority, whereby the actual policy was formulated and carried out at the local level by diverse political actors and institutions. This model of the "domain" state was replaced in much of Europe by a fiscal-military state. Carlo Capra has described the shift as one from justice to administration.[4] And administration, of course, relied on, and itself generated, a lot of documentation, information inscribed on paper. This shift to paperwork, the grist for the bureaucratic mill, was just as prevalent in constitutional states as it was in absolutist ones.[5] The famed rise of the early modern state could be measured as much by its generation of paper as by any other metric. As Max Weber might have said: "no paper, no bureaucracy." For many of those within early modern bureaucracies, there was an "iron cage" of paperwork.

The rise of paperwork was driven by the widespread adoption of a "politics of inscription," which saw the expressions, institutions, and personnel of state power rest and depend on paper-based transactions. Princes and other state authorities, seeking to achieve mastery over information about their rule, realms, and subjects, saw paper instruments as the means by which to do so. They sought full representation of their power on paper as an essential step toward assertion of their power in practice. Early modern states, and the bureaucracies (literally, "rule by the desk") that arose to serve them, relied on documents to represent virtually the lands and populations over which they had authority. As a matter of course, sovereigns and states directed more and more resources to the shepherding of these documents, committing new personnel with the requisite competencies to the business of writing, new institutions to the management of the resulting documentation, and new physical spaces for its preservation and storage. The state, in early modern Europe, became an information manager.

Because so much of politics was now mediated by the drafting, circulation, and deployment of paper instruments, writing itself became a political activity. Politics, of course, remained at its core about the exercise of power, but the paper of politics was now invested with that

---

[4] Carlo Capra, "Governance." In Hamish Scott, ed., *Oxford Handbook of Early Modern European History*, Vol. II (Oxford: Oxford University Press, 2015), 478–511.
[5] A point made in Thomas Ertman, *Birth of the Leviathan. Building States and Regimes in Medieval and Early Modern Europe* (Cambridge: Cambridge University Press, 1997).

power, and became its embodiment. The assertion of authority was routinely mirrored and justified by writing on paper. Writing's representative role meant that, in many ways, statecraft became a virtual activity, whereby the reality perceived by secretaries, ministers, diplomats, and other agents of the state was inscribed in their written records, acts, and correspondence. The resulting paper subsequently became essential to construction of what was deemed "real" within state institutions. It became, in a formulation put forward by David Dery, a "papereality."[6] In circulating their paper, political individuals and institutions ended up relying on written instruments to epitomize their world. Early modern political life saw the emergence of a new sociability whose modality was documents, establishing as essential to government a wide range of writing practices and creating new roles for professionals of political writing.

Political information in early modern Europe, as Maria Rosa has suggested, was fed by diverse channels and many different articulations: "a chain of figures but also an inexhaustible circuit of information" combined to create a political "knowledge."[7] The increase in state paper was partly a procedural outcome: governance was increasingly carried out with recourse to paper instruments, and to letters in particular. Paper became a necessary mediator for the exercise of political power and a written residue accompanying most political acts. It could be carried easily by agents of the state as a vector of its power: the political authority of an individual rested not only in his person but also in the paper that he carried. Paper, too, could be preserved in large quantities in spaces dedicated to that purpose, specifically in the burgeoning state archives of the period, reflecting the widely shared inclination to preserve and a determination to establish a real-time record of rule and a database of precedent.[8] The ultimate goals of this commitment to rule by paper were little different than they had been among rulers for centuries, before paper became an essential medium of political exchange: to establish

---

[6] David Dery, "Papereality" and learning in bureaucratic organizations." *Administration and Society*, 29.6 (1998), 277–289.
[7] "Una catena di figure, ma anche un circuito inesauribile di informazioni che, se intendevano appagare nell'immediato una interessata sete di conoscenze o soltanto una semplice curiosità, finivano col raffigurare in ogni caso, dove più dove meno, anche al di là e la di sotto dei livelli più alti, un 'sapere' politico, che sempre più andava circolando, nel flusso contingente degli evvenimenti, tra gli scenari mobili e inquieti della società europea." Maria Rosa, Preface to Elena Fasano Guarini and Rosa, eds., *L'informazione politica in Italia (secoli xvi–xviii)* (Pisa: Scuola Normale Superiore, 2001), ix–x.
[8] On the impetus to archive, see Markus Friedrich, *Die Geburt des Archivs. Ein Wissensgeschichte* (Munich: Oldenbourg Verlag, 2013); as well as Paul Dover, "Deciphering the diplomatic archives of fifteenth-century Italy." *Archival Science*, 7.4 (2007), 297–316; and Filippo De Vivo, "Ordering the archive in early modern Venice (1400–1650)." *Archival Science*, 10 (2010), 231–248.

legitimacy, reinforce sovereignty, facilitate the collection of revenue, optimize one's position vis-à-vis neighboring states, and, ultimately, assert control over one's territories and populations. In the pursuit of these ends, they were fated to achieve at best partial triumphs; in the generation of massive amounts of paper, however, they were dizzyingly successful.

4.1 Writing the Medieval State

The connection between writing and the state has always been close. Jack Goody sees the earliest written governments as exploiting "the capacity to communicate at a distance, to store information in files, and to tend to depersonalize interaction."[9] The promulgation and circulation of public documents in medieval societies served to reinforce uniformity and standardization. The work of Michael Clanchy on the medieval English monarchy has been especially illuminating of the importance of writing to the authority of the state. Per Clanchy, the state is formed at the conjunction of coercion, charisma, and routinization – writing, he suggests, is essential to all three of these.[10] As a political tool, writing was "the most powerful instrument of standardization."[11] The repeated writing of a regularized, written language implicitly conveys political ideology. Writing detaches language from its inscriber, thus depersonalizing it, which in turn aids in the propagation of a fundamentally impersonal entity, the state. Indeed, Clanchy suggests, by externalizing knowledge and by disassociating it from a specific person, writing in effect creates information and makes that information dependent on a particular information technology. Goody calls writing a "technology of the intellect."[12] In medieval England, Clanchy insists, the application of this technology, and the resulting proliferation of documents, increased the power of the state, even far from the king's presence.[13]

The growth in state documentation in the late Middle Ages was a feature across Western Europe in what John Watts has called "a huge

---

[9] Jack Goody, *The Logic of Writing and the Organization of Society* (Cambridge: Cambridge University Press, 1986), 89.
[10] Charisma, according to Clanchy, depends on feeling and supernatural authority and in order for it to endure, it must be replicable through logical ordering and definition. That is how charisma comes to be routinized.
[11] Michael Clanchy, "Does writing construct the state?" *Journal of Historical Sociology*, 15.1 (2002), 68–70 (here 68).
[12] Jack Goody, *The Logic of Writing*.
[13] Michael Clanchy, "Literacy, law and the power of the state." In *Culture et idéologie dans la genèse de l'État moderne. Actes de la table ronde de Rome (15–17 octobre 1984)* (Rome: École Française de Rome, 1985), 25–34.

multiplication in the formulaic records of government."[14] The sources of this increase in documentation were multiple. Across Western Europe, there was an increase in taxation, which naturally produced more records, as did the advent of paid armies, which incrementally replaced feudal musters. These military commitments were extremely expensive and required bureaucratic shepherding, both of which drove the need for paper records. In the thirteenth and fourteenth centuries, there was a marked increase in the offices and personnel associated with government, engaged in activities more often than not mediated by writing. Among the most important institutions to expand were law courts and government chanceries; in both of these, writing and record-keeping were essential, and both were institutions that committed themselves to the preservation of documents that could be used in the future. In France in 1314, a mere four councilors handled the *requêtes du palais*, the petitions coming in from subjects. By 1343, that number was up to twenty-nine. In the same period, there was a doubling of the notaries working in the royal chancery, and a tripling of the councilors attached to the Parlement. Similar developments could be seen elsewhere. The administrative footprint of the papal *curia* doubled in the years of its residence in Avignon (1303–1378). The English crown began keeping systematic records of letters and judgments in the first decade of the thirteenth century.

Another medieval monarchy dedicated to written government was the Kingdom of Aragon. But while English documents had been rendered chiefly on parchment, in Aragon we see an administration that embraced the use of paper, supplied by the local paper industry. In 1257, King Jaume I (r. 1213–1276) opted to employ locally sourced, relatively high-quality paper for the running of his administration. This made him the first European monarch to use paper in the daily functioning of his government (certain Italian communal governments were using paper at about the same time). The use of paper as a recording and communication device was essential to the operation of the Aragonese chancery, and the use of this abundant, flexible, durable, and relatively inexpensive material led, as it would in many other subsequent cases, to the appearance of an official culture of compulsive record-keeping. The primary reason for this, as Stephane Péquignot has demonstrated in his work, is that letters were fundamental to the practice of government and diplomacy in the late Middle Ages, and the availability of paper, produced in abundance locally in Jaume's kingdom, chiefly by Muslim artisans, served

---

[14] John Watts, *The Making of Polities. Europe 1300–1500* (Cambridge: Cambridge University Press, 2009), 124.

to facilitate the flow of letters. Officials in Jaume's archives maintained sophisticated records of the letters sent out and received, and developed document location tools. They served as an active data bank for governance. Jaume was thus opting to base his rule on paper, writing, and archives. The Kingdom of Aragon was genuinely a "paper state" *avant la lettre*.

This commitment to running the kingdom with paper was shared by his son, Pere, and even more so by his grandson, Jaume II (r. 1291–1327), whose reign left one of medieval Europe's largest repositories of paper. With ready, local access to a supply of paper, Jaume II's officials kept copious records, including rough drafts and copies of letters entered in registers. His archives include sophisticated records of letters sent out and received, as well as a complex set of document location tools.[15] Nor was Jaume the only Spanish sovereign to use paper as a tool of governance – his contemporary King Alfonso X of Castile also used it, if not as broadly. As remarkable as Jaume's "information system" was, the paper documents generated by the institutions of his government would be dwarfed by those of even a mid-sized Italian city-state in the fifteenth century. The bureaucracies of the sixteenth- and seventeenth-century monarchies would dwarf these still further.

Written government and abundant use of paper came early to the medieval Italian communes. Italian cities between the twelfth and fourteenth centuries underwent a "politicization of the word" or a "verbalization of politics," whereby governance was largely conducted via written instruments. It was part of what Enrico Artifoni, in describing the Italian communes of the thirteenth century, has called an "inexorable process of growth in writing."[16] By the middle of the fourteenth century, across many towns in the realm of *Latinitas* there had been a significant takeoff in institutional urban literacy. The clearest indication of this transformation was a corresponding rise in the volume and diversity of written records created and preserved by civic institutions in the course of their self-government. The civic chancery in many Italian communes became, according to Claude Gavard, not only a *place de pouvoir* but also a *place de mémoire* – a storehouse as well as an instrument of political authority.[17] The preservation of documents necessitated their management: it required systems of storage to prevent wastage and loss, but also

---

[15] Stéphane Péquignot, *Au nom du roi: pratique diplomatique et pouvoir durant la règne de Jacques II d'Aragon, 1291–1327* (Madrid: Casa de Velázquez, 2009).

[16] Enrico Artifoni, "Podestà professionali e la fondazione retorica della politica communale." *Quaderni storici*, 63 (1986), 687–719.

[17] Claude Gavard, "Conclusion." In Kouky Fianu and DeLloyd J. Guth, eds., *Écrit et pouvoir dans les chancelleries médiévales: espace français, espace anglais* (Turnhout: Brepols, 1997), 333–342 (here 335).

protocols for determining access and secrecy, and finding aids and indices for locating the appropriate records. It also required the dedicated service of a cadre of literate individuals versed in "the profession of the pen" (*mestiere della penna*).[18]

Important precursors of early modern developments were the political bodies of *quattrocento* Italy, notable for their growing and increasingly uniform production, circulation, and storage of public written records. There was a corresponding rise in the number, and variety, of offices and officials who were involved in this activity.[19] Of particular importance was the role of the chancery, which had to tackle the documentary demands of the Italian Renaissance state, especially the paper flows generated by diplomatic activity. As Andrea Guidi has put it: "the chancery is genuinely the central point of the system of communication at the base of the management and conduct of state affairs."[20]

The surge in documents was a function of a number of shared factors: the widespread availability of regionally sourced paper, an attitude toward documentary production and preservation linked to new state offices, the desire of princes and dominant patriciates to legitimize their rule through the establishment of a paper trail, and increased diplomatic activity. In the words of Alessandro Silvestri: "Authoritative control over the writing, dispatching and storage of standard series of records became a necessity for rulers, since the physical expansion of states and the increased specialisation of administration extended the areas in which documents were required."[21] Administrative correspondence; letters to and from chief executives; complaints and petitions to the prince, his proxies, and central administrative bodies; records of official appointments; minutes of the meetings of important councils; lists of office-holders; and various legislative documents, as well as drafts and copies of many of these, gathered as files and bundles of paper in the documentary repositories that were now a feature of nearly every administrative center in Italy. This new inflow of documentation was generated chiefly by the tasks of day-to-day

---

[18] This is the phrase used by Gianbattista Palatino to describe the job of secretaries and others dedicated to writing, in his *Compendio del gran volume de l'arte del bene et leggiadramente scrivere tutte le sorti di lettere et caratteri* (Rome: Heredi di Valerio et Luigi Dorici Fratelli Bresciani, 1566).
[19] Guido Castelnuovo, "Offices and officials." In Andrea Gamberini and Isabella Lazzarini, eds., *The Italian Renaissance State* (Oxford: Oxford University Press, 2012), 368–385.
[20] Andrea Guidi, *Un segretario militante. Politica, diplomazia e armi nel Cancelliere Machiavelli* (Milan: Mulino, 2009), 39: "Insomma, qui la Cancelleria è davvero il punto nodale del Sistema di communicazione alla base della gestione e della condotta degli affari di stato."
[21] Alessandro Silvestri, "Ruling from afar: government and information management in late medieval Sicily." *Journal of Medieval History*, 42.3 (2016), 357–381 (here 360).

administration, and was now combined with the existing documentary traditions of the communal period.[22] These trends were in evidence across all types of regime: seigniorial Ferrara and Mantua, republican Florence and Venice, ducal Milan, and pontifical Rome.

The chancery became a locale of central importance, the place that redacted and registered the rising tide of documentation, and managed the increasingly complex processes of generating, organizing, and conserving the paper of politics. Chanceries across Italy had to equip themselves to handle the documentary demands of the regional state. Thus the seigneurial regimes of Milan, Ferrara, and Mantua developed active chanceries that produced huge amounts of documentation related to both diplomacy and territorial administration. Under the Sforza, the Milanese Duchy became one of Italy's most sophisticated bureaucracies; Duke Francesco Sforza (r. 1450–1466) declared that he wished to "govern by documents."[23] It was the context of the chancery that informed the political thought of Niccolò Machiavelli (1469–1527), the second chancellor of the Florentine Republic from 1498 to 1512. His daily handling of paper, as much as his diplomatic missions and deep reading in ancient history, is what shaped his famous outlook on political life.[24]

The commitment to written government was most pronounced in northern Italy, but one of the most striking examples was the *Conservatoria* of King Ferdinand I of Aragon (r. 1412–1416) in Sicily. All the documents pertaining to royal property in Sicily had to pass through this body. Its clerks maintained an extensive series of administrative books, each of which covered a different area of paperwork: fiefs and privileges, grants, salaries, accounts, customs, commissions, castles, and debts. Then, within each book, the information was organized according to rubrics, and in many cases clerks added marginal notations. All this was deemed essential in asserting authority over a royal province separated from the royal seat in Barcelona by the Tyrrhenian Sea.[25]

The developments in Italy gradually created a cadre of what we might call "professionals of a culture of public writing." Humanistically trained chancellors and humanists oversaw the implementation of widely shared administrative techniques, cultural practices of letter writing, and stewardship of state documents. The shared competencies and cultural skills of these individuals afforded them political clout and a degree of social mobility, redeemable in administrative milieus across the Italian political

---

[22] Castelnuovo, "Offices and Officials," 382.
[23] Francesco Senatore, *"Uno mundo di carta": forme e strutture della diplomazia sforzesca* (Naples: Liguori, 1998); Axel Behne, "Archivordnung und Staatsordnung im Mailand der Sforza-Zeit." *Nuovi Annali della Scuola per Archivisti e Bibliotecari*, 2 (1988), 93–102.
[24] Guidi, *Un segretario militante*.   [25] Silvestri, "Ruling from afar."

landscape.[26] Their roles in the oversight of the papers of state assured them access to political power – they were precursors to the *letrados*, *intendants*, and other members of the *noblesse de robe* that would play such important roles in the political life of early modern Europe in the centuries to follow.

Among the important transformations in the written culture of Italy in the *Quattrocento* was the "gradual change from the notary-chronicler to the (notary-) chancellor-humanist."[27] The great output of documents that characterized medieval Italian communes had chiefly been the work of notaries. The development of political writing in the regimes of late medieval Italy saw a gradual breakdown of the bright line between notarial practice and the writing of the chancery. Those working in chanceries were responsible for what Attilio Bartoli Langeli has called a "communal diplomatics" that served the political consolidation and legitimization of regimes that were constantly at risk of being destabilized by internal rivalries between political factions and external threats from geopolitical rivals.[28] Composing and managing documents for the benefit of the commune, the written output of chanceries was dynamic and varied, reflecting the complex of political activities of these urban polities. Despite this complexity, there was a creeping uniformity in the format, production, and usage of public written records across the various fifteenth-century Italian states.[29] Diplomatic and administrative correspondence, the letters of princes and other sovereigns, petitions from subjects, *cahiers de doléances*, records of appointments and minutes of meetings, lists of offices, documents pertaining to legislation, receipts, fiscal surveys: all of these could be found in the holdings of most Italian states, overseen by professionals of the written word. "The 'documentary tradition and the history of the city' combined, in a decisive way, with new written records of a purely administrative character."[30]

---

[26] See the example of Antonio da Trezzo, who served both the Duchy of Milan and the Kingdom of Naples, in Paul Dover, "Royal diplomacy in Renaissance Italy: Ferrante d'Aragona (1458–1494) and his ambassadors." *Mediterranean Studies*, 14 (2005), 57–94 (here 91–92). Another example is Giovanni Lanfredini, who served as Lorenzo de' Medici's ambassador in Naples and Rome, who also cultivated close ties with a number of other Italian sovereigns. See Elisabetta Scarton, *Giovanni Lanfredini: uomo d'affari e diplomatico nell'Italia del Quattrocento* (Florence: Olschki, 2007).

[27] Castelnuovo, "Offices and Officials," 382.

[28] Attilio Bartoli Langeli, "Premessa." In Bartoli Langeli, Andrea Giorgi, and Stefano Moscadelli, eds., *Archivi e comunità tra medioevo ed età moderna* (Rome: Ministero per i beni e le attività culturali, 2009), vii–xiv.

[29] On this process, see the studies in the special edition of *Reti medievali*, 9 (2008), edited by Isabella Lazzarini, *Scritture e potere. Pratiche documentarie e forme di governo nell'Italia tardomedievale (XIV–XV secolo)*.

[30] Castelnuovo, "Offices and Officials," 382–383. See also Paolo Cammarosano, *Tradizione documentaria e storia cittadina. Introduzione al "Caleffo Vecchio" del Comune di Siena* (Siena: Accademia senese degli Intronati, 1988).

The city archive went from being simply a depository for notarial documents, to an active node of the paper flow of everyday governance, bringing together the records of individual offices and enlarging to accommodate the documentation that accompanied the expansion of political activity. Again, this consolidation and expansion of archives was not confined to major territorial states; it was pursued in communes, rural communities, towns subject to larger polities, ecclesiastical bodies, and major families, all of which perceived the benefit of keeping hold of their documents. We see the widespread establishment of protocols for the storage of documents; regulations for drafting different types of document; and rules for access, retrieval, and removal. It was customary for the chancellor, often a trained humanist, to oversee the archives and formulate rules for maintenance and access. The sophistication of the record-keeping differed from state to state, as did the level of centralization. In the Italian *signorie*, the balance between the "communal" records and those of the ruling family differed from locale to locale, but generally the regimes oversaw the preservation of documents related to public functions associated with the princely court.[31] In Milan, Francesco Sforza ordered the regrouping of documentary series and the reworking of inventories, so that the archives of the Sforza could be used and consulted regularly. The Gonzaga in Mantua, meanwhile, had systematic inventories of their documents by the middle of the fifteenth century, betraying an almost obsessive commitment to writing for a small territorial state.[32] Similar inventories became commonplace across Italy, an indication of a commitment both to written government and the preservation of documents for future consultation. Even smaller political centers developed systematic documentary and archival models.[33] This "urge to archive," as we shall see, became a staple of early modern political life. Indeed, many of the documentary practices of written government that were typical of *Quattrocento* Italian states would become prevalent in Europe outside of Italy after 1500. Writing would now accompany most political actions, and it is the residue of these that filled the archives of early modern states, leaving a paper trail that dwarfed that produced by medieval polities.

---

[31] Gian Maria Varanini, "Public written records." In Andrea Gamberini and Isabella Lazzarini, eds. *The Italian Renaissance State* (Oxford: Oxford University Press, 2012), 385–405.

[32] Axel Behne, *Antichi inventari dell'Archivio Gonzaga* (Rome: Ministero per i beni culturali e ambientali, Ufficio centrale per i beni archivistici, 1993).

[33] B. Pagnin, *I formulari di un notaio e cancelliere padovano del sec. XV* (Padua: Istituto di storia medievale e moderna, 1953).

4.2 From Notaries to Secretaries

Developments in the Italian city-states of the Renaissance presaged a broader commitment among early modern European states to the offices, practices, and personnel of a culture of official writing and the production of documents as a central function of the state. The flow of documents and the archives that stored them demanded tasks of administration that were secretarial rather than notarial, giving rise across Europe to what I have called elsewhere an early modern "age of secretaries."[34] Secretaries were everywhere in early modern Europe, and were tasked with writing and documentary oversight in all manner of contexts, but particularly within political institutions. In the simplest terms, secretaries were information managers. Secretaries distinguished themselves as operatives with a particular skill set related to the drafting, production, and archiving of documents. Their emergence marks a shift from the fundamentally notarial culture of the Middle Ages, where a premium was placed on the recording and copying of relatively small numbers of largely statutory written instruments.

Secretaries acted as the custodians of the state institutions that emerged or expanded to capture, manage, and maintain documentary records. The shift in engaging secretaries as state personnel was mirrored by the emergence of chanceries akin to those in late medieval Italy. The chancery, of course, was above all a place of writing, the engine room for the redaction, registration, and reproduction of documentation. This was the institutional backdrop for the rise of the secretary as an essential figure in early modern politics. Archives and chanceries, sites for information management, became some of the most important organs of the state apparatus. They would become foundational pillars of the emerging state bureaucracies.

In his 1594 treatise *Il secretario*, Battista Guarini identified paper as the raw material of the secretary. Paper is to the secretary as marble is to the sculptor.[35] Writing is therefore his *arte*, his particular skill. The expansion of chancellery offices and secretariats in the sixteenth and seventeenth centuries was accompanied by a rash of treatises concerned with the makeup of the ideal secretary.[36] There was a broad recognition that the office of secretary was one consumed by the continual use of pen and paper in the service of prince and state. The secretary had to know and

---

[34] Paul Dover, "Introduction: the age of secretaries." In Dover, ed., *Secretaries and Statecraft in the Early Modern World* (Edinburgh: Edinburgh University Press, 2016), 1–15.
[35] Battista Guarini, *Il secretario. Dialogo di Battista Guarini. Nel qual non sol si tratta dell'ufficio del Segretario, et el modo del compor Lettere* (Venice: Ruberto Megietti, 1594), 10.
[36] See Benedict Buono, "La trattatistica sul 'segretario' e la codificazione linguistica in Italia fra Cinque e Seicento." *Verba*, 37 (2010), 301–312.

keep the seals, ciphers, and other tools surrounding the production of letters. In 1543, Francesco Priscianese wrote that the office of secretary included making sure that no written instruments coming in and going out were lost and that all were registered, with the incoming letters kept in files according to the day, month, "and sometimes hour" that they were received.[37] One popular and frequently plagiarized treatise, *Del secretario* (1565), by Francesco Sansovino, deems the management of documents within the prince's chancery as especially important. The secretary must "keep the drafts of [the letters] he writes, and also keep the completed letters in alphabetical order so that in every case he can show one thing or another. [He must] conserve the letters written to the Prince and the indications of from where and when they were sent."[38]

The role of secretaries as managers and mediators of information on behalf of the prince was a regular point of emphasis in this wave of treatises. In the language of the day, secretaries were "channels," "pipes," "conduits," or "paths" for information. They were also characterized in terms of the prince's anatomy, as the "throat" or neck," or as residing in the "stomach of the king," helping to guide his will and thoughts. They were there to ensure that the prince had access to the news necessary for everyday governance and effective communication.

The secretary was, according to Vincenzo Gramigna, writing in 1620, a *dicitor di penna*, a "pen-speaker."[39] The secretary's oversight of the paper of politics – recording his patron's correspondence, its organization and safe-keeping – granted him a key role in shaping the authority of the prince and in the effective formation of the state itself. Indeed, the secretary to Duke Alfonso II d'Este (r. 1559–1597), Giovanni Battista Nicolucci (1529–1575) (who wrote under the name il Pigna), in his treatise *Il principe*, declared that the secretary played a role in "forming" the very being of the prince.[40] In this role, the secretary needed not only to

[37] Francesco Priscianese, *Del governo della corte d'un Signore in Roma. Dove si ragiona di tutto quello, che al Signore, & à suoi Cortigiani si appartiene di fare. Opera non manco bella, che utile, & necessaria* (Rome: Francesco Priscianese, 1543), 30–31: "Del rimanente poi, che s'appartiene à cotale ufficio, come lo esser bello intenditore di cifere, & molto accurate, & diligente, che niuna cosa de gli scritti suoi si perda, & registrare il tutto, & tenere le lettere ricevute in filze, ò mazi per ordine, co'l notarvi il giorno, e'l mese, & molte volte l'hora della ricevuta."

[38] Francesco Sansovino, *Del secretario di M. Francesco Sansovino libri Quattro* (Venice: Francesco Rampazetto, 1565), 4v: "Tenga le minute di ciò che si scrive, & tenga anco le lettere distese per ordine d'alfabeto, accioche in ogni caso si possa mostrar l'una cosa & l'altra. Serbi le lettere scritte al Principe, & le segni di fuori dal luogo donde vengono, e li dì della data." An extensive discussion of how a secretary should keep registers of letters is in Angelo Ingegneri, *Del Buon Segretario Libri Tre di Angelo Ingegeri* (Rome: Guglielmo Faciotto, 1594), 98–103.

[39] Vincenzo Gramigna, *Opuscoli del signor Vincenzo Gramigna segretario* (Florence: Pietro Cecconcelli, 1620).

[40] Giovan Battista Pigna, *Il principe di Giovanni Battista Pigna* (Venice: Francesco Sansovino, 1561).

be a diligent scrivener, but also a virtuoso in the politics of inscription. An analog invoked on multiple occasions in seventeenth-century treatises was that between the secretary and Proteus, the Greek sea-god who could contort his body into any shape. Gabriel Perez del Barrio Angulo, in his *Secretario y Consegero de Señores y Ministros* (1645), compared the secretary to a musical instrument, called on to play different tunes according to the needs of the prince.[41] In an English manuscript treatise entitled *Il secretario qualificato* (1606), attributed to H. Parnell and housed in the Folger Library, we read that the secretary should "be readye to lepp out of one shape into another, as the diversitie of occurrences shall reqyre."[42] The pen was the primary tool for the secretary's Protean capacities. The secretary needed to be flexible, adaptable, and fluid in his writing.[43]

This profusion of prescriptive works pointed toward the growing range of expertise and professionalism expected of the state secretary. As Giulio Cesare Capaccio wrote in his treatise *Il Secretario* (1599):

[J]ust as with his tongue every man expresses the treasures of his mind, so too [the secretary] makes clear and distinct that material which was first conceived in form by other people, and in a simulacrum of a letter brings splendor to that mysterious idea that, receiving light and spirit from their voices, makes distant things appear to be present, facilitates negotiations, aligns the times, stabilizes memory, and in that place to which the letter arrives, shrinks the world.[44]

This is a long and imposing list, indicative of the centrality of the secretary to state business.

Secretaries, therefore, were chiefly concerned with paperwork. One of the important themes of the political history of this period is Europeans coming to grips with the potential and possibilities, as well as the limits

---

[41] Gabriel Perez del Barrio Angulo, *Secretario y Consegero de Señores y Ministros: Cargos, Materias, Cuydados, Obligaciones y curioso Agricultor de quanto el Govierno, y la Pluma piden para cumplir con ellas: El indice las toca, y estan ilustradas con sentencias, conceptos, y curiosidades, no tocadas* (Madrid: Francisco Garcia de Arroyo, Impressor del Reyno, 1645).

[42] Folger Shakespeare Library, Washington, DC, Mss. V.a. 554 *Il secretario qualificato*. Attributed to H. Purnell, 1606.

[43] Salvatore Nigro, "The secretary." In Rosario Villari, ed., *Baroque Personae*. Trans. by Lydia Cochrane (Chicago: University of Chicago Press, 1995), 82–99.

[44] *Il Secretario. Opera di Giulio Cesare Capaccio Napolitano. Ove quanto conviene allo scriver Familiare. Cioè All'ornato del dire. All'ortografia. Alla materia dei Titoli, delle Cifre, dello scriver Latino, brevemente si espone*. 3rd ed., expanded and amended (Venice: Niccolò Moretti, 1599), 2; " come con la lingua ogni uomo i tesori della mente esprime, così egli con la penna fa Chiara e distinta quella materia prima informa dell'altrui concetto; et in un simolacro di una lettera reca splendore a quella tenebrosa idea che, dalle sue voci ricevendo luce e spirito, fa le cose lontane parer presenti, facilita i negozii, accorda i tempi, stabilisce la memoria, et in quell luogo ove giunge la lettera riduce il mondo."
See also Salvatore Nigro, "Il segretario: precetti e pratiche dell'epistolografia barocca." In Nino Borsellino and Walter Pedullà, eds., *Storia generale della letteratura italiana*, Vol. VI. *Il secolo barocco. Arte e scienza nel Seicento* (Milan. Federico Motta Editore, 1999), 507–530.

and hazards, of paperwork. The embrace of paperwork ultimately meant that the early modern state, in its claims to authority, in the realm of its responsibilities, and in the personnel that it required and employed to pursue these, was something unprecedented and fundamentally different from its medieval precursors. Now the authority of the prince or other sovereign body, in addition to being premised in the soundness of his claims to sovereignty and in his capacity to project violence, was also dependent on the comprehensiveness with which state power could be expressed and encompassed instrumentally by paper.

The rise of secretaries and of paperwork was especially evident in the realm of diplomacy and international relations. The regularity and increasing complexity of interstate politics and the need to mediate the incumbent masses of paper (much of which was made up by the correspondence of ambassadors) helped encourage the emergence of the office of secretary of state and its various analogs. It may be true, as Franca Leverotti has suggested, that the diplomatic history of this period should be seen as a "history of men," rather than a history of systems and institutions.[45] But by the end of the sixteenth century, it is equally clear that diplomacy had, in most European polities of any size, become a permanent sector of the state's activities. If, in 1500, diplomacy was chiefly a praxis rather than an institution, by 1700 the reverse was true.[46] The state organizations that emerged in tandem with these changes were, above all, bodies for information management. A variety of foreign offices and secretariats of state, under a great variety of names, were now tasked with overseeing the large volumes of information and intelligence coming forth from representatives abroad and other sources.[47]

These ministries, often headed by foreign ministers or secretaries of state, were in large measure dedicated to processing the paperwork of international statecraft, which was generated chiefly through epistolary exchange with correspondents abroad. Secretaries of state became important figures across a variety of regimes, not so much for their shaping of policy, which remained the preserve of the prince, but in their shepherding of the diplomatic paper trail.

---

[45] Franca Leverotti, *Diplomazia e governo: i "famigli cavalcanti" di Francesco Sforza (1450–1466)* (Pisa: GISEM-ETS Editrice, 1992), 10.
[46] This is the formulation of Daniela Frigo in "Corte, honore et ragion di stato: il ruolo dell'ambasciatore in età moderna." In Frigo, ed., *Ambasciatori e nunzi. Figure della diplomazia in età moderna*. Special issue of *Chieron. Materiali e strumento di aggiornamento storiografico* (1999), 13–55.
[47] Alessandra Contini, "L'informazione politica sugli stati italiani non spagnoli nelle relazioni veneziane a metà conquecento (1558–1566)." In Guarini and Rosa, eds., *L'informazione politica*, 1–58.

In France and Spain, by the mid-sixteenth century, secretaries of state were among the most powerful ministers in the government. Their authority rested not only on their intimacy with and proximity to the prince himself, but on their access to and control of important state documents. They often played a role in determining what documents the prince would see.[48] The secretary of Holy Roman Emperor Charles V, Francisco de los Cobos (1477–1547), sifted through the incoming correspondence and had the clerks in his charge compose summaries to share with the Emperor. In this way, los Cobos in part determined what would pass before the Emperor's eyes. Imperial ambassadors, aware of this practice, sometimes sent copies of their dispatches to the Emperor directly to the secretary, in the hope that los Cobos reading it twice would improve the odds of Charles receiving the information they wished him to see. Reporting on los Cobos's triage of imperial correspondence, the Venetian ambassador Bernardo Navagero (1507–1575) observed that "when he is with the Emperor, everything goes through his hands, and when the Emperor is absent, in all important matters he is the ruler through the Council and his own judgment."[49] Los Cobos's power, therefore, rested on his management within the imperial government of both essential relationships and important documents.

Across Europe from the early sixteenth century onward, we witness the establishment of ruling councils, with varying nomenclature – the Council of State in Spain (from 1522) and the "Privy" Council in England (from 1540) and Spain (from 1557). These councils tended to be narrow in their composition, made up of men in whom the prince had confidence. They were generally the source of the so-called royal favorites, figures close to the prince who aggregated authority into their own hands. Favorites were deemed a necessary reaction to the expanded demands of early modern statecraft, including the stewardship of state documents, which were well beyond the capacity of a head of state to encompass. The most prominent of these figures, such as Richelieu and Mazarin in France, Olivares in Spain, and Buckingham in England are well known, but there were analogous figures in smaller states as well. They oversaw many of the cumbersome tasks, including the onerous paperwork associated with early modern government, for, as King

---

[48] John Headley, *The Emperor and his Chancellor: A Study of the Imperial Chancellery under Gattinara* (Cambridge: Cambridge University Press, 1983) and Rebecca Ard Boone, "Empire and medieval simulacrum. A political project of Mercurino Arborio di Gattinara, Grand Chancellor of Charles V." *Sixteenth century Journal*, 42.4 (2011), 1027–1049.

[49] Quoted in Howard Kenniston, *Francisco de los Cobos: Secretary of Emperor Charles V* (Pittsburgh: University of Pittsburgh Press, 1958), 348.

Philip IV of Spain (r. 1621–1640) once remarked: the "task could scarcely be performed by the king in person, since it would be incompatible with his dignity to go from house to house to see if his ministers and secretaries were carrying out their orders promptly."[50] By the eighteenth century, the rather inchoate roles of the favorite were replaced by defined government offices, such as first minister or foreign secretary, supported by staffs attending to associated paperwork.[51]

4.3 The Politics of Inscription and the "Letterocracy"

All of this paperwork was chiefly the result of what I call a "politics of inscription." The inscription of political ideas, instructions and descriptions of subjects, scenarios, and events expanded greatly and shaped European governance and statecraft. Building on medieval medial forms, but also developing new ones, early modern European states produced documents possessing multiple and simultaneous functions. Documents are inscribed not only to preserve, but also to show and inform – the word "document" itself is, as I pointed out earlier, derived from the Latin *docere*, to inform, show, or instruct. Documents are thus fundamentally representations, designed to demonstrate something to the viewer, usually about something that has happened in the recent past. Documents of all sorts, therefore, served as tools of mediation between government and governed and between metropole and periphery, but also, in important ways, between past and present (often with a view toward their deployment in the future). They also supplied connective sinew between intention and action, and thus between aspirations and implementation. They were the containers for writing's "conserved energy," and mechanisms for storing political potential.

In practice, inscription usually meant description. A great many of the documents that political bodies created during this period were essentially descriptive in nature – regular diplomatic dispatches providing accounts of the situation abroad; the census reports and tax surveys carried out by state bodies; responses to surveys sent out to ascertain information about one's realm, subjects, and possessions in the New World; and reports from the likes of *intendants* or provincial governors. It was this descriptive material that accumulated in enormous volumes in

---

[50] Quoted in Francisco Tomás Valiente, *Los validos en la monarquía española del siglo XVII* (Madrid: Istituto de Estudios Políticos, 1963), 181.
[51] Hamish Scott, "The rise of the first minister in eighteenth-century Europe." In Timothy Blanning and David Cannadine, eds., *History and Biography: Essays Presented to Derek Beales* (Cambridge: Cambridge University Press, 1996), 21–52.

files and swamped the statutory documentation that constituted much of medieval records.

The politics of paper in Europe were also chiefly epistolary. In a pattern that had been present in medieval regimes, state institutions, chiefly chanceries, developed and expanded chiefly to meet the challenge of receiving, copying, registering, and storing incoming letters, and then drafting, composing, and dispatching outgoing ones. The exchange of letters was an indication of political activity.

The early modern European political scene already operated as a "letterocracy," in which the everyday conduct of governance, negotiation, diplomacy, and the exercise of authority were chiefly mediated through correspondence.[52] The sheer number of letters written by and to statesmen in early modern Europe is a clear indication of how epistolarity came to govern local, regional, and international politics. Assigning preeminent roles to sender and recipient, the letter as a paper technology had manifold competencies: among other things, it could inform of decisions, confer authority and safe passage, transmit orders and requests, mobilize and coordinate multiple agents of authority, send news and descriptions of circumstances, and express opinion. Rather than the finished product of the political process, letters were the written testimony of the ongoing process of governing. They were also a form of writing that, as a matter of course, generated yet more writing, because letters naturally prompted responses. This is in keeping with a broader development that Jürgen Herold has located in the late Middle Ages, which saw a gradual change in thinking about the nature of the letter and its communicative role. From being *fidelis nuntia* ("faithful messenger") between sender and recipient, the letter was now conceived as a component of conversation between two parties, *sermo scriptus* (a "written conversation").[53] Administration via correspondence, chiefly through the maintenance of a series of these written conversations, became commonplace in regimes across Europe. Most of the paper that came across the desks of Europe's "paper princes" was in the form of letters: the early modern sovereign ruled by correspondence.[54] And a great many of these letters that statesmen had to wade through were fully or in part actually

---

[52] Dover, "Introduction: the age of secretaries."
[53] Jürgen Herold, "Von der "tertialitas" zum "sermo scriptus." Diskurswandel im mittelalterlichen Briefwesen und die Entstehung einer neuen Briefform von der Mitte des 13. bis zum Ende des 15. Jahrhunderts." In Christina Antenhoffer and Mario Müller, eds., *Briefe in politischer Kommunikation vom Alten Orient bis ins 20. Jahrhundert* (Göttingen: V&R Unipress, 2008), 83–113.
[54] "Paper princes" is a term coined by Meg Williams. See her ongoing project at www.paperprinces.org.

"letters about letters" – details on what had arrived and had been sent, the details of carriage, and what one should expect to receive.

There were at least four important modalities of the letter as a political tool. First, it allowed a connection between political actors who were at a distance from one another. It allowed the transference of information and legitimacy and in theory facilitated the elaboration, coordination, and implementation of policy by multiple actors. The availability of a communicative mechanism that did not require face-to-face interaction greatly multiplied the potential paths and outcomes of political activity, conducted across great distances.

Second, the exchange and circulation of letters allowed discussion, negotiation, and debate around the sovereign that was unbound by space, in what we might call a "virtual court." Decision-making was often mediated by the consultation of letters from individuals far from the metropole. Proximity to the prince was still vital in many circumstances, of course, but recourse to correspondence expanded the circle of those with a voice in the discussion. The letter acknowledged the reality of the distance that existed between correspondents: each letter was a monologue that was pretending to be a dialogue. Letters shrank distance between writers, but they could also be used deliberately to create distance and obfuscation. The participants in a dialogue carried out in a series of monologues could take advantage of the gaps in time and geographical distance that lay between them to carve out space for political autonomy.[55]

Third, letters are an extraordinarily flexible medium of communication and governance. They are simultaneously a form of expression, a means of conveying information, and a spur to action. Different types of letter serve to effect political action in different ways and under different circumstances. This was reflected in the publication of numerous treatises for secretaries and letter writers that detailed guidelines for composing dozens of varieties of letter tailored for particular circumstances. Works like Bartolomeo Zucchi's *L'idea del segretario* (1600), which stretched to three volumes, largely consisted of reproductions of actual letters between famous correspondents that were representative of the many categories of correspondence.[56] As Roger Chartier has described it: "Free and codified, intimate and public, suspended between secrecy and sociability, the letter, more than any other expression, brings together social bond and subjectivity."[57]

---

[55] Reinhard Nickisch, *Brief* (Stuttgart: Metzler, 1991), 9–10.
[56] Bartolomeo Zucchi, *L'idea del segretario dal signore Bartolomeo Zucchi da Monza. Rappresentata in un Trattato de l'Imitatione, e ne le lettere di Principi, e d'altri Signori* (Venice: Compagnia Minima, 1600).
[57] Roger Chartier, "Avant-propos." In Chartier, Alain Boureau, Cécile Dauphin, and Michel Demonet, eds., *La correspondance. Les usages de la lettre au XIXe siècle* (Paris:

Finally, letters offer a real-time record of governing and, when preserved, a reservoir of precedent and information that can be referenced and deployed for present and future action. Of course, the commitment to preservation meant that these letters soon accumulated in enormous volumes, leading to new requirements of the state related to recordkeeping. As we shall see, "seeing like a state" (to borrow the phrase of James Scott) meant a dedication to archives that preserved the records of the processes of governance, chiefly in the form of letters.[58]

For all of these reasons, correspondence came to mediate most of the day-to-day operations of early modern governments. Letters both reinforced and pulverized the distance between political actors, between the governors and the governed, with the work displaced to the desk, to the office, and to the archive.

The "letterocracy" was composed of many epistolary formats, but the building block for this politics of correspondence (and indeed of a broader cultural embrace of letter writing) was the *littera clausa*, a dated letter from an identifiable sender to a precise recipient, the form of which was rooted in the Renaissance Italian chancery letter. Literate men and women, first in Italy and then elsewhere in early modern Europe, came to believe that *litterae clausae* containing news, from the personal and familial to the public and political, from the minute to the general, were essential for controlling, understanding, and acting in their world. Such an outlook created a "society of letter writing," one that was accustomed to the regular exchange of letters, to the production and diffusion of documents, and to the conservation of writings in governmental and institutional archives. This complex of epistolary communication had intertwined roots in merchant practice and in political forms that emerged in the late Middle Ages.

Despite the emerging importance of *litterae clausae* between named, individual senders and recipients, the composition and circulation of letters in early modern Europe were complex. Letters were rarely the stable and transparent vehicles of interpersonal communication that they might seem at first glance: they were dispatched and then subject to a different interface each time they were read.[59] Perhaps because they became the chief means by which the affairs of court and state were

---

Fayard, 1991), 7–13 (here 9): "Libre et codifée, intime et publique, tendue entre secret et sociabilité, la lettre, mieux qu'aucune autre expression, associe le lien social et la subjectivité."

[58] James Scott, *Seeing Like a State: How Certain Schemes to Improve the Human Condition Have Failed* (New Haven, CT. Yale University Press, 1998).

[59] This is a point stressed in Heather Wolfe and Alan Stewart, *Letterwriting in Renaissance England* (Washington, DC: The Folger Shakespeare Library, 2004).

transacted, they were nearly always the result of the coproduction of multiple individuals, and subject to reading by many beyond the addressee indicated.

Shepherding a letter from conception to receipt usually involved many people. In archives across Europe from this period, it is common to find multiple copies of the same letter, sometimes assuming different forms and stages of completion. In some cases, this was because compositors were seeking to guard against loss or determined to send copies of the letter via different routes to assure passage. But many of these letters were also drafts, working papers, and copies, only a small portion of which must ultimately have been deemed worthy of storage: a reminder that an official epistolary exchange or royal letter created far more paperwork than merely the final product itself, and that the composition, circulation, and reception of a letter were all joint, multistep processes, involving the work of numerous people beyond the sender: secretaries, clerks, scribes, translators, and other intermediaries.

The flexibility and multi-functionality of correspondence rendered it particularly essential for the operation of complex political formations that were compelled to rule at a distance, such as the Holy Roman Empire under the Habsburgs. The head of the imperial Privy Council under Ferdinand I, Bernhard Cles (1484–1539), was an early example of a statesman who relied on the capacity of letter writing to exercise political control over an extensive state. Marino Cavalli, in a 1550 treatise on the office of the ambassador, recalled Cles as operating a sort of mobile chancery: "I remember seeing the Cardinal of Trent Bernardo da Cles, the chancellor of the present emperor Ferdinand, who was at that time King of the Romans, carrying with him a velvet bag on the saddle of his mule, with a pen, paper and writings inside for the insignia and standard of the notary."[60] Capitalizing on the availability of paper, Cles operated a "chancellorship by correspondence." As Cavalli remarked, Cles was rarely seen without paper and pen and was constantly receiving and dispatching letters of state. The paper flows he oversaw were essential to the governance of Ferdinand's empire, and allowed Cles to bring the authority of the emperor to bear, even over the great distances of the Habsburg patrimony. Megan Williams estimates that, by 1530, the Austrian Court Chancery was using twice the amount of paper on a weekly basis as the Imperial Court Chancery, a considerably larger

---

[60] Marino Cavalli, *Informatione dell'offitio dell'ambasciatore di Marino de Cavalli il Vecchio* (1550) ed. Tommaso Bertelè (Florence: Olschki, 1935), 90–91: "Et mi racordo io vedere il Cardinal di Trento Bernardo da Cles, Canceliero dello presente Imperator Ferdinando, che era all'hora Re de Romani, portarci sempre un carniero di velutto all'arzone della sua mulla, con un calamaro, carta et scritture dentro per insegna et standardo della nottaria."

body, had been using in the 1470s. In 1555, that same Court Chancery was using four times the paper it had twenty-five years earlier.[61]

The increase in the circulation of letters began at the very top. There was a great increase in the letter writing between monarchs in this period, both to representatives of their own state and to other princes. Letter writing by medieval monarchs had been comparatively rare, as it was generally considered to be beneath the station of the ruler, fit instead for delegation to a lesser light. Letter writing by princes had been an exercise in the assertion of authority and dominance, rather than a function of day-to-day governance. The foundations of this attitude began to erode in the late Middle Ages. The archives of state for fifteenth-century Italy are full of letters between the princes of the peninsula. By the sixteenth century, monarchs such as Elizabeth I of England (r. 1558–1603) and Philip II of Spain (r. 1556–1598) regularly dispatched holograph letters. Elizabeth was an enthusiastic letter writer, and operated a two-tier form of diplomacy that included both her epistles and those of her diplomats. In her letters to Henri II of France (r. 1547–1559), for example, it becomes evident that she felt that, while her ambassadors should oversee relations according to the *lex gentium*, she should correspond directly with Henri in the spirit of a code of royal honor and reciprocity.[62] Policy was thus negotiated in the space between these twin flows of correspondence, with her counselors, secretaries, and ambassadors fully aware of her readiness to exchange letters directly with other princes. In this regard, her "authorship" of letters was an important component in the projection of her authority. Sheets of paper understood to be issued directly from the hand of the monarch were endowed with especial importance, not only as one-off declarations of political dominance, but also as routine indications of princely intentions, a matter-of-course article of early modern governance. The results of this shift can be seen in cases like that of King Henri IV of France (r. 1598–1610), whose extant correspondence runs to nearly 10,000 letters.[63] By the time of his reign, writing letters was an essential component of princely rule. As Rayne Allison has put it:

The expectation that rulers should be involved in the production of letters (an idea that had not been current during the medieval period) had important implications for how political power was exercised: in order to stay in control of state and diplomatic affairs, rulers had become clerks in their own court, ruining their eyesight as they worked into the night (as Philip II routinely did) ... Sixteenth century monarchies

---

[61] Megan Williams, "This continuous writing": the paper chancellery of Bernhard Cles." In Dover, ed., *Secretaries and Statecraft*, 63–89 (here 64).
[62] Rayne Allinson, *A Monarchy of Letters: Royal Correspondence and English Diplomacy in the Reign of Elizabeth I* (Basingstoke: Palgrave Macmillan, 2012), 51.
[63] Berger de Xivrey, ed., *Collection de documents inédits sur l'histoire de France· recueil des lettres missives de Henri IV*, 9 vols. (Paris: Imprimerie Royale, 1843–1858).

were built on letters, and their exchange facilitated the emergence of the nation-state.[64]

Princes were writing more letters than ever before in the course of their governing, but it was the diplomats serving them who wrote more letters than anyone else practicing early modern statecraft. This was a function of the profound transformations in diplomatic practice in the early modern period, building upon developments first seen in fifteenth-century Italy. The bulging diplomatic folders in evidence in last few decades of the fifteenth century in Italy were filled chiefly by the expansion of letter writing by ambassadors and the princes and bodies that dispatched them abroad. The letters coming in and out of the chancery of the Milanese dukes run by the first secretary Cicco Simonetta (1410–1480), who oversaw the fifteenth century's most extensive diplomatic network, created, in the words of one Milanese official in the ducal administration, a "world of paper."[65]

A diplomatic mission created a paper trail at several levels. There were the instructions sent at the outset of the mission (known as *istruzioni*); the letters sent to the ambassador in the course of the mission (the *missive*); the copies of those outgoing letters collected in registers (the *copialettere*); the files of the letters received (the *responsive*, which also included copies of letters from other correspondents attached to the ambassador's correspondence); decrees nominating individuals to diplomatic offices; and, in some locales, *relazioni*, or summations, on the completion of an embassy.[66] Thus, in Milan and in other Italian states in the second half of the fifteenth century, the conduct of diplomacy generated stacks of paper, which required constant management.

Diplomats were generally expected to operate in three areas of competency: representing their sovereigns, negotiating agreements, and gathering information. A good summation was offered by the Venetian ambassador Bernardo Navagero, who described in his *relazione* of 1558 from Rome what he felt he was being expected to do:

I have learned in the missions on which it has pleased your Serene Highness to send me that the job of the ambassador is divided in three parts: in listening and advising, for which diligence is necessary; in negotiating, for which deftness is extremely useful; and in reporting, where judgment is of great importance, speaking of the necessary and useful things and leaving out the empty and useless.[67]

---

[64] Allinson, *A Monarchy of Letters*, 192–193.   [65] Senatore, "*Uno mundo di carta*."
[66] See Paul Dover, "Deciphering the diplomatic archives," 299.
[67] "Ho imparato nelle legazioni nelle quali per molti anni è piacuto a Vostra Serenità servirsi di me che l'uffizio dell'ambasciatore è diviso in tre parti: nell'intendere ed avvisare, nel che è necessaria la diligenza; nel negoziare in che giova mirabilmente la destrezza, e nel riferire, ove il giudizio importa grandamente parlando delle cose necessarie ed utili e lasciando le vane e inutili." Eugenio Albèri, ed., *Relazioni degli ambasciatori veneti al Senato*, Series II, Vol. III (Florence: Società editrice fiorentina, 1846), 369.

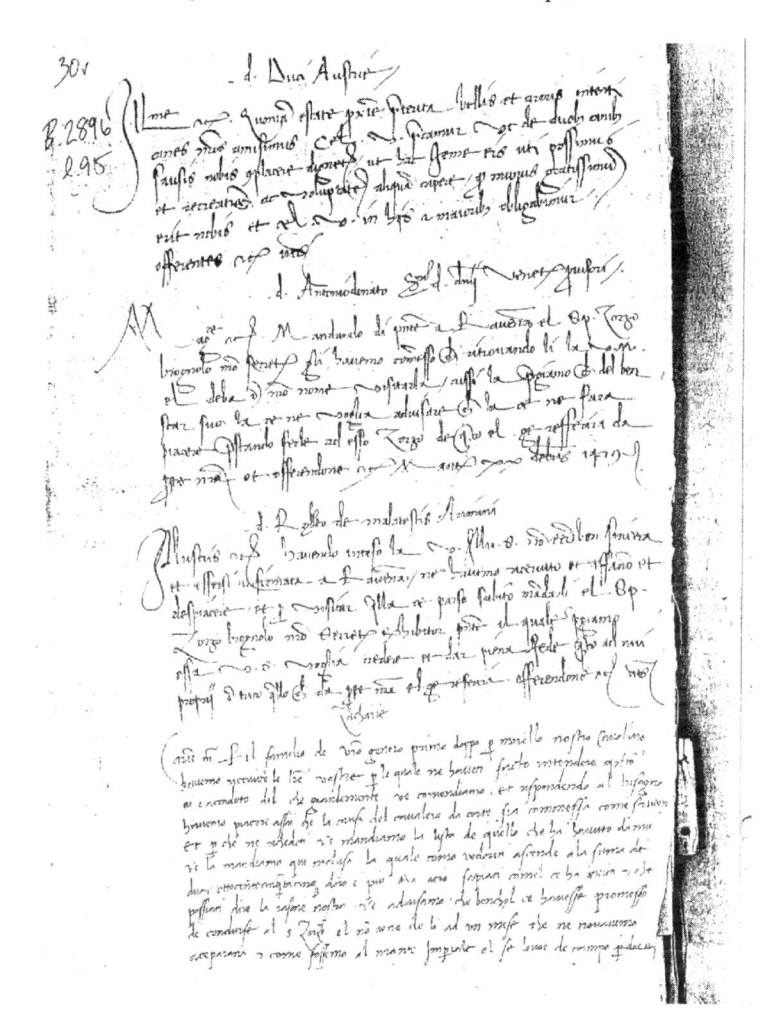

4.1 Early modern archives filled up with registers of copied outgoing letters, such as this one from the chancery of the Marquis of Mantua in December 1479. Archivio di Stato di Mantova, Archivio Gonzaga, *Copialettere*, B.2896, L.95, 30v (reproduced with permission of the Archive).

It was especially the last of these, the reportage of news, that filled the pages of countless letters written by early modern ambassadors. Regular political correspondence from ambassadors and other informants fed a growing expectation that princes and governments should be kept abreast of the latest international developments.

The most important of all the transformations in diplomacy in this period was residency.[68] Beginning in the fifteenth century in Italy, especially after the formation of the Italian League in 1455, it became customary for envoys to reside for longer periods of time, a practice that serviced all three of the imperatives identified by Navagero. The tendency to lengthen diplomatic deployments had multiple origins, and in some cases developed into the practice of permanent resident embassies, for which Italy has again rightly been identified as the progenitor.[69] Residence in diplomacy was, in the long term, a sea change in the practice of statecraft, but it should be seen as merely one component of a complex of information networks that spanned Renaissance Italian politics. Italian chanceries sent out and received huge numbers of letters to and from diplomats, but also corresponded widely with private citizens, especially merchants and commercial agents.[70]

Resident ambassadors across Italy were instructed to gather and report whatever information they were exposed to – leading to a near-daily data dump. News, rumor, and speculation became the currency of diplomacy and access to information deemed vital for large and small actors alike. Like merchants and natural philosophers, ambassadors were observers,

---

[68] On the emergence of the resident ambassador in Italy, see the classic account of Garrett Mattingly, *Renaissance Diplomacy* (London: Cape, 1955). For a fuller account of the meaning and importance of residence, see Vincent Ilardi, "The first permanent embassy outside Italy: the Milanese Embassy at the French Court, 1464–1483," in Malcolm Thorp and Arthur Slavin, eds., *Politics, Religion and Diplomacy in Early Modern Europe: Essays in Honor of Delamar Jensen* (Kirksville, MO: Sixteenth Century Journal Publishers, 1994), 1–18. For the particularities of resident embassies in the oligarchic republics, see Riccardo Fubini, "La figura politica dell'ambasciatore negli sviluppi dei regimi oligarchici quattrocenteschi." In Sergio Bertelli, ed., *Forme e tecniche del potere nella città (secolo XIV–XVII). Annuario della Facoltà di Scienze Politiche dell'Università di Perugia. 16 (1979–1980)*. (Perugia: Università di Perugia, 1982), 33–59. See also his "Diplomacy and government in the Italian city-states of the fifteenth century (Florence and Venice)." In Daniela Frigo, ed., *Politics and Diplomacy in Early Modern Italy. The Structure of Diplomatic Practice, 1450–1800* (Cambridge: Cambridge University Press, 2000), 25–48. Fubini has sought to undermine the importance of resident ambassadors in fifteenth-century Italian diplomacy, and he rightly points out that there is precious little evidence that resident ambassadors occupied clearly defined offices. It is also undoubtedly the case that a large portion of diplomacy in the fifteenth century was not carried out by resident ambassadors. This latter point is stressed in Michael Mallett, "Italian Renaissance diplomacy." *Diplomacy and Statecraft*, 12.1 (2001), 61–70, esp. 64–66.

[69] Riccardo Fubini, "La 'résidentialité' de l'ambasadeur dans le mythe et dans la réalité: une enquête sur les origines." In Lucien Bély, ed., *L'invention de la diplomatie* (Paris: Presses universitaires de Paris, 1998), 27–35.

[70] Isabella Lazzarini, *Communication and Conflict Italian Diplomacy in the Early Renaissance, 1350–1520* (Oxford: Oxford University Press, 2015), 31–48.

and, like them, they engaged in lengthy description of their observations, with which they filled up their routine dispatches.

The pioneering Sforza dukes in Milan routinely emphasized the information gathering of their ambassadors. Francesco Sforza, concerned from the outset of his reign in 1450 about his tenuous legitimacy and with the manifold threats to his state, insisted repeatedly that he be "advised of everything." The anonymous set of recommendations for ambassadorial service by a Venetian nobleman from the sixteenth century is revealing of this zeal for information: take care that the information you gather is from reputable and/or corroborated sources, but whatever news you have, report it nonetheless.[71] "The job of ambassadors," two Florentine ambassadors wrote in 1450, "is, day by day, hour by hour, to inform those who sent them what they have heard, from whom, and in what manner," as ambassadors larded their dispatches with details.[72]

This urge to report news became a self-fulfilling prophecy, as the acquisition of information abetted yet further demands for news and intelligence. Especially at major information exchanges such as Rome,

---

[71] The author of the treatise writes: "Deve però sempre havere riguardo a questo di non scrivergli cosa alcuna per certa di quelli con gli quali si negotia che non ne habbia testimonia di lettere ò di huomini alli quali il Padrone presti fede, perché molte volte la variatione loro potrebbe causare sdegno et mala opinione el padrone, et quando mai non havesse sospetto di fede, haverebbe sinistra opinione di leggerezza ò di poco prudenza. Però sarà sempre lodato di fare più che non scrisse, et dare buona speranza dove espediente prima che dire la cosa per ferma." Donald Queller, "How to succeed as an ambassador: a sixteenth-century Venetian document." *Studia Gratiana*, 15 (1972), 655–671 (here 669).

On information gathering as a competency of fifteenth-century Italian ambassadors, see Michael Mallett, "Ambassadors and their audiences in Renaissance Italy." *Renaissance Studies*, 8.3 (1994), 229–243; Isabella Lazzarini, "L'informazione politico-diplomatica nell'età della pace di Lodi: raccolta, selezione, trasmissione. Spunti di ricerca dal carteggio Milano-Mantova nella prima età sforzesca (1450-1466)." *Nuova Rivista Storica*, 83 (1999), 247–280; Paul Dover, "The resident ambassador and the transformation of intelligence gathering in Renaissance Italy." In Eunan O'Halpin, Robert Armstrong, and Jane Ohlmeyer, eds., *Intelligence, Statecraft and International Power: Papers Read before the 27th Irish Conference of Historians held at Trinity College, Dublin, 19–21 May 2005* (Dublin: Irish Academic Press, 2006), 18–34; Paul Dover, "Good information, bad information and misinformation in fifteenth-century Italian diplomacy." In Mark Crane, Richard Raiswell, and Margaret Reeves, eds., *Shell Games. Studies in Scams, Frauds, and Deceits (1300–1650)* (Toronto: Centre for Reformation and Renaissance Studies, 2004), 81–102. See also the chapters on communication and information in Lazzarini, *Communication and Conflict* and Catherine Fletcher, *Diplomacy in Renaissance Rome. The Rise of the Resident Ambassador* (Cambridge: Cambridge University Press, 2015).

[72] Giovanni Pandolfini and Francesco Sacchetti to the Signoria of Florence, 5 May 1450: "L'ufficio degli imbasciatori ... è giorno per giorno, hora per hora, secondo che intendono, et da chi in che modo, dare notitia a chi gli manda." Francesco Senatore, ed., *Dispacci sforzeschi da Napoli*, Vol. I: *1444–2 luglio 1456* (Naples: Istituto italiano per gli studi filosofici, 1997), 51.

Venice, or Milan, the volume of information left ambassadors charged with its gathering (as well as the statesmen who received the letters), perplexed, bewildered, and exhausted.[73] Serving at a distance and judged largely by its capacity to keep the prince informed, a resident embassy was only as valuable and successful as its paper trail.

Such practices, as a matter of course, generated simply enormous quantities of documentation. It is not uncommon to find 300 dispatches from a single ambassador in a single year in the second half of the fifteenth century.[74] The numbers continued to rise in the sixteenth century, with the general increase in the incidence of extended resident embassies. Between May 1503 and April 1504, the Venetian ambassador in Rome, Antonio Giustinian, wrote 472 dispatches from his post.[75] One rough estimate is that between 1565 and 1613, ambassadors sent the Venetian Senate a quarter of a million pages, with a similar volume of replies. In the case of Venice, the sheer amount of news coming into the Senate could prove vexing, as the Venetian noble Girolamo Priuli (1486–1567) once observed in his *Diarii*:

[T]oday indeed so many recent letters have been read in the Venetian Senate that ended up here in this present and past days from so many places and of so many different types and kinds that it would be rather difficult to judge; and ... reading lasted for five hours without interruption until half past one in the night; thus having listened to so many letters, and being focused on what they said, my head was all perturbed and confused.[76]

Priuli's confusion was not an isolated instance. As early as the late fifteenth century, Italian statesmen frequently expressed their difficulty in navigating the thicket of contradictory or indeterminate information, making clear-minded decision-making more, rather than less, difficult. That some chanceries did alter, manipulate, or outright falsify the content of letters muddied the waters even further and heightened suspicion about the reliability of information. The pursuit of more and better information, rather than clarifying and resolving conflicts, could serve to complicate and deepen them. Melissa Bullard has identified such

---

[73] For example, for the case of the papal court at Rome, see Paul Dover, "Saper la mente della soa Beatitudine": Pope Paul II and the ambassadorial community in Rome (1464–71)." *Renaissance and Reformation*, 31.3 (2008), 3–34. For the case of Milan, see Lazzarini, "L'informazione politico-diplomatica."

[74] In 1461, the Mantuan ambassador in Milan, Vincenzo della Scalona, wrote more than 360 to the Marquis of Mantua and his wife Isabella Lazzarini, ed., *Carteggio degli oratori mantovani alla corte sforzesca (1450–1500)*, Vol. III *(1461)* (Rome: Ministero per I Beni e le Attività Culturali, 2000).

[75] Pasquale Villani, ed., *Dispacci di Antonio Giustinian, ambasciatore veneto in Roma dal 1502 al 1505* (Florence: Successori le Monnier, 1876).

[76] Quoted in Lazzarini, *Communication and Conflict*, 50.

anxieties in the diplomatic arena of late fifteenth-century Italy, coinciding with the expansion of resident diplomacy in the peninsula. Contradictory news and information abounded. Bullard has shown just how challenging it was for Lorenzo de' Medici in Florence to establish the reasoned basis (*fondamento*) that he desired for his important decisions. He often simply did not know what to believe.[77] In an age of information saturation marked by high-profile intelligence failures and plagued by fake news, Lorenzo's frustration should be a familiar one.

These patterns of diplomatic representation, which were widely shared across Italy by the final decades of the fifteenth century, gradually spread outside of Italy. The first permanent resident embassy outside of Italy was the representative of Duke Francesco Sforza of Milan to France, dispatched in 1463. Ferdinand of Aragon (r. 1479–1516) was among the first non-Italian princes to commit himself to the use of resident ambassadors, with representatives in Rome, the Holy Roman Empire, Venice, Portugal, Genoa, France, Savoy, and Milan by 1513. The extended conflagration of the Italian Wars (1494–1559), with the concomitant need for alliances (which often shifted with dizzying rapidity), and the desire for up-to-date information, all suggested the utility of resident ambassadors, and in the first half of the sixteenth century we see a growing number of European states embracing them. By the time of the death of King Francis I (r. 1515–1547) in 1547, there were ten permanent French embassies abroad, with the likes of Honoré de Caix serving for twenty-three years at the court in Lisbon. The French commitment to systematic resident diplomacy was challenged by the convulsions of the French Wars of Religion in the second half of the sixteenth century, but even in the war-racked years of 1559–1600, some seventy-two French ambassadors served in missions abroad.[78] Building upon the preceding efforts of Ferdinand of Aragon, the real heirs to the Italian diplomatic system were the Habsburgs under Charles V and then, especially, Philip II. Philip's global diplomatic and informational network was an essential component of the Spanish king's desire to be "informed of everything."

The adoption of residency was gradual and not universal, and episodic bilateral relations remained the norm in many places. Short-term missions, dispatched for limited and discreet ends, remained essential to interstate relations. Still, by the seventeenth century, resident ambassadors had

---

[77] Melissa Meriam Bullard, *Lorenzo il Magnifico: Image and Anxiety, Politics and Finance* (Florence: Olschki, 1994), as well as Bullard, "The Language of Diplomacy in the Renaissance." In Bernard Toscani, ed., *Lorenzo de' Medici: New Perspectives* (New York: Peter Lang, 1993), 263–278.

[78] Delamar Jensen, "French diplomacy and the wars of religion." *Sixteenth-century Studies Journal*, 5.2 (1974), 23–46 (here 44).

become commonplace in relations between the leading European states, and among the chief concerns of the constituent parties remained the provision of timely and pertinent information, to be ready for any incipient threats and opportunities during an age of near-ceaseless war.[79] The petering out of the extended period of religious warfare by the middle of the seventeenth century, along with the confessional tensions that had driven the conflict, saw the reciprocal exchange of resident ambassadors become entrenched. The leading continental power, the France of Louis XIV (r. 1643–1715), operated an extensive and vigorous pan-European diplomatic network, predicated on the use of resident ambassadors and their gathering of information. Even a state like Sweden, which had largely practiced diplomacy ad hoc in the service of her military aspirations during the Thirty Years' War, under the guidance of Axel Oxenstierna (1583–1654), began to station ambassadors at most of the leading European capitals.[80] Such developments reflect an emerging reality that diplomacy was less reactive than it was an organic and constant feature of interstate relations, with state officials committed to the prosecution of foreign policy, and bureaucracies that managed the immense quantity of paperwork that it all entailed. Like so much else in early modern Europe, the conduct of diplomacy was in large part about information management. The case of France at the end of seventeenth century is illustrative. At the outset of Louis XIV's personal rule in 1661, a single coach was all that was needed to transport the foreign minister and his secretaries. By 1715, the Marquis of Torcy, Jean-Baptiste Colbert the Younger (1665–1746), required twenty coaches to carry his personnel, which included clerks, notaries, translators, codebreakers, cryptographers, and archivists.[81]

Early modern diplomacy, therefore, was largely about the exchange of paper. In his treatise *Del segretario* (1629), Panfilo Persico described ambassadors as "the eyes and ears of the prince" who "should inform [them] about everything that is happening that is worthy of note ... he must leave nothing out, but advise himself of every move and every novelty."[82] Ambassadors often played the role of what Daniela Frigo

---

[79] A work that focuses especially on the importance of reliable intelligence during the war-torn early decades of the seventeenth century is Alain Hugon, *Au service du roi catholique: honorables ambassadeurs et divins espions. Représentation diplomatique et service secret dans les relations hispano-françaises de 1598 à 1635* (Madrid: Casa de Velazquez, 2004).

[80] Erik Thomson, "Axel Oxenstierna and Swedish diplomacy in the seventeenth century." In Dover, *Secretaries and Statecraft*, 140–154; Heiko Droste, *Im Dienst der Krone: schwedische Diplomaten in 17. Jahrundert* (Berlin: LIT Verlag, 2006).

[81] John Rule and Ben Trotter, *A World of Paper. Louis XIV, Colbert de Torcy and the Rise of the Information State* (Montreal: McGill-Queen's University Press, 2014).

[82] Panfilo Persico, *Del segretario del signor Panfilo Persico, Libri Quattro etc.* (Venice: Damian Zenaro, 1629), 196.

has called the "silent resident" (*residente del silentio*), when they were expected to focus especially on observing and reporting what they had heard, and the resulting volume of letters could be vast.[83]

The Venetian *relazioni*, the famous summaries of the political and social landscape of the state in which an ambassador was posted, and composed upon the ambassador's return to Venice beginning in the early sixteenth century, illustrate the need for distillation in the information-rich environment of early modern diplomacy. They interrupted the ongoing rush of ordinary correspondence of the ambassador, as one ambassador gave way to another, providing an informational snapshot. In the course of the sixteenth century, they became a part of the written memory of the Venetian chancellery and were regularly consulted by the Venetian Senate in its decision-making. Other states began to emulate this form of reportage – the Republic of Lucca began to produce its own *relazioni*, starting in the 1580s.[84]

In the spirit of the *relazione*, other state chanceries produced summaries of the information coming in and circulated them among ambassadors and statesmen. The Milanese *Consiglio Segreto* was already producing them in the fifteenth century.[85] Such efforts, or *sommari*, which became commonplace across Italy by the sixteenth century, represented examples of information triage in the face of documentary abundance. They were often inscribed on the verso of the letter itself or alongside the address, such that they would be visible when the letter was folded and placed in files, facilitating documentary retrieval. In the Milanese chancery in the fifteenth century, secretaries had collated such summaries into notebooks that resembled notarial registers, thus not only highlighting information contained in dispatches, but organizing it into categories.[86] Summarizing diplomatic dispatches became a common practice in chanceries across Italy. In the Duchy of Ferrara, starting in the 1560s, summaries of incoming and outgoing letters were arranged under headings, then copied into registers which repeated the summaries verbatim but also sorted them thematically and chronologically. It was clear that these were created by secretaries for subsequent use.[87] In sixteenth-century Venice, secretaries in the Senate wrote summaries of dispatches in special ledgers called *rubricari*, which were eventually divided into separate volumes for

---

[83] Daniela Frigo, "Corte, honore et ragion di stato," 31.
[84] Guarini and Rosa, *L'informazione politica*, 15.
[85] Alfio Rosario Natale, ed., *Acta in Consilio Secreto in castello Portae Jovis Mediolani*, 3 vols. (Milan: A. Giuffre, 1963–1969); Archivio di Stato di Venezia, Archvio de Senato, Deliberazioni Segrete (Senato Secreta).
[86] Senatore, *"Uno mundo di carta,"* 108.
[87] Laura Turchi, "Storia della diplomazia e fonti estensi: note a margine." *Quaderni Estensi*. 6 (2014), 368–395.

incoming and outgoing dispatches for each embassy abroad.[88] Extraordinarily time-consuming, such efforts did not reduce the amount of paper on hand, for while the volumes of summaries were kept readily available for quick consultation, the original dispatches were nonetheless filed away in the archive.

Along with chanceries, the embassies themselves, comprising ambassadors and their secretaries, devoted considerable time to information management. Embassies of any length maintained their own mini-archives. According to Cavalli, an ambassador's secretary had to be *laborissimo et diligentissimo* in his writing, exhibiting the skills of an outstanding notary.[89] For Jean Hotman, the Marquis of Villiers-Saint Paul (1552–1636), writing in 1603, the job of the embassy secretary was to relieve the burden of the ambassador's office by attending to his paperwork: penning his dispatches; keeping the register of letters; faithfully keeping the drafts, ciphers, and other important papers; and attending to the expenses of the ambassador's residence, all essential components of a successful embassy[90] Giulio Cesare Capaccio, in his 1597 treatise *Il secretario*, wrote that, in ordering the embassy's papers into cabinets, the diplomatic secretary was also engaged in ordering memory. He recommended the use of commonplaces to simplify access for both himself and the ambassador – a strategy, as we shall see, that was also adopted by merchants, scholars, and naturalists.[91]

4.4 Knowing the State

Effective government came to presuppose the effective provision of information. In part, the growth in letter writing in early modern politics was a function of the increased enthusiasm of the state for information about its lands and subjects. This information arrived at the metropole in many different forms, of varying degrees of systematization. Peter Burke, for example, has called the early modern period "an age of questionnaires." Parish visitations, various *catasti* and other forms of census-taking, the spiritual "accounting" of members conducted by the Society of Jesus, the

---

[88] Filippo de Vivo, "Archival intelligence: diplomatic correspondence, information overload, and information management in Italy, 1450–1650." In Liesbeth Corens, Kate Peters, and Alexandra Walsham, eds., *Archives and Information in the Early Modern World*. Proceedings of the British Academy 212 (Oxford: Oxford University Press, 2018), 53–85 (here 72).
[89] Cavalli, *Informatione dell'offitio dell'ambasciatore*, 88.
[90] Jean Hotman Sieur de Villiers, *De la charge et dignité de l'ambassadeur* (Paris: J. Périer, 1603), 22.
[91] Capaccio, *Il secretario*, 15v.

queries of French *intendants*: all of these evince institutions' thirst for information.

Medieval regimes had rarely traded in information in the abstract sense. Despite efforts such as the ambitious 1427 *catasto* in Florence, in the Middle Ages councils and parliaments rarely discussed what we would today call information or data, except perhaps to enumerate the number of fighting men at hand or to number those who had managed to escape taxation. They might be aware of incidents of large-scale mortality or labor shortages, but they did not count them or seek to represent them as numbers. Medieval governments had only vague ideas about their balance of payments, the number of subjects that they had, or general information on prices or wages.[92]

By the sixteenth century in Italy, the census (known by a variety of names: *anagrafo, catasto, estimo*) had become a regular undertaking for governments. Rome had a census in 1526; Florence in 1527, 1552, and 1556; Venice in 1509, 1540, and 1581; Naples in 1547 and then again in the 1590s. Officials often relied on the ecclesiastical infrastructure, organizing by parish and thrusting responsibility onto the parish priest to collect the requisite information. Such reckonings were undertaken for tax purposes, of course, but also to assess welfare requirements and population losses due to plague and other calamities. It was not always human souls that they sought to enumerate: some recorded agricultural animals, guns in private hands, or gondolas (as did a seventeenth-century Venetian census). The collection of such data led to the need to categorize it, as well: by gender, by age, by profession, by place of origin, by wealth. These were early signs of the bureaucratic impulse not only to count, but also to classify subjects. The story of censuses in Italy reveals that the collection of information created its own logic, leading to a perceived need for more information, and for accompanying systems of categorization and organization. This is suggestive of a waxing "numerate mentality" born from the need to speak of volumes of information in abstractions.[93]

In some locales, recourse to the printing press allowed the queries to become routine: the Venetian government in the seventeenth century devised printed forms (known as *facciate*), divided into columns and rows, for its officials to use when gathering information, and before

---

[92] See, for example, Olive Coleman, "What figures? Some thoughts on the use of information by medieval governments." In Donald Cuthbert Coleman and Arthur Henry John, eds., *Trade, Government and Economy in Pre-Industrial England: Essays Presented to F.J. Fisher* (London: Weidenfeld and Nicolson, 1976), 96–112.

[93] Peter Burke, "Classifying the people: the census as collective representation." In *The Historical Anthropology of Early Modern Italy* (Cambridge: Cambridge University Press, 1987), 27–39.

long, states across Europe mobilized the capacity of the printing press to generate such information-gathering tools.[94] There was an increasingly widely shared understanding that the collection of information about subjects was essential for the effective functioning of state institutions, in both the immediate and the long term.

In the *Tesoro politico* (1602), attributed to Comino Ventura, we read that just as a good horseman must know the nature and qualities of his horse, so a prince must have complete knowledge of the nature and affections of his own people.[95] For example, the sixteenth-century so-called Tudor Revolution in Government was dependent on effective information gathering and dissemination. English monarchs justified their actions with proclamations and pronouncements, exploiting the printing press and postal networks to broadcast the desired information. The nailing of printed royal proclamations onto doors in public places is well attested in sixteenth-century England.[96] The functional political space of England was admittedly a rather narrow one, dependent on gathering and managing information from a relatively small number of people, but, starting under Henry VIII (r. 1509–1547), the Tudors undertook extensive efforts to collect information about their lands and subjects.[97] One of the first was Thomas Cromwell's (1485–1540) compilation of the *Valor Ecclesiasticus*, a comprehensive survey of church assets in England. Notably, Cromwell also instructed all parish clergy to keep registers of the baptisms, burials, and marriages in their parishes, to create a running demographic record of English communities. A series of enclosure commissions collected detailed information on the plots of land involved; the 1549 Parliament ordered a census of the sheep of the realm. Taken together, these efforts constitute a committed effort to gather information on the territory and inhabitants of England.

Henry VIII's daughter, Elizabeth I, took further steps to establish an informational profile of her realm. Her clerk of the Privy Council, Robert Beale (1541–1601), thought it essential that the Crown gather what information it could on the realm's gentlemen and consolidate it in a single book. Her councilor William Burghley, Lord Cecil (1520–1598),

---

[94] Peter Burke, "Postfazione: Che cos'è la storia degli archivi?" In Filippo de Vivo, Andrea Guidi, and Alessandro Silvestri, eds., *Archivi e archivisti in Italia tra medioevo ed età moderna* (Rome: Viella, 2015), 359–372.
[95] Comino Ventura, *Tesoro politico in cui si contengono Relationi, Istruttioni, Trattati, & varii Discorsi, pertinenti alla perfetta intelligenza della ragion di stato* (Vicenza: Giorgio Greco, 1602), 10r.
[96] Colin Richmond, "Hand and mouth: information gathering and use in the later Middle Ages." *Journal of Historical Sociology*, 1.3 (1988), 233–252.
[97] Geoffrey Elton, *The Tudor Revolution in Government: Administrative Changes in the Reign of Henry VIII* (Cambridge: Cambridge University Press, 1953).

frequently obtained customs figures on exports, imports, and the balance of trade, and in 1563 proposed the establishment of county registry offices to house parish register transcripts. The Privy Council, in 1563, sought statistics on clergy in every diocese and the population of every parish. In 1577, there was a census of all the inns in the country.[98] These various efforts were not coordinated in any meaningful way, but, without question, they reflect a desire to collect precise information, with a view to creating a picture of the realm on paper.

Among other things, the gathering of data allowed comparison between countries. The widely circulated political treatises of Jean Bodin (1530–1596) and Giovanni Botero (1544–1617) stressed the importance of national wealth and power and the desirability of measuring them. In *England's View in the Unmasking of Two Paradoxes*, published in 1603, Gerald Malynes (ca. 1552–1641), a merchant who served as assay master of the Mint, employed various facts and figures, such as geographical size and population, to compare France and England.[99] By the second half of the seventeenth century in England, as Paul Slack has shown, the Crown regularly gathered political "arithmetick" (a term coined by the economist and naturalist William Petty (1623–1687) in the 1670s) and employed it for the purposes of government. These "mathematicians" operated according to the conviction that efficient gathering of information on the realm's land, people, wealth, and trade, and the storage of that information for subsequent consultation, were of essential importance to the state. In the spirit of Francis Bacon's call for "useful knowledge," England boasted, by the Restoration of the monarchy in 1660, many so-called "men of numbers" (a moniker employed by the diarist Samuel Pepys (1633–1703)), who were fascinated with the potential of deploying numerical data for political purposes. This group included men like Petty, who had conducted the cadastral Down Survey of Ireland in 1654–6, and Thomas Osborne, Lord Danby (1632–1712), who instituted the Compton Census of 1676, a questionnaire distributed to communicants. By 1695, the Compton Census was gathering data on fully half of the 9,500 parishes of England and Wales – this information, gathered together by bishops and archbishops, soon accumulated in great "bundles of paper" which the census board struggled to organize and use. By the end of the seventeenth century in England, there was, according to Slack, "a disjuncture between the intoxication of new computations and

[98] These examples are taken from David Palliser, *The Age of Elizabeth: England under the Later Tudors* (London: Routledge, 2014), 372–373.
[99] Gerald Malynes, *England's View in the Unmasking of Two Paradoxes* (London: Richard Field, 1603).

hard-headed calculation of their utility in the everyday practice of politics."[100]

In Spain, the establishment first of a pan-European patrimony and then a global empire created wide-ranging informational demands that dwarfed those in England. The opening up of the New World, and the encounter with heretofore unknown people, plants, and animals, encouraged a commitment to observation, description, and the accumulation of facts. The Spanish crown assumed what we might call an empirical approach to governance, gathering massive quantities of information about lands and subjects on both sides of the Atlantic Ocean. The outlook was fed by streams of scientific, commercial, and state activities that recognized the importance of observation and data collection. After the first few decades of conflict, conquest, and accommodation, Spanish royal authorities dedicated impressive efforts to supplying themselves with information about the New World, in so doing entrenching an empirical approach to Empire. Every time an *encomienda* changed hands, information was gathered anew. In 1533, King Charles V requested that his officials in New Spain gather "complete information (*entera noticia*) about the things of that land and its qualities."[101] Fulfilling such requests demanded the development of new mechanisms for gathering and organizing information. What began as general inquiries gradually became more precise in targeting particular types of information.

The reign of Philip II is the epitome of the early modern monarch who demanded information and then found himself overwhelmed by the paper his demands generated. Philip's information-gathering schemes were manifold and diverse. Early in his reign, in 1566, he enlisted Pedro de Esquivel, a professor of mathematics at the University of Alcalá, to prepare a comprehensive geography of Spain. Esquivel was instructed to provide descriptions of "all places." One contemporary described it as "the most careful and accurate description ever to be undertaken for any province since the creation of the world ... Your Majesty has ordered that not a hand's breadth of land is to pass without inspection ... so that the truth of everything can be established."[102] These grand ambitions were never fulfilled, as first Esquivel and then his successor died in quick succession, but through his manifold efforts, Philip became perhaps the best-informed sovereign in

---

[100] Paul Slack, "Government and information in seventeenth-century England." *Past and Present*, 184 (2004), 33–68 (here 58).
[101] Arndt Brendecke, "Papierbarrieren. Über Ambivalenzen des Mediengebrauchs in der Vormoderne." *Mitteilungen des Sonderforschungsbereiches* 573 "Pluralisierung und Autorität in der Frühen Neuzeit" 2 (2009), 7–15 (here 9).
[102] David Goodman, *Power and Penury. Government, Technology and Science in Philip II's Spain* (Cambridge: Cambridge University Press, 1988), 65.

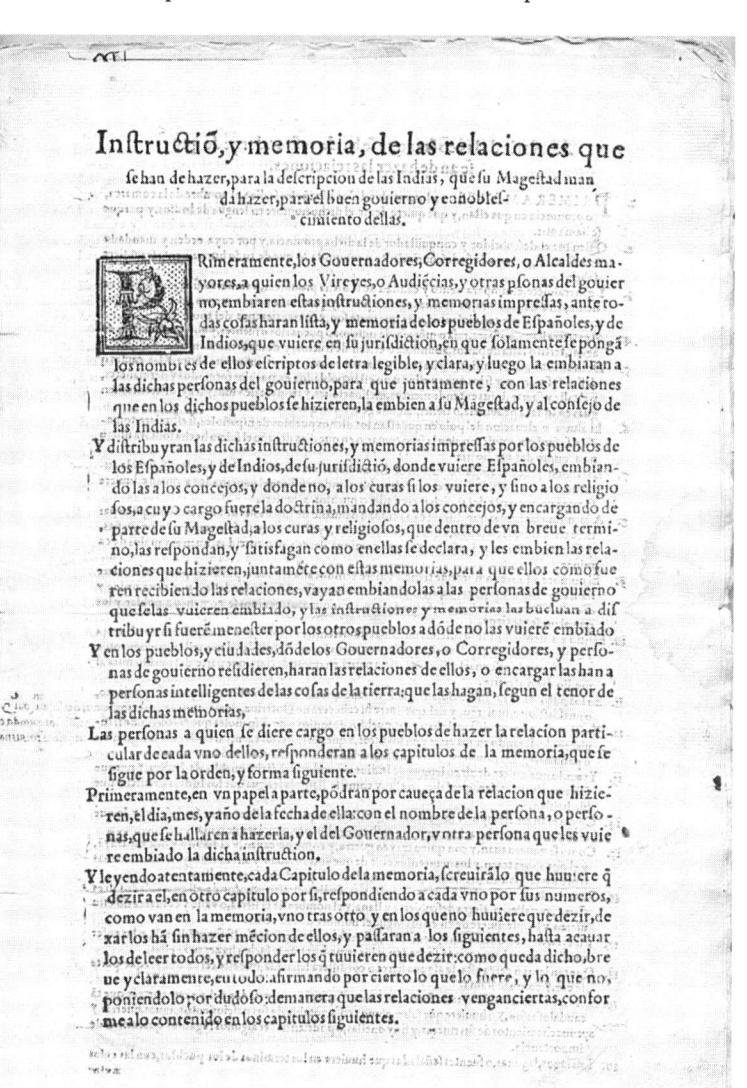

4.2 Instruction for the *Relaciones geograficas* (1577) ordered by Philip II to gather information about New Spain. Benson Latin American Collection, Library of the University of Texas-Austin (reproduced with permission of the Library).

all of Europe, even though it proved difficult for the king to get a reliable picture of his possessions in the Americas, for a number of reasons.

In 1566, Luis Sánchez, a low-level cleric who had lived in the colonies for eighteen years, composed a report on conditions in the Americas, in response to a request from the president of the Council of the Indies. He identified several reasons in particular why it was so difficult to understand the Americas fully. First, there were the size, diversity, and distance away of the regions involved, which made a complete picture virtually impossible to achieve. Most of those who were overseeing royal policy in the Americas had never been there and had to depend on the incomplete impressions of others. He also suggested that many of those who were informing the Crown about the Americas were generally interested only in their own gain, and thus the information they provided could not be trusted.

Juan de Ovando (1515–1575), appointed to Philip II's Council of the Indies in 1569, had a "fever" for gathering information about the life and history of the New World, demonstrated in his program to assemble the so-called *Relaciones geograficas*. Recognizing that there was no comprehensive system for reporting such information, he established a permanent office to oversee its collection and centralization, institutionalizing a process that had previously been ad hoc in nature. Ovando composed a lengthy list of questions, at first directed towards matters concerning the administration of New Spain and the archbishoprics established there. The project involved a great deal of copying, as it called for duplicates of all the official documents related to the ecclesiastical jurisdictions, ranging from a list of all bishops currently serving to rules for the choirs. He sought the acts and minutes of synods and lists of all those who attended, copies of the instructions given to *visitadores* to dioceses and religious orders, copies of the catechisms being used, and the financial records of cathedrals and other churches. He demanded descriptions of all church buildings and information on who built them and when, as well as who patronized them. He wanted details on New World benefices and ecclesiastic offices, and on their past and current holders. The Archbishop was also to furnish a description of each town and an estimate of the number of both Spaniards and Indians living in dioceses. By 1571, the questionnaire had 200 questions; from 1577, the questionnaire was printed, accompanied by a royal decree that required a response from the overseas colonies. Many of the completed surveys survive to this day, a massive haul of information about the Americas. Much of what he asked for from the archbishops would be brought together in his *Descripción del Arzobispado de México*.[103]

---

[103] Clinton Edwards, "Mapping by questionnaire: an early Spanish attempt to determine New World geographical position." *Imago Mundi*, 23 (1969), 17–28.

Ovando was clearly convinced that effective governance in the Indies rested in large part in receiving as much information about the Indies as possible on paper. Comprehensive knowledge, according to Ovando, had to precede comprehensive control.[104] Efforts like these represent a confluence of the attitudes of naturalists and state actors: a desire for information about newly discovered lands; the privileging of experience and description; and the compilation of reports in writing, resulting in data banks available for subsequent consultation. There is scant evidence, however, that much use was made by the Crown of the information that the *relaciones* compiled. Most appear to have remained untouched in files, until they were rediscovered in the late eighteenth century.[105]

The efforts to encompass in writing an empire as sprawling and diverse as the Spanish Empire, and to manage the resulting yield of information, were mirrored by countless similar smaller-scale efforts by other European polities in the decades that followed. There was an increasingly important flow of documents produced by states of all sizes seeking to learn more about their populations. Early modern bureaucracies gradually sought to systematize and institutionalize such information. They also sought to organize and present that data in forms that afforded ease of location and extraction. These efforts to mediate information were both preparatory and post hoc. Especially toward the end of the early modern period, states exploited the capacity of the printing press to mass-produce questionnaires, tables and columns. Such "fill-in-the-blank" paper technologies carried out some of the information management ahead of time, by channeling it into prescribed categories that facilitated tabulation and calculation. In 1688, for example, the Prussian government began keeping *Populationlisten*, which recorded all baptisms, marriages, and deaths. By 1722, Prussian administrators were keeping *Historische Tabellen*, which included rubrics for twenty-four different categories of information. These tables were then condensed into *Generaltabellen*, which sought to encapsulate the state of the whole monarchy on a single sheet of paper.[106]

As this discussion suggests, the marshalling of information by the state was designed to make two important things possible: comparison and planning for the future. The information gathered, and often represented as numbers, could be employed to argue for particular policies. Aggregate

---

[104] Stafford Poole, *Juan de Ovando. Governing the Spanish Empire in the Reign of Philip II* (Norman, OK: University of Oklahoma Press, 2004).
[105] Howard Cline, "The Relaciones Geograficas of the Spanish Indies, 1577–1648." *Handbook of Middle American Indians*, 12 (1972), 183–242.
[106] Otto Behre, *Geschichte der Statistik in Brandenburg-Preussen bis zur Gründung des Königlichen Statistischen Bureaus* (Berlin: Topos, 1905), 273.

figures could be cited (and manipulated) for government purposes. In a later age, such figures would be referred to as statistics. The politics of inscription abstracted political reality by representing it in writing; the emergence of numerical and statistical information meant abstracting that reality even further. In this, men of government were representative of the broader embrace of information collected as facts and figures: an attitude increasingly evident among merchants, scholars, and scientific virtuosi. Just as accessing accumulated data banks was an established feature of commerce, scholarship, and natural philosophy, so too did questions of proper and effective governance come to involve the collection, collation, and interpretation of information. In this way, "political arithmetic" was merely a manifestation in the political sphere of a broader social and cultural inclination, and the emerging "information state" a by-product of attitudes and practices related to the management of information.

4.5 Overload?

These demands for information created new pressures and demands on governing officials, who often struggled to digest all that they had received. The classic example of this quandary was Philip II of Spain, whose informational challenges have been the subject of Geoffrey Parker's magisterial treatment of Philip's management style. In pursuit of the universal knowledge he professed to desire, the king at any given time had huge amounts of paperwork crossing his desk, despite his employment of a private secretary. In Spain, each of the many councils that oversaw the functioning of the composite monarchy generated and were in receipt of large numbers of documents: petitions, complaints, and reports from viceroys, governors, and other officials.[107] The opinions of these councils were summarized in *consultas*, drafted by the conciliar secretaries, and then presented to the king. The king registered his own opinion on the *consulta*, usually through marginal notation, after which it was returned to the corresponding council. The appropriate secretary then drafted a letter, which was signed by the king and sent to the corresponding viceroy or governor, and any other interested parties. This process was designed to meet the challenges of asserting central control over distant and particularist jurisdictions, and, as one might imagine, created a vast paper trail. This was hardly a recipe for rapid

[107] Manuel Rivero Rodríguez, *El Consejo de Italia y el gobierno de los dominios italianos de la monarquía hispana durante el reinado de Felipe II (1556–1598)* (Madrid: Universidad Autónoma de Madrid, 1992), 219; Geoffrey Parker, *The Grand Strategy of Philip II* (New Haven, CT: Yale University Press, 1998), 13–45.

administrative responses.[108] It is little wonder that Philip garnered the moniker of *rey papalero*.

In March 1571 alone, Philip was said to have personally handled more than 1,250 petitions, prompting him to lament about "these devils, my papers."[109] Philip brought these devils on himself, as he had a marked preference for conducting royal business in writing as opposed to in person. This meant that the *consultas a boca* that regularly occurred under his father Charles became increasingly rare. The *despacho por escrito* was the chief way by which Philip interacted with royal officials, petitioners, and his subjects. The dialogue of rule was conducted largely within the margins of these documents, in the form of the king's comments and sometimes those of his private secretary. Virtually every aspect of the king's rule was mediated through paper and writing. The situation was made worse by Philip's notorious unwillingness to delegate these tasks. Nor did the king's obsessive and controlling nature help matters. He often allowed himself to be consumed by the relatively trivial, and his mistrust of his employees made him generally unwilling to delegate. Philip sought to extend "rule at a remove" to the scale of a global empire, as he himself remained sequestered in Madrid. He endeavored, according to Luis Cabrera de Córdoba, to "move the world by means of paper," ruling the sprawling domains "which he never actually set foot on."[110]

After 1573, Mateo Vázquez de Leca (1542–1591) acted as a sort of information manager for Philip, performing triage on the paper coming into the king. Vázquez warned the king that if he did not reduce the prodigious volume of his reading and writing, his health would be at risk.[111] Vázquez's tasks included filtering the king's correspondence, providing minutes of the meetings of the various ruling councils known as *juntas*, relaying the king's instructions to these bodies, and drafting the king's responses to the many *consultas* he received. But even with Vázquez acting as a documentary filter and as an intermediary between the king and his secretaries, a huge amount of information still ended up accumulating on the king's desk. It proved extremely difficult, amid the massive

---

[108] John Huxtable Elliott, *Imperial Spain, 1469–1716* (New York: St. Martin's Press, 1964), 177.
[109] Arndt Brendecke, "'Diese Teufel, meine Papiere ...' Philipp II von Spanien und das Anwachsen administrativer Schriftlichkeit." *Aventinus. Die Historische Internetzeitschrift von Studenten für Studenten*, 5 (2006), n.p. See also his *Empirical Empire: Spanish Colonial Rule and the Politics of Knowledge* (Berlin: De Gruyter, 2016), 18.
[110] Antonio Castillo Gómez, "The new culture of archives in early modern Spain." *European History Quarterly*, 46.3 (2016), 545–567 (here 557).
[111] Geoffrey Parker, *Imprudent King. A New Life of Philip II* (New Haven, CT: Yale University Press, 2014), 72.

amount of paper produced in governing his global empire, to decide what was genuinely important enough to put before Philip himself. The Spanish Council of War produced an average of two bundles of documents a year in the 1560s; by the 1590s, it was generating more than thirty bundles. This meant that the king received 2,000 letters a year covering military and naval affairs alone. The chief body serving as a conduit for information from the Americas was the Council of the Indies, which dedicated enormous amounts of time to reading the letters coming in from across the Atlantic.

Whatever his intent in demanding information, Philip II often found himself seriously discomfited by the sheer volume he received. Between March 1572 and March 1573, Philip was away from Madrid for 161 days, and during that time his couriers brought him more than 500 packets of letters, most of them from secretaries of the various royal councils.[112] The predictable result, as it almost always is with executives who refuse to delegate, was that Philip was overwhelmed. In demanding to know "all" (or, as he once described it, "complete information on the present state of affairs in all areas"[113]), which is of course impossible, he simply ended up knowing "too much" to engage in effective decision-making.

Philip II was in many ways a unique case: in scope, in administrative complexity, and in personality. But his struggles were representative. Governments and their ministers, even in states far smaller than the global empire of Spain, struggled to navigate this maze of paper – it became evident that the perceived benefits of the politics of inscription were accompanied by a batch of challenges. The accumulation of government documents in the State Paper Office under Queen Elizabeth had, by the end of the sixteenth century, left Robert Cecil (1563–1612) in "blindness and uncertainty" when he tried to make sense of the collections related to royal finances. He added that even the relatively narrow documentary record on royal forests left him "in a wood indeed."[114] By the end of the sixteenth century, ministers across Europe were inhabiting the "worlds of paper" that had vexed the ministers of fifteenth-century Milan. It was easy for European statesmen, like so many of us, amid a flood of data, to become so consumed with the particulars, that they lost sight of the general.

4.6 Archives

One notable expression of the importance of information to early modern governance was the waxing commitment to the systematic preservation of

---

[112] Parker, *Imprudent King*, 72–73. [113] Parker, *Imprudent King*, 300.
[114] Slack, "Government and Information," 39.

records. There emerged in Europe a broadly shared consensus that the public authority of the state, in the interest of its own political legitimacy, must conscientiously conserve, manage, and certify its paper. The links between ruler, state, and archives became considerably more explicit and concrete in the early modern period. These connections were reinforced by the increasingly sedentary nature of early modern courts and associated institutions, a departure from the itinerant courts that prevailed in the Middle Ages. Archives, stuffed with the paper records of governance, were not merely the products of the exercise of power but its embodiment.[115] The commitment of a polity to systematic recordkeeping and information management, however, was not necessarily an indication of political power and confidence. Many of the states who experimented with new forms of what Filippo de Vivo calls "archival intelligence" did so out of a marked sense of political weakness and insecurity.[116] Possession of, and access to, political information was conceived as a means of making up for anxieties about contested sovercignty or geopolitical vulnerability.

All manner of documents accumulated within early modern political archives: registers, rolls, account books and ledgers, tax records, charters, contracts, treaties, histories, transcriptions of ancient documents, privileges, reports of *intendants* and other agents, censuses, newssheets, and printed tomes, along with many other forms of writing. For all this diversity, however, the bulk of their contents was made up by letters, reflecting the letterocracy I described earlier. European chanceries thus developed new ways of managing the documents accumulating from current activity while also devising means to access the records from the past, along with dedicating new spaces to the storage of both.

The early modern period thus saw a widespread expansion in the institutions of the state dedicated to the preservation of documents that it received and produced. Robert-Henri Bautier has called this the "crucial phase in the history of archives."[117] Archives became the "arsenals of authority," with buildings, bureaucratic institutions, and personnel committed to the preservation of the documents of politics. All these were accompanied by secretarial practices that preserved and managed a great volume and variety of information related to governance, with recourse to

---

[115] Elizabeth Yale, "The history of archives: the state of the discipline." *Book History*, 18 (2015), 332–259 (here 336–337).
[116] Filippo de Vivo, "Archival intelligence."
[117] Robert-Henri Bautier, "La phase cruciale de l'histoire des archives. La construction des dépôts d'archives et la naissance de l'archivistique (XVIc – début du XIXe siècle)." *Archivum*, 18 (1968), 139–149.

repositories ordered to facilitate both storage and access. As Randolph Head's book on European political archives shows, while the practices of information management across Europe remained heterogeneous, between 1400 and 1700, European secretaries and archivists, in seeking to bring order to the morass of records, employed a common batch of media technologies, including lists, notebooks, inventories, and indices.[118] To put it simply, in a pattern followed in other areas of European society in this period, "archives evolved from repositories of old documentary proofs into information-management institutions."[119]

New scholarship on archives (the so-called "archival turn") has insisted, rightly, on considering them not as neutral repositories of information, but instead as expressions of individual and institutional outlook and intent, whereby their structure and content were the result of choices, deliberate and unconscious, which reflected the active exercise of power. In short, record-keeping and archiving are social practices.[120] Foucault regarded the archive as a figurative, rather than physical, space. Recent studies have, thankfully, reversed Michel Foucault's formulation, and focused on the material and organizational shape of the archives and on the practices that governed their construction and use. This hard work of trudging through the archives, hard work which Foucault studiously avoided, has revealed much about the circumstances under which documents were produced and preserved, and about changing attitudes toward information. Archives were, to be sure, symbolic representations of societies' power dynamics, but they were also spaces in which the practical decisions and everyday drudgery of information management transpired. Early modern archives were the product of deliberate and discriminating choices, but also of the incidental and accidental.

States in the Middle Ages had maintained archives, of course. Already in the thirteenth century, the papacy (and ecclesiastical institutions more broadly) had committed themselves to extensive record-keeping. City-states across Italy were devoting considerable efforts to maintaining records and archiving the business of governing.[121] Most medieval

---

[118] Randolph Head, *Making Archives in Early Modern Europe* (Cambridge: Cambridge University Press, 2019).
[119] Filippo de Vivo, Andrea Guidi, and Alessandro Silvestri, "Archival transformations in early modern European history." *European History Quarterly*, 46.3 (2016), 421–434 (here 423).
[120] Eric Ketelaar, "Records out and archives in: early modern cities as creators of records and as communities of archives." *Archival Science*, 10 (2010), 201–210 (here 201).
[121] Paolo Cammarosano, *Italia medievale: struttura e geografia delle fonti scritte* (Rome: La Nuova Italia Scientifica, 1991); Jean-Claude Maire Vigueur, "Révolution documentaire et révolution scripturaire: le cas de l'Italie médiévale." *Bibliotheque de l'École des Chartes*, 153.1 (1995), 177–185.

polities established dedicated physical spaces to the preservation of important documents. In Italy and the Low Countries, a general archival consciousness, manifested in a commitment to collecting, arranging, and archiving documents, was shared by even the smallest towns and rural communities. Local elites, for example the *podestà* of small towns and statelets, felt compelled to maintain records, filing away not only statutes but also, increasingly, routine administrative documents, mostly letters. Although many of the Italian communes had lost their independence by the fifteenth century, the influence of their archival and material practices proved durable.

As the regular writing and systematic record-keeping that had prevailed in late medieval Italy became commonplace across Western Europe, the new offices and personnel of the early modern state generated more and more working papers, which, as we have seen, were mostly varieties of correspondence. Many of these papers were produced by, and captured in writing, the day-to-day functions of government, as opposed to the primarily statutory and legal "deposits" that characterized the materials of the medieval archive.[122] This division reflected a distinction in the archives that was already becoming evident in the Middle Ages. Documents resulting from the active business of government were *Urkunden* (again, chiefly letters) and represented a different species of writing from the *Akten*.[123] Another way of characterizing this distinction is one between an institutional "functional" memory (in the sense of a "current" archive) and a "deposit" memory (or "sedimentation" archive).[124] The documentation of functional memory, among other things, was produced in much greater volumes that that of deposit memory, and it created logistical and organizational challenges of an altogether new scale.

If there was a typical response among state archivists of this period, it was to preserve these *Urkunden*, and regimes engaged in a constant battle against the "entropy of the archive," which was especially vexing when new material came into the archive for which there might not be an existing mechanism of organization or category for ready filing.[125]

---

[122] This is the characterization of Aleida Assmann, *Erinnerungsräume: Formen und Wandlungen des kulturellen Gedächtnis* (Munich: Beck, 1999).
[123] On this distinction, see Varanini, "Public written records," 389, as well as Andrea Guidi, "The Florentine archives in transition: government, warfare and communication (1289–1530 ca.)." *European History Quarterly*, 46.3 (2016), 458–479 (here 463).
[124] Filippo Valenti, *Scritti e lezioni di archivistica, diplomatica e storia istituzionale* (Rome: Ministero per i beni e le attività culturali, ufficio centrale per i beni archivistici, 2000), 89–103.
[125] This is the term used in Roscoe Hill, "Reforms in shelving and numbering in the Archivio de las Indias." *Hispanic American Historical Review*, 10 (1930), 520–524.

Similarly, in some locales, archivists struggled to know what to do with "non-current" materials, documents that were not directly related to the current concerns of governance. These were often shunted off into far-off rooms, moldering in a confused, disordered existence.[126]

In the early modern period, regimes built spaces or designated existing ones to the tasks of preserving and organizing state papers. This growth was rarely systematic and planned deliberately; the piecemeal expansion of government activities and the paper they produced meant that the coverage and physical footprint of the associated repositories advanced in a similarly fitful fashion. The expanded documentary footprint of government was underway before the establishment of fixed capitals that took place in the course of the sixteenth century. Holy Roman Emperor Charles V, for example, had an itinerant court, and his itinerancy meant that the important stakeholders in the imperial administration had to be kept up-to-date with his movements and decisions. And in order to make decisions that were informed, his mobile chancery processed the correspondence that it was receiving. This complex system supported the exchange of letters and embassies, and made correspondence and the epistolary record essential to the functioning of imperial government, as those who might normally be side by side were far apart from one another, connected only by a regular exchange of letters. Thus, the primary archives holding the correspondence from Charles's reign, in Vienna, Simancas, and Brussels, still contain more than 120,000 letters written to and by Charles and his immediate advisers. "They contain the actual stream of information, questions, advice, decisions and orders that enabled the composite monarchy to achieve its unity of action. The regents and chief advisors in the diverse states formed the mainstay of this correspondence, of which the surviving copies alone point to an average of 8.5 letters sent per day during the 40-year reign."[127]

The development of the Spanish imperial archive at Simancas reflects the waxing urge to gather, record, and manage the paper trail as an expression of state authority. The Kingdom of Spain was especially pioneering in the development of paper-based administration, so the need for documentary management by the mid-sixteenth century was imperative. In 1545, Charles V transferred his *trésor de chartes*,

---

[126] See, for example, Alessandro Silvestri, "Archivi senza archivisti. I maestri notai e la gestione delle scritture nel Regno di Sicilia (prima metà XV sec.)." In De Vivo, Guidi, and Silvestri, eds., *Archivi e archivisti*, 43–69.

[127] Wim Blockmans, *Emperor Charles V 1500–1558* (London: Arnold, 2002), 133. See also Geoffrey Parker, *Emperor. A New Life of Charles V* (New Haven, CT: Yale University Press, 2019), especially his fascinating discussion of sources, 569–595.

a collection composed of items typical of a medieval royal treasury, to Simancas. The repository established there changed fundamentally in character, however, after the appointment by Philip II, Charles's successor, of Diego de Ayala as royal archivist. A guide for the archival operations at Simancas that Ayala drew up for the king in 1588 declared that the goal of the repository was "to conserve the [writings] that touch on the patrimony, state, and royal crown of these realms and to its rights of patronage" and to "gather all information that would be useful for the effective direction of current affairs, and of those affairs which may occur every day."[128]

Arndt Brendecke has questioned whether Simancas was in fact an active archive, noting the small number of document requests arriving from Madrid. Philip II sent numerous locked chests of documents to Simancas for storage, but kept the keys himself, so that not even the archivist had access to them. Simancas was used as a prison, and Beinecke suggests that it became one for documents as well as for people. Still, even if documents were sent there to be cloistered, they would be stored there in uninterrupted series until the French Revolution.[129]

In England, in the wake of the Tudor Revolution in Government initiated by Thomas Cromwell, the government amassed archives unprecedented in English history, stuffed with the paper residue of everyday governance: correspondence of many sorts, memoranda, minutes of meetings, notes, and policy documents.[130] A number of archival series of the English crown began in the first half of the sixteenth century, including the journals of the House of Lords (beginning in 1509) and the House of Commons (from 1547). Cromwell's efforts to undertake administrative reforms, especially in the area of record-keeping, were granted particular urgency by the pressures related to the dissolution of more than 600 monasteries.[131] The efforts of Cromwell created the

---

[128] José Rodríguez de Diego, ed., *Instrucción para el gobierno del Archivo de Simancas* (Madrid: Ministerio de Educación y Cultura, 1988), 97, quoted in Head, *Making Archives*, 224.

[129] Robert-Henri Bautier, "La phase cruciale de l'histoire des archives." 141–142; José Luis Rodríguez de Diego and Julia T. Rodríguez de Diego, "Un archivo no solo para el rey, significado social del proyecto simanquino en el siglo XVI." In José Martínez Millán, ed., *Felipe II (1527–1598). Europa y la monarquía católica* (Madrid: Editorial Parteluz, 1998), 463–475. The case of Brendecke is summarized in Arndt Brendecke, "Knowledge, oblivion, and concealment in early modern Spain: the ambiguous agenda of the Archive of Simancas," in Corens, Peters, and Walsham, eds., *Archives and Information*, 131–149.

[130] Geoffrey Elton, *The Tudor Revolution in Government*.

[131] Vanessa Harding, "Monastic records and the dissolution: a Tudor revolution in the archives?; *European History Quarterly*, 46.3 (2016), 480–497.

136   The Information Revolution in Early Modern Europe

foundations in England for "a new kind of government in which bureaucracy became a guiding principle."[132]

The systematic collection and storage of government papers in England began at Whitehall Palace in the reign of Henry VIII – the first real evidence of an English state archive. Elizabeth I codified this commitment to the preservation of the government's papers with the institution of the State Paper Office in 1578. A clerk of the papers was appointed, in charge of an office in Whitehall, located beneath the Banqueting House.[133] These steps were a response to what Maggie Yax has called an "explosion of government activity," and an indication of the importance of documents to Tudor government.[134] Thomas Wilson (ca. 1560–1629), at the State Paper Office under Elizabeth's successor King James I (r. 1603–1625), applied his considerable expertise in the collection, organization, and circulation of state documents. Wilson sought to collect and preserve, but also wished the State Paper Office to be a tool that actively aided governance, applying a system of preservation that would accord a place for each document as it arrived. The Keepers who followed Wilson built upon his efforts in order to stay on top of the proliferation of paper, and regarded standardized record-keeping as a function of good government.

The Medici dukes in Florence issued legislation reunifying all of the various notarial registers into a single, common depot in 1569. Pope Pius V (r. 1566–1572), in 1568, commenced the process of gathering together all of the papal archives into a single location, the Castello Sant'Angelo, which would ultimately lead to the creation of the unified Vatican Archives in 1610.[135]

Even small polities had to face the challenge of the accumulation of large piles of paper – storing and (even more so) organizing these retained records was everywhere a daunting task. Johann Heinrich Waser, who became *stadtschreiber* of Zurich in the mid-seventeenth century, wrote in his *Autobiography* of indexing the city's archive: it was "endless labour ... in both chanceries and in the council chambers, everything is more than filled; item, there was also a room in the town hall next to the accounting office that was full of papers, likewise the old boxes in the Fraumünster were stuffed, with many boxes stacked on top of one another out of

---

[132] Geoffrey Elton, *The Tudor Revolution in Government*, 126.
[133] Angela Andreani, *The Elizabethan Secretariat and the Signet Office* (New York: Routledge, 2017), 42.
[134] Maggie Yax, "Arthur Agarde, Elizabethan archivist: his contributions to the evolution of archival practice." *American Archivist*, 61 (1998), 56–69 (here 68).
[135] Bautier, "La phase cruciale," 141–144.

place."[136] Such anxieties reflected a dual transformation in European political archives: the expansion of records and the concurrent attempts to bring order to them.[137]

This expanded galaxy of documents, given its diversity, also came to be stored and registered in ways other than the straightforwardly chronological, which proved impractical, given the great expansion in daily documentation. The sixteenth-century ordinances of the Imperial Austrian *Kanzlei*, for example, reveal a frequently repeated concern that order in the archives would not be kept and that documents must be stored in a manner such that they could be located and retrieved easily and quickly.[138] Documents were thus often bound into book form, or tied together with a string, or a "file," in the terminology of the day.[139] Every archive deployed some combination of sacks, trunks, cases, or cabinets to the storage of documents, employed with the competing ends of secrecy and accessibility in mind. The expansion of archives in early modern Europe was the result of a sufficient number of decision-makers deeming the preservation of political paper not only desirable, but "useful."

The relentless arrival of new material into the archive forced archivists to furnish their collections with classificatory schemes and finding aids.[140] They resorted to the employment of "little tools of knowledge" (a term coined by Peter Becker and William Clark): indices, inventories, registers, compendia, and other navigational tools, an indication that archives, at least in theory, were being filled in order to be used.[141] These "little tools" became essential to the "culling, condensing and consulting" that took place in early modern European archives.[142]

Early modern archivists and secretaries introduced or further developed a range of paper tools to manage and navigate the documents that accumulated in the archives. These included notebooks, registers,

---

[136] Randolph Head, "Knowing like a state: the transformation of political knowledge in Swiss archives, 1450–1770." *The Journal of Modern History*, 75.4 (December 2003), 745–782 (here 762).
[137] De Vivo, Guidi, and Silvestri, "Archival transformations," 421.
[138] Megan Williams, "Zu Notdurfft der Scheiberey." Die Einrichtung der frühneuzeitlichen Kanzlei." In Dagmar Freist, ed., *Diskurse – Körper – Artefakte. Historische Praxeologie in der Frühneuzeitforschung* (Bielefeld: Transcript Verlag, 2015), 335–372.
[139] See Heather Wolfe and Peter Stallybrass, "The material culture of record-keeping in early modern England." In Corens, Peters, and Walsham, eds., *Archives and Information*, 179–208.
[140] On such challenges, see also Roscoe Hill, "Reforms in shelving"; and Donald Kelley, "Jean du Tiller, archivist and antiquary." *Journal of Modern History*, 38 (1966), 337–354.
[141] Peter Becker and William Clark, eds., *Little Tools of Knowledge: Historical Essays on Academic and Bureaucratic Practices* (Ann Arbor, MI: University of Michigan Press, 2001).
[142] De Vivo, "Archival Intelligence," 83.

inventories, and indexes. Nicholas Faunt (ca. 1578–1608), a member of the inner circle of Francis Walsingham (1532–1590), the chief secretary of Queen Elizabeth I, advised in his treatise, *Discourse Touching the Office of the Principal Secretary of Estate*, that the state secretary employ a set of notebooks to keep track of the papers in the archive. One would record all of the incoming and outgoing correspondence, while another, which he called a "memorial book," would list matters that required immediate action. He also advised that the secretary systematically record vital information from correspondence and other documents (which he called "loose papers"), and gather them in a series of notebooks, organized by subject areas, thus removing the need to pore through the original hoard.[143]

The president of the Parlement de Paris, Jean le Nain (1609–1698), filled more than 200 volumes with copies of documents in the Parlement's archives. For these copybooks he then created a multi-volume index, which researchers still use as a guide to the contents of these archives. In order to create this index, le Nain generated thousands of tiny slips of paper upon which were written summaries of documents' contents. He placed these slips in thematic order, pinned into some eighty-three separate books. He then copied this reorganized information in his own handwriting to create a thematic index. His efforts serve as a reminder that information management is hard work.[144]

The archivist therefore became an institutional information manager. As the role of the archivist expanded, standard administrative practices emerged. Albertino Barisoni, in his *De archivis commentarius*, written in the 1620s or 1630s and one of the first works dedicated entirely to the subject of archives, identified two "noble ends" for the archive: first, that they preserve the records of the state "uncorrupted" and second, that they allow these records to be found quickly and as often as they are needed.[145] At about the same time, another treatise on archives, the *De archivis* (1632) of Baldassare Bonifacio, came to similar conclusions. Bonifacio identified the usefulness of the archive as an informational resource, "a well constituted store of volumes and documents and records" employed to "instruct and teach," "clear up and illustrate obscure matters," and "conserve patrimonies and thrones." Access to the information stored in the archive,

---

[143] Charles Hughes, ed., "Nicholas Faunt's discourse touching the office of the Principal Secretary of Estate." *English Historical Review*, 20 (1905), 499–508.

[144] Markus Friedrich, "How to make an archival inventory in early modern Europe: carrying documents, gluing paper and transforming archival chaos into well-ordered knowledge." *Manuscript Cultures*, 10.10 (2017), 160–173 (here 170).

[145] Lester Born, "The *De archivis commentarius* of Albertino Barisoni (1587–1667)." *Archivalische Zeitschrift*, 50/51 (1955), 13–22.

he posited, was more important to the state's flourishing than navy yards and munition factories. Archives had to be organized in a manner that minimized the labor of searching, by the employment of indexes and filing systems organized according to geographical provenance, alphabetization, and chronology. State archives were not only a locus for capturing the paper trail of the state in past and present, but also an informational resource for the future, a store of precedent for use by the prince.[146]

Cornelia Vismann has identified the sixteenth century as the "epoch in which the modern filing system arises."[147] The period 1400–1700 Randolph Head has called the "era of the chancellery book," an item singularly committed to tracking a document through its lifetime in a chancery, from arrival (or dispatch), to active use, to storage. Across the Holy Roman Empire, princes organized their archives as *Registraturen*. These *Registraturen* were designed not only to facilitate the storing and finding of documents but also to allow the ongoing processing of documents as they were produced or arrived. Thus, in the *Hofregistratur* of the Archduke Ferdinand of Tyrol (1529–1595) in Innsbruck, by the second half of the sixteenth century every document had to be examined, recorded in a journal and in indexes, and then placed in the right order. In the 1570s, only a few volumes of such journals existed, but by the turn of the century there were more than forty dedicated to both incoming and outgoing documents.[148] This enormous profusion of secondary paper, of information about information, was yet another indication that efforts at information management, though designed to bring order to abundance, ended up generating a great deal more paper.

The idea that state archives were a public resource scarcely existed in this period. Nor were there clear lines about what should be kept in a state archive, and what could remain in the collections of individuals. While

---

[146] These trends, incidentally, were not exclusive to the European context. Political formations outside of Europe that were committed to government by paper were also faced with the challenges of storing and organizing large volumes of documentation. In Qing China, for example, the driving force of the regime's archival practice was apparently to save everything, even things that had no evident interest to the government. The notion of weeding out documents before archiving was unknown to the Qing archivists. The key decisions of the archivists were not over what to keep but rather what should be circulated. Predictably, with so many documents on hand, sorting through them and making such determinations was a challenging task. In the Yongzheng period, documents associated with the imperial court were divided into three categories: "published," "yet to be published," and "not to be published." See Beatrice Bartlett, "Qing statesmen, archivists and the question of memory." In Francis X Blouin Jr. and William Rosenberg, eds., *Archives, Documentation and Institutions of Social Memory (the Sawyer Seminar)* (Ann Arbor, MI: University of Michigan Press, 2006), 417–426.
[147] Cornelia Vismann, *Files: Law and Media Technology*. Trans. by Geoffrey Winthrop-Young (Stanford: Stanford University Press, 2008), 91.
[148] Randolph Head, *Making Archives*, 249–266.

there was a broadening expectation that the accumulation of records was one indicator of the authority of the state, there was rarely an accompanying consensus among the ministers that produced them that these records should end up as the preserve of the state. There were also significant hurdles to gathering all related state papers in central archives, as there remained legal and operative uncertainties concerning the ownership of ministers' papers. Efforts to centralize locales for storage invariably came up against the resistance of ministers who felt that their papers were rightly their personal or family property, and should remain in their possession. For example, all the great ministers of the seventeenth century in France – Sully, Mazarin, Richelieu – maintained control of their own archives. The same was true of Jean-Baptiste Colbert (1619–1683), the first minister of Louis XIV; his son, the Marquis de Seignelay (1651–1690), inherited his archive upon his father's death, rather than it becoming property of the French state.[149] Thomas Wilson in the English State Paper Office waged a constant battle to enforce regulations requiring that state counselors and officials deposit their papers at the Office.[150]

The story of archives in early modern Europe reveals the central importance of information management to the political history of the period. The organization and composition of archives reflected the priorities of the political system: what was retained depended on how the administration functioned, just as the modes of access depended on who used what documents, and how, when, and where. All of this should remind us that the history that we write about this period is very much dependent on how the information we discover in its archives was recorded and preserved. As Randolph Head has observed: "An archive is thus more than a heap of parchment and paper; it is also a structure of knowing manifest not only in the disposition of documents within the archive but also more visibly in the inventories, physical containers, and other tools that an archive's users employed."[151]

Despite the great expansion of archives, preservation was naturally a selective process.[152] That a document made it into an archive is, in some way, an indication of its importance, at least at the time that the decision was made to preserve it, rather than dispose of it. At the same time, however, the decision to archive a document meant that it was of

---

[149] Jacob Soll, *The Information Master: Jean Baptiste Colbert's Secret State Intelligence System* (Ann Arbor, MI: University of Michigan Press, 2009), 153.
[150] Nicholas Popper, "Archives and the boundaries of early modern science." *Isis*, 107.1 (2016), 86–94 (here 90–91).
[151] Head, "Knowing like a state," 749.
[152] On selective preservation, see Arnold Esch, "Überlieferungs-Chance und Überlieferungs-Zufall als methodisches Problem des Historikers." *Historische Zeitschrift*, 240.3 (1985), 529–570.

waning importance, that it could be removed from circulation, away from the eyes of active policy makers. Whatever their effectiveness as tools of governance, political archives provided states and sovereigns with a sense of control, or at least helped project an image of control to their subjects, rooted in the appearance of omniscience. The role that archives played in the attempts to encompass the state in writing often betrayed extremely grand ambitions, ones that transcended time and distance and purported to encompass "all" the writing related to the state. Such ambitions were doomed to fail, of course, an early indication of something we are repeatedly reminded of in our own day: that information does not translate seamlessly into power.

4.7 Rule at a Remove and its Limits

Many of the letters and other documents that filled archives had, in their lives, traveled long distances. The paper of politics was deployed in part to achieve control away from the center. The Society of Jesus, for example, saw the exchange of paper as the essential means by which the central office in Rome could keep in touch, and ultimately control, its far-flung chapters across the globe. Epistolary exchanges were a means for the Society of establishing an institutional scaffolding that spanned great distances. From its very beginning, the Jesuit order relied on a dense network of correspondence – as early as 1542, Ignatius Loyola (1491–1556) spoke of seeing "250 letters in a few days only."[153] The letters that traveled to and from the provinces were the sinew of a deeply hierarchical model that aspired to assert control over the periphery through epistolary exchange. Thus, in 1666, Father General Gianpaolo Oliva (1600–1681) remarked that while ubiquitous presence was the preserve of God Himself, "[our only resource is] the loyal and sincere diligence of our administrators which, through the means of ink and paper, is able to connect Orient and Occident and moves both Indies closer to Rome."[154]

Such ambitions to assert control and assure obedience through long-distance information flows were as a matter of course limited by the vagaries of early modern communication on a global scale. Reports of letters arriving in tatters, or not at all, were legion. The Jesuit missionary stationed in Mexico, Petrus Thomas Van Hamme (1651–1727), lamented that of the thirteen or fourteen letters sent to him by a fellow

---

[153] Paolo Quattrone, "Accounting for God: accounting and accountability practices in the Society of Jesus (Italy, XVI–XVII centuries)." *Accounting, Organizations and Society*, 29 (2004), 647–683 (here 667).
[154] Markus Friedrich, "Governance in the Society of Jesus: 1540–1773. Its Methods, Critics, and Legacy Today." *Studies in the Spirituality of the Jesuits*, 41.1 (2009), 1–42 (here 13).

Jesuit in Leuven, in the Low Countries, only one actually arrived. Nor could the veracity of the news that did arrive be assured, confirming a popular Castilian proverb that "from long journeys, come long lies." There were thus built-in limitations to what has been called "an intelligence system unequalled by any state in Europe at the time," operating on a truly global scale.[155] The governor-general might aspire to total knowledge and control via paper, but time and space remained undefeated.

This period furnishes many examples of how information management came to be deemed critical to effective governing at a distance and to strengthening control from the center. The *politique proche* of traditional, face-to-face interactions, which had always been at the core of political life, remained important, but was now supplemented and in some cases supplanted by additional connections maintained by medium- and long-distance correspondence. The composition of letters, often enforced by superiors, was understood, often naively, to militate against the fissiparous tendencies of delay and distance, and of mastering the space between. Correspondence condensed distance, allowing what we might call "rule at a remove." Fernand Braudel famously declared, in his panorama of the sixteenth-century Mediterranean world, that distance was "enemy number one." In early modern politics, correspondence was the chief tool to combat that enemy. In his treatise, *Dell'arte delle lettere missive* (1674), Emanuele Tesauro wrote that "the missive letter is nothing more than a brief discussion between two people far apart from each other, brought together by the miracle of a piece of paper."[156] The politics of inscription abetted government at a distance. In early modern Europe, distance was not eliminated as it has been in the digital age, but the exchange of correspondence eroded its significance significantly. Regular letter writing as an essential feature of governance, as we have seen, along with the use of inscription as an indispensable means of representing and projecting power and authority, combined to dissolve, almost miraculously, the distances between the political metropole and peripheries, with significant repercussions for the real and perceived means and scope of the authority of the state.

The rule of Philip II of Spain over his global empire can credibly be described as a virtual one, carried out from the depths of the Escorial through a never-ending exchange of letters arriving from points of varying remove from the body of the king, with the responses to them bearing the

---

[155] The claim of Donald Lach and Edwin van Kley, *Asia in the Making of Europe*, Vol. I: *The Century of Discovery* (Chicago: University of Chicago Press, 1965), 315.

[156] Emanuele Tesauro, *Dell'arte delle lettere missiue del conte, e caualier Gran Croce D. Emanuele Tesauro* (Venice: Paolo Baglioni, 1674), 360: "Che se la Lettera Missiva, come si disse à principio, altro non è che un breve Ragionamento frà due Persone lontane, avvicinate per miracolo di una Carta."

4.3 Colbert, looking pleased with his papers. Claude Lefèbvre, *Jean Baptiste Colbert* (1666). Museum of the History of France, Versailles (Getty Images).

tell-tale signature *Yo, el Rey*. Unlike his father, Charles V, who was largely itinerant, Philip chose chiefly to remain in Madrid, requiring the dispatch, on a daily basis, of hundreds of reports, letters, and instructions. Philip may have garnered the moniker of *rey papalero*, the "paper king," but Boutier, Landi, and Rouchon have revised this label to specify the nature of all that paper, to "the epistolary prince, surrounded by secretaries, governing by correspondence."[157] Philip was seeking to control, through correspondence, often with great frustration, a polity that was genuinely

---

[157] Jean Boutier, Sandro Landi, and Olivier Rouchon, "Introduction." *Politique par correspondence. Les usages politiques de la lettre en Italie (XIVe–XVIIIe siècle)* (Rennes: Presses universitaires de Rennes, 2009), 13. The classic treatment of Philip II and the

global in its extent. But *le gouvernement épistolaire*, as Boutier, Dewerpe, and Nordman have termed it, was pursued in early modern polities both large and small.[158]

We might see, toward the end of the seventeenth century, the efforts of Jean-Baptiste Colbert in France as the early modern apotheosis of the ambitions of political paper, the mobilization of information in the pursuit of political control, and the aspirations to "rule at a remove." Colbert sought to "master" information, seeing correspondence, reports, ledgers, accounts, and files of every description as levers of political power. As much as anyone in early modern Europe, he perceived the benefits of paperwork. Indeed, he seemed to enjoy it. Many of the concurrent streams of early modern informational culture came together in the person and activities of Colbert. He drew upon the humanistic culture of writing and its classical models of letter composition. His Jesuit education inculcated in him an appreciation for the skills and methods of accounting, as well as the Society's dedication to institutional control through paper-based information management. As a young man, he apprenticed with the Mascranni banking firm, in so doing becoming acquainted with its diligent financial record-keeping. In all that he did he showed that he had adopted, and instilled in his *intendants*, the observational ethic that had taken hold of early modern natural philosophers and statesmen alike, although he did reject categorically, in the pursuit of narrow state interests, the spirit of openness that characterized the European *respublica litterarum*. Colbert was also a keen note-taker and collector of documents. He sought written records on an array of subjects related to the authority of the Crown, gathering the information from his *intendants*, *commissaires*, and other agents, into "portfolios" and "registers" that might run to hundreds of pages. These were known as the "Mélanges Colbert," and embodied the zeal with which Colbert sought to marshal information for the benefit of the French state.

Colbert sought, therefore, in the service of his king, to be "informed of everything," in order to establish a massive bank of information that could be used to extend the Crown's authority in the face of particularist claims of nobles and others within France, and to place France in a better position in relation to its rivals abroad; for Colbert, information was genuinely "useful."[159] Colbert's zeal for the collection of information was

informational challenges of managing a global empire is Parker, *The Grand Strategy of Philip II*, esp. 11–75.
[158] Jean Boutier, Alain Dewerpe, and Daniel Nordman, *Un tour de France royal: le voyage de Charles IX, 1564–1566* (Paris: Aubier, 1984), 213–235.
[159] Soll, *The Information Master*, 59.

married to a comparable enthusiasm for triaging, organizing, and taxonomizing what he gathered. Jacob Soll has called him the "information master," but Colbert was equally an information manager – he was a political pioneer in the composition of reports and dossiers, summarizing and distilling large quantities of information into manageable, digestible formats for consultation by the king. He instructed his *intendants* and his son, the Marquis of Seignelay, to produce extracts of the information that they had gathered. Colbert had his reports filed according to a call system so that he could use them effectively. He saw that information could be deployed to the Crown's advantage, and that it should be stored and accessible for future use, with the most important and frequently consulted stored in his personal archive. The administrative archive of Colbert he built essentially from scratch, seeking to allay the haphazard and accretive nature of other state archives. He wanted the vast paper trail of the French crown to be navigable and usable as an effective tool of royal power.[160]

Colbert, at the tail end of the period covered in this book, sought to represent the French state in documents, to produce a written simulacrum of the kingdom. Statecraft for him, and for his successors, was primarily a matter of paperwork; government was as much about writing as it was about anything else. It is another reminder that early modern Europe invented bureaucracy and invested power in it, with the embodiment of state authority moving from a sovereign atop a horse to a secretary behind a desk.

The efforts of Colbert were consolidated under his successors. A large recent study of the French foreign ministry, led by Colbert's nephew, Colbert de Torcy, has shown how this was the case. The ministry continued to be organized around the systematic intake, triage, and analysis of information. This administrative apparatus had paper instruments as its lifeblood, to such an extent that it has been estimated that Colbert de Torcy's office generated twice as much paperwork on a daily basis as had that of his father, the Marquis de Croissy (1625–1696), successor to the *grand Colbert*. The skillful production and handling of documents were the calling cards of Colbert de Torcy's officials. They were above all managers of information, and were serving an "information state."[161] The bureaucracy established under Louis XIV, staffed by his *intendants*, men of talent and administrative thoroughness, was a lasting one. The central royal ministries and each of his *intendants* were attended upon by secretaries, who managed many "worlds" of paper, and these individuals

---

[160] Jacob Soll, "How to manage an information state: Jean-Baptiste Colbert's archives and the education of his son." *Archival Science*, 7 (2007), 331–342.
[161] Rule and Trotter, *A World of Paper*.

were chief reasons why Louis XIV could (supposedly) say on his deathbed: "Je m'en vais, mais l'état demereura toujours." It would be fifty years after the death of Louis before the word *bureaucratie* entered the French language, appearing for the first time in print in 1764 in Melchior von Grimm's serial *Correspondance littéraire*, as a means of describing the fifth form of government after monarchy, oligarchy, aristocracy, and democracy. But with its intimate embrace of paper and of information, Louis XIV's administration was a bureaucracy *avant la lettre*.

The aspirations of early modern administrators and state-builders, intrinsic to their efforts to govern via a culture of writing and supported by the deployment of growing numbers of "information professionals," were invariably outsized in comparison to the results. Nobles and other regional power brokers might employ informational strategies of their own. They marshalled the power of paperwork as well, keeping their own records and maintaining their own archives, in part as a mechanism to counter the claims of the state. Giora Sternberg has shown, for example, how French aristocrats, in the seventeenth century, deployed their own documents to respond to the official ceremonial record that was maintained by Colbert. These nobles sought copies of records from the archives of the master of ceremonies, but also, more importantly, dedicated themselves to writing and the production of news, registers, and letters which chronicled their participation in various ceremonies, rather than leaving the record-keeping entirely in the hands of the Crown. "Information technologies were open to other political actors," rather than just to the state, and such parallel centers of documentary production created their own heaps of paper.[162]

A great many people wanted and generated political paper in early modern Europe. This paper, exchanged across links of kinship, patronage, and economic connection, expressed interests as much as it did information. Many wished to be in the know, and recognized the value of current political material and of news from abroad, in order to be better positioned to advance their own interests.

* * *

---

[162] Giora Sternberg, "Manipulating information in the Ancien Régime: ceremonial records, aristocratic strategies, and the limits of the state perspective." *Journal of Modern History*, 85 (2013), 239–279 (here 277). For a slighter later period, see Markus Friedrich, "The rise of archival consciousness in provincial France: French feudal records and eighteenth-century seigneurial society." *Past and Present*, 230 (2016), Supplement 11. *The Social History of the Archive: Record-Keeping in Early Modern Europe*. Ed. by Alexandra Walsham, Liesbeth Corens, and Kate Peters, 49–70. See also, for a German case, Mareike Menne, "Confession, confusion and rule in a box? Archival accumulation in Northwest Germany in the age of confessionalization." *Archival Science*, 10 (2010), 299–314.

Why did early modern states demand and collect so much information? We should not assume that their efforts were necessarily or primarily directed toward the streamlining of governance. Nor should we assume that it was in order to have on hand the largest possible base of empirical data on which to found informed decisions and establish the best policy. The establishment of the most substantive and reasoned foundation of knowledge for governance figured only partly in their minds. Instead, their goals were manifold, shaped by personalities, personal rivalries, institutional contexts, and the desire among individuals to establish their indispensability. These efforts were, in the words of Arndt Brendecke, "meant to ensure opportunities for control, to keep arbitrariness within narrow confines, and to ensure that politically shrewd decisions were made, i.e. to take on-site claims and interests into account."[163] The demands for *entera noticia* were as much about the impression of watchfulness and control exercised by the ruler as they were about achieving the comprehensive acquisition of all the available information. The demands themselves were meant to assert the plenitude of power, reinforce hierarchies, and embody the ruler's claim over his territory.

In every demand for information made by the state, it was in the state's interest that the response be honest and complete, but this was rarely true for the respondent. The position of respondents at a distance from the metropole, where they invariably knew more about local conditions than did the center, provided far-flung subjects with certain advantages. This informational asymmetry was a source of autonomy. Agents of the center, such as diplomats, might deem it advantageous to provide a "total" picture. But officials on the periphery often deliberately limited the extent of the information that they provided. In some cases, local officials, such as governors, *podestà*, or *intendants*, might provide fulsome responses to requests not because they were intent on keeping the recipient well informed, but in order to demonstrate to the center their own authority, competence, or omniscience. In this way, supplying information could empower actors on the periphery, not just in the metropole. In the end, the picture the center had was dependent on the information that the periphery chose to provide. So while we can speak confidently of the emergence of the "information state," it is important to remember that political information is never raw data; it is always cooked. Often, such information represents little more than laundered interests.

These realities are reminders of the limitations of the ineluctable "rise of the early modern state" long associated with early modern Europe. The "state," of course, is an abstraction, and the "paper state" an abstraction

---

[163] Brendecke, *Empirical Empire*, 134.

of that abstraction, representing a necessarily incomplete picture of political reality. The aphorism that "knowledge is power" does not apply unless that knowledge can be rendered actionable from the information gathered and presented in documents. Neither, then, is information power, nor does it necessarily confer sovereignty and control. That is as true today, when state institutions struggle to distill knowledge from an ocean of information about their subjects and adversaries, as it was for the early modern statesmen exploring the promise and perils of what Philip II called "these devils, my papers."

5 Revolutionary Print

In 1586, Tomaso Garzoni published a sprawling survey of the professions, *La Piazza Universale di Tutte le Professioni del Mondo, e Nobili et Ignobili*. His entries on dozens of professions are as much opportunities to hold forth on related questions of interest to him as they are detailed discussions of the professions themselves. In his lengthy entry on printers (*stampatori*), Garzoni pauses to offer an extended reflection on the impact of the printing press in his century. He asserts that, without the printing press and the "miraculous art of print," much learning would remain asleep in the shadows. Print greatly reduced the "intolerable price" of books and made them accessible to many more people for whom they had been out of reach: "Today everyone can learn." He compares the printing press to the ring of Angelica (from Torquato Tasso's *Orlando Furioso*), which broke the spells of ancient philosophers, who had held the people rapt with foolishness (Anaxamander), follies (Heraclitus), pretenses (Democritus), vanities (Melissus), and idiocies (Carneade), as well as writings of philosophers in his own century, who are no less arrogant and crazy. The press opened the eyes of the blind and provided light to the ignorant – "a truly rare, stupendous and miraculous art," one that separates gold from lead, the rose from the thorns, the wheat from the chaff.[1]

On and on he goes, in an extraordinary paean to the influence of the printing press and of its inventor, Johannes Gutenberg (c. 1400–1468). Garzoni's rhetoric is flamboyant, but his twin emphases – the abundance and affordability of books, making them available to a much larger reading population, and the resuscitation and rescue of authors who otherwise would have remained in the shadows – are echoed by other early modern commentators. The humanist and historian Polydore Vergil (c. 1470–1555) stressed precisely these points in his *On Discovery*: "Books in all disciplines have poured out to us so profusely from this invention that no work can possibly remain wanting to anyone, however needy. Note too that this

---

[1] Tomaso Garzoni, *La piazza universale di tutte le professioni del mondo, e nobili et ignobili* (Venice. Giovan Battista Somascho, 1586), 847.

invention has freed most authors, Greek as well as Latin, from any threat of extinction."[2] Similarly, the prominent French humanist Henri Estienne (c. 1531–1598) in his work on the Frankfurt Book Fair, also stressed how the printing press had made "an abundance of books" available "to all the lands of the globe" and rescued the Muses from exile, giving them the strongest protection (*firmissimum praesidium*) against loss.[3]

There is little doubt that, in the public imagination at least, early modern Europe is regularly associated with the invention of Gutenberg. When I describe this book project to others, they invariably mention the printing press. "The age of print," the advent of "print culture," and the "coming of the book" are phrases routinely invoked in descriptions of the early modern period. Such designations both overstate the pervasiveness of the printing press's influence, and overlook the impact of factors unrelated to the press. We must move away from the medieval–early modern bifurcation between manuscript and print, to recognize that the print revolution was only part of, and in many ways symptomatic of, broader transformations in information generation and exchange.

Recognizing the enduring importance of manuscript, including manuscript books, is essential for understanding the early modern period. There is also no question that the work of cultural historians and historians of the book (foremost among them Adrian Johns) in questioning some of the claims made by Elizabeth Eisenstein about the pervasive influence of the printing press has proven to be salutary.[4] Doing these things forces us to acknowledge significant continuities from the pre-print period and recognize that some of the transformations attributed to the printing press are better understood as reflections of transformations already underway. Eisenstein's claim, for example, that the printing press was responsible for a novel "fixity" in Renaissance culture, where knowledge and authorship were codified by the preservative power and reproducibility of print, has been effectively challenged, in the recognition that the world of print was in fact a largely unregulated bacchanal of contested authorship, unattributed borrowing, and unstable content.[5] Copiers, typesetters, and printers made mistakes;

---

[2] Polydore Vergil, *On Discovery*. Trans. and ed. by Brian P. Copenhaver. I Tatti Renaissance Library, 6 (Cambridge, MA: Harvard University Press, 2002), II.7.

[3] James Westfall Thompson, ed., *The Frankfort Book Fair: The* Francofordiense Emporium *of Henri Estienne* (Chicago: The Caxton Club, 1911), 172–173.

[4] Elizabeth Eisenstein, *The Printing Press as an Agent of Change. Communications and Cultural Transformations in Early Modern Europe*, 2 vols. (Cambridge: Cambridge University Press, 1979) and then the abridgment, with a new afterword addressing some of the critiques, as *The Printing Revolution in Early Modern Europe* (Cambridge: Cambridge University Press, 2005).

[5] The chief critique of Eisenstein's claims along these lines is by Adrian Johns, *The Nature of the Book. Print and Knowledge in the Making* (Chicago: University of Chicago Press, 1998); see also the *American Historical Review* Forum, "How Revolutionary Was the Print

and supposedly identical versions of a text often betray variations, sometimes significant ones, meaning that "variant copies were the norm."[6] Accuracy in printed replication was a concern from the very beginning. Even Martin Luther (1483–1546), who recognized and exploited the potential of print as much as anyone in sixteenth-century Europe, lamented the absence of authorial control over what made its way into print: "I know my wish doesn't count, since what will be done is what the press wants and not what I want."[7] He complained: "I do not even recognize my own books ... They leave things out, they put things in the wrong order, or they falsify the text or fail to correct it."[8] Luther sought to counteract these annoyances by having his printers include Luther "logos," a lamb and a flag or a rose with a cross in the center, to act as a mark of authenticity. Galileo Galilei (1564–1642), too, saw his work appropriated without his consent. His landmark images of the lunar surface, first published in Venice in 1610, were reprinted in editions in Frankfurt and London, from woodcuts that produced non-identical images each time they were used.

It was for such reasons that Desiderius Erasmus (1466–1536) was among those expressing ambivalence regarding the printing press. He worried especially about quality control in the helter-skelter world of sixteenth-century publishing. He described it as "an invention designed to be the greatest blessing to learning and education [that] tends through the errors of those who misuse it to become a serious threat." Erasmus was nonetheless perfectly happy to exploit its potential for furthering his reputation and notoriety. The risk of errors was especially present when books were printed in a hurry. A printer from Parma in 1473 sought forgiveness for the numerous errors in one of his editions by claiming it had been produced faster than it took asparagus to be cooked, in order to bring it to press ahead of his competitors.[9]

In the early age of print, there were *texts* rather than *a* text. As Paul Nelles has put it: "When approached from the point of view of the production and consumption of print, it is clear that in no way was print a stable, univocal medium."[10] But the "preservative power" of print

---

Revolution?": Introduction by Anthony Grafton, Exchange between Elizabeth Eisenstein and Adrian Johns, *American Historical Review*, 107.1 (2002), 84–128.

[6] David McKitterick, *Print, Manuscript and the Search for Order, 1450–1830* (Cambridge: Cambridge University Press, 2003), 123.

[7] Quoted in Sachiko Kusukawa, *Picturing the Book of Nature. Image, Text and Argument in Sixteenth-Century Human Anatomy and Medical Botany* (Chicago: University of Chicago Press, 2012), 93.

[8] Quoted in John Flood, "The book in Reformation Germany." In Jean-François Gilmont and Karin Maag, eds., *The Reformation and the Book* (Aldershot: Ashgate, 1998), 21–103 (here 51–52).

[9] Sigfrid Henry Steinberg, *Five Hundred Years of Printing* (New York: Penguin, 1974), 119.

[10] Paul Nelles, "Reading and memory in the universal library: Conrad Gessner and the Renaissance book." In Donald Beecher and Grant Williams, eds., *Ars reminiscendi*

highlighted by Eisenstein was nonetheless real and transformative. The interpolation of printing errors did not preclude a waxing permanence in associations of textual and authorial identity. Episodes such as the famous 1631 bible that omitted the "not" from the seventh commandment, leaving the reader with "Thou shalt commit adultery," should not distract us from this new reality. There was a print revolution, and it transformed the informational landscape of Europe in numerous important ways, if not in the ways generally attributed to it, especially in the years after 1500, when the volume, variety, and social and geographic range of readership of printed books expanded voluminously. The best estimates, from the British Library Incunabula Short Title catalog, is that there were nine million printed books in circulation before 1500. The increase in output in the sixteenth century was exponential – the Universal Short Title Catalog from the University of St. Andrews estimates at least 345,000 separate editions and more than 180 million printed books. If nothing else, this was at least a quantitative revolution. There was no part of the world in the same time frame that came anywhere near to this level of production.

Accustomed as we are to the world of print, we might find the capabilities of medieval scribes to produce manuscript books in large volumes surprising. In short spurts, they could write with great rapidity. From the eleventh century onward there had been an expansion in the scriptoria across Europe, chiefly in response to the demand of ecclesiastical institutions. But for most ecclesiastical libraries, the demand for books was generally restrained, for once the need for books essential to the life of the monastery had been fulfilled, production in the scriptorium would slow down, or even cease altogether for a period of time.[11] By the thirteenth century, there is ample evidence of professional scribes operating apart from the ecclesiastical realm, reflecting the increased demand for writing outside of the Church. Town governments and universities, in particular, created niches for professionals of the written word.

The presence of professional scribes, the advent of cursive scripts, and the availability and affordability of paper all contributed to the increased supply of books in the late medieval, pre-print context. Once again, the use of paper was a game changer. It was many times cheaper than parchment, and this allowed many more and different people to buy books, bringing diversity to a market that had been dominated by relatively expensive products intended

mind and memory in Renaissance culture (Toronto: Centre for Reformation and Renaissance Studies, 2009), 147–169 (here 149).
[11] Michael Gullick, "How fast did scribes write? Evidence from Romanesque scripts." In Linda Brownrigg, ed., *Making the Medieval Book: Techniques of Production: Proceedings of the Fourth Conference of the Seminar in the History of the Book to 1500* (Los Altos Hills, CA: Anderson Lovelace, 1995), 39–58 (here 48).

for a niche clientele. This expanded production included works in the vernacular, especially cheaply made educational and religiously themed books, intended for the personal use of the purchaser. Paper, which had become standard in documentary production, was commonplace in continental book production by the section half of the fourteenth century (and by 1400 in England), several decades before the printing press.[12] The *pecia* system, whereby university staff and students would enjoin scribes to copy required texts for use in their courses, saw the relatively rapid production of books, especially if scribes were working with cursive scripts, and using paper as a surface. Some surviving contracts from the University of Paris stipulate the production of at least one leaf a day, but anecdotal evidence suggests that far higher rates of writing were possible, including a report that a student, working from before dawn to shortly before midnight, produced twenty-three leaves of Ovid's *remedia amoris*.[13] Nor were large production runs of individual manuscripts unheard of. The scriptorium of Diebolt Lauber at Hagenau in the fifteenth century produced sufficient copies of German vernacular literature that customers could purchase them from stock.[14]

A good monastic scribe could probably generate, it has been estimated, something on the order of 200 lines, or two to three leaves, of text in a single day; although, in most monastic settings, scribes would not work a full day, given their other in-house obligations. In English Benedictine houses, this might mean five hours a day; at Moissac, a Cluniac house, scribes rarely worked more than three hours a day writing.[15] None of these medieval precursors could compare with the rate of production made possible by the printing press, where a twelve-hour day of work might generate multiple thousand printed sheets. The radical transformation in the speed and volume of book production is an unassailable fact.

The great increase in the volume of printed paper was accompanied by a great diversification of the material. Print created altogether new types of intellectual communities, actual and virtual, and transformed access to

---

[12] Malcolm Parkes, "The literacy of the laity." In David Daiches and Anthony Thorlby, eds., *Literature and Western Civilization*, Vol. 2: *The Mediaeval World* (London: Aldus, 1973), 555–577.
[13] Johan Peter Gumbert, "The speed of scribes." In Emma Condello and Giuseppe de Gregorio, eds., *Scribi e colofoni: le sottoscrizioni di copisti dalle origini all'avento della stampa* (Spoleto: Centro Italiano di Studi sull'Alto Medievo, 1995), 57–69 (here 68). On the *pecia* contracts, see Hugues V. Shooner, "La production du livre par la pecia." In Louis Bataillon, Bertrand Guyot, and Richard Rouse, eds., *La production du livre universitaire au Moyen Âge* (Paris: CNRS, 1988), 17–37.
[14] John Flood, "The printed book as a commercial commodity in the fifteenth and early sixteenth centuries." *Gutenberg Jahrbuch*, 76 (2001), 172–182 (here 174).
[15] Jean Dufour, *La bibliothèque et le scriptorium de Moissac* (Geneva: Librairie Droz, 1972), 35–37. David Knowles, *The Monastic Order in England* (Cambridge: Cambridge University Press, 1950), 450–451.

information, scholarly and otherwise. Printed books, chapbooks, pamphlets, posters and certificates, and a great variety of hybridized forms, became everyday items, part of the fabric of early modern society, especially in urban settings. Put simply – and this is a point of great significance for the themes of this book – the printing press injected huge quantities of information into European society. The medium may not be the message, as suggested by Marshall McLuhan, but the medium of print shaped methods of presentation, distribution, and recombination of information in early modern Europe. It also compelled Europeans to undertake new and different efforts at managing the information issuing forth from the presses.

5.1   Early Print

Roger Chartier has downplayed the print revolution relative to the digital revolution because, he claims, the printing press did not change the medium or the format in which one encountered writing; the container remained the book.[16] Familiar types of book could now be produced in previously unimaginable numbers: clerical handbooks, service books for monasteries, psalters, and books of hours for use in the Church; student grammars, Latin wordbooks, and other texts for practical instruction for use in education. It is unsurprising that intellectuals and scholars, like those cited at the outset of this chapter, would emphasize how the printing press had transformed the world of books they knew so well. But Chartier's argument undervalues the many ways in which the printing press did change the formats in which early modern Europeans encountered the written word (and images, for good measure). Many of the books that the printing presses churned out in no way resembled the familiar forms taken by medieval manuscript books. Cheap handbooks, abridgments of ancient standards, and how-to manuals, generated without a specific patron or customer in mind, were entirely new to the age of print. They were a reflection of a very important change brought about by printing, a fundamental transformation in the relationship between producer and consumer: the latter was now almost always unknown. Only very rarely was a printed book generated for the specific use of a single customer.

What is more, the print revolution was only partially about books. Much, perhaps most, of what came off early modern printing presses was never intended to be bound into a book. As Peter Stallybrass has helpfully reminded us: "printers do not print books. They print sheets of

---

[16] See Roger Chartier, "Languages, books, and reading from the printed word to the digital text." *Critical Inquiry*, 31 (2004), 133–152; and "The printing revolution: a reappraisal." In Sabrina Alcorn Baron, Eric Lindquist, and Eleanor Shevlin, eds., *Agent of Change. Print Culture Studies after Elizabeth L. Eisenstein* (Amherst: University of Massachusetts Press, 2007), 397–408.

paper."[17] A singular focus on books limits the range of the historical gaze and understates the extent of the impact of the printing press. A great many early printed items had no real medieval analogs: pamphlets, corrantoes, broadsides, printed notices and proclamations, bureaucratic forms and documents, single-page devotional images, among many other printed devices. These were novel formats that print had made possible, or at least made immeasurably easier to produce. The market for printed material was much broader and more diverse, in part because books were only a portion of what early printers produced.

Because they survive in such small numbers, especially relative to the massive volumes of them that were produced, it is easy to overlook how important single-page printed instruments were to the early print

5.1 Much of the work of the earliest printing presses was dedicated to the production of cheap, high-volume items. Especially lucrative was the printing of indulgences, like this one printed by Johannes Gutenberg in 1455 (Getty Images).

[17] Peter Stallybrass, "Printing and the manuscript revolution." In Barbie Zelizer, ed., *Explorations in Communication and History* (New York: Routledge, 2008), 111–118 (here 111).

industry. The enormous output of indulgence certificates is a case in point – the great late medieval boom in the preaching of indulgences happened to coincide with the advent of printing. Mid-fifteenth-century indulgence campaigns were among the very first organized efforts to mobilize the potential of the printing press. It is widely known that in 1454–5 Gutenberg suspended his printing of his famous bible in order to pick up a lucrative order to print 2,000 copies of a thirty-nine-line, single-page indulgence.

The press's ability to reproduce identical forms quickly and in profusion was a boon for the indulgence trade. As early as 1455, an indulgence campaign under the name of Paulinus Chappe was employing printed thirty- and thirty-one-line letters of indulgence. Printing houses across Germany, in Cologne, Mainz, Strasbourg, Lübeck, Basel, and Erfurt, became involved in major indulgence campaigns. The Cardinal Raymund Peraudi (1435–1505) oversaw, at the height of his German indulgence campaign of 1488–1490, the production of as many as thirty editions of his single-page indulgence letters, emanating from multiple cities. Some of these editions ran between 5,000 and 20,000 copies.[18] A decade later, in 1499–1500, the printer Johann Luschner printed 142,950 indulgences for the Benedictines at Montserrat.[19] Printers competed tooth and nail for such commissions, as their high volume and relative lack of complexity assured high profit margins.

The likes of Peraudi also mobilized print to publicize their indulgence sales: printed broadsides announcing indulgence campaigns posted in public places became essential means of communication for marketers. Printers would also often produce indulgence catalogs and calendars, as well as sermons, brochures, and guidebooks to churches, relics, and festivals associated with certain indulgences. The growth in the indulgence trade after 1500, which so infuriated Luther, would have been impossible without the printing press, a technology itself closely linked to Luther's revolt.

Indulgences were only one category of low-cost, high-volume items that made the Church such a good client of the earliest printers. Michael Giesecke tells of clerics at Regensburg and Freising in 1487 pouring through hundreds of newly printed missals to make sure that they were

[18] Falk Eisermann, "The indulgence as a media event." In Robert Swanson, ed., *Promissory Notes on the Treasury of Merits: Indulgences in Late Medieval Europe* (Leiden: Brill, 2006), 309–330 – this is a translation and abridgment of "Der Ablass als Medienereignis: Kommunikationswandel durch Einblattdrucke im 15. Jahrhundert; Mit einer Auswahlbibliographie." In Rudolf Suntrup and Jan Veenstra, eds., *Tradition and Innovation in an Era of Change*, Vol. 1 of *Medieval to Early Modern Culture* (Frankfurt: Peter Lang, 2001), 99–128.
[19] Stallybrass, "Printing and the manuscript revolution," 112.

all in fact identical.[20] The Augsburg printer Jodocus Pflanzmann printed a whopping 20,000 certificates of confession (four to be cut from each sheet) for a church in Nördlingen in 1480. It took him six weeks to complete the job.[21] The nature of church business inclined itself to such "jobbing" contracts, which were especially prized by printers.

The higher survival rate of the larger, more expensive editions almost certainly skews the picture we have of the landscape of early print. Of the original 2,520 copies of the famed *Nuremberg Chronicle*, with its elaborate cityscape illustrations, printed in 1493 by Hartmann Schedel in Nuremberg, nearly half, or 1,200, have survived to the current day.[22] Of Gutenberg's famous forty-two-line bible, some forty-nine complete or partial copies survive (out of a print run of perhaps 200). The consensus among scholars now, however, is that the work that Gutenberg chose to print first was Aelius Donatus's *Ars Minor*, which was, by the middle of the fifteenth century, a standard beginner's grammar text. This was short, cheaply produced, and met a built-in market demand; the vast majority of copies were used into extinction.[23] The twenty-four exemplars of this text that survive represent a tiny percentage of a much larger total print run. At about the same time, Gutenberg also printed an edition of the *Sybilline Prophecies*, an ancient poem. All that remains of this printing project is a single postcard-sized fragment discovered in 1892, inside the cover of an account book.[24] Gutenberg, in fact, was chiefly what we would call a "jobbing" printer, most of whose projects were similarly small and inexpensive. His "Admonition to Christendom against the Turks," the oldest surviving dated printed item of any sort (December 1454), was an example of the cheap, breathless *Türkenkalendar*, mass-produced to meet the demand of a reading public anxious for news from the East.

Printing was a commercial concern and presses tended to appear where large quantities of information circulated. Towns that had significant legal, governmental, or educational institutions tended to have more extensive printing facilities. This was evident early on in Italy, with its commitment to written government, its thriving epistolary culture, and its

---

[20] Michael Giesecke, *Der Buchdruck in der frühen Neuzeit. Eine historische Fallstudie über die Durchsetzung neuer Informations- und Kommunikationstechnologien* (Frankfurt: Suhrkamp, 1991), 145.
[21] Flood, "The printed book as a commercial commodity," 173.
[22] Andrew Pettegree, *The Book in the Renaissance* (New Haven, CT: Yale University Press, 2010), 42.
[23] Wolfgang Schmitt, "Die Ianua (Donatus): Ein Beitrag zur lateinischen Schulgrammatik des Mittelalters und der Renaissance." *Beiträge zur Inkunabelkunde*, dritte Folge, 4 (1969), 43–80.
[24] John Man, *The Gutenberg Revolution. How Printing Changed the Course of History* (New York: Random House, 2010), 155–156.

large ecclesiastical footprint. The best estimates are that between 36 and 44 percent of all incunabula were of Italian origin.[25] These numbers do not include the copious editions of placards, posters, pamphlets and indulgence certificates that have disappeared without a trace. Venice, in particular, soon emerged as a major printing hub, such that, by 1471, one-third of all the printed books produced in Europe emanated from Venice.[26] By the sixteenth century, more than 100 Italian towns had printing presses. In the last two decades of the fifteenth century, the printing press became a commonplace in towns across northern Italy, the Rhineland, and Low Countries. By the early sixteenth century, all the major cities of Western Europe had printing presses, with Venice, Paris, and Lyons as the leading centers. In the decades that followed, German printing underwent rapid expansion. The British Library's *Short title catalogue of Books printed in Germany up to 1600* shows 150 distinct German and Austrian towns with publishing or printing activities. For Italy, the number was 130 locales.

A great deal of the work on these early printing presses was directed toward the fulfilment of orders for relatively simple, inexpensive printed instruments. Because paper constituted at least half of the total cost of production, selling large numbers of such slight volumes offered considerably higher profit margins. A well-organized printshop could churn out 500 copies of an eight-page pamphlet per day. Uwe Neddermayer has calculated that nearly half a million copies of 661 separate editions of student grammars were produced in the Holy Roman Empire alone *before* the year 1500.[27] As with indulgences, it is likely that there are no remnants of hundreds of these earliest editions and their existence thus remains unknown to us. This is despite the fact that they were printed in press runs that might number in the thousands. Stocks of scholarly books might last for years, while cheap items like these were priced to move. The Augsburg bookseller George Willer (1514–1594), famed for his catalogs of the Frankfurt Book Fair, ordered 22,000 calendars in a single year. Publishers not infrequently followed the publication of an expensive, heavily illustrated Latin text, likely to sell in small numbers to a select clientele, with short vernacular editions in order to recoup their investment. Tessa Watt has estimated that the survival rate for sixteenth-century English ballads is one in every 10,000 copies printed, or one

---

[25] Philippe Nieto, "Géographie des impressions européennes du XVe siècle." *Revue française d'histoire du livre*, 118–121 (2003), 125–173.
[26] Pettegree, *The Book in the Renaissance*, 54.
[27] Uwe Neddermeyer, *Von der Handschrift zum gedruckten Buch. Schriftlichkeit und Leseinteresse im Mittelalter und in der frühen Neuzeit. Quantitative und qualitative Aspekte* (Wiesbaden: Harrassowitz Verlag, 1998), II, 794.

exemplar of every ten editions.[28] In the sixteenth century, grammar school students in Germany could purchase inexpensive printed pages that included reading exercises that could be hung up in the home or in the schoolhouse – virtually none have survived.

Books, too, surprisingly early on, came to cater to a more popular, more cost-conscious clientele. Although many of the books to come off the printing press in its earliest decades were produced for narrow, learned audiences, such as the Church, it did not take long for printers to recognize the potential diversity of the book-buying public. It has been estimated that as much as one-third of incunabula printed in Italy were in the vernacular – most of these were popular, religious works: devotionals, prayer books, and other works of piety. Again, few have survived.[29] The printing press may have been a boon to scholars and churchmen, but it also put books into the hands of those outside the traditional reading cadres. The *Flugschriften* (literally, 'flying writings') that did so much to publicize the person and ideas of Martin Luther after his revolt against the Catholic Church were among the most famous examples of such rapidly produced, inexpensive items, often replete with provocative illustrations. Both by and about Luther, these circulated in the hundreds of thousands in the 1520s, playing a vital role in the creation of what Andrew Pettegree has called "Brand Luther," one of Europe's first multimedia campaigns. Luther became the most famous man in Germany, even though he almost never left Wittenberg. In the 1520s, there was a veritable "pamphlet war" between Luther and his opponents, as friendly printers saturated the market, confident that their publications would be snapped up by eager partisans. In the period 1520–1525 alone, printers churned out more than 7,000 editions of *Flugschriften*. Figures tabulated by Pettegree suggest that, by 1522, Luther's German-language works had already been published in 828 separate editions; by the end of that decade, there would be 1,245 more, for a grand total of about two million distinct copies.[30] Luther's Small Catechism, in particular, proved to be an extremely flexible printed product. It was printed as a short book, but publishers also released versions in the form of wall charts and school texts. It appeared in German and Latin, but also in French, Dutch, and Danish translations.

[28] Tessa Watt, *Cheap Print and Popular Piety* (Cambridge: Cambridge University Press, 1991), 141.
[29] Ann Schutte, "Printing, piety and the people in Italy: the first thirty years." *Archiv für Reformationsgeschichte*, 71 (1980–1), 5–19; Lotte Hellinga, "The Gutenberg revolutions." In Simon Eliot and Jonathan Rose, eds., *A Companion to the History of the Book* (Oxford: Blackwell, 2003), 207–219.
[30] Andrew Pettegree, *Brand Luther: 1517, Printing and the Making of the Reformation* (New York: Penguin, 2015), 144.

Flugschriften were appealing to printers chiefly because they used, relative to most editions, so little paper. The competencies that printers employed in early ecclesiastical "jobbing" they could easily apply to other forms of publication. By the beginning of the sixteenth century, woodcut illustrations were common in print publications, and were especially well suited for short, sensational items intended for a popular audience – a great many of the *Flugschriften* dealing with Reformation controversies would include them, thus transmitting visual information in tandem with the textual.

Particularly revealing of the emerging and shifting emphases of the market for print around the turn of the sixteenth century is the five-decade career (1482–1532) of the Strasbourg printer Johann Grüninger (1455–1533). During that time, Grüninger produced more than 500 editions of immense diversity, including religious, humanist, legal, and scientific works, as well as popular literature such as practical handbooks and news pamphlets covering the controversies of the day. His output was made up by works in both Latin and German, by historical and contemporary authors. The nature of his publications, however, changed over time, and closely reflected the changing market. Initially, in the 1480s, Grüninger focused on religious texts almost exclusively, including Latin and German bibles, collections of sermons, the *Speculum vitae Christi* of Ludolf of Saxony, and high-volume contracts to print breviaries for the Church. By the second decade of the sixteenth century, while he continued to publish in Latin (especially medical texts), Grüninger focused far more on works in the vernacular. By 1520, Grüninger was tapping into the Reformation controversies and published both pro- and anti-Lutheran tracts. This trajectory shows a printer keenly aware of the shifting tastes of the public, adapting his output accordingly.[31]

As the book trade came of age in the sixteenth century, the variety of works published expanded and books began to assume distinctive (and often regional) looks and formats, as publishers were now less concerned with producing editions that looked like their manuscript forbears, and introduced features unique to printed books, such as tables of content, indices, and paratextual sections such as introductions, prologues, and dedications. Printers continued to produce older, traditional texts, which circulated in ever greater numbers, but also sought to explore the potential of the medium. Gradually, the market for print underwent

---

[31] Jacqueline Daillon, "Jean Grüninger, imprimeur-éditeur à Strasbourg." *Arts et métiers graphiques*, 65 (1938), 41–46; Jürgen Schulz-Grobert, *Das Straßburger Eulenspiegelbuch: Studien zu enstehungsgeschictlichen Voraussetzungen der ältesten Drucküberlieferung* (Tübingen: De Gruyter, 1999), 77–109.

segmentation, with different editions and formats aimed at different purchasing publics, and publishers carving out expertise in particular types of texts. Deluxe, large-format editions of ancient and patristic authors, often ringed by extensive commentaries, were paralleled by popular editions of the most sought-after classical works by the likes of Cicero, Virgil, and Terence. Similarly, reference works that sought to provide expurgated access to classical learning, such as the *Adagia* of Erasmus, first published in 1500, were produced in print runs that ran into the thousands.

Items such as these were essential transmitters of information from and about the ancient world, reaching a broad early modern reading public, beyond those in the rarified air of humanist scholarship. There was, in the second century of print, a vast effort at *translatio studiorum*, which saw the bequest of antiquity rendered in common languages. This broad effort to translate the chief works of antiquity widened the channels of information about the ancient world flowing into early modern society. One of the more provocative contentions of Elizabeth Eisenstein's print revolution was that it made the Renaissance of early modern Europe "permanent," marking a fundamental difference from the previous Carolingian and twelfth-century renaissances. The works of the ancients were now in private studies, classrooms, and the pockets of lay readers, and were unlikely ever to be lost again. This is suggestive of the genuinely revolutionary transformations in both permanence and access made possible by print.

5.2   The Maturation of the Market

As the market for print matured in the course of the sixteenth century, an increasing proportion of production was of vernacular literature, including condensed versions of popular tales that might run to only ten or twelve leaves. How-to literature, in both Latin and the vernacular, became extremely popular, especially in Italy, catering to a book-buying public of the middle orders of society. Printers also responded to broad demand for pamphlets, posters, newssheets, almanacs, and printed icons, which were produced in incalculable numbers, each print run injecting more and more paper into everyday life.

Printers and sellers had to manage a central tension: how to take advantage of the relatively low marginal cost of each additional copy of an item printed or ordered, while avoiding being left with unwanted stock. A notarized inventory of a printer's workshop in Milan from 1570 suggests that access to popular printed items such as broadsides, calendars, schoolbooks, catechisms, and other religious pamphlets was extremely widespread and that these items circulated in very large numbers in the sixteenth century. The stationer Girardone focused especially on works used regularly in local schools, convents, and confraternities; these were likely to be reliably salable. Students in Italy's many private and communal schools regularly purchased basic ABCs, alphabet tables, grammar primers, and elementary math manuals, and Girardone clearly sold a great many of these: he had more than 3,000 schoolbooks in his 1570 inventory. He also carried a huge stock of single-sheet religious images, including 2,250 copies of the Passion alone. There was plenty of secular material as well, from astrological calendars to recipe books to a variety of how-to manuals. He also sold many playing cards (printed on heavier paper), along with treatises on how to play them.[32]

Print injected written information into European society across a broad spectrum. Few Europeans built up large, personal libraries, but many of them acquired inexpensive printed items from a printing industry that recognized in them vital components of a lucrative market. Both stationers and booksellers sold a range of things related to writing: blank paper, ink, and notebooks.[33] This is an indication of widespread written literacy and regular recourse to writing. Full, functional literacy may have remained rare in the sixteenth century, but it was a skill shared by a growing minority of European men and women.[34] Printing meant, among other things, that there was more writing about, visible in public, to be read, shared, or heard.

The printing press transformed the business of the book, creating altogether new structures and pathways for the production, sale, and distribution of books. Initially, the distribution of printed books was reliant on the existing business structures of the stationers and their guilds and sets of privilege. But once print had established itself, it moved outside the confined markets of the Church, universities, and legal institutions, and expanded to meet the multiple nodes of demand across European society. The emergence of the bookfairs is a good illustration of this. Especially in the first century and a half of print, these were essential events for the marketing, sale, and exchange of books. Lyons

---

[32] Kevin Stevens, "Vincenzo Girardone and the popular press in Counter-reformation Milan: a case study (1570)." *Sixteenth Century Journal*, 26.3 (1995), 639–659.

[33] Megan K. Williams, "The apothecary, the secretary, and the diplomat: apothecaries as purveyors of paper, ink, and information." Paper delivered as part of the panel, "Paper as a Material Artifact of Governance and Trade, 1500–1800," Renaissance Society of America Annual Convention, Berlin, March 26, 2015.

[34] Two works that suggest a high level of literacy include David Cressy, *Literacy and the Social Order, Reading and Writing in Tudor and Stuart England* (Cambridge: Cambridge University Press, 1980); and Sara Nalle, "Literacy and culture in early modern Castile." *Past and Present*, 25 (1989), 74–98.

had established a bookfair decades before the printing press. Antwerp had one by the end of the fifteenth century. The most important of the fairs by far, however, was the Frankfurt Book Fair, the economic footprint of which was significant enough to drive the schedule and output of printers across Europe. Some sort of book exchange had been present in Frankfurt since the thirteenth century, but it was only with the advent of print that it became a major event, international in its notoriety. Prefaces to early modern printed books often made mention of the Fair, even apologizing for errors that might have slipped into the text as printers scurried to get a book out in time for the Fair. In 1522, the Zürich publisher Christoph Froschauer (1490–1564) famously transgressed Lenten prohibitions on eating meat by feeding his workers sausages in his printshop, indirectly leading to the Zwinglian Reformation, in his efforts to get printing projects done in time for Frankfurt. In 1530, Erasmus found himself overburdened with work as he sought to produce new texts before Frankfurt, and his publisher in Basel, Froben, operated six presses day and night in order to get them all in print.

An event on the scale of the Frankfurt Fair could not have existed without the printing press; the Fair began meeting twice yearly in 1485. It depended on volume and variety, an economy of scale and choice. It became an essential rendezvous for publishers, book dealers, and sellers. So many books were there assembled, Henri Estienne suggested, that a fair-goer could, in a single visit, procure a library on par with the celebrated princes of antiquity. In 1611, the Englishman Thomas Coryatt (1577–1617) said that Frankfurt brought together an array of books that "surpassed ... literally anything I have ever seen on my travels, by so much that it seemed to me to be the epitome of all the most significant collections in Europe."[35] In the 1610s, an average of 1,000 new Latin publications were appearing at Frankfurt yearly.

The Frankfurt Book fair gave tangible, physical form to the brave new world of abundant printed books.[36] The trade in books, especially those in the *lingua franca* of Latin, was genuinely pan-European. Books were not terribly unlike commodities, traveling between regions according to a calculus of local supply and demand. And, like commodities, books became more impersonal objects, produced for a market instead of a specific patron or owner in mind.

It is interesting to note that the word in German for "publisher" is *Verlag*, which literally means "money man," the individual who laid out

---

[35] Quoted in Peter Weidhaas, *A History of the Frankfurt Book Fair*. Trans. and ed. by Carolyn Gossage and W. Aldis Wright (Toronto: Dundurn Press, 2007), 63.

[36] Alexander Marr, "A Renaissance library rediscovered: the "Repertorium librorum Mathematica" of Jean I du Temps." *The Library: the Transactions of the Bibliographical Society*, 9.4 (2008), 428–470.

the necessary funds to finance the printing. Printshops were media companies, responding to perceived needs and filling market niches. Much, perhaps most, of what was printed was what was expected to turn a profit. This calculus privileged information of certain types and formats. Producers ranged in scale from the print "factory" of Christophe Plantin (1520–1589) in Antwerp, which employed as many as 150 people to run its presses, to countless (and often nameless to history) small shops that churned out printed items of fathomless variety and quality. Few publishers were involved only in the publishing aspects of the book trade and some assumed an array of informational roles. Some acted as printers for the texts of other publishers, acted as booksellers in their own right, served as postal agents or moneychangers, or as hosts and patrons for scholars.[37] In the early sixteenth century, an especially important figure in the European book trade was the *marchand libraire*, literally the "merchant-bookseller." They chose the projects to pursue, arranged the financing, and oversaw the printing process, if not always carrying it out themselves. Among the better known examples are the Giunti family in Florence and Jean Petit in Paris. Individual, small-scale booksellers often specialized in certain categories of items. Sellers of scholarly books often set up shop across the street from law schools and universities. In Paris, for example, Simon Vostre, at his shop on the rue Neuve-Nostre-Dame, focused on the sale of books of hours.[38]

As in the life story of other media, as books and other printed materials became part of the daily fabric of European society, the formats, modes of sale, and channels of distribution became increasingly diverse. Like so many other products that sell at a variety of price points, many different types of sellers ended up plying their trade. Few vendors sold the whole gamut of printed materials, so many niches of supply emerged. In 1678, representatives of the Amsterdam booksellers guild sent a request to the city authorities asking that they take action against peddlers, who were "too lazy to work" and had resorted to hawking books, newspapers, and printed libels on the streets, products that guilds did not have.[39] By the second half of the seventeenth century,

---

[37] Ian Maclean, "The market for scholarly books and conceptions of genre in Northern Europe, 1570–1630." In Georg Kaufmann, ed., *Die Renaissance im Blick der Nationen Europas* (Wiesbaden: Harrassowitz, 1991), 17–31 (here 20–21).

[38] David Shaw, "The book trade comes of age: the sixteenth century." In Eliot and Rose, eds., *Companion*, 220–231 (here 230).

[39] Roeland Harms, Joad Raymond, and Jeroen Salman, "Introduction: the distribution and dissemination of popular print." In Harms, Raymond, and Salman, eds., *Not Dead Things. The Dissemination of Popular Print in England and Wales, Italy and the Low Countries, 1500–1820* (Leiden: Brill, 2013), 1–30 (here 9).

there was a genuine market for information, segmented by producers and consumers.

The landscape of religious publishing is illustrative. The Church, which needed service books, specialist theological and legal texts, missals, preaching manuals, books of hours, as well as indulgence certificates by the thousands, generated huge volumes of printed material. After the Council of Trent, new liturgies and position statements required the reprinting of old service books, as well as the composition of new ones. Trent's reiteration of the role of saints contributed to a surge of printed hagiographic literature and of single-sheet depictions of favorite saints, in what was known as the "century of saints." The religious controversies of the sixteenth century created new market niches for religious publications, and not just among Protestants, who snatched up vernacular Bibles, psalters, prayer books, and polemics. Catholics, too, printed works in great numbers for both lay and clerical readers. Religious polemic on both sides remained an important component of printed output into the era of confessionalization.

The volume of print production continued to increase into the seventeenth century, but regional differences become evident, generally reflecting the intensity of regional economic activity. As commercial products, books traveled along the same trading circuits that connected markets with each other, often stored and shipped in barrels alongside other goods.[40] Printing would see exponential gains in England after the removal of government censorship in 1695; a Printing Act introduced by the Crown in 1662 had sought to limit the number of master printers in England to twenty-four, but by 1705, there were seventy operating in London alone! Dror Wahrman has described the takeoff in English printing in the second half of the seventeenth century as "Print 2.0," whereby the proliferation of printed items in England, many associated with the political upheavals of the Civil War and then the Glorious Revolution, made print "new" to a great many people.[41]

By the final decades of the seventeenth century, in many parts of Europe, print played an important role in creating a crowded media environment where the written world might be accessed in manifold formats, now including newspapers, learned journals, and other periodical publications. The oldest learned journal was the French *Journal des savants*, edited by Denis de Sallo and published for the first time in 1665. Similar literary journals appeared in Italy in 1668 (*Giornale dei letterati*)

---

[40] James Raven, "Selling books across Europe, c. 1450–1800. An overview." *Publishing History*, 34 (1993), 5–19.
[41] Dror Wahrman, *Mr. Collier's Letter Racks. A Tale of Art & Illusion at the Threshold of the Modern Information Age* (Oxford: Oxford University Press, 2012).

and in Germany in 1682 (*Acta eruditorum*).[42] A great array of scientific and literary periodicals, the bulk of them in the vernacular, began to appear in many parts of Europe. Books had also assumed many of the forms familiar to us today, including novels. These developments were essential in creating the preconditions for what Rolf Engelsing has called the *Lesenrevolution* of the eighteenth century, by which time a mass national and international trade in books, linked to a reading public based in urban formations, had become a reality.

The print revolution, too, offered new ways of transmitting visual information. Woodcuts and engravings became common features of printed books, and the inclusion of illustrations and maps a selling point for publishers. Print allowed unprecedented reproduction of visual depictions of people, places, things, and ideas. This capacity could have important consequences. In the creation of "Brand Luther" described earlier, one of the most telling pieces of information that circulated across Germany about Luther was his visage. Potentially sympathetic individuals across Germany could easily put a face with a name, as Lucas Cranach's (1472–1533) depictions of Luther circulated widely. Luther became one of the most recognizable faces in European history up to that point, in a world before photographs, film, and video.

The transmission of visual information in printed form remained for some time, however, experimental and unreliable. Images and text often did not work seamlessly with one another – they were rarely composed by the same person and author and illustrator might work at cross-purposes. Printers often took stock images and redeployed them for various purposes. Illustrations were expensive, and complicated the typesetting and order of the text. But as the print industry matured, the use of illustrations was synchronized with the textual content, particularly in disciplines where the visual representation of reality was deemed epistemologically important. This was especially the case in the realm of natural history, where the waxing authority of the observational ethic supported the marshalling of arguments that were visual as well as textual, overturning long-influential arguments about the epistemological value of images by Aristotle, Pliny, and Galen. The works of Leonhard Fuchs (1501–1566) on botany, Conrad Gessner (1516–1565) on zoology, Andreas Vesalius (1514–1564) on anatomy, and Galileo Galilei (1564–1642) on astronomy, all evince a complementary relationship between text and image, where visual information is understood to be demonstrative and persuasive evidence. The advent of instruments such as the telescope and

---

[42] Rietje van Vliet, "Print and public in Europe 1600–1800." In Eliot and Rose, eds., *A Companion*, 247–257.

microscope, which related truths exclusively in a language of images, made the inclusion of visual information even more essential. Medical students and their professors, for example, now had access to more detailed and elaborate anatomical prints, including the so-called "fugitive sheets," which were printed sheets of the human form with lift-up flaps to reveal the structures beneath.[43] This systematic use of images in scientific treatises bolstered the growing conviction that the use of images, as a fruit of observation, was a key component of the effective reading of the books of nature.[44]

The scientific images in scholarly treatises and depictions of saints in cheap print are reminders that this remained a multimedia culture, one that found meaning in image as much as it did in text. Images remained essential conveyors of meaning to both the non- and semi-literate and to learned milieus that increasingly recognized the authority of observation. Print was thus multipronged in its delivery of information.

5.3 The Abundance of Books and the Expansion of Libraries

For early modern readers, by far the most obvious impact of the print revolution was the sheer number of books there now were. For the first time, a technology was available that made it possible for individuals to own more books than they could read. One set of estimates has put the number of manuscript books produced in Western Europe in the twelfth century at 769,000, rising to 1.761 million in the thirteenth, 2.746 million in the fourteenth, and 4.999 million in the fifteenth. Before the advent of print, urban institutions such as universities "had taken over the role as the main engines of the process of manuscript production in the Latin West," replacing monastic scriptoria.[45] Practices such as the *pecia* system, whereby a single manuscript was copied several times in short order by scribal professionals, combined with the availability of inexpensive paper, allowed the large-scale reproduction of books.

The most important effective truth in all this was that the technology of the printing press meant a great many more books in circulation. An estimate of five million manuscripts produced in Western Europe in the fifteenth century, became 12.56 million printed books for the period 1454–1500, 215.9 million for the sixteenth century, and 518.64 million

---

[43] Mary Lindemann, *Medicine and Society in Early Modern Europe* (Cambridge: Cambridge University Press, 2010), 143.
[44] On this, see especially Kusukawa, *Picturing the Book of Nature*.
[45] Eltjo Buringh, "The role of cities in medieval book production: quantitative analyses." In Marco Mostert and Anna Adamska, eds., *Uses of the Written Word in Medieval Towns* (Turnhout, Belgium: Brepols, 2014), 119–177 (here 149).

for the seventeenth century.[46] The printing press was not the sole reason for this spectacular rate of increase – growing prosperity, urbanization, and literacy all played a role – but these numbers suggest, quite simply, an altogether different world of books.

Both the abundance and the variety of books available were unprecedented. Books were now products, printers were producers, and readers were consumers, both of the physical item of the book and of the information that it contained. As it became immeasurably easier for individuals to seek out and acquire books, so too did it become possible for them to establish collections of their own. Institutional and personal libraries grew in size and scope as a matter of course. Our picture of the books that filled these collections is necessarily incomplete. Only a very small sample, perhaps fewer than 1 percent, of the books printed in the first century of print survive today. Some categories of books may have disappeared entirely, especially as individuals and libraries had a tendency to keep the same sorts of books.[47] It was now possible for an individual, should they have the means, to acquire more books than he or she could profitably read. Early modern scholars, librarians, and archivists now had to contend with the sheer volume of books, and the circulation, organization, and use of the information they contained.

Early modern scholars, antiquarians, and librarians were well aware of the brave new world of publishing in which they lived and frequently remarked on the immense profusion of books, which they acknowledged with enthusiastic praise but also with great bewilderment. The anxiety was especially evident from the mid-sixteenth century forward, when the infrastructure of print was sufficient to produce a volume of books (and hence information) that defied efforts to encompass it.[48] The abundance of books was widely remarked upon, with wonder and appreciation, to be sure, but also with wariness and suspicion. "So many books are being printed now/There's not a soul but boasts he is a sage!," the peasant Barrildo explains in Lope de Vega's play *Fuenteovejuna* (1614), which was actually set in the year 1476. Tellingly, Vega has a student from the University of Salamanca – who, unlike Barrildo, lives in the world of books – respond: "It seems to me they know less than before/Because the great excess of books creates/Confusion in the minds of readers

---

[46] Eltjo Buringh and Jan Luiten Van Zanden, "Charting the "Rise of the West": manuscripts and printed books in Europe, a long-term perspective from the sixth through eighteenth centuries." *Journal of Economic History*, 69.2 (2009), 409–445 (here 417).
[47] A point made by Eugenio Garin, *L'educazione in Europa, 1400–1600: Problemi e Programmi* (Bari: Laterza, 1957), 15–16.
[48] This is a periodization proposed by McKitterick, *Print, Manuscript and the Search for Order*.

now ... the world got on without it very well/For many centuries and this one/there is no St Jerome or Augustine."[49]

Scholarship was transformed by the availability of printed books, which now accumulated in the libraries of scholars, and which Alexander Pope described as "a scourge for the sins of the learned," away from monasteries and courts. In 1627, George Hakewill (1578–1649), looking back over a century of print, saw the press as redeeming books from their "bondage" in monastic libraries.[50] Some of the libraries of individual humanists, scholars, and professionals came to dwarf the collections of even the largest monastic repositories. In keeping with the spirit of Renaissance humanism, scholars were deeply interested in preserving the information passed down from antiquity and responded by "stockpiling it, by sharing it, with others in manuscript and print, and by encouraging the foundation of great libraries by wealthy princes and patrons."[51] The nature and loci of libraries thus changed significantly, and the venues for information exchange through books correspondingly expanded.

Broad-based private access to large numbers of books had important ramifications for the approaches to education in early modern Europe. Humanist educators in the fifteenth century, like Vittorino da Feltre (1378–1446) and Guarino da Verona (1374–1460), had focused their curricula on a relatively small number of texts and their lectures on word-by-word exegesis of these works, and the linguistic lessons they could yield. The focus was on a narrow range of texts that were rare and expensive, and dependent on the teacher imparting information to the students.

The underlying assumptions that informed this approach evaporated with the advent of print. Organization and distillation of knowledge now became more important than in the pre-print world. Encyclopedic works that gathered together the essential knowledge from ancient texts stood in for recitation by a master teacher. Because books were now far easier to come by, dictation, the spoken word, and in-class close reading were less imperative. Students of means could now assemble libraries of their own, something exceedingly rare in the age before print. Reading expectations focused on breadth more than depth, and the intellectual practices and paper instruments of learning emphasized the location, organization, and categorization of knowledge garnered from reading. These were the emphases of educational strategies developed by the likes of Petrus

---

[49] Cited in Roger Chartier, "Languages, books, and reading," 140.
[50] Julia Crick and Alexandra Walsham, "Introduction: script, print and history." In Crick and Walsham, eds., *The Uses of Script and Print 1300–1700* (Cambridge: Cambridge University Press, 2004), 1–26 (here 1).
[51] Ann Blair, *Too Much to Know* (New Haven, CT: Yale University Press, 2010), 22.

Ramus (1515–1572), who subjected the greatly expanded world of knowledge to speciation and classification.[52] The greater availability of books due to print made Ramist educational approaches appealing because teachers could assume access to, and familiarity with, a broader array of texts, and thus focus on ideas and themes that recurred across authors and texts.

Although sizable private libraries did exist in the age before print, in general medieval libraries were vanishingly small by comparison to early modern ones. As books became more widely available, the social role of libraries as displays of wealth and prestige declined. They ceased to be baubles of cultural exclusivity. In the fifteenth century, at least, some prominent collectors continued to insist on stocking their libraries with manuscript books, most famously the King of Hungary, Matthias Corvinus (r. 1458–1490), and Duke Federico da Montefeltro (r. 1444–1482) in Urbino.[53] Such resistance, however, was patchy and, ultimately, short-lived, even among curators of monastic libraries, who soon took interest in the new technology and sought to employ it to enhance their own holdings and serve the interests of their scholarly communities.[54] Institutions and collectors were more than happy to add printed books to their manuscript collections, even in some cases binding them together. That being said, over time the emergence of print meant the disappearance of massive numbers of manuscripts, many of them repurposed for other uses or disposed of altogether, deemed inferior to the slick, new print version. It is impossible to gauge with any precision how much was lost. Manuscript books from the Middle Ages that had been the focus of regular use now assumed a very different status, either as redundant or as the object of an antiquarian bibliophilia.

Book ownership underwent profound changes, both in the type of books owned and in the people who owned them. Henri-Jean Martin has studied book ownership in Valencia for the period 1474–1550 and found that nine out of ten ecclesiastics owned a book, three-quarters of all professionals, one-half of aristocrats, one-third of all merchants, one-seventh of textile workers, and one-tenth of manual workers.[55]

---

[52] See Anthony Grafton and Lisa Jardine, *From Humanism to the Humanities: Education and the Liberal Arts in Fifteenth and Sixteenth-Century Europe* (Cambridge, MA: Harvard University Press, 1986).

[53] Andrew Pettegree, "The Renaissance library and the challenge of print." In Alice Crawford, ed., *The Meaning of the Library* (Princeton: Princeton University Press, 2015), 72–90.

[54] Barbara Halpoer, "Libraries and printers in the fifteenth century." *The Journal of Library History*, 16.1 (1981), 134–142 (here 139–140).

[55] Henri-Jean Martin, *The History and Power of Writing* (Chicago: Chicago University Press, 1994), 347.

Numbers such as these were considerably less weighted toward clerics in the century that followed. One estimate suggests that private libraries increased tenfold in size in the early modern period.[56] Even then, it is likely that we underestimate the number of books in private ownership in early modern Europe, because many of these books (and in some cases, entire collections) eventually ended up in institutional libraries as a purchase or bequest following the death of the original owner, thus obscuring initial ownership.

Individuals established these large libraries for a variety of reasons. Some built them as utilitarian repositories for their scholarship or polemicizing. Members of the professions, especially lawyers and doctors, assembled them as a professional resource. Nobles might regard them as a treasure or ornament for their residence, or as a totem that would associate them with wisdom and learning. Princes had both the resources and inclination to expand their libraries, as both reservoirs of knowledge and expressions of power and authority. Duke Albrecht V of Bavaria, for example, during the years of his reign (1550–1579) built up a library of more than 11,000 volumes from almost nothing, purchasing books and acquiring other collections, including that of Johann Jakob Fugger (1516–1575), for which he paid 50,000 florins, as well as that of his uncle, Ernst.[57] His was the second largest in all of Germany, trailing only the imperial library in Vienna.

Private libraries served as important nodes in the information networks that emerged between scholars in the early modern Republic of Letters.[58] Especially in the period after 1500, humanists, exploiting the vistas of knowledge that the printing press had opened up, acquired for themselves printed versions of both modern and classical works. The riches of the monastic or university library relocated away from those institutional halls to the intimate confines of the personal study.

The personal libraries of prominent and well connected scholars could grow very large indeed. The Swiss humanist, reformer, and polymath Joachim Vadian (1484–1551) acquired a library that at its height numbered 1,200 volumes. Michel de Montaigne (1533–1592) was complaining

---

[56] Ann Blair, "Organizations of knowledge." In James Hankins, ed., *The Cambridge Companion to Renaissance Philosophy* (Cambridge: Cambridge University Press, 2007), 287–305 (here 297).

[57] Otto Hartig, *Die Gründung der Münchener Hofbibliothek durch Albrecht V. und Johann Jakob Fugger* (Munich: Verlag der Königlich-Bayerischen Akademie der Wissenschaften, 1917); Felix Strauss, "The 'Liberey' of Duke Ernst of Bavaria (1500–1560)." *Studies in the Renaissance*, 8 (1961), 128–143.

[58] An opposing view on the role of private libraries, that they were "not involved in that network of relations through which sixteenth-century French intellectual elites disseminated knowledge across space," is offered in Adi Ophir, "A place of knowledge: the library of Michel de Montaigne." *Science in Context*, 4, 1 (1991), 163–189 (here 184).

that he could not possibly familiarize himself with more than a thousand books on the shelves of his own library. The posthumous inventory of the books of the French humanist and philologer Isaac Casaubon (1559–1614), widely considered to be Europe's most well-read man, recorded a collection of 2,050 printed books, 1,200 of which he had with him in London and another 850 that he had left in Paris.[59] Casaubon employed literary agents in his pursuit of titles he desired, and consulted Gessner's *Bibliotheca universalis*, and a variety of catalogs, including those of the Frankfurt Book Fair. In some cases, Casaubon purchased multiple copies of the same book, filling them with notes from separate readings, a practice that would have been unthinkable in the age before print. Most of his books were festooned with his copious notes, memoranda, key words, and intratextual references. His library was thus a resource, a database to be used as much as read.[60]

Casaubon's Italian contemporary, the humanist, botanist, and mentor of Galileo, Gian Vicenzo Pinelli (1535–1601), was an even more omnivorous bibliophile. His library contained upwards of 10,000 books, in print and manuscript, but also masses of additional handwritten material, including lessons from professors at the University of Padua, reams of his correspondence, copies of catalogs from libraries, sketches and drawings, collections of recipes, genealogical tables, bibliographies, travelogues, and even rough drafts of works written by others.[61] He also collected an enormous number of *avisi*, the handwritten news pamphlets produced in profusion in Italy in the sixteenth century, which he organized for ease of consultation[62] Pinelli filled numerous notebooks with observations from his reading and correspondence and covered his books with annotations. Acquaintances, Galileo among them, regularly came to Pinelli's library to read them. Pinelli sought news from correspondents near and far and collected parcels of news as *scritture*, which he organized into subject-based dossiers, indexed by numerical and alphabetical notation. Pinelli was thus an information aggregator, organizer, and manager. Pinelli's library became, in concentration, the very picture of the early modern secular scriptorium.[63] Perhaps what is most striking

---

[59] Thomas Anthony Birrell, "The reconstruction of the library of Isaac Casaubon," in Arnold Croiset van Uchelen, ed., *Hellinga Festschrift. Feestbundel: Forty-Three Studies in Bibliography to Prof. Wytze Hellinga on the occasion of his retirement from the Chair of Neophilology in the University of Amsterdam at the end of the Year 1978* (Amsterdam: Nico Israël, 1980), 59–69.
[60] Mark Pattison, *Isaac Casaubon, 1559–1614* (London: Longmans, 1875), 429.
[61] Angela Nuovo, "Manuscript writings on politics and current affairs in the collection of Gian Vincenzo Pinelli (1535–1601)." *Italian Studies*, 66.2 (2011), 193–205.
[62] The Biblioteca Ambrosiana acquired the collection of *avisi* upon Pinelli's death.
[63] Nuovo, "Gian Vincenzo Pinelli," 196.

about this concentration of information in the collection of Pinelli is that he was a notorious homebody; he never traveled himself. The case of Pinelli is eloquent testimony to the manifold ways in which information circulated in sixteenth-century Italy. Pinelli displayed "a lifelong habit of retaining every useful scrap of paper" and embraced an encyclopedic approach to learning that the new media landscape of paperwork and print had made possible.[64]

Isaac Casaubon's friend and fellow bibliophile, Jacque-Auguste de Thou (1553–1617), possessed an even larger private library, perhaps the largest in all of Europe at the time.[65] De Thou was part of a number of paper sodalities, as he was among the foremost figures of the network of relations that made up the seventeenth-century Republic of Letters, in which he exchanged correspondence and books with the likes of Casaubon, Justus Lipsius (1547–1606), and Joseph Scaliger. His personal connections and his many travels augmented his library, which appears to have grown as large as 9,000 books during his lifetime, reaching 13,000 volumes under the stewardship of his son. The content reflects de Thou's efforts to create an up-to-date research library, more humanist than legal, with history, belles-lettres, theology, and science particularly well represented in its contents. De Thou's project, continued by his son, is a monument to what over a century of print had made possible, a late humanist effort to bring together the far fields of learning that were now captured in printed books.

These libraries were often more than just places for storage and contemplative retreat; they were also important nodes for cultural exchange. In the early modern *respublica litterarum*, such "private" libraries were just as likely to be loci of sharing, where reading might take place physically in the presence of others or virtually through the exchange of correspondence. The exchange of books and other materials found in these libraries traced a sort of information road map of the Republic of Letters.[66]

Doctors and lawyers, too, immersed themselves in the printed word and accumulated large personal book collections from the sixteenth

---

[64] Marcella Grendler, "Book collecting in Counter-Reformation Italy: the library of Gian Vincenzo Pinelli (1535–1601)." *Journal of Library History*, 16.1 (1981), 143–151 (here 147).
[65] Antoine Coron, "*Ut posint aliis*: Jacque Auguste de Thou et sa bibliothèque." In *Histoire des bibliothèques françaises*. Tome II: *Les bibliothèques sous l'Ancien Régime, 1530–1789* (Paris: Promodis – Éditions du Cercle, 1988), 100–125; Anna Maria Raugei, "Deux collections humanistes: la bibliothèque de Thou et la bibliothèque Dupuy." In Gilles Bertrand, Anne Cayuela, Christian Del Vento, and Raphaële Mouren, eds., *Bibliothèques et lecteurs dans l'Europe moderne (XVIIe–XVIIIe siècles)* (Geneva: Droz, 2016), 225–242.
[66] Angela Nuovo, "*Et amicorum*: costruzione e circolazione del sapere nelle biblioteche private nel Cinquecento," in Rosa Maria Borraccini and Roberto Rusconi, eds., *Libri, biblioteche e cultura degli ordini regolari nell'Italia moderna attraverso la documentazione della Congregazione dell'indice* (Vatican City: Biblioteca Apostolica Vaticana, 2006), 105–127.

century onward. Lawyers in early modern Europe, like those today, lived and worked among books and records. The Florentine politician and historian Francesco Guicciardini (1483–1540), in one of his *Ricordi*, wrote that "it is necessary for practicing doctors [of the law] to want to see what everyone has written; and so the time they would put into thinking is consumed instead in reading books resulting in exhaustion of the spirit and body, such that it has more in common with hard labor than with scholarship."[67] Examining posthumous inventories, Pierre Aquilon has estimated that the typical lawyer in Picardy in the sixteenth century owned 116 books.[68] Lawyers were frequently zealous bibliophiles with large personal libraries. The historian and bibliographer Ludovico Muratori (1672–1750) wrote in his *Dei difetti della giurisprudenza* (1743) of "the flood of books that make up the libraries of lawyers."[69] These predictably contained many specialized legal texts but also books on a great range of other subjects: oratory, poetry, history, and the works of classical authors were all well represented.[70] The Milanese lawyer and notary Giovanni Battista Bianchini (1613–99) maintained an expansive private library of more than 2,000 printed and 110 manuscript volumes.[71] Scholars regularly visited his library and upon his death, his collection became part of the monastic library of the Cistercians of Saint Ambrose. Lawyers such as Bianchini were *fils du livre*, as Lucien Febvre has described the jurists of the Franche-Comté in the sixteenth century.[72]

[67] "[P]erò e dottori che praticano, sono necessitati volere vedere ognuno che scrive; e cosí quello tempo che s'arebbe a mettere in speculare, si consuma in leggere libri con stracchezza di animo e di corpo, in modo che l'ha quasi piú similitudine a una fatica di facchini che di dotti." Series C, no. 208: http://digilander.libero.it/il_guicciardini/guiccardini_ricordi_serie_C.html. My translation.
[68] Pierre Aquilon, "Petites et moyennes bibliothèques 1530–1660." In *Histoires des bibliothèques françaises*, Tome II: *les bibliothèques sous l'Ancien regime 1530–1789* (Paris: Editions du Cercle de la Librairie, 1998), 180–205.
[69] Ludovico Antonio Muratori, *De i difetti della giurisprudenza* (Naples: Stamperia Muziana, 1743): "quell diluvio di libri, che formano le Biblioteche de' legisti, in cadauna nondimen delle quali, non ostante la gran copia de' volumi, più son quei che mancano, che quei che vi fanno comparsa."
[70] Pierre Aquilon, "Quatre avocats angevins dans leurs librairies (1586–1592)." In Aquilon and Henri-Jean Martin, eds., *Le livre dans l'Europe de la Renaissance: actes du XXVIIIe Colloque international d'études humanistes de Tours* (Paris: Promodis – Editions du Cercle de la Librairie, 1998), 503–549; Rodolfo Savelli, "Giuristi francesi, biblioteche italiane. Prime note sul problema della circolazione della letteratura giuridica in età moderna." In Mario Ascheri and Gaetano Colli, eds., *Manoscritti, editoria e biblioteche dal medioevo all'età contemporanea: studi offerti a Domenico Maffei per il suo ottantesimo compleanno* (Rome: Roma del Rinascimento, 2006), 1239–1270.
[71] Maria Antonietta Conte, "La biblioteca di Giovanni Battista Bianchini (1613–1699): fra i Cisterciensi di S. Ambrogio e il collegio dei notai di Milano." *Archivio storico lombardo*, 118 (1992), 405–470.
[72] Lucien Febvre, *Philippe II et le Franche-Comté: la crise de 1567, ses origines et ses conséquences: étude d'histoire politique, religieuse et sociale* (Paris: H. Champion, 1912), 345–349.

Doctors, too, acquired large libraries. It has been estimated that, in the course of the sixteenth century, the number of medical titles in circulation increased by a factor of more than one hundred and the total number of copies by an even greater percentage. These titles were well represented in the growing personal libraries of physicians. Nicolò Leoniceno (1428–1524), who taught mathematics, medicine, and philosophy at the University of Ferrara for almost sixty years in the late fifteenth and early sixteenth centuries, amassed a personal library of at least 340 volumes, over half of which were manuscripts.[73] The Augsburg doctor, mathematician, and historian Achilles Pirmin Gasser (1505–1577) accumulated a collection of 3,000 books, all but 200 of which were printed. Gasser's collection, like those of many physicians, ranged well beyond medicine; several hundred of the titles were historical or geographical in nature. He systematically sought to update his collection with the most recent publications, ordering the latest scientific titles from publishers in the Netherlands.[74] The Nuremberg physician Georg Palma (1543–1591) had a library of 800 volumes, covering medical volumes, but also humanist tracts and astrological works.[75] The library of Thomas Lorkyn (ca. 1528–1591), the Regius Professor of Physic at Cambridge, at his death included more than 400 medical titles, a portion of one of the largest private libraries in Britain.[76] One survey has estimated that doctors in seventeenth-century Paris owned an average of 220 books. These collections predictably contained many medical texts, but, like those of lawyers, extended into other subjects such as natural history, military science, and, increasingly, literature in the vernacular. Print was a boon for disciplines such as medicine, that relied on visual, as well as written, information.

Book ownership and the accumulation of personal libraries were not confined to such professionals. Marino Zorzi has undertaken a census of the *postmortem* inventories of libraries in Venice for the period 1527 to 1599, and found that most of them did not exceed 100 volumes and belonged to individuals who were neither clerics nor professionals.[77] Print undoubtedly made book ownership more attainable for university

---

[73] Daniela Mugnai Carrara, *La Biblioteca di Nicolò Leoniceno. Tra Aristotele e Galeno: Cultura e libri di un medico umanista* (Florence: Olschki, 1991).

[74] Bernd Lorenz, *Allgemeinbildung und Fachswissen. Deutsche Ärzte und ihre Privatbibliotheken* (Herzogenrath: Verlag Murken-Altrogge, 1992).

[75] Hannah Murphy, "Common places and private spaces: libraries, record-keeping and orders of information in sixteenth-century medicine." *Past and Present*, 230. Supplemental Issue 11 (2016): *The Social History of the Archive: Record-Keeping in Early Modern Europe*, Alexandra Walsham and Liesbeth Corens, eds., 253–268.

[76] Peter Murray Jones, "Reading medicine in Tudor Cambridge." In Vivian Nutton and Roy Porter, eds., *The History of Medical Education in Britain* (Amsterdam: Rodopi, 1995), 153–183.

[77] Marino Zorzi, "La circolazione del libro a Venezia nel Cinquecento. Biblioteche private e pubbliche." *Ateneo Veneto*, 177 (1990), 155–163.

students than it had been under the *pecia* system that predominated in the Middle Ages.

Students at the University of Paris in the sixteenth century owned an average of twenty volumes, while the famously bibliophilic novices of the Society of Jesus owned between thirty and forty. Joan Davies has examined the inventory of one student at the University of Toulouse, Antoine Lagarde, who owned more than 150 books, almost all of them printed, as well as a large quantity of manuscript materials: letters, papers, and notebooks.[78] Lagarde's collection was indicative of how a student with sufficient resources could exploit the new opportunities offered by print. It testifies to the life of a student awash in paper: a predicament that would surely find sympathy among students ever since.

For some individuals, the creation of a vast personal library became a chief life concern. This was apparently the case of Don Hernando Colón (1488–1539), the second son of Christopher Columbus. Hernando's so-called Biblioteca Colombina came to number 15,300 volumes, more than 90 percent of which were printed (as well as more than 3,000 prints and many pamphlets he felt it worth preserving), and was staffed by full-time specialists in Hernando's employ.[79] The librarians compiled numerous inventories of the library's content, organized according to author, content, place of publication, and other criteria. Hernando made several months-long trips to seek out books, in Italy, the Low Countries, Germany, and France, as well as exploiting a broad network of booksellers, merchants, diplomats, and other acquaintances. In his will, Fernando gave extremely detailed instructions for the preservation of the collection as well as for future acquisitions, leaving it to his cousin Don Luis. The ambitions of Hernando, made possible by print, are revealed in a letter that he sent to Charles V in 1536:

[T]here should be in the kingdom a certain place where all the books of every branch of knowledge which treat of the Christian world and even outside of it should be collected ... So that in time the library will come to possess all the books that can be obtained and all that is written can be reduced to alphabetical order in other books as stated above to the end that each [visitor] may be easily instructed in what he wishes to know.[80]

---

[78] Joan Davies, "Student libraries in sixteenth-century Toulouse." *History of Universities*, 3 (1983), 61–86.
[79] Ilaria Caraci Luzzana, ed., Geoffrey Symcox, trans., *The History of the Life and Deeds of the Admiral Don Christopher Columbus. Repertorium Columbianum*, Vol. XIII (Turnhout, Belgium: Brepols, 2014), 10–11. Also see Edward Wilson-Lee, *The Catalogue of Shipwrecked Books. Christopher Columbus, His Son, and the Quest to Build the World's Greatest Library* (New York: Scribner, 2019).
[80] Quoted in William Sherman, "A new world of books: Hernando Colón and the *Biblioteca Colombina*." In Ann Blair and Anja-Silvia Goeing, eds., *For the Sake of Learning. Essays in Honor of Anthony Grafton*, Vol. I (Leiden: Brill, 2016), 404–414 (here 412).

On the tomb that Hernando shares with his father in Seville Cathedral, Hernando's escutcheon depicts four open books, representing the four chief categories of the main catalog of his library: authors, subjects, epitomes, and materials.

The efforts to create universal libraries were both physical and virtual. The Swiss polymath Conrad Gessner sought to achieve comprehensiveness virtually in composing his *Bibliotheca Universalis*, the first two volumes (of a planned three) of which appeared in Zürich in 1545 and 1548. In the first volume, Gessner described in form and content some 10,000 texts, presenting them alphabetically by author, and supplying details on the date and place of publication. In his second volume, Gessner then sought to organize the knowledge contained in this mass of books, employing thematic keywords, or *loci communes*, to do so. Such commonplaces were designed to help the reader classify knowledge as it was acquired. Gessner organized his commonplaces according to a tree of twenty-one classifications, with headings such as "grammar" and "theology." His envisioned third volume was to be an alphabetic index to all twenty-one classifications but never appeared, as the publisher begged off the expense.

Although he recognized that some works were more worthy and useful than others, Gessner's tastes were omnivorous: "I scorn no work," he declared. Gessner sought out inventories and catalogs of books – his *Bibliotheca* was thus something of a sixteenth-century union catalog. He undertook a trial run of sorts by composing for Christoph Froschauer, the Zürich printer, the catalog of the 1543 spring Frankfurt Fair, which was a clearinghouse for the latest information on the European book trade, and what was available in print.[81] Gessner's project to encompass every book was representative of how, in the age of the printed book, scholarship compelled not only reading but also the organization and classification of the knowledge obtained. Gessner was seeking to organize the "abundance of books" into what one of his chief interpreters, Helmut Zedelmaier, has described (in an artful but appropriate anachronism) as "sixteenth-century metadata."[82] Laurent Pinon has called the *Bibliotheca universalis* the "Noah's Ark of the Renaissance."[83] The Protestant Gessner's work, ironically, was used both as a guide for the compilation of the Catholic Church's Index of Prohibited Books and for assembling the library of the Most Catholic King, Philip II of

---

[81] Paul Nelles, "Conrad Gessner and the mobility of the book: Zurich, Frankfurt and Venice (1543)." In Daniel Bellingradt, Paul Nelles, and Jeroen Salman, eds., *Books in Motion in Early Modern Europe. Beyond Production, Circulation and Consumption* (Basingstoke, UK: Palgrave Macmillan, 2017), 39–66.

[82] Helmut Zedelmaier, "Suchen und Finden vor Google: Zur Metadatenproduktion im 16. Jahrhundert." in Blair and Goeing, eds., *For the Sake of Learning*, Vol. I, 423–440.

[83] Laurent Pinon, *Livres de zoologie de la Renaissance: une anthologie (1450–1700)* (Paris: Klincksieck, 1995), 34.

Spain.[84] The Index, like the *Bibliotheca universalis*, was organized alphabetically.[85] Both were also exemplars of an increasingly common type of publication: "books about books." These took forms that did not exist in the Middle Ages, such as school textbooks, printed commonplace books, and a variety of reference books targeted at both specialist and general audiences.

The French scholar and bibliophile Gabriel Naudé (1600–1653), the embodiment of late humanist polymathy, was known as a "living library," but he also boasted a massive non-living one. Louis Jacob, in his *Traicté des plus belles bibliothèques publiques et particulieres* (1644), estimated that Naudé's library contained more than 8,000 volumes.[86] The full inventory has been lost, but three extant partial inventories testify to the sprawling nature of Naudé's acquisitions. Three-quarters of the books are in Latin and a similar percentage are of "modern" authors from the sixteenth and seventeenth centuries. This was not merely an effort to assemble the indispensable authors, a sort of *bibliothèque choisie*; instead, Naudé apparently sought to amass all he could. In his *Instructions concerning Erecting a Library* (1622), there was scarcely anything written or printed that Naudé felt should not be included. The little books one might regard as "mean baubles and pieces of no consideration" are sometimes "the most curious pieces of the whole library."[87]

Naudé's approach was one he extended into his tenure as librarian for Cardinal Mazarin (1602–1661), the chief minister for Louis XIII and Louis XIV. Mazarin was committed to assembling a library that would be the envy of Europe, and in Naudé, already an avid collector of books, he had a perfect partner. Naudé surprised observers by purchasing "many bad and very old pieces that no one ever asks for."[88] Naudé sought out books in every way available to him: he would sometimes purchase hoards of books by weight rather than examining the individual volumes, and it was said of Naudé he would leave bookshops as if they had been visited by a whirlwind. Under Naudé's guidance, Mazarin's library grew to 40,000

---

[84] Alberto Moreni, "La bibliotheca universalis de Konrad Gessner e gli Indici dei libri proibiti." *La Bibliofilia*, 88 (1986), 131–150; Gregorio de Andrés, *La real Biblioteca de El Escorial* (Madrid: Aldus, 1970).
[85] A point made in Zedelmaier, "Suchen und Finden."
[86] Estelle Boeuf, *La bibliothèque parisienne de Gabriel Naudé en 1630* (Geneva: Droz, 2007).
[87] Gabriel Naudé, *Instructions Concerning Erecting a Library* (Cambridge, MA: Houghton, Mifflin and Company, 1903), 94.
[88] "M. Naudé a deja fait un fort grand amas de livres. Chacun s'estonne des livres qu'il achette et particulièrement nos libraires qui se defont de beaucoup de mauvaises pièces et fort vielles que l'on ne demande jamais." From a letter of Christophe Dupuy of 31 July 1645, in Kathryn Willis Wolfe and Philip Wolfe, eds., *Humanisme et politique. Lettres romaines de Christophe Dupuy à ses frères (1636–1645)* (Paris and Seattle: Papers on French Seventeenth Century Literature, 1988), 200–201.

volumes.[89] Naudé called it "the work of my hands and the miracle of my life" and elsewhere referred to it as his "daughter." He intended the collection to be a civic resource, open to the public. When he argued against its planned dispersal by the Paris Parliament during the political disruptions of the Fronde (1648–1653), he emphasized that its contents offered utility for every sort of reader: "there is no Book whatsoever, be it never so bad or decried but may in time be sought for by some person or other." Naudé regarded the library as an information resource, a *bibliotheca universalis* made possible by the reproductive power of print, and compared it with the meadow of Seneca, where every living creature is able to find what is proper for them to live. It was, after all, according to Naudé "much easier at present to procure thousands of Books than it was for the Ancients to get hundreds."[90]

Naudé envisaged the library as an *instrumentum* for learning, for evaluating perceived knowledge, and for indulging curiosity, but in order for a library to be an effective tool toward those ends, the information within it had to be subjected to organization. At a time when early scientists were mining the repository of nature in their pursuit of *historia naturalis*, the library was the testing ground for *historia litteraria*. Naudé's vision of the library is an early systematic envisioning of the library as a tool of research, an institution with pretensions to encyclopedic comprehensiveness, but with tools for navigation that would mirror the order of knowledge itself.[91]

The perceived need to group and categorize books led to the beginning of modern bibliography. Thus, we see book lists, disciplinary segmentations, and catalogs. François de la Croix du Maine (1552–1592) and Antoine du Verdier (1544–1600) compiled a *Bibliothèque française* in 1584, which promised 100 "buffets" of 100 volumes (themselves divided into 10 sections), for a total of 10,000 volumes of a "perfect and complete library."[92]

---

[89] John Cotton Dana and Henry W. Kent, eds., *Two Tracts Written by Gabriel Naudé*. (Chicago: McClurg, 1907), 28.

[90] Gabriel Naudé, *Advis pour dresser une bibliothèque* (Paris: François Targa, 1627), 40–41: "personne de jugement ne peur douter qu'il ne nous soit maintenant plus facile d'avoir des milliers de livres qu'il n'estoit aux anciens d'en avoir des centaines ..."; quoted in Elizabeth Eisenstein, *Divine Art, Infernal Machine: the Reception of Printing in the West from First Impressions to the Sense of Ending* (Philadelphia: University of Pennsylvania Press, 2012), 86.

[91] Paul Nelles, "The library as an instrument of discovery. Gabriel Naudé and the uses of history." In Donald Kelley, ed., *History and the Disciplines: The Reclassification of Knowledge in Early Modern Europe* (Rochester, NY: University of Rochester Press, 1997), 41–57.

[92] Henri-Jean Martin, "Classements et conjonctures." In Roger Chartier and Martin, eds. *Histoire de l'édition française*. Vol. 1: *Le livre conquérant. Du Moyen Âge au milieu du XVII siècle* (Paris: Fayard, 1989), 429–457 (here 437).

Roger Chartier has called the proliferation of catalogs and bibliographies in early modern Europe "the new order of books." Medieval library catalogs had been designed primarily for inventory control rather than for search and recall, once the size of collections expanded. But when Gottfried Leibniz (1646–1716) was creating the catalog for the Herzog August Bibliothek in Württemberg, he drew explicit parallels between the library catalog and the account books of the merchant: "if the purpose of a businessman is garnering profits from his products, deploying certain technologies such as double-entry accounting, the comparison concedes that a library full of books remains worthless as long as it does not maintain a single book about these books."[93] Print had expanded libraries such that their contents could not be mastered by any one person – catalogs had to resolve the library's great range of texts with its usability. Naudé recognized the libraries in his day had grown to a size where the human mind could no longer encompass the information that they contained. "Because it is altogether impossible," he wrote, "that we should, by our own industry, learn and know the qualities of so vast a number of Books," one should look at the various ways that librarians had catalogued their collections. A library that is not given a proper ordering system, he insisted, was like an army that had not been placed in regiments, or a pile of stones that had not yet been formed into a palace or house. He described his ideal classificatory scheme as "always that which is the easiest, the least confusing, the most natural, useful, and which followed the faculties of theology, medicine, jurisprudence, history, philosophy, mathematics, humanities and others, all of which one has to subdivide according to their various parts."[94] As Thomas Hyde (1636–1703) declared in his preface to the catalog of Oxford's Bodleian Library (1674), after noting the great size of his undertaking: "if they examine this catalogue they will see that diversity at once expressed and reconciled."[95] The English Parliamentarian and essayist Samuel Pepys (1633–1703),

---

[93] Markus Krajewski, *Paper Machines. About Cards and Catalogs, 1548–1929*. Trans. by Peter Krapp (Cambridge, MA: MIT Press, 2011), 22.

[94] Naudé, *Advis*, 29: "Finalement à cause que nous ne pouvons pas par nostre seule industrie sçavoir et cognoistre les qualitez d'un si grand nombre de livres"; and 134: "je croy que le meilleur est tousjours celuy qui est le plus facile, le moins intrigué, le plus naturel, usité, et qui suit les Facultez de Théologie, Médecine, Jurisprudence, Histoire, Philosophie, Mathematiques, Humanitez, et autres, lesquelles il faut subdiviser chacune en particulier, suivant leurs diverses parties."

[95] Elisabeth de Rijk, "Thomas Hyde, Julia Pettee and the development of cataloging principles; with a translation of Hyde's 1674 Preface to the Reader." *Cataloging & Classification Quarterly*, 14.2 (2010), 31–62 (here 52). The first printed catalog of the Bodleian, published in 1605, was organized first according to subject matter, then by size, and only then by the names of the authors.

for his part, sought to resolve this conundrum by organizing his library of more than 3,000 by the size of the book![96]

By the beginning of the sixteenth century, there was demand for accumulated bibliographical information among scholars and book collectors. Manuscript library catalogs actually circulated in surprisingly large numbers, serving as collective snapshots of the books that were out there, and a road map for books they might wish to acquire themselves. It was now, in the new landscape of print, a reasonable expectation that bookhunters would be able to acquire the texts listed in these catalogs. Catalogs became something akin to an informational road map of the terrain of the *respublica litterarum* in the age of print, guidebooks to the possibilities of research and *collezionismo* in the sixteenth century. They were representative of the new dimensions of humanism and scholarly life that had been opened up by the abundance of printed books.

5.4   Print as a Spur to Manuscript

Earlier, I suggested that the "age of print" was in fact a "new age of manuscript." Print was a significant spur to more manuscript writing. The writing of early modern Europeans, in fact, was often, directly or indirectly, a response to print. These responses took many forms. The flood of early printed books was met with "an avalanche of manuscript notes and codices which contained extracts from, and even entire copies of printed volumes."[97]

Printed books are a combination of type and blank space. This allowed for the addition of manuscript notes, annotations that served as criticism, commentary, and marginal indices. The surface of the early modern printed book was not a sacrosanct space – it was often the locus of a dialogue between print and manuscript; manuscript continued to be the vehicle through which readers of printed books sought to categorize and commit to memory the information that they encountered in print. A considerable amount of recent scholarship has shown that early modern readers used books' blank spaces as loci for conversations with the book, and between the book and other books. Humanist heroes like Plutarch and Erasmus emphasized the importance of employing marginalia and it

---

[96] Jane Hughes, *The Pepys Library and the Historic Collections of Magdalene College Cambridge* (New York, Scala, 2015), 29; Kate Loveman, *Samuel Pepys and His Books: Reading, Newsgathering, and Sociability, 1660–1703* (Oxford: Oxford University Press, 2015), 46.

[97] Isabelle Charmantier and Staffan Müller-Wille, "Worlds of paper: an introduction," *Early Science and Medicine*, 19 (2014), 379–397 (here 386).

was an admonition that early modern readers took to heart, noting useful vocabulary, remarking on parallels with other authors, offering reflections on the substance of what they were reading, or registering their disagreement or distaste.[98] In an age that increasingly emphasized note-taking as a strategy for managing information and the challenges to human memory, these marginal notes are the best preserved evidence that we have of real-time readers' interface with and response to what was before them, and a further indication of how the printed word abetted handwritten words.

Anyone who has spent any meaningful time with early modern printed books has encountered the marginalia that appear in profusion in their margins, in-between the lines, and on blank pages. These marginalia were often more than mere notes. They reveal reading as a social activity, a means by which to enter into conversation with other works, readers, and with contemporary events. In my own work on annotated sixteenth-century books, I have witnessed how the first owner of a 1503 Aldine *Divine Comedy* engaged in profane rants against the Republic of Venice and Pope Alexander VI, prompted by the substance of Dante's poem. The same reader also saw it fit to recount his own near-contemporary travels and experiences, including the unearthing of the Laocoön statue in Rome and the annular eclipse of 1502.[99] I have also examined how a young Heinrich Bullinger (1504–1575), later the prominent Zürich Reformed theologian and pastor, handwrote into the margins of his copy of *Polyhistor*, by the late antique geographer Solinus, hundreds of cross-references from more than sixty other works taken directly from the extensive printed scholia of a different, sprawling edition of *Polyhistor*, compiled by Johannes Camers. The result is pages and pages of tightly packed handwriting, wedged into every available space, in an attempt to recreate in his own copy, in manuscript, the printed glosses he was reading in Camers's edition.[100]

---

[98] The scholarship on marginalia and what they tell us about early modern reading is growing rapidly. Generally, see William Sherman, *Used Books: Marking Readers in Renaissance England* (Philadelphia: University of Pennsylvania Press, 2008); Heather Jackson, *Marginalia: Readers Writing in Books* (New Haven, CT: Yale University Press, 2001); some specific case studies include Anthony Grafton, "*Discitur ut agatur:* how Gabriel Harvey read his Livy." In Stephen A. Barney, ed., *Annotation and Its Texts* (Oxford: Oxford University Press, 1991), 108–129; Jacob Soll, "The hand-annotated copy of the *Histoire du gouvernement de Venise*, or how Amelot de la Houssaie wrote his history." *Bulletin du Bibliophile*, 2 (1995), 279–293.

[99] Paul Dover, "Reading Dante in the sixteenth century: the Bentley Aldine Divine Comedy and its marginalia." In *Studies in Medieval and Renaissance History*, 3.14 (2017), 199–228.

[100] Paul Dover, "How Heinrich Bullinger read his Solinus: reading ancient geography in 16th-century Switzerland." In Kai Brodersen, ed., *Solinus: New Studies* (Heidelberg: Verlag Antike, 2014), 171–195.

Owen Gingerich's chronicle of his multi-year effort to track down and catalog all the extant copies of the first and second print editions of Copernicus's *De revolutionibus* reveals how reader annotations could have lives that extended beyond the personal use of their authors. He tells the story of how a curious marginal note regarding the anonymous preface to the copy of *De revolutionibus* owned by the astronomer Michael Maestlin (1550–1631) was actually a third-hand transcription of the same manuscript gloss that had been copied twice before, first by the mathematician Peter Apian (1495–1552), and then by his son Philipp (1531–1589). The annotations of an individual migrated across multiple print copies of the same work, owned by different individuals.[101] Examples such as these reveal how printed books offered up opportunities and spaces for hybridized exchanges of information and knowledge.

Europe's printing presses also churned out a great many pages with spaces left blank deliberately, intended to be filled in after purchase. In such cases, the resulting item ended up being a hybrid of printed and manuscript text, where print guided the format and content of the appended handwriting. As Peter Stallybrass has put it:

> I would argue that printing's most revolutionary effect was on manuscript. If we define manuscript in terms of all writing by hand as opposed to the kind of manuscripts that have been the main subject of study, we might begin to see that the history of printing is crucially a history of the "blank" (that is, of printed works designed to be filled in by hand).[102]

The indulgence certificates discussed earlier in this chapter, and printed in the hundreds of thousands, are a good example of this calculus: they were printed documents with blank spaces to be completed by hand. They served as prototypes for ecclesiastical and governmental forms that the early modern Church and state employed with increasing frequency, for gathering information on their parishioners and subjects. Early modern Europe invented the "to-be-completed" bureaucratic form, a format that has accumulated in colossal quantities ever since. It is hard to imagine modern government, law, or commerce without it.

By the second half of the sixteenth century, printers were publishing pamphlet editions of classical texts intended for student use that incorporated wide spaces between the lines of text so that notes could be added.[103]

---

[101] Owen Gingerich, *The Book Nobody Read: Chasing the Revolutions of Nicolaus Copernicus* (New York: Walker and Company, 2004), 158–159.

[102] Peter Stallybrass, "Little jobs. Broadsides and the printing revolution." In Sabrina Alcorn, Eric Lindquist, and Eleanor Shevlin, eds., *Agent of Change: Print Culture Studies after Elizabeth Eisenstein* (Amherst: University of Massachusetts Press, 2007), 315–341 (here 340).

[103] Anthony Grafton, "Teacher, text and pupil in the Renaissance classroom: a case study from a Parisian classroom." *History of Universities*, 1 (1981), 37–70.

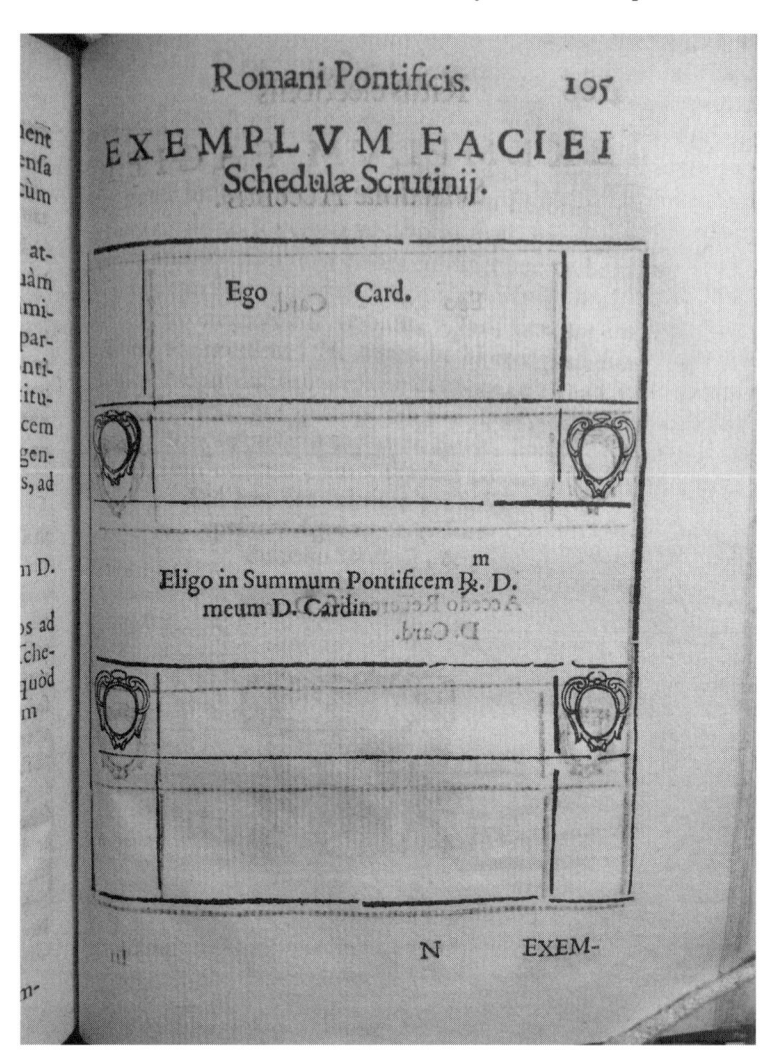

5.2 Much early printed material was designed to be written on, like this papal election ballot. *Caeremoniale continens ritus electionis Romani Pontificis* (Rome, 1667). Folger Shakespeare Library, Washington, DC, 176214.2 (reproduced with permission of the Folger).

Printed herbals not infrequently contained blank pages in order to allow the owner to record his own observations from the field. The binding process, too, might make allowances for space in which to append notes. The English poet John Donne (1572–1631) owned a copy of Nicholas Hill's *Epicurean*

Philosophy, one which had previously belonged to Ben Jonson (1572–1637). It had been bound with blank pages between the printed ones, allowing for commentary and refutation.[104]

Almanacs, printed and sold in profusion starting in the sixteenth century, are a prominent example of this phenomenon. They were often sold by street vendors (known as *merciers* in France), as well as by booksellers, a reflection of the broad demand among the purchasing public. They were specifically designed to be written on, functioning as diaries as much as books. Some included writing tables, with spaces to be populated with the requisite data. Because many of the pages in an almanac were date-specific, owners of these texts often cut or tore out individual pages or sections for limited-time use. It has been estimated that, by the 1640s, 300,000 almanacs were sold in England every year, each between forty and fifty pages long and costing about two pence, well within the price range of a laborer.[105] By the second half of the seventeenth century, it has been estimated that one in three English households purchased their own almanac.[106] Almanacs accounted for 40 percent of the English Stationers' Company's paper budget between 1673 and 1682. Many pieces of paper included in the almanacs were deliberately left blank in the printing; the most popular printed text in Restoration England was an almanac that was designed to be filled out in manuscript.[107] One quarter of all titles published in Sweden in the seventeenth century were almanacs.[108] The Venetian printer Girolamo Albizzi, working with the friar Vincenzo Coronelli, starting in the 1660s, produced a tourist yearbook and almanac that would remain in print for forty-three years.[109] This publication incorporated blank spaces for travelers to recount their own experiences while visiting the locales covered in the text.

Designed to be used, and rarely retained beyond the year in question, rather than simply read, such items survive in extremely small numbers in relation to the vast numbers of them originally produced. For example, Leonard Digges's *A Prognostication Everlasting*, first published in 1555, went through thirty-three editions by the year 1619. It offered predictions

---

[104] Piers Brown, "'hac ex consilio meo via progredieris': courtly reading and secretarial mediation in Donne's *the Courtier's Library*." *Renaissance Quarterly*, 61.3 (2008), 833–866 (here 837–838).
[105] Jeremiah Dittmar, "Information technology and economic change: the impact of the printing press." *Quarterly Journal of Economics*, 126.3 (2011), 1133–1172.
[106] Wahrman, *Mr. Collier's Letter Racks*, 8.
[107] Stallybrass, "Printing and the manuscript revolution," 113–114.
[108] Robert Allan Houston, *Literacy in Early Modern Europe. Culture and Education 1500–1800* (Harlow: Longman, 2002), 200.
[109] Brendan Dooley, *The Social History of Skepticism. Experience and Doubt in Early Modern Culture* (Baltimore, MD: Johns Hopkins University Press, 1999), 65.

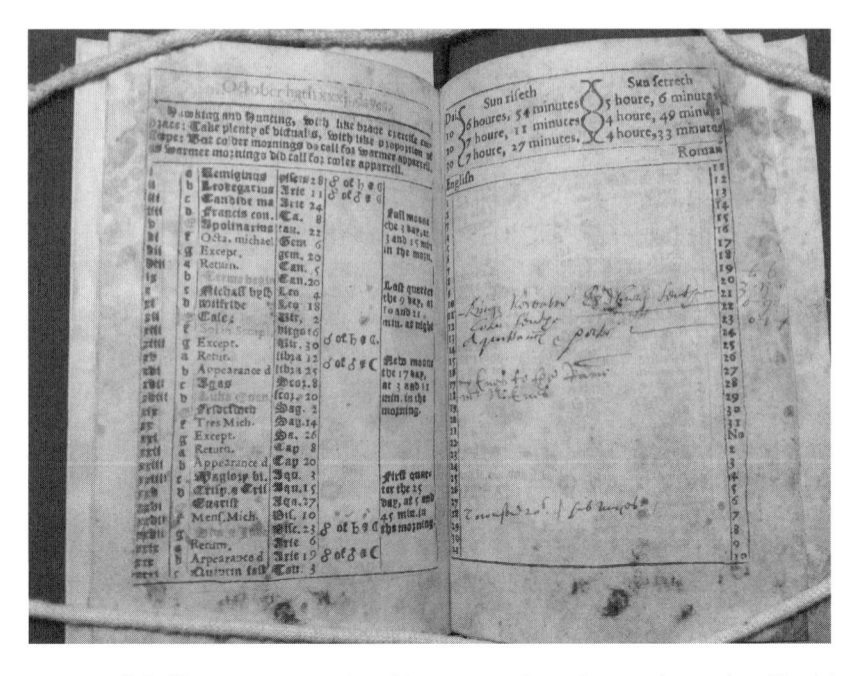

5.3 Almanacs were printed in vast numbers, but rarely survive. Daniel Browne, *A new almanacke and prognostication, for the yeare of our Lord God 1628* (London, 1628). Folger Shakespeare Library, Washington, DC, STC 421 (reproduced with permission of the Folger).

of weather via astrology, as well as recommendations as to when to bleed, purge, and bathe, along with a wealth of practical information regarding sunrises, sunsets, and moon phases. Of the 1576 edition, only seven are known to have survived.[110] David McKitterick has discovered that of all the sheet almanacs printed at Cambridge University before 1640, only a single, imperfect, copy has survived. This is despite the fact that in the years 1631–1633 alone, approximately 30,000 of them were printed, and then presumably marked up in manuscript by their owners.[111]

All this handwriting is a reminder that manuscript clearly retained considerable advantages in a world transformed by print. Print did not attenuate inscription by hand; instead, it created new opportunities for it.[112] It is

---

[110] Folger Shakespeare Library 6864: Leonard Digges, *A Prognostication Everlastinge of Right Good Effecte* (London: Thomas Marsh, 1576).
[111] David McKitterick, *A History of Cambridge University Press*, Vol. 1: *Printing and the Book Trade in Cambridge 1534–1698* (Cambridge: Cambridge University Press, 1992), 203.
[112] On the enduring importance of script versus print, see, among others: Harold Love, *The Culture and Commerce of Texts. Scribal Publication in Seventeenth-century England* (Oxford:

undoubtedly true that manuscript copying became increasingly rare as a means of book reproduction, given the availability of print versions.[113] But scribal production of many varieties remained essential, in some regards becoming more important than ever, in administrative and bureaucratic circles, in record-keeping of all sorts, in letter writing, and in scholarly work. It allowed, in a way print did not, real-time preservation of information that cost next to nothing. And it could take advantage of a wide range of paper surfaces: notebooks, loose sheets, blank spaces in books and pamphlets, and leftover scraps.

It is also the case that publication, in the sense of making texts or ideas public, did not necessarily involve printing. Print publication was not necessarily the intended end of the production of handwritten texts, or the most cost-effective method. Manuscript publications continued to occupy an important niche in the circulation of knowledge. Filippo de Vivo and Brian Richardson have rightly emphasized that "[t]o neglect manuscripts means distorting both our understanding of the strategies available to authors in reaching their public and our notion of who was reading what at the time."[114] Authors frequently passed around manuscript drafts among acquaintances and target audiences. Manuscript allowed for circulation among limited groups of known individuals; provided greater latitude for editing, correction, and criticism; and afforded room for direct communication between writer and readers. Assembled reflections and notes, partial or incomplete manuscript texts, handwritten miscellanies and commonplaces, collections of letters received and sent, and full copied texts (often from printed versions) were regularly gathered together within book bindings, finding themselves placed alongside printed works on the shelves.

In England, some Stuart-era political tracts remain extant in more than forty manuscript copies. This was partly due to the undeveloped nature of the printing infrastructure in England, but was also reflective of a robust culture of manuscript publishing, spearheaded by what C.W. Brooks has

---

Oxford University Press, 1993); Gerald Tyson and Sylvia Wagonheim, eds., *Print and Culture in the Renaissance: Essays on the Advent of Printing in Europe* (Newark, DE: University of Delaware Press, 1986); Anthony Grafton and Ann Blair, eds., *The Transmission of Culture in Early Modern Europe* (Philadelphia: University of Pennsylvania Press, 1990); Sandra Hindman, ed., *Printing the Written Word: the Social History of Books, c. 1450–1520* (Ithaca, NY: Cornell University Press, 1991); Arthur Marotti and Michael Bristol, eds., *Print, Manuscript, and Performance: the Changing Relations of the Media in Early Modern England* (Columbus, OH: Ohio State University Press, 2000).

[113] Armando Petrucci, "Copisti e libri manoscritti dopo l'avvento della stampa." In Condello and Gregorio, eds., *Scribi e colofoni*, 57–69; Joseph B. Trapp, *Manuscripts in the Fifty Years After the Invention of Printing* (London: Warburg Institute, 1983).

[114] Filippo de Vivo and Brian Richardson, "Preface." *Italian Studies*, 66.2. *Special issue on cultural transmission in early modern Italy* (2011), 157–160 (here 158).

called a "clerical underworld" of "underclerks, scriveners, and servants."[115] Some inflammatory and explicit handwritten political pamphlets from the period are preserved in the thousands, as citizens saw the production of such items as a means of participating in political life.[116] In England, where printing was tightly controlled under the Stationers' Company in London, reproduction by hand offered a means of production that was decentralized and flexible, and depended on more informal connections of friendship and commerce. The audience for manuscript publication was more targeted than the open space of print publishing. But this did not mean, as the evidence from seventeenth-century England shows, that certain manuscript libels, pamphlets, and polemics did not circulate in large numbers.[117]

There were many important complete works that circulated chiefly or solely in manuscript form – Galileo, for example, given the sensitivity of his claims, had several works that were "published" this way. In some cases, several versions of the same text existed and circulated at the same time. Nick Wilding has shown that in Galileo's case this was deliberate – it was a means of evading censorship and allowed for greater textual flexibility in specific contexts. Wilding provides the example of the famous *Lettera a Madama Cristina*, which is extant in at least thirty-four manuscript copies, in addition to the sixty copies from the first print edition. We must assume, therefore, a large readership for such manuscript "publications," and regard them not as works that failed to make it into print but instead as a parallel, alternative, and sometimes complementary form of information circulation.[118]

All this evidence of the enduring importance of manuscript writing in a supposed "age of print" should dissuade us from easy bifurcations. After all, the label "manuscript" itself depended on the existence of printed material. In this sense, "print" invented "manuscript." Before the advent of the printing press, Europeans did not conceive of something called "manuscript" (or *manoscritto*, or *manuscrit*, or *Handschrift*), because what was written was necessarily written by hand. It was not until the 1674 catalog of the university library at Leiden that we see a clear division made in cataloging between manuscript and printed books.[119] As Margaret Aston has suggested, it is more accurate to speak of the interaction of

---

[115] Christopher W. Brooks, *Pettyfoggers and Vipers of the Commonwealth* (Cambridge: Cambridge University Press, 1986), 157.
[116] On scribal publication's enduring importance, see Love, *The Culture and Commerce of Texts* and Fernando Bouza, *Corre manuscrito: Una historia cultural del Siglo del Oro* (Madrid: Marcial Pons, 2001).
[117] Noah Millstone, *Manuscript Publishing and the Invention of Politics in Early Stuart England* (Cambridge: Cambridge University Press, 2016).
[118] Nick Wilding, "Manuscripts in motion: the diffusion of Galilean Copernicanism." *Italian Studies*, 66.2 (2011), 221–233.
[119] McKitterick, *Print, Manuscript and the Search for Order*, 13.

print and manuscript than by focusing solely on the "impact" of print on an existing world of manuscript.[120] The production of a book required a great many moments, interventions, and processes, involving numerous actors, discharged chiefly in manuscript. Anthony Grafton, pointing out how often early modern authors marked up by hand their printed texts in order to revise and refine subsequent printings, has compared the printing press to a word processing tool, albeit one with slower processing speeds than we are used to in the computer age.[121] In this fashion, manuscript and print worked together in both the diffusion and composition of texts. To call early modern Europe an "age of print," therefore, is to apply a historical misnomer, one that belies the true nature of information production, preservation, and exchange.

* * *

The revolution wrought by print looks different now than it did when Eisenstein first offered her provocative thesis. It looks different partly because we no longer equate print with books. Print, in its early centuries, enabled the creation of a grand variety of media forms other than books, and many of the most important repercussions of the printing press had little or nothing to do with the production and circulation of books. It also looks different because we no longer recognize an "Age of Gutenberg" or an "Age of Print," which displaced a preceding "Age of Manuscript." It is also evident that the printing press did not authenticate good content, provenance, and authorship. Information after Gutenberg remained shifting, unstable, and uncertain. The capacity to reproduce in large quantities at great speed did not change this and, in many ways, accentuated these realities.

A different revolution, then. But a revolution nonetheless. It is far too reductive to insist, as McLuhan would have us do, that the "medium is the message." Nor did the colossus of McLuhan's "typographic man" sweep all before him. But the medium did matter, and its use did have substantial repercussions for the course of European history. Looked at from the perspective of information, the assimilation of the printing press into European society was a profound agent of change (to borrow, deliberately, a phrase employed by Eisenstein). As suggested earlier in this chapter, the large-scale production of printed material, especially from about 1500 onward, effected an enormous increase in the amount of

---

[120] Margaret Aston, "Epilogue." In Crick and Walsham, *The Uses of Script and Print*, 275–289 (here 275).
[121] Anthony Grafton, *The Culture of Correction in Renaissance Europe* (London: British Library, 2011)

written information in circulation, as well as a great expansion in the breadth of access to that information. Books, which had heretofore resided chiefly in social and institutional niches, assumed an altogether new role in everyday life. And so too did other printed formats: pamphlets, price lists, posters, advertisements, official forms and questionnaires, and ultimately journals and newspapers. All of these medial forms injected new information flows into the lives of Europeans, and helped introduce news and data as objects of acquisition and discussion. None of this meant that oral and manuscript information became vestigial – in fact, printed material often prompted the creation of yet more oral and handwritten communication. Print was thus an information accelerant and catalyst, and in filling these roles, offers echoes of the more recent digital revolution. After all, digitization has not meant that we have stopped reading books, writing things down, or engaging in conversation – at least not yet. As in the digital revolution, a new technology combined with existing ones to reinforce some means of communication, modify others, and create altogether new ones.

For European scholars, including the increasing number who sought understanding of the natural world, print forged a new world of learning, one that compelled them to construct new tools to navigate the seas of information contained in the book of nature and in the books of man. It is to that story that we turn in Chapter 6.

6 The Book of Nature and the Books of Man

In 1607, Tommaso Campanella, the Italian philosopher and naturalist (1568–1639), seeking to distinguish his approach from those that came before him, remarked:

> I learn more from the anatomy of an ant or a grass (not to mention the miraculous anatomy of the world as a whole) than from all the books written from the beginning of time to the present, since I learned to do philosophy and to read God's book. I use this exemplar to correct the books of men, which have been badly and arbitrarily copied.[1]

His remarks capture an unmistakable shift in the course of the early modern period toward privileging the book *of* nature, sometimes at the expense of, but more often along with, books *about* nature. The waxing emphasis in these centuries on thorough investigation of the book of nature as an essential component of the library of knowledge would have far-reaching consequences, with new methodologies and epistemologies.

Whether the early modern period witnessed a genuine "scientific revolution" and the systematic pursuit of knowledge about the world via "scientific method" remain questions of vigorous debate. Steven Shapin famously began his survey of the Scientific Revolution with these words: "There was no such thing as the Scientific Revolution, and this is a book about it."[2] Historians have debated vociferously over when, where, and whether a genuinely scientific ethic, as we moderns would understand it, emerged in early modern Europe. Many of the recent scholarly treatments of the Scientific Revolution have tended to find fewer traces of modernity among early modern scientific knowledge and practice than they have identified means by which practitioners sought to reconcile their methods and findings with long-standing, preexisting traditions. These studies have cast doubt on whether we can identify a widely shared

---

[1] Quoted in Ann Blair and Anthony Grafton, "Reassessing humanism and science." *Journal of the History of Ideas*, 53.4 (1992), 535–540.
[2] Steven Shapin, *The Scientific Revolution* (Chicago: University of Chicago Press, 1996), 1.

experimental approach to ascertaining truth about the natural world, which most agree is an essential hallmark of modern science, before the eighteenth century. In as far as they move us away from lazy teleologies, such approaches are welcome, as they assess practitioners and knowledge systems in their own terms and contexts. I do not wish to wade into this debate here, but rather simply affirm something that many contemporaries expressed: that the early modern period was in many ways a *nova aetas*. And much of what was new related to the centrality of observation, information, and data. The most consequential transformations all concerned the means by which practitioners gathered, recorded, and circulated information about their discoveries, along with the tasks of organizing and taxonomizing it, fundamental steps in establishing knowledge about the natural world.

The important shifts in the pursuit of natural knowledge, it seems to me, can be broadly divided into four categories. First, there was a growing commitment to observation and description as central to natural philosophy. It is essential to remember that observations survive the moment of their occurrence only through description and, in some cases, depiction, generally through inscription on paper. As these descriptions accrued, they created new banks of what we today would call "data." Over time, this data achieved an authority of its own, and became the basis for natural knowledge itself, displacing preexisting axioms and paradigms. Early modern scholarly life was lousy with descriptive particulars: it was full of lists; detailed descriptions of plants, animals, and experiments; and collections of commonplaces. Giving form to these particulars became a paramount concern for early modern savants, as expressed by Francis Bacon (1561–1624) in *Novum Organum* (1620):

A natural and experimental history is so diverse and disconnected that it confounds and confuses the understanding unless it is stopped short, and presented in an appropriate order. So tables must be drawn up and a coordination of instances made, in such a way and with such organization that the mind may be able to act upon them.[3]

Second, the pursuit of science was transformed by the availability of books in print. Natural philosophy, like other areas of scholarship, could not help but be transformed by the haul of information, ideas, and approaches harvested from the recovery, publication, and circulation of books, old and new. It was both a boon and a burden, and they employed paper and pen to distill useful information from their reading. William Gilbert (1544–1603), in his influential text on magnetism, *De magnete*

[3] Francis Bacon, *The New Organon*. Trans. and ed. by Lisa Jardine (Cambridge: Cambridge University Press, 2000), 109.

(1600), emphasized the need "to seek knowledge not from books only but from things themselves," but nonetheless stressed the necessity to work through "so vast an Ocean of Books by which the minds of studious men are troubled and fatigued."[4]

Third, as numerous recent studies have emphasized, early modern science was frequently conducted across networks of sociability, through the exchange of correspondence, books, specimens, and experimental data. There was a real sense among many practitioners that the pursuit of natural knowledge was a collaborative and cumulative venture, made possible by face-to-face meetings and, even more so, by the virtual sodalities scaffolded by the regular exchange of paper. There emerged a broadly shared understanding that progress in scientific understanding would occur only if knowledge of observation and experiment circulated among friends and colleagues near and far. This spirit of exchange was behind various new scientific societies that emerged in the seventeenth century. These were places for scientific discovery, but even more so for the publication (in the broadest sense of the word) of results, the affirmation of social ties between scholars, and the confirmation of information about the natural world.

Finally, scientific knowledge was shaped in important ways by those other than the celebrated scientific experts, the so-called *virtuosi*, and there has been a growing recognition of the varied social origins of new thinking about the natural world and the locales in which the studies took place. The study of the natural world no longer originated in the universities, as it had in the Middle Ages. Its polygenesis extended now to princely courts, which were free of many of the intellectual constraints of the university, as well as to informal academies and scientific societies. Information also circulated between these bodies and broader communities of merchants, autodidacts, and artisans.[5] Francis Bacon, for one, saw the enterprise of natural history as one that relied on the contributions of a great many individuals: "the materials on which the intellect has to work

---

[4] "Sed quid ego in tam vasto Librorum Oceano, quibus studiosorum ingenia perturbantur, fatiganturque." William Gilbert, *De magnete, magnetisque corporibus, et de magno magnete tellure* (London: Peter Short, 1600), This English rendering is from the 1990 translation by S. P. Thompson (www.gutenberg.org/files/33810/33810-h/33810-h.htm). Gilbert later explains that he had read everything available on the subject before setting out on his experiments, and begins the book proper with what we might call a literature review. Both this reading and his research into "things themselves" were essential for the composition of his treatise.

[5] On these broader social origins, see Robert Iliffe, "Material doubts: Hooke, artisan culture and the exchange of information in 1670s London." *The British Journal for the History of Science*, 28.3 (1995), 285–318; Steven Shapin and Simon Schaffer, *Leviathan and the Air Pump: Hobbes, Boyle and the Experimental Life* (Princeton, NJ: Princeton University Press, 1985); Deborah Harkness, *The Jewel House: Elizabethan London and the Scientific Revolution* (New Haven, CT: Yale University Press, 2008).

are so widely spread that one must employ factors and merchants to go everywhere in search of them and bring them in."[6] The transformation of science involved a great many places, as well as people. Ports, marketplaces, workshops, and (new to early modern Europe) coffee shops served as venues of information exchange between *virtuosi* and the "non-scientific" public. Such individuals may have been on the fringe of established cultural circles, but they could participate in the world of science through print, and shared a commitment to empiricism and to the authority of experience and observation.

All four of these themes concern the generation, organization, and circulation of information about the natural world. These particulars, which today we might call "facts" or "data," became the raw material, the building blocks of scientific knowledge. As in other areas of early modern European life, information management became a habitual concern and point of emphasis, and was itself a driver in the transformation of scientific learning.

Still, the world of science at the beginning of eighteenth century was not our own. Experiment was not yet the dominant form of scientific inquiry, and scientific method was applied intermittently. Much knowledge remained categorized by its ends (as it had been by Aristotle), and thorough systematic categorization and speciation based on observable features remained in the future. What is more, the modern separation of natural and human sciences was scarcely underway. Nevertheless, science in 1700 was already concerned with observing and collecting particulars, and then storing and sorting them, as the recognized building blocks of knowledge about the natural world. These particulars – what today we would call "evidence" – were the *historia* of natural history and were elevated alongside the universals of *philosophia*, and, increasingly, seen as helping to shape the universals themselves. In short, science in 1700 was rooted in information, information about the natural world gathered from experience, experiment, and study. Science had been transformed by a revolution in information across the previous two centuries, whether or not we choose to speak of a Scientific Revolution.

6.1 The Importance of Observation

Early modern naturalists gradually came to embrace observation as an essential means of understanding their subject matter; ultimately,

---

[6] From *Parasceve ad historiam naturalem et experimentalem* (1620), cited in Peter Antsey, "Locke, Bacon and natural history." *Early Science and Medicine*, 7 (2002), 65–92 (here 71).

everything became worthy of the human gaze. Francis Bacon described the new science, rooted in such observations, as *venatio*, a hunt: collecting data came first and attention should be paid to every observable detail. As he explained in his influential *Novum Organum* (first published in 1620), this process of collection must run its course before any theorizing could take place and be undertaken without the intention of confirming preexisting ideas. Virtually no one in the early modern period was a fully paid-up Baconian, perhaps not even Bacon himself. Even the most empirical observers adhere to set programs, seek to store up established notions, and privilege some facts over others. Nonetheless, Bacon's admonitions reflect a sensibility, widespread by his lifetime, that privileged the power of observation and recognized the worth of the resulting data. So, by 1667, the English diarist and naturalist John Evelyn (1620–1706), in a letter to Abraham Cowley, was declaring that "the Heavens, the Seas, the Whole globe of Earth (from the variously adorned surface, to the most hidden Treasures in her bowels), all God's visible workers, are your Subject."[7] Daston and Park describe this approach as follows: "Fearful of excluding anything, the natural philosophers strained every nerve to catch everything."[8] In this sense, it was the world itself that expanded.

This early modern emphasis on observation and experiment offered challenges to Aristotelian science, so long predominant. *Experientia* and *observatio* were now brought into contrast with Aristotelian "opinion." Experience, for Aristotle, was essential in establishing what was familiar and accepted as the basis for premises. What observation did take place was largely undertaken to understand phenomena that were already accepted as "common knowledge." Scholastic natural philosophers did not really intend, therefore, to observe new facts or "make discoveries." In this sense, the Aristotelian paradigm was not about seeking to add new information to the system; it operated in what was essentially a closed universe.

The commitment to observation and particulars changed this calculus. No longer would the empirical gaze be restricted to the "common" experience emphasized by Aristotle. It must encompass those things that departed from the familiar, the "deviating instances," as Francis Bacon called them, as well as the banal and quotidian. An intellectual disposition to pay heed to all sorts of information was therefore required, injecting huge quantities of particulars into the networks of knowledge

---

[7] Douglas Chambers and David Galbraith, eds., *The Letterbooks of John Evelyn*, Vol. 2 (Toronto: University of Toronto Press, 2014), 435.
[8] Lorraine Daston and Katharine Park, *Wonders and the Order of Nature* (New York: Zone Books, 1998), 316.

and discovery, compelling scientists and scholars to develop methods for processing the resulting data.

The cosmological finitude of Aristotle was thus exploded. The world, and the range of things to know about it, expanded geometrically. Even when scientific investigation was guided by Aristotelian categories and imperatives (which it largely was, well into the seventeenth century), the new experiential and observational approach yielded great accumulations of particulars. The early modern world simply contained a great many more things. The prevailing assumption that the writings of the ancients had delineated everything was proven dreadfully wrong: the visions of Pliny, Theophrastus, and Ptolemy were shown to be restricted and woefully incomplete. The obliteration of the confines of this former world was also spatial, as the geographical horizons of European collection and observation extended into newly explored lands.

Experience, therefore, became a "caustic solvent" of established beliefs.[9] Subjected to observation and description, the things of the world yielded information, the management and classification of which became central to the scientific transformations of the early modern world. The end of finitude, the manifold new discoveries, and the change in the scale of nature combined to pose an urgent epistemological question: do you fit new knowledge into existing categories and interpretative schemes or do you create new "types" in which to group them? Discovery in early modern Europe not only meant "uncovering" something that was previously unknown – a new species, a new land, a new process in nature – it also meant accommodating that piece of knowledge within a system that connected it in meaningful ways with what was already known.[10] The "emblematic view of nature," in which plants, animals, and natural phenomena were categorized chiefly according to moral and literary traditions, was no longer tenable.[11] New taxonomies were required.

Experience, in the Aristotelian mold, needed to be subjected to logic in order produce knowledge that was analytically solid. By contrast, the observational ethic, even when it was employed in order to confirm existing axioms, was all about the recording and accumulation of data; this included the results of experiment but also scholarly practices such as excerpting and note-taking. Developments in the field of medicine, whose

---

[9] This is the expression employed in David Wootton, *The Invention of Science* (London: Allen Lane, 2015), 270.
[10] This is a point made by Peter Dear in *Revolutionizing the Sciences. European Knowledge and its Ambitions*, 2nd ed. (Princeton: Princeton University Press, 2009), 126.
[11] William Ashworth, "Natural history and the emblematic world view." In David Lindberg and Robert Westman, eds., *Reappraisals of the Scientific Revolution* (Cambridge: Cambridge University Press, 1990), 303–332.

practitioners were particularly inclined toward an observational ethic, are exemplary of these trends. The authority of Galen (130–210 CE), whose writings on anatomy were rediscovered (and published in a Greek edition by Aldus Manutius) only in 1525, stood in equipoise with personal observation. As early as 1522, Jacopo Berengario da Carpi (1460–ca. 1530), in his *Isagoge Breves Prelucide ac Uberime in Anatomiam Humani Corporis*, was declaring that observation was the sole route to anatomical truth. While Galenic texts framed many of the medical questions, the emphasis on observation undermined Galen's authority. Doctors and empirics were committed observers and recorders of the particulars of case studies, and they regularly shared and compared case records to assemble knowledge and acquire insight.[12] In a 1579 medical text, Thomas Muffet (1553–1604) exhorted his readers: "Nor is it ever too late to change to better ways: even in this old age of yours, sell your estates, take to the sea, go abroad, build laboratories, study chemistry, cultivate the new medicine that does not float about on a sea of opinion but is established by the evidence of the senses."[13]

By the seventeenth century, sense experience and scientific experimentation were widely acknowledged as the keys to medical knowledge – by that time, empirical observation in medicine had acquired a positive connotation. Shortly after 1700, the Dutch physician and botanist Herman Boerhaave (1668–1738) was insisting that scientific knowledge could not be "based on theoretical speculation without any reference to practical experience" and that nature was the "sole guide" for the perfection of medicine.[14] It is not an accident that a number of the most important philosophers of the early Enlightenment were also physicians: John Locke (1632–1702), Julien Offray de la Mettrie (1709–1751), and Bernard Mandeville (1670–1733).

The embrace by naturalists of new ways to collect, observe, describe, and classify, was accompanied by copious writing.[15] Writing on paper was the chief means by which they created and organized knowledge and then exchanged it with one another in networks of scholarly sociability. The observatory, laboratory, and theater of nature were essential locales for the pursuit of scientific learning, but so too was the blank space of the page. The

---

[12] Pamela Smith, "Laboratories." In Katherine Park and Lorraine Daston, eds., *The Cambridge History of Science, Vol 3: Early Modern Science* (Cambridge: Cambridge University Press, 2006), 291–305.
[13] Quoted in Peter Murray Jones, "Reading medicine in Tudor Cambridge." In Vivian Nutton and Roy Porter, eds., *The History of Medical Education in Britain* (Amsterdam: Rodopi, 1995), 153–183 (here 176).
[14] Quoted in Harold Cook, *Matters of Exchange: Commerce, Medicine, and Science in the Dutch Golden Age* (New Haven, CT: Yale University Press, 2007), 409.
[15] See Paul Delaunay, *La zoologie au seizième siècle* (Paris: Hermann, 1962).

writing produced and circulated by natural philosophers was manifold in its format: records and accounts of experiments; drawings, plans, and diagrams; accounts of conversations with fellow practitioners; travelogues; speculative notes and offhand observations and reflections written into the margins of books; commonplace books designed to categorize information taken from reading and experience; treatises in varying degrees of completion; loose notes and scribbles of every variety; and the letters to and from others members of the scientific *respublica litterarum* (which will be discussed in Chapter 7). In early modern science, the paper piled up relentlessly.

Francis Bacon, perhaps the most consistent advocate for the empirical outlook, stressed the importance of writing, in its various forms, to the pursuit of knowledge about the natural world. He wrote in his *De augmentis*:

> The great help to the memory is *writing*; and it must be taken as a rule that memory without this aid is unequal to matters of much length and accuracy; and that its unwritten evidence ought by no means to be allowed. This is particularly the case in inductive philosophy and the interpretation of nature; for a man might as well attempt to go through the calculations of an Ephemeris in his head without the aid of writing, as to master the interpretation of nature by the natural and naked force of thought and memory, without the help of tables duly arranged.[16]

Naturalists were thus motivated by a desire to preserve their thoughts on paper, to protect them against loss and destruction, and to have at hand a repository that would support and spur their memories. A great many of the tools, techniques, and implements that scientists and scholars employ to augment their memories – catalogs, indexes, digests, charts and tables, glossaries, lexicons, and of course taxonomies and other brands of speciation – date from the early modern period.[17] Some believed the accumulation of particulars overburdened memory and was a threat to clear thinking. This was the view of Descartes, who insisted that "the fewer items we fill our memory with, the sharper we will keep our native intelligence for increasing our knowledge." Luckily (he wrote elsewhere), "human ingenuity has given us that happy invention – the practice of writing. Relying on this is an aid, we shall leave absolutely nothing to memory but put down on paper whatever we have to retain."[18] Many branches of natural philosophy embraced copious writing alongside (and as a function of) the

---

[16] *De augmentis*, ch. 5. Quoted in Andrew Hiscock, *Reading Memory in Early Modern Literature* (Cambridge: Cambridge University Press, 2011), 224.

[17] A point made by Richard Yeo, "Between memory and paperbooks: Baconianism and natural history in seventeenth-century England." *History of Science*, 45 (2007), 1–46 (here 3).

[18] The first quote is from a 1640 letter to Cornelis van Hogelande, the second from Descartes' *Rules for the direction of the mind*, rule 16. Both of these are cited by Yeo, "Between memory and paperbooks," 21.

ethic of observation and empirical spirit. And the exchange of both manuscript and printed information multiplied the impact of their observations about the natural world.

6.2 Historia et Experientia

The growing commitment to the observational ethic thus injected large quantities of data into the European community of natural philosophers. But it is a mistake to set this empirical bent wholly against a preceding world of books. "Experience" for early modern naturalists was as much about the experience of reading as it was the processes of observation and experiment. There was, in early modern natural philosophy, what Hannah Murphy has labeled a "hybrid hermeneutics."[19] The great abundance of books made available by print was as transformative for science as it was for other areas of scholarship, as accounts of the natural world compiled by both ancients and contemporaries were shared in print to an unprecedented degree. In this fashion, early modern science was in part an exercise in philology, and its practitioners shared the routines and methods of Renaissance humanists.

Many Renaissance naturalists saw their undertakings chiefly as a reworking of classical traditions, accessed through reading. Nicolaus Copernicus (1473–1543) and Andreas Vesalius (1514–1564) state as much in their works. Copernicus, in his seminal *De revolutionibus orbium coelestium* (1543), reports that he had scoured all the available ancient authorities for references to the earth moving. Similarly, Vesalius, often considered the epitome of the observational ethic, presents his *De humani corporis fabrica* (1543) as a revisiting of ancient practice and even collaborated in the publication of a new edition of Galen.

Reading was the foundation of much early modern natural philosophy, and critical reading invariably meant responsive writing that added to the paper trail, in the form of responsive notes – in the margins of books, on scraps of paper, and in dedicated waste and commonplace books. In early modern natural philosophy, there was not so much a rejection of the value of books as there was a reconsideration of which books should be read, and what use should be made of them. We can see this combined commitment to experience and humanistic reading in some of the paradigmatic figures of early modern science. Take Johannes Kepler (1571–1630), the figure perhaps most associated with the creation of the "new astronomy," characterized by rigorous physical observation

---

[19] Hannah Murphy, "Common place and private spaces: libraries, record-keeping and orders of information in sixteenth-century medicine." In *Past and Present*, 230.11 (2016). Supplemental issue on "The social history of the archive: record-keeping in early modern Europe." Ed. by Alexandra Walsham and Liesbeth Corens, 253–268.

and mathematical calculation. Galileo once wrote to Kepler bemoaning those philosophers who confined themselves to books: "This kind of man thinks that philosophy is a sort of book like the *Aeneid* and *Odyssey*, and that truth is to be found not in the world or in nature but in the collation of texts ... I wish I could spend a good long time laughing with you."[20] But the denigration of book learning could profitably only go so far. Anthony Grafton has emphasized that Kepler's praxis focused as much on his commitment to humanistic reading as it did on his observation of the heavens. Kepler was a keen reader and interpreter of classical and biblical texts and he brought to them a critical and often skeptical mien typical of his Renaissance humanist forbears. It is evident that Kepler's exploration of the skies frequently transpired by staring down at his books, and the discrimination he applied to this reading paralleled the care he gave to his collection of astronomical data. Many of the methods of naturalists to record and organize their information were inspired by or borrowed from Renaissance humanism. Like other scholars of the age, natural philosophers inhabited a world of paper, inscribed in manuscript and print. Even as they focused increasingly on "things," chiefly things observed, it was impossible for them to abandon the words in books. "The normal early modern scientist resembled a book worm dragging its endless length down endless book stacks rather than Cesi's lynx fiercely scrutinizing the secrets of nature."[21] As Grafton has written elsewhere: "the laboratory could not exist without the library."[22] Early modern naturalists were book beavers as much as they were lab rats.

The commitment to *historia*, in the form of pillaging books and observing nature, meant that naturalists were drawing particulars from both past and present. If *Historia* meant anything, it meant abundance. Arno Seifert has called *historia* the namesake (*Namengeber*) of early modern empiricism.[23] The *historia* of "natural history," terminology that began to appear regularly in the sixteenth century, meant a collection of information about nature, drawn from both texts and observation. This is implicit in its appearance in titles about the natural world such as Conrad Gessner's *Historia animalium* (1551–1558), José de Acosta's *Historia Natural y Moral de las Indias* (1590), and Claudius Clusius's *Rariorum plantorum historia* (1601).

---

[20] Quoted in Richard Yeo, *Notebooks, Virtuosi, and Early Modern Science* (Chicago: University of Chicago Press, 2014), xii.

[21] Anthony Grafton, "Kepler as a reader." *The Journal of the History of Ideas*, 53.4 (1992), 561–572 (here 564–565).

[22] Anthony Grafton, *Commerce with the Classics: Ancient Books and Renaissance Readers* (Ann Arbor, MI: University of Michigan Press, 1997), 227.

[23] Arno Seifert, *Cognitio historica: die Geschichte als Namengeberin der frühneuzeitlichen Empirie* (Berlin: Duncker & Humblot, 1976).

To capture the spirit of *historia* as information gathering from multiple sources, we can again look to the field of medicine. Already in the fourteenth century, coinciding with the regular availability of paper, physicians kept manuscript records of their cases. Doctors often kept casebooks that documented details of their encounters with patients, as well as pharmacological records. Beginning in the sixteenth century, physicians amassed empirical patient histories, which were collected in large volumes of *observationes*.[24] The manuscript writing produced in the service of medicine dwarfed all of the new writing about human physiology, disease, and treatment in early modern printed books. We are now accustomed to paperwork as a bugbear of modern medical practice, but it turns out this is not a modern problem. Medical practitioners were especially zealous observers and record keepers, and enthusiastic users of a variety of paper technologies to collect, format, select, reduce, compare, and sort.

Physicians accumulated case studies from their own practice, but also from the experiences of colleagues and correspondents, and from their own reading of medical literature. These *observationes* would become the basis for vast projects in commonplacing undertaken by medical specialists, comprising both contemporary medical texts and first-hand observation. Observation gradually gained authority, chiefly because it proved more useful in practice. Charles Estienne (1504–1564), in his 1545 anatomical treatise *De dissectione partium corporis humani*, declared that "he who writes the *historia* of the human body should take care, among other things, to know from direct experience the things he will describe."[25] By the second half of the sixteenth century, *observatio* had become an epistemic genre that embodied the embrace of empirical observation. Accumulating in numbers, *observationes* created packets of information that could be exchanged and circulated with colleagues within the profession, thus promoting a sense of shared, collective empiricism, a sort of *respublica medica*. This practice had parallels in established humanist practice, where scholars collected *exempla* from texts for their teaching, as in Mario Mizolio's *Observationes in Marcum Tullium Ciceronem*, first published in 1535.

The great numbers of medical *observationes* that accumulated were an indication of the information glut that could result from a commitment to

---

[24] See Johanna Geyer-Kordesch, "Medizinische Fallbeschreibungen und ihre Bedeutung in der Wissensreform des 17. und 18. Jahrhunderts." *Medizin, Gesellschaft und Geschichte*, 9 (1990), 7–19.

[25] Quoted in Gianna Pomata, "*Praxis Historialis*: the uses of *historia* in early modern medicine." In Pomata and Nancy Siraisi, eds., Historia : *Empiricism and Erudition in Early Modern Europe* (Cambridge, MA: MIT Press, 2005), 105–146 (here 107).

empiricism. Starting in 1584, Pieter van Foreest (1521–1597), the "Dutch Hippocrates," published his *Observationum et curationum chirurgicarum* in a staggering thirty-two volumes! By the next generation, the surgeon Wilhelm Fabry von Hilden (1560–1634) (Latinized Fabricius Hildanus), the "father of German surgery," published some six *centuriae* of *Observationes et curationes chirurgicae*, bringing together nearly sixty years of reading and medical practice. Here he cited 348 separate colleagues who had shared their observations with him in person, in print, or through correspondence. There was theoretically no limit to how expansive such projects could become.[26]

The *observatio*, then, was a piece of empirically gathered information that could be combined with other *observationes*, could be shared with other individuals, and tended to accumulate in great numbers. It became a staple of a range of disciplines, not only medicine, but also law, astronomy, and other branches of natural philosophy, as a unit of exchange between scholars and naturalists, and, by the end of the seventeenth century, the fruit of "experimental philosophy," gathered under controlled conditions.

6.3 Description

The emphasis on observation, over time, required greater and greater precision in description. Much of the information resulting from the commitment to observation was not strictly what we might today call "data," but instead information of a descriptive nature. Naturalists recorded, shared, and sometimes published detailed descriptions of plant and animal species (including the ones seen for the very first time in the New World), of human physiology, of visions revealed by telescope and microscope, of a great variety of natural phenomena, and of the results yielded by a growing commitment to experiment. These descriptions filled the notebooks of naturalists, the communication that they shared with interested colleagues, and the printed books that they published. The inclination to description thus generated a new *copia*, a common store of information about the natural world that offered opportunities for comparison, correlation, and categorization. The shift to description, in this way, proved in the long run to be epistemologically disruptive.

---

[26] On medical *observationes*, see the articles by Gianna Pomata : "Sharing cases: the *observationes* in early modern Medicine." *Early Science and Medicine*, 15.3 (2010), 193–236; and "Observation rising: birth of an epistemic genre, 1500–1650." In Lorraine Daston and Elizabeth Lunbeck, eds., *Histories of Scientific Observation* (Chicago: University of Chicago Press, 2011), 45–80.

Certain branches of the natural sciences particularly embraced copious description. Botany in early modern Europe, for example, became what Brian Ogilvie has called a "science of describing."[27] "Botanizing" was necessarily about experience, as it involved describing plants that one had seen in person. Description and, when available, depiction, became the bases for the pursuit of botanical knowledge. The commitment to observation and description led to a transformation of botanical knowledge and practice, chiefly because of the resulting influx of new information about the world's plant life. This hoard, reflected in the many new printed books with lengthy and detailed descriptions and illustrations, demanded a new catalog of nature.[28] Early modern botanists, like many contemporary scholars, were inveterate "sorters" of knowledge. A corresponding botanical taxonomy became an important concern in the course of the sixteenth century. Botanists became information managers, too.

At first, botanical description aimed at identifying the species that had been described by ancient authorities, such as Theophrastus (fourth century BCE) and Dioscorides (first century CE). But such deference to ancient authorities did not preclude an observational ethic. Gonzalo Fernández Oviedo (1478–1557), author of the *Historia general y natural de las Indias* (the first part of which was published in 1535), might have described Pliny as the "foremost of all historians," but Oviedo himself was an exceptional witness of what he encountered in the Indies and his *Historia* repeatedly emphasizes the importance of good and reliable testimony.

Eventually, systematic observation overwhelmed the limited and familiar varieties of plants contained in ancient texts. The New World opened up a hemisphere's worth of plants to exploration and description, most of which were entirely unknown to European experience and unattested in the ancient sources. If botanists could not undertake fieldwork themselves (and very few could make a trip to the New World), they had to rely on reports of the observations of others and on access to specimens provided by colleagues.

This meant, as Steven Harris has put it, that "European knowledge of the natural world depended increasingly upon expert practitioners who were entrusted with providing reliable information and authentic natural specimens while traversing ever larger and more remote geographical tracts."[29] It

---

[27] Brian Ogilvie, *The Science of Describing: Natural History in Renaissance Europe* (Chicago: University of Chicago Press, 2006).
[28] The circulation of illustrations of plants was an especially valuable and consequential feature of print, as it was something that manuscript could not really produce with any accuracy or consistency.
[29] Steven Harris, "Networks of travel, correspondence and exchange" in Park and Daston, *Cambridge History of Science*, 341–362 (here 341).

is quite striking, however, how long it took for even partial knowledge of New World plants to become incorporated into European botany. Henry Lowood has highlighted the remarkable case of Jerome Bock's *Kräuterbuch*, published in 1539, which describes maize, but makes no mention of its New World origins, instead speculating, based on his reading of Pliny and Dioscorides, that it originated in India. Bock even gives it the name *frumentum asiaticum*! The American origins of corn, in fact, would not be firmly acknowledged by a prominent botanist until Pietro Mattioli (1501–1577) did so in 1570.[30]

The integration of descriptions from personal botanizing, of the growing book knowledge of plants made accessible by print, and the sharing of samples, forced a recalibration of plant categories and multiple exercises in information management. The influx of New World information was highly disruptive in this regard, especially after the systematic efforts to describe and catalog New World biota undertaken by the Spanish crown, starting in the 1570s.[31] In 1571, King Philip II sent Francisco Hernández (1514–1587) to compose a natural history of New Spain. Hernández spent several years gathering material and making observations and then returned with sixteen volumes of largely inchoate notes and illustrations. Philip then instructed Nardo Antonio Recchi (ca. 1540–1594) to provide this morass with some order, at which Recchi was only partly successful. His efforts were not published until 1651, long after the deaths of both Philip and Nardo, through the efforts of Francesco Stelluti at the *Accademia dei Lincei* in Rome, as the *Tesoro Messicano*, representing only a portion of the mountain of notes collected by Hernández.[32]

Particularly illuminating were the endeavours of one prominent Dutch botanist who never made the trip across the Atlantic, Carolus Clusius (1526–1609), to gather together news about European and American plant life. He drew upon various printed travel narratives, examined botanical gardens, collected samples, and conducted a correspondence with other botanists, including the Spanish naturalist Juan de Castañeda, who, over several years, provided him with samples and news of the latest curiosities arriving in Seville.[33] In lieu of personal collecting and experience in the Americas, Clusius rested on information supplied by others. In so doing, Clusius furnished his works, published by Christophe Plantin

---

[30] Henry Lowood, "The New World and the European Catalog of Nature." In Karen Odahl Kupperman, ed., *America in European Consciousness, 1493–1750* (Chapel Hill, NC: University of North Carolina Press, 1995), 295–323 (here 300–301).

[31] Teresa Huguet-Termes, "New World *Materia Medica* in Spanish Renaissance medicine: from scholarly reception to practical impact." *Medical History*, 45 (2001), 359–76.

[32] This story is covered in David Freedberg, *The Eye of the Lynx: Galileo, His Friends, and the Beginnings of Modern Natural History* (Chicago: University of Chicago Press, 2002).

[33] Antonio Barrera-Osorio, *Experiencing Nature: The Spanish-American Empire and the Early Scientific Revolution* (Austin, TX: University of Texas Press, 2006), 126–127.

in Antwerp, with the latest information about plant life from both sides of the Atlantic. Like so many other naturalists, Clusius was forced to think about where all this fit into the catalog of nature. In his botanical garden at the University of Leiden, Clusius made a curious choice about classification. Faced with such *copia*, he organized the plants geographically, dividing his beds by continent.[34]

Clusius's geographical sorting was but one answer to the abundance.[35] Another approach can be seen in the *De plantis* of Andrea Cesalpino (1519–1603), published in 1583. Although he was largely guided by Aristotle and Theophrastus, Cesalpino tellingly classified plants by their fruits and seeds, rather than by their pharmacological properties, as had been customary. It was a taxonomy based on his own observations, often in the botanical garden in Pisa that he tended himself.

In all, Cesalpino described and classified some 1,500 plants. This number was three times the 500 listed in the natural history of Dioscorides, the first-century Greek thinker, who remained the greatest botanical authority at the time of *De plantis*'s publication. In 1623, Caspar Bauhin (1560–1624) catalogued more than 6,000 plants in his *Pinax theatri botanici*.[36] Only eighty years after that, John Ray (1627–1705), in summarizing the state of botanical knowledge, compiled a catalog of 20,000 plants. Ray's contemporary, Joseph de Tournefort (1656–1708), made the recommendation in his *Élements de botanique* (1694) that botanists use a new, more inclusive, taxonomical unit – the genus – to encompass all known plants in 600 types. This meant that, after a century and a half of committed observation and description by botanists, there were now more genera of plants than there had been varieties of plants at the outset![37]

Similar trends appeared in zoology, where massive, encyclopedic works on the animal world began to appear in the sixteenth century. Ulisse Aldrovandi's (1552–1605) description of birds stretched into the three

---

[34] Paula Findlen, "Anatomy Theaters, Botanical Gardens, and Natural History Collections." In Park and Daston, *The Cambridge History of Science*, Vol. 3, 272–289 (here 283). On the life and career of Clusius more broadly, see Florike Egmond, *The World of Carolus Clusius: Natural History on the Making, 1550–1610* (London: Pickering and Chatto, 2010).

[35] Alix Cooper, *Inventing the Indigenous: Local Knowledge and Natural History in Early Modern Europe* (Cambridge: Cambridge University Press, 2007) and Sabine Anagnostou, *Missionspharmazie. Konzepte, Praxis, Organisation und wissenschaftliche Ausstrahlung* (Stuttgart: Steiner Verlag, 2011).

[36] Brian Ogilvie, "Enyclopedism in Renaissance botany: from *historia* to *pinax*," in Peter Binkley, ed., *Pre-modern Encyclopaedic Texts. Proceedings of the Second COMERS Congress, Groningen, 1–4 July 1996* (Leiden: Brill, 1997), 87–97.

[37] Lowood, "The New World and the European Catalog of Nature." In his *The Wisdom of God Manifested in the Works of Creation* (1691), Ray also enumerated 150 quadrupeds, 500 birds, 1,000 fishes, and 10,000 insects.

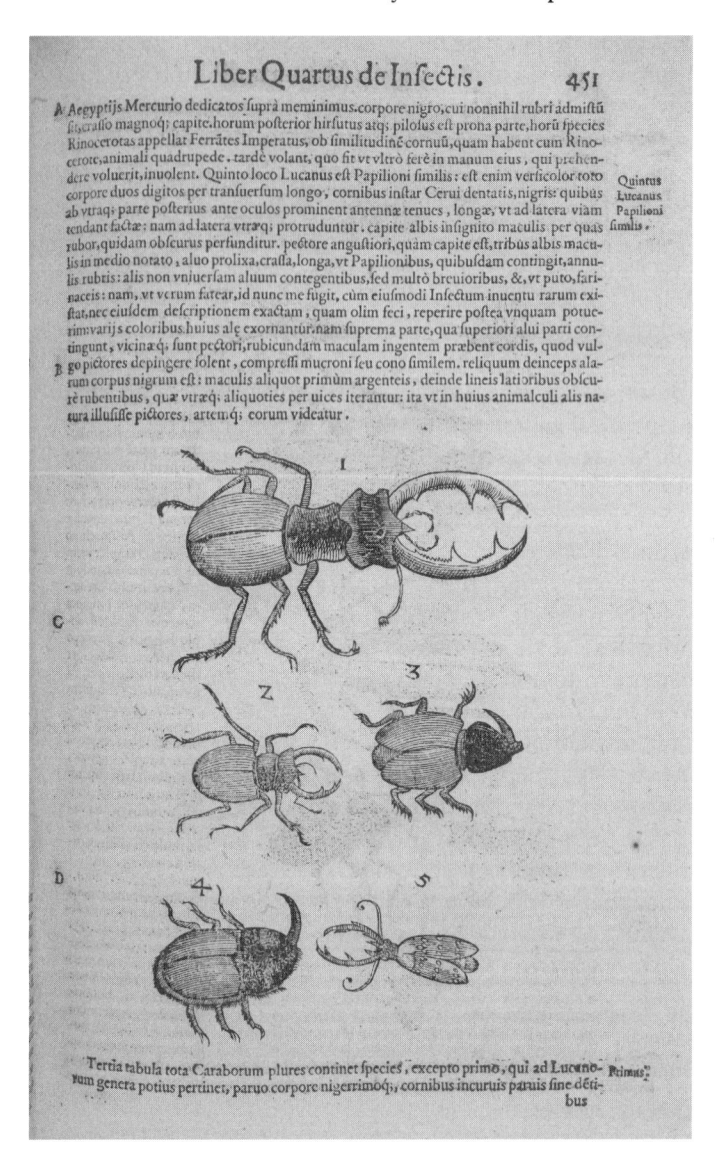

6.1 Observation, description, depiction. Ulisse Aldrovandi epitomized the new zeal to capture the expansiveness of the natural world, here in his section on beetles in *De animalibus insectis libri septem* (Bologna, 1605). (Alamy).

volumes of the *Ornithologia* (1600) and detailed 390 species. Aldrovandi aimed to compile an encyclopedia that was based on the accumulation of observational particulars, most of them supplied by others. The result was a sprawling compendium, of which Jean-Baptiste Chevalier de Lamarck remarked in the nineteenth century: "by eliminating everything useless or irrelevant to the subject, one could reduce it to a tenth of the original."[38] Such were the hazards of the accumulative instinct and a commitment to precise description.

It was the same predisposition toward collection and preservation that saw specimens accumulate in jumbles in the European museums that began to appear in the course of the seventeenth century. Museums were the physical embodiment of the accumulation of particulars, which offered a physical rather than a textual encounter with nature and provided spatial embodiment of the newly expansive universe. As Paula Findlen has written:

6.2 The accumulation of particulars. *Ferrante Imperato and his son Francesco showing visitors their cabinet of curiosities.* Engraving from the *Dell'historia naturale* (Naples, 1599). (Getty Images).

---

[38] Quoted in Ernst Mayr, *The Growth of Biological Thought: Diversity, Evolution and Inheritance* (Cambridge, MA: Harvard University Press, 1982), 168.

"Museums forced scholars to think of nature as a group of objects whose material specificity mattered very much in understanding them. Rather than contemplating nature as an abstract universal, collectors reveled in its particularities. Such things were the facts born of experience."[39] Resembling cabinets of curiosities and *Wunderkammern*, museums, like notebooks, and like archives, were places in which to warehouse knowledge.

Aldrovandi, who embraced *copia* in both his writing and in his accumulation of physical objects, seeded the first genuine public science museum, which opened in 1617 in Bologna. It gathered together 11,000 distinct animals, plants, and minerals, as well as an additional several thousand pressed specimens. Museums like Aldrovandi's sought to represent nature in its totality. In the 1681 catalog of the Royal Society's repository at Gresham College, Nehemiah Grew (1641–1712) wrote that the collection brought together "not only things strange and rare but the most known and common amongst us."[40] As places where the particulars of nature were gathered, sorted, and presented to a public audience, museums brought into relief the pressing need to classify and bring order to the contents of the world in all its abundance and variety.

6.4 Note-taking

Resting on a novel combination of observation, description, and broad reading of newly accessible texts, natural philosophers generated their own *copia*, prompting concerns about how to organize and keep tabs on all these particulars. To cope with the surfeit of information, interventions were required both at the stage of discovery, through personal experience or exposure to the writing of others, and then at the subsequent stage of knowledge categorization and classification. We have already seen how the great accumulation of printed books compelled the production of catalogs and encyclopedias, as well as the disciplinary classification of knowledge. But the explosion of the enclosed Aristotelian universe would end up requiring efforts of an entirely different sort and scale.

These various attempts to provide route finders and signposts within the tangled thicket of information available proceed from some shared principles. One is that genuinely useful knowledge could be distilled from the

---

[39] Findlen, "Anatomy Theaters," 287. [40] Findlen, "Anatomy Theaters," 288.

mass of texts with the effective application of reading strategies: these programs often employed metaphors of bees producing honey from nectar or harvests yielding fruit from the forest, rendering the mass of learning manageable and meaningful. A second is that human memory could be subjected to effective systemization with the application of logic, the essential tool for organizing knowledge. Ordered reading, focused study, and itemization of information were essential for learning. To express it in terms that we might use in the current day: they needed to acquire the means to understand the data they had before they could determine what it meant.

The need for information management that concerned, and bedeviled, so many people and institutions in early modern Europe, was of especial importance to natural philosophers, who, perhaps more than anyone, relied on precedent and an accumulation of evidence that they would need to consult subsequently. In order to keep up with the accumulating particulars central to the pursuit of *historia*, naturalists both borrowed the techniques of humanists and developed original and idiosyncratic means of keeping notes and tracking observations. The resulting loose-leaf manuscript reading notes, paper notebooks, and commonplace books were forms rare or nonexistent in earlier periods. Whether at the scale of recording a single experiment or of an institutional archive, these devices were means of carrying out tasks for which the human mind is not suited. Human memory, we now know, is socially and spatially networked, with memories linked to one another in a complex relational lattice. It is decidedly not structured like an account book, a register of experimental results, or a cabinet of documents.

The memory-aiding practices that proliferated among early modern scholars and scientists in many cases had medieval origins, spanning from the deeply practical protocols of merchants to the more abstract pursuits of scholars and students, and all of these were made more regular and workable by the availability of paper. Medieval commentaries and the copious philological glossing undertaken by Renaissance humanists were forms of note-taking, as were the commonplace books students kept in the course of their studies. By the early modern period, the pursuits that suggested, or required, note-taking expanded further. Doctors, for example, were avid note-takers, recording the observations of consultations and the results of treatments.[41] Lawyers had manifold occasions to take notes: trials, depositions, and commentaries on preceding case law.

---

[41] Jacob Soll, "Healing the body politic: French royal doctors, history and the birth of a nation 1560–1634." *Renaissance Quarterly*, 55 (2002), 1259–1286; and Soll, "The uses of historical evidence in early modern Europe." *Journal of the History of Ideas*, 64.2 (2003), 149–157.

Printers and publishers also had frequent recourse to taking notes, as part of the preparatory work to producing editions. These were designed to enhance memory but also helped categorize and store data for subsequent consultation and analysis.

Paper facilitated writing things down, for others, for oneself, and for posterity. Writing things down became synonymous with scholarly work, and especially as an activity that accompanied reading. This is what Pierre Gassendi (1592–1655) wrote of his mentor, the astronomer, antiquary, and savant Nicolas-Claude Fabri de Peiresc (1580–1637):

> He was so unwearied with writing, that he presently noted down whatever he met with. To say nothing of his letters, which were very many in number, most full of learning and commonly very large ... Moreover, whatsoever he noted down, he did it upon a new or fresh leaf of paper that if anything were afterwards to be added, it might be done without confusion. And he always wrote on the top of the leaf, or the upper part of the margin, the Subject or Title of what he was to note down, in a large character (with which he commonly inserted paper names, and other words, which in the ordinary letter, could not so well be read, or so soon found out) and he added the year and the day, and if he received it from some other, he premised the Author's name.[42]

In Gassendi's description of his friend's writing practices, we see two features of Peiresc's scholarly habits that became widespread – a commitment to writing things down (read, observed, experienced, or otherwise), and the adoption of practices to cut through the resulting thicket of information. The case of Peiresc's archives provides ample evidence of where such a dedication to scribbling could get you – it has been estimated that Peiresc's archive contains more than 77,000 pieces of paper, many of which were originally kept loose and then tied up into bundles (they are bound today). There are seventeen volumes of Peiresc's correspondence (with other scholars, but also with merchants, diplomats, and mariners), as well as 107 volumes of his "works in progress," which include a diverse array of notes, draft essays, and memoranda. Peiresc's commitment to description is evident in the observations he made of nature and of human affairs, and in his reading of history. He applied the same observant eye and descriptive pen to funerals as he did to the movement of Jupiter.[43] Peter Miller calls this vast trove of material "paperware," a database upon which Peiresc drew for his published work and for letters with his many correspondents.[44]

---

[42] From *Mirrour of True Nobility* (1657), quoted in Peter Miller, *Peiresc's Mediterranean World* (Cambridge, MA: Harvard University Press, 2015), 13.

[43] Peter Miller, "Description terminable and interminable: looking at the past, nature and peoples in Peiresc's archive." In Pomata and Siraisi, eds., *Historia*, 355–397.

[44] Miller, *Peiresc's Mediterranean World*, 15.

Gassendi's comments also reveal that Peiresc was committed to a particular brand of writing, note-taking, the aim of which was to distill large amounts of information, and which became widespread in a range of pursuits and disciplines from at least the sixteenth century. Notes, of course, are generally created in order to be disposed of. We are therefore left to speculate as to the full extent to which they were used. Rare cases of survival indicate how a dedication to regular note-taking could generate piles of paper. The German doctor, mathematician, and logician Joachim Jungius (1587–1657), a professor at the universities of Rostock and Helmstedt and then at a secondary school in Hamburg, generated personal papers that ran to 150,000 pages, about a third of which remain extant. Much of this comprises notes taken in the course of his reading, teaching, and professional practice.[45]

Note-taking in the early modern world was a variegated scribal practice in which a great many people participated. The practices of merchants, financiers, and scholars suggest that note-taking became, in a world awash in paper, an essential intermediate step in the creation of large data banks and thus of knowledge. As Jacob Soll has written: "Even when they are destined for disposal, notes are a first step in the chain of information gathering, central to the history of large-scale data banks and information, as well as to the evolution of script into print, or from informal notes to formularies."[46] Ann Blair has identified the essential process involved in note-taking as the 4 S's: storing, sorting, summarizing, and selecting.[47] Note-taking became (and remains) yet another form of information management, essential to many.

Note-taking brought together a range of manuscript traditions: extracting and commonplacing from texts, various strands of *ars memoria*, accounting financial transactions, the observational ethic of natural philosophers, and the jotting down of travelers, ranging from words scribbled on scraps to systematically recorded and organized notebooks. In the increasingly numerous information systems that were in use in this period, notes served as building blocks for data banks and triggers for memory and as means of distilling and categorizing masses of information. Notes, were, in the words of Jeremias Drexel (1581–1638), in his 1638 treatise on excerpting and note-taking, *medicamentum oblutionis*

---

[45] Christoph Meinel, "Enzyklopädie der Welt und Verzettelung des Wissens: Aporien der Empirie bei Joachim Jungius." In Franz Eybl, Wolfgang Harms, Hans-Henrik Krummacher, and Werner Welzig, eds., *Enzyklopädien der frühen Neuzeit. Beiträge zu ihrer Forschung* (Tübingen: Niemeyer, 1995), 162–187.
[46] Jacob Soll, "From note-taking to data banks: personal and institutional information management in early modern Europe." *Intellectual History Review*, 20.3 (2010), 355–375 (here 365).
[47] Ann Blair, "Note taking as an art of transmission." *Critical Inquiry*, 31.3 (2004), 85–107.

nobilissimum, a noble "medicine against forgetfulness." In truth, though, they were a license to forget. Drexel believed that the taking of notes amplified one's ability to exercise judgment, as it prompted slow, careful, and attentive reading, constraining the reader to evaluate and compare. Even if one had a fantastic memory, one must make extracts, because forgetting was inevitable.[48] These paper technologies were, in the words of Alberto Cevolini, "forgetting machines."[49] Forgetting became both necessary and inevitable, as the volume of information pressing upon the memories of early modern scholars became overwhelming. The pressure was especially keenly felt by men of science, who required accuracy about their particulars. Notes and notebooks were means of retaining these details with exactitude and permanence, two essential features of the particulars of the new science.

A good memory remained desirable or valuable in the early modern period and there were many examples of individuals' prodigious memories being celebrated: the likes of Isaac Casaubon (1559–1614)[50] and Joseph Scaliger (1540–1609)[51] were praised for their capacious memories. There was, however, a broad recognition that God-given memory was insufficient to encompass the large quantities of detailed information from reading, observation, and experiment that needed to be recorded with precision. Notes, excerpts, and commonplaces were all forms of external memory (often described as *memoria secondaria* in the literature of the day) that relieved the burden on intrinsic memory. They also acted as a prompt to recollection, and freed up the human mind to expend its energies on things other than the labors of remembering. Notes were not chiefly, then, a replacement of memory but instead a means of augmenting it, akin to adding an additional external battery to a laptop.

Hunting and apian metaphors for note-taking were common, echoing the advice of Seneca in *Moral Epistles to Lucilius*, No. 84:

---

[48] Helmut Zedelmaier, "Johann Jakob Moser et l'organisation érudite du savoir a l'époque moderne." In Élisabeth Décultot, ed., *Lire, copier, écrire: les bibliothèques et leurs usages au XVIIIe siècle* (Paris: CNRS, 2003), 43–62.

[49] Alberto Cevolini, ed., *Forgetting Machines: Knowledge Management Evolution in Early Modern Europe* (Leiden: Brill, 2016).

[50] Hugo Grotius remarked on Casaubon's capacious memory, interestingly in the context of Casaubon's ability to recall things by glancing at the notes he had written in the margins of his books. This from a letter to Joachim Camerarius of 1628, cited in Anthony Grafton and Joanna Weinberg, *"I Have Always Loved the Holy Tongue": Isaac Casaubon, the Jews and a Forgotten Chapter in Renaissance Scholarship* (Cambridge, MA: Harvard University Press, 2011), 14.

[51] It is notable that Scaliger himself declared that he had not a good memory but a good power of reminiscence: *Memoriam voco huiusce cognitionis conservationem. Reminiscentiam dico, repetitionem disciplinae, quae e memoria delapsa fuerat.* He described himself as such in *Aristotelis Historia de Animalibus, Julio Cesare Scaligero Interprete* (Toulouse, 1619), 30.

We should follow, men say, the example of the bees, who flit about and cull the flowers that are suitable for producing honey, and then arrange and assort in their cells all that they have brought in; these bees, as our Vergil says: "pack close the flowing honey, And swell their cells with nectar sweet ...

... We also, I say, ought to copy these bees, and sift whatever we have gathered from a varied course of reading, for such things are better preserved if they are kept separate; then, by applying the supervising care with which our nature has endowed us, – in other words, our natural gifts, – we should so blend those several flavours into one delicious compound that, even though it betrays its origin, yet it nevertheless is clearly a different thing from that whence it came.[52]

By the seventeenth century, numerous manuals on note-taking had appeared, Francesco Sacchini's *De ratione libros cum profectu legendi libellus* (1614), Jeremiah Drexel's *Aurifodina artium et scientiarum omnium excerpendi sollertia* (1638) and Vincent Placcius's *De arte excerpendi* (1689) among the best known. These guidebooks gave instructions on how best to take notes and record extracts from readings, but also how to organize the subsequent accumulations of data. They described practices that reinforced memory, by triggering the recall of things read or experienced, but also freed up the mind to expend its energy on other things. Placcius used the imagery of a "memory closet," where ideas and facts were stored, and which could be opened up to prompt recall.[53]

Where early modern notes do survive, it is often in notebooks. Brian Vickers has written that "the Renaissance was fundamentally a notebook culture."[54] Notebooks served as spaces for accumulating information and observations but also as thematic portfolios, as spaces in which information could be sorted and associated. The maintenance of multiple notebooks dedicated to the recording of specific categories of data had long been a common practice of merchants, and had been picked up by Renaissance humanist polymaths such as Rudolf Agricola (1443–1485), Desiderius Erasmus (1466–1536), and Juan De Vives (1493–1540). It proved to be a medium that served the ends of natural philosophers, lawyers, and doctors, among others, very well.

Such practices were essentially accounting applied to scholarship and science, a means of managing data. In their most basic form, the notes of merchants were known as *adversaria* (so-called because they appeared on

---

[52] Translation from the Loeb Classical Library edition, Vol. 2 (Cambridge, MA: Harvard University Press, 1920). Trans. and ed. by Richard Mott Gummere. Online version can be found at https://en.wikisource.org/wiki/Moral_letters_to_Lucilius/Letter_84.
[53] Blair, "Note taking as an art of transmission," 106. On the "art of excerpting" generally and the creation of such "machines," see Helmut Zedelmaier, "Johann Jakob Moser et l'organisation erudite."
[54] Brian Vickers, ed., *Francis Bacon: The Major Works* (Oxford: Oxford University Press, 1996), xlii.

facing pages of an open notebook), or, as they are sometimes called, "waste-books." The German theologian Heinrich Salmuth (1522–1576) described the *adversaria* as intermediate catchalls to aid fallible memories: "These *adversaria* are chaotic tables, or little books of notes and charts which they write quickly, lest something slip their memory. Later these could be edited into correct and permanent tables."[55]

Like merchants and financiers undertaking accounting of their activity, many scholars and naturalists kept notebooks of two sorts. One followed the model of the *adversaria*, generally organized chronologically rather than according to any topical scheme. These often resembled diaries, providing a sequential recounting of observations, opinions, impressions, and experiences. Predictably, such collections could be massive, bringing together as they did largely undifferentiated data. The other would be a commonplace book, in which notes, textual abstracts, and observations were arranged into thematic categories.

Aldrovandi, for example, compiled thirty-two volumes of manuscript *Observationes*, following the model of the *adversaria*. In keeping these two sorts of notebooks, one on the model of a merchant's waste book and one that organized his *loci communes* alphabetically, Aldrovandi was imitating mercantile practices he knew from his years as a bookkeeper.[56] Neither did much to relieve the immense pressure of the accumulating information. When Aldrovandi sought to bring order to his notes, his efforts buckled under the weight of the accumulated information. His alphabetic manuscript encyclopedia, the *Pandechion Epistemonicon*, designed to provide shortcuts, became fantastically unwieldy in its own right, stretching to eighty-three shelf-groaning volumes. He used the world *selva* ('forest') to describe its contents, telling the Grand Duke of Tuscany that it was designed to

> find whatever the poets, theologians, jurists, philosophers, historians have written on any thing of nature or art one wishes to know or about which one wants to write ... and other [things] will be found that are not mentioned by the authors [and] that came to my attention through many documents, in a variety of places through a plenitude of authors.[57]

He (or a scribe working for him) took notes on small slips of paper, stored them in linen bags assigned to letters of the alphabet, and then pasted them into the corresponding page in a notebook. Robert Hooke

---

[55] Quoted in Vera Keller, "Nero and the last stalk of *Silphion*: collecting extinct nature in early modern Europe." *Early Science and Medicine*, 19 (2014), 424–447.

[56] Fabian Kraemer, "Ulisse Aldrovandi's *Pandechion Epistemonicon* and the use of paper technology in Renaissance natural history." *Early Science and Medicine*, 19 (2014), 398–423.

[57] Paula Findlen, *Possessing Nature: Museums, Collecting, and Scientific Culture in Early Modern Italy* (Berkeley: University of California Press, 1996), 64.

(1635–1703) used glue in a similar fashion, pasting loose slips into pages of notebooks.

Aldrovandi also maintained a commonplace book. In this device, notes, textual extracts, recorded observations, and transcribed documents were arranged into thematic categories, both to facilitate the location of information and as an interim step in the production of knowledge. In *De copia verborum*, his brief textbook on rhetoric and composition, Erasmus described the use of *loci communes* to categorize knowledge.[58] Erasmus's approach was an early example of what would become known as commonplacing, one of the most widely employed responses to the abundance of scholarly knowledge. For over a century, it remained a prominent means of organizing the fruits of one's reading and assembling ideas and text for future use. From their original associations with inquiry into the moral sciences, commonplace techniques migrated into related fields such as the natural sciences, theology, history, medicine, and law.[59] It became a shared cultural practice employed by a great variety of Europeans wanting to collate the information before them.

Philip Melanchthon (1497–1560), the Wittenberg humanist, reformer and friend of Luther, devised instructions of his own based on loci-collections, employing a batch of keywords.[60] His *Loci communes rerum theologicarum* (1521) reflected the dispositions of Lutheran theology, with headings such as "free will," "grace," and "justification." Conrad Gessner built upon the loci employed by Erasmus and Melanchthon and created a hierarchy of knowledge, running from the general to the specific. Petrus Ramus (1515–1572) then took the principle of commonplaces several steps further, offering logical schemes and elaborate *stemmae* for organizing knowledge according to branching categories. Ramist approaches were highly influential, beginning in the second half of the

---

[58] See J. Kelley Sowards, "Erasmus and the apologetic textbook: a study of the 'De Duplici Copia Verborum ac Rerum.'" *Studies in Philology*, 55.2 (1958), 122–135; Bert Roest, "Rhetoric of innovation and recourse to tradition in humanist pedagogical discourse." In Roest and Stephen Gersh, eds., *Medieval and Renaissance Humanism: Rhetoric, Representation and Reform* (Leiden: Brill, 2005), 115–149 (here 139–140). For examples of how prominent humanists in Zürich employed Erasmus's recommendations in their own note-taking, see Urs Leu, "Aneignung und Speicherung enzyklopädischen Wissens. Die Loci-Methode." In Christine Christ von Wedel and Leu, eds., *Erasmus in Zürich: eine verschwiegene Autorität* (Zürich: Verlag, Neue Zürcher Zeitung, 2007), 327–342.
[59] Ann Moss, "Power and persuasion: commonplace culture in early modern Europe." In David Cowling and Mette Bruun, eds., *Commonplace Culture in Western Europe in the Early Modern Period* (Leuven: Peeters, 2011), 1–18.
[60] Siegfried Wiedenhofer, *Formalstrukturen humanistischer und reformatorischer Theologie bei Philipp Melanchthon*, Vol. 1 (Bern: Lang, 1976).

6.3 Commonplacing politics. The page on "tyranny" from John Milton's commonplace book, begun 1608, British Library Add MS 36353 (Getty Images).

sixteenth century, representing, in the eyes of Walter Ong, the apotheosis of a "diagrammatic" approach to knowledge.[61]

By the end of the sixteenth century, the manuscript commonplace books in archives and personal collections reflect the influence of Ramist ideas, including *topoi* books with hierarchical heading systems.[62] It was not long before commonplace books, which in personalized, manuscript form proved so useful to individuals as repositories of the fruits of their reading, also began to appear in print. These were followed by what we might call "reference books" (in the sense that we still understand them), which sought to combine simultaneous commitments to comprehensiveness and concision.[63]

For those engaged in the study of the natural world, observed phenomena, descriptions of reality, recorded facts and numbers, and, eventually, experimental results, all lent themselves to commonplace organization.[64] Physicians were among those who would embrace commonplacing and indexing as means of organizing and presenting medical information. A profusion of medical texts, both ancient and modern, as well as a growing body of case studies, sometimes gathered and published in printed anthologies, compelled medical practitioners to organize and systematize the available medical knowledge. As in other areas of learning, it was imperative to achieve some sort of control over masses of reading. Girolamo Cardano (1501–1576), for example, in his *Contradicentium medicorum* (1545), organized data from medical disputations into analytical categories, writing that "these books were necessary, indeed useful, so that the memory of many authors could be gathered together at once." Cardano advocated a note-taking system, marking certain passages as not useful and indicating others as worthy of extraction into notebooks in manageable and retrievable excerpts, ready for subsequent consultation.[65]

Girolamo Mercuriale (1530–1606), the author of numerous medical treatises and an important figure in medical circles in Italy, published a guide for medical students on how to organize their studies. He regarded reduction and expurgation as essential to medical education,

---

[61] Walter Ong, *Ramus, Method and the Decay of Dialogue* (New York: Octagon Books, 1979, c1958).
[62] Ong, *Ramus, Method and the Decay of Dialogue*. See also Howard Hotson, *Commonplace Learning: Ramism and its German Ramifications, 1543–1630* (Oxford: Oxford University Press, 2007).
[63] On reference books, see the terrific book by Ann Blair, *Too Much to Know. Managing Scholarly Information before the Modern Age* (New Haven, CT: Yale University Press, 2010).
[64] Lorraine Daston, "Taking note(s)." *Isis*, 95 (2004), 443–448.
[65] Nancy Siraisi, *The Clock and the Mirror. Girolamo Cardano and Renaissance Medicine* (Princeton: Princeton University Press, 1997), 52–53.

emphasizing the importance of maintaining notebooks (*thesauri*), "so that if you find anything relevant to *materia medica*, or on the mores of physicians, or on the medical art, you can use it to add to your medical books, to adorn your knowledge of medical things opportunely."[66] Such advice recognizes the limitations of human memory in the face of the huge expansion of available medical information. Even the clearest and most focused mind, Mercuriale recognizes, will be insufficient without an accompanying written bulwark, in the form of notebooks and memoranda (*promptuaria*). These should be organized topically according to commonplaces: "following these steps, anything that is forgotten can then be recalled without a great deal of labor."[67] The assumption here is that forgetting is inevitable and that safeguards should be in place to ensure that what is important is not lost.

As a matter of course, projects in medical commonplacing mushroomed. The Genevan physician Théophile Bonet (1620–1689) composed his gargantuan *Sepulchretum sive Anatomica practica* (1679), which ran to a mind-numbing 1,716 printed pages. Bonet used the index as a template for the construction of his own book. It covered nearly 3,000 patient histories, extracted from 400 other physicians, stretching all the way back to Hippocrates. These narratives were then cut up and organized according to anatomical features; running from head to toe (which was typical for the medical practice of the age), cases appeared in more than one *observatio*, as the order of presentation was topical, rather than serial.[68] Bonet was seeking to achieve the elusive combination of comprehensiveness and navigability.

The widespread use of commonplacing came to an end by the close of the seventeenth century. Notebooks of other sorts, such as table books, journals, and diaries now predominated, as commonplace books came to be associated with rigidity and bygone pedagogies.[69] The last prominent treatise on the practice was authored by John Locke, who advocated an approach to creating commonplace books that afforded considerably more flexibility than those proposed by predecessors.

The widely shared commitment to commonplace practices had epistemic repercussions and shaped the information that scholars and naturalists preserved and circulated amongst each other. In recording particulars by the thousands, naturalists in essence created what we understand today

---

[66] Richard Durling, "Girolamo Mercuriale's *De modo studendi*." *Osiris*, 2.6 (1990), 181–195, here 193.
[67] Durling, "*De modo studendi*," 195.
[68] Volker Hess and J. Andrew Mendelsohn, "Case and series: medical knowledge and paper technology, 1600–1900." *History of Science*, 48 (2010), 287–314.
[69] Yeo, *Notebooks*, 23.

to be the "fact." Lorraine Daston sees the emergence of "militant empiricism" among natural philosophers, highlighting the work of Robert Boyle. Facts went from being singular, striking, or unusual events or items that were secret or resisted discovery, to mundane particularities easily replicated through experiment. In indulging their curiosity, naturalists paid attention to every particular, looking for revelatory contrasts. Over time, this emphasis on empirical observation revealed the epistemological importance of the mundane, the demonstrable, and the replicable, which divulged more about nature's truth than did the extraordinary, which defied replication and reproduction.

Daston has shown how this transformation manifested itself in the case of the French naturalist Charles François de Cisternay Dufay (1698–1737) in his work on luminescence. Dufay practiced a "new factuality of regularity," which emphasized the capacity to gather, accumulate, and replicate facts. He no longer idolized the extraordinary and outlandish, but instead recognized that genuine understanding of the natural world could most effectively be located in observation of the ordinary, repeatable, and reliable. The everyday became wondrous in its own right, and what was true about the natural world was what happens "all or most of the time."[70] The new brand of understanding typified by Dufay made facts regularities – when observed and accumulated in bulk, and then subject to some sort of quantification, they became "data": information in the sense that we understand it.[71]

These banks of data were the fruits of curiosity. Shedding some of its long-standing negative connotations, curiosity about the natural world gradually became desirable, even respectable. Thomas Hobbes (1588–1679), for example, was full of praise for curiosity, about the natural world and about the human sciences – he identified this, rather than Aristotle's reason, as the quality that separated man from beast. It was an innate human desire, but one directed toward the ends of knowledge, unlike bodily appetite or the pursuit of carnal pleasure.[72] As with "facts," curiosity underwent a metaphysical transition, becoming less tied to the explicitly wondrous or secretive. The ethic of detailed observation, description, and data accumulation fostered a curiosity that was directed at the everyday, in recognition that it was where the explanations for what and why things happened might lie.[73]

---

[70] A formulation of Mary Lindemann, *Medicine and Society in Early Modern Europe* (Cambridge: Cambridge University Press, 2010).
[71] Lorraine Daston, "The cold light of facts and the facts of cold light: luminescence and the transformation of the scientific fact." *Early Modern France*, 3 (1997), 17–44.
[72] *Leviathan* I iii.vi.
[73] On this, see Lorraine Daston, "Curiosity in early modern science." *Word & Image*, 11.4 (1995), 391–404.

Commonplaced observational data and reading excerpts were torn from their original contexts and then condensed into more digestible morsels (Ann Blair calls them "factoids") to fit the categories under which they were recorded. These scientific "facts" were "quotes" taken from the book of nature, which could then be applied to a variety of epistemic uses.[74] Removed from their original context by commonplacing, and stationed under headings determined by the preferences or concerns of an individual observer or reader, these items became information liable to subsequent reference, deployment, and critical reinterpretation.

Facts, in their brief form, offer numerous conveniences: they are shareable, and allow for collective learning, thus encouraging sociability among naturalists. Unlike opinion, facts are detached from any particular theory and do not exist chiefly to illustrate a general principle that has already been determined. This unmooring from any specific causative association meant that they became interchangeable, recombinable, applicable to multiple circumstances, and deployable for manifold arguments.[75] "Matters of fact" had long been important constituents of legal discourse, as the objects of inquiry, and this sense of "discovery" in the law became evident in the interrogation of nature.[76] Facts, by the end of the early modern period, were becoming the constituent particles of what we now call information.

Whether these various attempts to abbreviate, excerpt, organize, and categorize actually ended up genuinely reducing the strain of information overload is an open question. Those scholars and naturalists who suffered most from information overload were the ones who did the most to create it in the first place. There is no real limit to the notes one can take, and drawing boundaries around what is "relevant" information is often extremely difficult. Many of the scholarly practices and paper technologies that were designed to contain and compartmentalize information, in practice encouraged its production and duplication. Particulars ended up inhabiting numerous categories within information storage systems and were constituent parts of multiple relational manifolds. These afforded novel routes to advancing knowledge, but did little to confine and distill the available particulars, or to make them digestible.

---

[74] This formulation is offered by Michael Stolberg in "John Locke's 'New Method of Making Common-Place Books": tradition, innovation and epistemic effects." *Science and Medicine*, 19 (2014), 448–470 (here 469).

[75] See, in particular, Lorraine Daston, "Perché sono i fatti brevi?" *Quaderni storici*. New series 36, 108.3 (2011), 745–770.

[76] A point made in Lorraine Daston, "Strange facts, plain facts, and the texture of scientific experience in the Enlightenment." In Suzanne Marchand and Elizabeth Lunbeck, eds., *Proof and Persuasion: Essays on Authority, Objectivity and Evidence* (Turnhout: Brepols, 1996), 42–59.

Efforts at collating and classifying nature culminated, most famously, in the projects of speciation that occurred in the eighteenth century. The pioneering figure in this field was the Swedish naturalist Carl Linnaeus (1707–1778), whose binomial speciation of biota encapsulates both the early modern mania for data collection and many of the techniques used to manage it. Linnaeus was an inveterate accumulator of observations, data, and specimens. He was also at the center of a sprawling network of correspondence and knowledge exchange among naturalists. He routinely complained to his colleagues that he had difficulty staying on top of all this material, and he used a great array of techniques forged by his early modern predecessors in seeking to manage it.[77] As he gathered data about the natural world, Linnaeus constructed hundreds of lists and tables to sort through the morass. He used files and loose-leaf slips of paper resembling index cards, which boasted the benefit that he could shift them around to meet his immediate needs. He also compiled a great number of dichotomous diagrams, organized according to the characteristics of the various species of plants and animals that he identified. The use of such diagrams was well over a hundred years old by this time.[78] Dichotomous classifications of knowledge had been features of the work of both Ramus and Jean Bodin (1530–1596).[79] Linnaeus was also an eager annotator, filling the blank spaces in his books with observations and cross-references. All of these mental practices for mediating the information before him were strategies that had come into common use in the preceding two centuries. Linnaeus's great taxonomical innovations, genera and species into which to fit plants and animals, were outgrowths of his efforts to contain and organize his particulars on paper. As more and more information accumulated, these categories became increasingly complex and flexible. Linnaeus might have been a pioneer of speciation, but his collation of nature into networked classifications that encompassed every plant and animal rested on foundations of the early modern toil to manage great abundances of information.[80]

---

[77] See Nils Ekedahl, "Linnean method and the humanist art of reading." *Symbolae Botanicae Upsalienses*, 33.3 (2005), 17–59.

[78] Walter Ong, "From allegory to diagram in the Renaissance mind: a study in the significance of the allegorical tableau." *The Journal of Aesthetics and Art Criticism*, 17 (1959), 423–440.

[79] Ann Blair, *The Theater of Nature: Jean Bodin and Renaissance Science* (Princeton: Princeton University Press, 1997), 84–85.

[80] This summary of Linnaeus's information management rests largely on Isabelle Charmantier and Staffan Müller-Wille, "Natural history and information overload." *Studies in History and Philosophy of Biological and Biomedical Sciences*, 43 (2012), 4–15.

6.5 Scientific Record-keeping

Accompanying the huge amounts of paper generated by naturalists was the familiar early modern urge to preserve them: in personal collections (or "papers"), in archives, or in print publication. There were at least three reasons why the *virtuosi* of early modern natural philosophy, as well as the associated institutions that emerged to support scientific inquiry, were especially interested in preserving these records. First, natural inquiry was cumulative, and consultation of the accrued particulars of observation and experiment was essential for moving knowledge forward. The establishment of what we would call "databases" of particulars was thus of great importance, including the banal, the trivial, and the quotidian.

Second, the process was a collaborative one, and this reinforced the importance of the preservation of notes, experimental records, and scientific opinions, which could move among practitioners. Such sharing occurred when findings and data were published in print, but also via the circulation of personal papers and the consultation of records in archives.

Finally, in addition to being cumulative and collaborative, the search was also contingent and open-ended, constantly subject to revision: hence the maintenance of one's papers was a means of surmounting the interruption of one's project by death.[81] The nature of this empirical inquiry into the expanse of nature was such that it could not possibly be completed in a single lifetime.

Many early modern *virtuosi* generated and accumulated massive collections of papers, which they regarded, as much as their observations and experiments on the natural world, as the raw material of discovery, as fundamental tools in the production of knowledge itself.[82] The preservative sensibility exhibited by many naturalists meant that they preserved even "slips and scraps," perceiving a potential future utility in even the smallest and seemingly most inconsequential pieces of paper.

It is important to think about the papers of naturalists not solely in relation to the production of printed knowledge, but as central to knowledge creation in their own right. The archives of naturalists contained a dizzying array of descriptions, notes, batches of experimental data, drafts of essays, commonplace materials, copies of others' texts and

---

[81] A point made by Elizabeth Yale in "The book and the archive in the history of science." *Isis*, 107.1 (2016), 106–115 (here 108).

[82] Michael Hunter, *The Boyle Papers: Understanding the Manuscripts of Robert Boyle* (Aldershot: Ashgate, 2007); Arnold Hunt, "Sloane as a collector of manuscripts." In Alison Walker and Michael Hunter, eds., *From Books to Bezoars: Sir Hans Sloane and his Collections* (London: The British Library, 2012); Felicity Henderson, "Robert Hooke's archive." *Script & Print*, 33 (2009), 92–108; Sarah Dry, *The Newton Papers* (Oxford: Oxford University Press, 2014).

letters, and loose papers of every description. The German-English polymath Samuel Hartlib (1600–1662), whom contemporaries described as the "conduit pipe" of knowledge and the "hub of the axletree of knowledge" for his deep and broad network of connections and correspondents, accumulated a massive collection of personal papers. The extant archive amounts to seventy-two bundles, only a fraction of what it originally was. In addition, Hartlib maintained a diary, covering the years 1631–1660, which ran to a third of a million words. Hartlib was a zealous transcriber; he "treated books and manuscripts as objects not to be pondered but to be plundered. Books were to be methodized, epitomized, indexed, gutted of their information. He did not want to own them, but he wanted to record information from them of possible use to others." Hartlib's commitment to keeping an archive was very much inspired by his recognition of science as a collaborative venture.[83]

Some naturalists took a more systematic, archival approach to their records than did others.[84] The English natural philosopher and architect Robert Hooke, a man of manifold interests, at his death had a massive library of at least 2,500 titles, but also an extremely large collection of disordered papers on a "confused Variety of Subjects," written in Hooke's barely legible handwriting. As Secretary of the Royal Society, he was also the custodian of its collections, and appears to have taken far more care in managing them than his own. His personal papers included letters he sent and received as Secretary, varied diagrams and descriptions of inventions, reports on papers read to the Society, and results of experiments; as well as records in unfinished or in intermediate form: extracts and notes from reading and observations, off-hand calculations, and unfinished drafts of essays and arguments. It was a complex, tangled forest of paper, reflecting his own as well as the Society's interests and commitments.[85]

Other naturalists showed great concern for the posthumous survival of their papers, uncertain whether family members would attend to them with due care, or, as happened with Peiresc, they would employ the papers they found in his study as kindling to warm themselves.[86] At the end of his life, the English antiquary and natural philosopher John Aubrey (1626–1697),

---

[83] Mark Greengrass, "Archive refractions: Hartlib's papers and the workings of an intelligencer." In Michael Hunter ed., *Archives of the Scientific Revolution: The Formation and Exchange of Ideas in Seventeenth-Century Europe* (Woodbridge, UK: Boydell and Brewer, 1998), 35–47 (here 45).

[84] Elizabeth Yale, "With slips and scraps: how early modern naturalists invented the archive." *Book History*, 12 (2009), 1–36.

[85] Henderson, "Robert Hooke's archive."

[86] "On asseure que les heritiers de Monsieur de Peiresc, s'étoient chauffez pendant tout un hiver des papiers qu'on avoit trouvez dans son cabinet." Joseph Pitton de Tournefort, *Relation d'un voyage du levant*, 2 vols. (Lyon: Anisson et Poseul, 1717), I, 6.

who had no secure locale at which to preserve his papers, worried that they would be used to line piecrusts or clean guns. Ultimately, he was able to have them deposited at the recently founded Ashmolean Museum.[87] The astronomer Christiaan Huygens (1629–1695), perhaps wary of what might happen to them left in the hands of his family, donated his papers to the University of Leiden to ensure their preservation.[88]

Implicit in all of these reasons to preserve one's records was that scientific archives could be used by individuals other than those who generated them, including members of subsequent generations, the result of an increasingly shared instinct to preserve. The foundation of the Ashmolean collection, and other enterprises like it, indicate the emergence of a shared commitment to saving the information recorded on the paper, as essential for the pursuit of scientific knowledge. Like antiquaries, who relied on the survival of manuscripts for their own work, naturalists came to recognize that their work might benefit from access to the "scientific record"; and that their papers could also be a means of projecting the image one wished for oneself, in life and in death.[89]

The importance of maintaining comprehensive records as a platform for further scientific discovery was also manifest in the scientific societies that emerged in the early modern period. One of the aims of the Royal Society, founded in 1660, according to its first historian, Thomas Sprat (1635–1713), was to

> make faithful records of all the works of nature, or art, which come within their reach; that so the present Age and Posterity, may be able to put a Mark on the Errors, which have been strengthened by long prescription; to restore the truths, that have been neglected; to push on those, which are already known, to more various uses; and to make the way more passable, to what remains unrevealed.[90]

The motto of the society may have been *nullius in verba*, but its commitment to the written word was unmistakable. The Royal Society faithfully kept minutes of its meetings, as well as "Letter Books," recording all the

---

[87] Michael Hunter, "The importance of being institutionalised." In Hunter, ed., *Establishing the New Science. The Experience of the Early Royal Society* (Woodbridge, UK: Boydell Press, 1989), 1–14.

[88] In general on the topic of scientific and medical archives, see the recent Vera Keller, Anna Marie Roos, and Elizabeth Yale, eds., *Archival Afterlives: Life, Death and Knowledge-Making in Early Modern British Scientific and Medical Archives* (Leiden: Brill, 2018).

[89] Massimo Bucciantini insists this was the case with Galileo. See "Celebration and conservation: the Galilean Collection of the National Library of Florence." In Michael Hunter, ed., *Archives of the Scientific Revolution*, 21–34.

[90] Thomas Sprat, *History of the Royal Society* (1667). Ed. by Jackson Cope and Harold Whitmore (St. Louis, MO: Washington University Press, 1956), 61–62. Quoted in Palmira Fontes de Costa, *The Singular and the Making of Knowledge at the Royal Society of London in the Eighteenth Century* (Newcastle: Cambridge Scholars Publishing, 2009), 7.

letters read in the Society. The papers of members and the findings of outsiders were registered in manuscript volumes, which were then filed away by the secretary in the Society's archive. These records were often then subject to circulation or to print publication in a periodical entitled *Philosophical Transactions*.[91] Alongside similar institutions, the Royal Society became "the coordinator of all news in the world of science, a sort of 'central bank' for science, with the data based on the observation of nature its currency."[92] It was an enormous task to give structure to what Robert Hooke called "a rude heap of unpolish'd and unshap'd Materials." For the first fifty years, the Society did not have a physical home, and early secretaries had to take home many of the papers they were charged with recording, making copies and registers at their own desks.[93] Only in 1677 was the step taken to keep all the records in a depository. The preservation of these records, in the archive or in published printed form, was regarded as vital to the pursuit of scientific knowledge, and concern for it became almost obsessive. It acted as a bridge to scientists to come, an institutional recognition that the quest for natural knowledge spanned lifetimes. Sprat described the contents of the Society's registry as being passed on to the "next generation of men." It was, as an information resource, a testament to the cumulative, collaborative, and continuous process of discovery, propelled by the observations, descriptions, notes, and experimental records that together formed the epistemic foundations of early modern science.

* * *

By the end of the seventeenth century, those engaged in the search for knowledge about the natural world were undertaking something fundamentally different from their medieval predecessors. There was a growing, if not universal, consensus that the old edifice of deference to received authorities had to be torn down and replaced. The new approach privileged observation and experience as routes to understanding, and increasingly saw experiment as the means by which to observe and experience; naturalists had ready access, thanks to two centuries of printed books, to the insights and findings of naturalists present and past; they had recourse to a new array of scientific instruments, such as the telescope and microscope, that furnished them with data; they were inclined toward

---

[91] Adrian Johns, "Reading and experiment in the early Royal Society." In Kevin Sharpe and Steven Zwicker, eds., *Reading, Society, and Politics in Early Modern England* (Cambridge: Cambridge University Press, 2003), 244–271.

[92] Marie Boas Hall, "The Royal Society's role in the diffusion of information in the 17th century," *Notes and Records of the Royal Society of London*, 29.2 (1975), 173–192 (here 184).

[93] Mordechai Feingold, "Of records and grandeur: the archive of the Royal Society." In Hunter, *Archives of the Scientific Revolution*, 171–184.

a critical attitude to the established authorities; they belonged to new communities and societies of learning, real and virtual, that were networked by paper and face-to-face exchanges; and they employed a novel language, one that emphasized evidence, numbers, and facts. Taken together, these transformations, whether or not they represent a "scientific revolution," constitute radical change in how Europeans came to understand the natural world. Of especial importance was the role of information in achieving knowledge about nature. Morsels of information, or "facts," which, when aggregated, became "data," were on their way to becoming the foundational evidentiary units of knowledge about nature. The changing role of information impacted the specifics of scientific practice, definitions of scientific truth, and the composition and conduct of communities of scientific learning. The Scientific Revolution, if there was one, was, as much as anything else, a revolution in information. Those who resolved to achieve understanding were faced with a novel set of tasks related to the massive new quantities of particulars about the universe now available: among them, quantification, distillation, and categorization. The sheer quantity of data about a heretofore bounded cosmos was bewildering to behold for some, such as Blaise Pascal (1623–1662), who offered this reflection: "I see the terrifying spaces of the universe hemming me in, and I find myself attached to one corner of this vast expanse without knowing why I have been put in this place rather than that, or why the brief span of life allotted to me should be assigned to one moment rather than another of all the eternity which went before me and all that which will come after me."[94]

The obliteration of a finite universe; the avalanche of particulars generated by observation, reading, and scholarly exchange; the acres of scientific "papers," archives, and journals generated as a function of ready access to paper recording instruments: all added to the wealth of information. Science might not yet have been subject to the data saturation of today but, as in other areas of early modern life, information management – its generation, its classification, its storage, and its sharing – and the related challenges of turning information into knowledge became chief concerns of its practitioners. Nature was now *copia*, abundance, and the character of the scientific tools and practices in place meant that the abundance would only grow moving forward.

---

[94] "Je vois ces effroyables espaces de l'univers qui m'enferment, et je me trouve attaché à un coin de cette vaste étendue, sans que je sache pourquoi je suis plutôt placé en ce lieu qu'en un autre, ni pourquoi ce peu de temps qui m'est donné à vivre m'est assigné à ce point plutôt qu'à un autre de toute l'éternité qui m'a précédé de toute celle qui me suit." *Pensées*, Sellier 681.

7 Writing Others and the Self

Early modern Europe was witness to a great age of letter writing, so much so that some have suggested that it saw an "epistolary revolution."[1] The seventeenth century, in particular, has been labeled the golden century of correspondence, and the "great century of discussion,"[2] abetted by the availability of paper and the expansion and systematization of postal systems across Europe. The great increase in epistolary traffic in early modern Europe was seeded by medieval practices. Starting in the eleventh century, there had been a rebirth in the art of epistolary rhetoric, which had ultimately led to the conventions of the *ars dictaminis*, which governed letter writing within the church and became important mediators in the exercise of political power. Between the twelfth and fifteenth centuries, the epistolary art migrated from the public to the private sphere, remaining formalized but becoming increasingly personalized. The *dictamen* of the late Middle Ages emphasized the value of *amicitia*, a chosen relationship rather than a dependent or contractual one.[3] The emergence of administrative writing and pragmatic literacy in late medieval towns positively encouraged and abetted writing by individuals. Most letters written by Europeans were now a product of daily necessity, personalized and employed for private communication. The stylistic prescriptions of the *dictatores* remained influential and continued to shape exchanges, especially between those of unequal social standing, but the greater frequency of epistolary exchanges that were private and in the vernacular made the strictures of *ars dictaminis* less applicable.[4]

---

[1] Jean Boutier, Sandro Landi, and Olivier Rouchon suggest this term should be used alongside the "print revolution": *Politique par correspondence. Les usages politiques de la lettre en Italie (XIVe–XVIIIe siècle)* (Rennes: Presses universitaires de Rennes, 2009).
[2] Émile Bréhier, *Histoire de la philosophie. Tome II: La philosophie moderne* (Paris: Librairie Félix Alcan, 1928), Part I: Le dix-septième siècle.
[3] Alain Boureau, "La norme épistolaire, une invention medievale." In Roger Chartier, ed., *La correspondance: les usages de la lettre au XIXe siècle* (Paris: Fayard, 1991), 127–157.
[4] For England, with insights that apply elsewhere, see Malcolm Richardson, "The Fading Influence of the Medieval *Ars Dictaminis* in England after 1400." *Rhetorica*, 19 (2011), 225–247.

Letters now took on an unprecedented mediatory function in interpersonal relationships, and extended the reach and definition of friendship. They were essential components in the thickening web of communication, by which parcels of information were packaged and then exchanged with acquaintances, forming the foundations of Europe's many virtual communities. By the fourteenth century, in much of Europe the letter had ceased to be chiefly a literary medium and had become a transactional and communicative instrument employed by the literate elements of society.[5] There is a clear connection here between the rise of the familiar letter, an epistle from one named correspondent to another, and the availability of paper after about 1300. In England, for example, all of the letters of the famed fifteenth-century collection of the Paston family were written on paper (whereas most of their formal legal documents were inscribed on parchment).[6] Paper clearly facilitated letter writing for many more people, and many more types of people (including sizable numbers of women of the noble and middling orders).

The early modern epistolary network has been a focus of much recent scholarship.[7] The widespread commitment to letter writing among merchants, scholars, and scientists dissolved distance and created virtual sodalities connected by common ends and interests. For literate Europeans, letters were the primary means of keeping informed of the latest learning and developments of consequence. The production of knowledge was far more decentralized in the early modern world than today, making the writing of letters an essential skill for keeping up to date, securing needed materials, and building and maintaining essential ties of sociability in the pursuit of learning.

Despite the advent of printed books, newspapers, and journals as conduits of information between interested parties, correspondence remained the chief way that written information and knowledge were shared between literate parties. As we have seen, correspondence was the lifeblood of long-distance trade, written government, and international institutions like the Society of Jesus and East India Companies. Like the paper they were now

---

[5] John Taylor, "Letters and letter collections in England." *Nottingham Medieval Studies*, 24 (1979), 57–70 (here 57).
[6] Jennifer Douglas, "'Kepe wysly youre wrytyngs': Margaret Paston's Fifteenth-Century Letters." *Libraries and the Cultural Record*, 44.1 (2009), 29–49 (here 32).
[7] For example, Hans Bot and Françoise Wacquet, *La République des Lettres* (Belin: De Boeck, 1997); Anthony Grafton, "A sketch map of a lost continent: the Republic of Letters." *Republic of Letters: A Journal for the Study of Knowledge, Politics and the Arts*, 1.1 (2009) (https://arcade.stanford.edu/rofl/sketch-map-lost-continent-republic-letters); Mark Greengrass, "Mapping structures of the intellectual field using citation and co-citation analysis of correspondences." *History of European Ideas*, 36 (2010), 330–339; and Peter Burke, "Erasmus and the Republic of Letters." *European Review*, 7.1 (1999), 5–17.

invariably written on, letters were highly flexible; varying in form, length, and content; and amenable to a great variety of uses. Letters retained their traditional purposes – currying favor, recommending acquaintances, confirming fealty and clientage, and displaying rhetorical virtuosity – but their far greater frequency and familiarity meant that they focused on the exchange of news and knowledge more than ever before; once again quantity and frequency ended up shaping format and content. The "letterocracy" that I described in Chapter 4 actually consisted of numerous, overlapping epistolary worlds. Letters in early modern Europe took a great many forms: the epistle sent by a single individual and designed for private reading, letters of safe conduct and credence, letters of recommendation, ecclesiastical bulls, pastoral letters, letters intended directly for publication, and letters aimed at multiple audiences, were all among the forms that letters took. Letters were also subjected to a range of secondary usages: annotation, copying, summarization, sharing, and redistribution into letter books, commonplace books, and printed editions.

Scholarly correspondents looked to imitate classical forbears like Cicero, whose famous letters circulated widely. Renaissance humanists, building upon, but also looking beyond, the *ars dictaminis*, experimented with the medium, creating an arsenal of styles, forms, and language for every occasion. The volume of letters was also a natural symptom of the period's bureaucratization, creation of commercial and intellectual networks, density of political exchanges, and desire to record thoughts and observations. But the greatest impulse to exchange letters originated in more mundane and practical concerns, accompanying all sorts of transactions and interchanges.

The Spanish playwright and poet Lope de Vega (1562–1635) once wrote to the duke of Sessa: "I do not know who claimed that letters are mental speech to those absent, but he spoke rightly, for, as one writes, one is thinking of the person to whom one is writing and speaks with him in one's mind, where his image is represented as if alive."[8] This sense that letters could transport one into the presence of others was a common refrain. The Dutch classical scholar Gerardus Vossius (1577–1649) once wrote to Archbishop James Ussher (1581–1656): "Because you understand that what is known far and wide as the Republic of Letters, as well as the friendship of those who belong to it, dissolve the distance between regions into nothing."[9] Erasmus wrote a treatise on letter writing (one of

---

[8] Fernando Bouza, *Communication, Knowledge and Memory in Early Modern Spain*. Trans. by Sonia López and Michael Agnew (Philadelphia: University of Pennsylvania Press, 2004), 8.

[9] "Scis enim, quam latè pateat Respublica Literaria, atque ut amicitiam eorum, qui ad hanc pertinent, nulla dissolvant regionum spatia." Letter 429, n. d., in *Gerardi Joan. Vossii*

at least 150 known treatises on the topic written in the Renaissance)[10], in which he emphasized the idea of exchanging insights and information with absent friends and colleagues, in so doing creating a virtual, cooperative sodality, a sort of sixteenth-century Facebook group.[11]

The production of some of the sixteenth-century's more prolific letter writers was simply astounding. Erasmus was one of the great letter writers of the age, but his epistolary portfolio was dwarfed by others.[12] The chief figures of the Reformation were especially avid letter writers – Luther has left us more than 3,500 letters (but only forty-seven of them from the pre-1517 period, an indication of the tendency of people to keep the letters of those who have become famous), Zwingli thousands more. Even before the 1517 indulgence controversy made him famous, Luther complained: "I would require two secretaries, for I do nothing almost all day but write letters."[13] John Calvin was at the center of a network of reformed churches and penned letters of support, counsel, and encouragement on a near daily basis to numerous correspondents.[14] Scholars have only begun to process these bucketloads of letters. Johannes Kepler (1571–1630), who was a devoted humanist as well as an astronomical pioneer, generated some six volumes of correspondence, half in German and half in Latin.[15] The modern edition of the correspondence of the Flemish humanist and stoic philosopher Justus Lipsius (1547–1606) runs to thirteen volumes, that of the early seventeenth-century polymath Hugo Grotius (1583–1645) to seventeen volumes. By the second half of the seventeenth century, we have Gottfried Leibniz (1646–1716), the German philosopher, whose epistolary output extends to some 15,000 letters to nearly 1,000 correspondents. The *Nachlass* of Leibniz in its entirety amounted to more than 200,000 pages of written and printed

et Clarorum Virorum ad Eum Epistolae (Augsburg: Sumptibus Laurentii Kronigeri, 1691), 427.

[10] Judith Rice Henderson, "Erasmus on the art of letter-writing." In James Murphy, ed. *Renaissance Eloquence: Studies in the Theory and Practice of Renaissance Rhetoric* (Berkeley, CA: University of California Press, 1983), 331–355.

[11] See Judith Rice Henderson, "Erasmus's *Opus de Conscribendis Epistolis* in sixteenth-century schools." In Carol Poster, ed., *Letter-writing Manuals and Instruction from Antiquity to the Present* (Columbia, SC: University of South Carolina Press, 2007), 141–177; also Erika Rummel, "Erasmus' manual of letter-writing: tradition and innovation." *Renaissance and Reformation*, 13(1989), 299–312.

[12] See Anthony Grafton, in his typical erudition, in "A sketch map of a lost continent."

[13] In a letter of 26 October 1516 to the Prior at Erfurt, Johann Lang, in *The Letters of Martin Luther*. Trans. and ed. by Margaret Currie (New York: Macmillan, 1908), 10.

[14] Elsie McKie, "A month in the life of John Calvin." In Murray Rae, Peter Matheson, and Brett Knowles, eds., *Calvin: The Man and the Legacy* (Hindmarsh, Australia: ATF Theology, 2014), 61–77.

[15] Anthony Grafton, "Kepler as a reader." *Journal of the History of Ideas*, 53.4 (1992), 561–572.

material, the full publication of which extended into fifty-seven volumes. One wonders whether he ever put his pen down.[16]

Even these numbers undoubtedly understate the frequency and volume of letter writing in the period. Only a small proportion survive, and the destruction of letters at the time was common.[17] Only some letters and sets of exchanges were deemed worth saving. In most cases, we have only some of the constituent letters of a series, rendering full understanding of their contents challenging; the picture we get from what remains of individual and institutional correspondence is necessarily patchy, episodic, fleeting, and incomplete.

7.1 The *Respublica Litterarum*

For early modern scholars, the exchange of material paper made possible genuinely pan-European networks of learning and information sharing and extended the notion of *amicitia*: letters were a bonding agent for scholarly friendships.[18] The regular exchange of letters among naturalists and scholars was especially suited to an age that increasingly embraced a sensibility privileging observation, description, and depiction, rather than the debate between antagonists, usually over knowledge already established, that characterized medieval dialectic.

Interactions between colleagues and the pursuit of knowledge were often founded on the exchange of correspondence, which supplemented or even replaced face-to-face encounters. These virtual communities had their own codes of conduct and social conventions. Epistolary interfaces served a wide array of purposes. Some were finely structured attempts to establish or maintain friendships or curry favor with patrons. Some sought to gather or disseminate news or opinion; some intended to secure manuscripts or (in the case of naturalists) desired specimens. All involved the exchange of information.

For those seeking knowledge about the natural world, letters were essential for fully exploiting the fruits of empiricism, because one needed to take advantage of observations and descriptions other than merely

---

[16] See Francisco Bethencourt and Florike Egmond, "Introduction." In Bethencourt and Egmond, eds., *Correspondence and Cultural Exchange in Europe 1400–1700*, Vol. III of *Cultural Exchange in Early Modern Europe*, General ed. Robert Muchembled (Cambridge: Cambridge University Press, 2007), 1–30.

[17] A point made by Arnold Hunt, "'Burn this letter': preservation and destruction in the early modern archive." In James Daybell and Andrew Gordon, eds., *Cultures of Correspondence in Early Modern Britain* (Philadelphia: University of Pennsylvania Press, 2016), 189–209.

[18] A point made in Ann Goldgar, *Impolite Learning: Conduct and Community in the Republic of Letters, 1680–1750* (New Haven, CT: Yale University Press, 1995).

one's own. Conrad Gessner's encyclopedic efforts to encompass all plants and animals of the world were unthinkable without correspondence with a network of more than 100 learned contacts, who regularly supplied him with information, observations, and manuscripts; he was, after all, a mere small-town physician. He regularly thanked these individuals in the dedications to his publications.[19] The maintenance of a flow of letters was essential for those, like Gessner, who found themselves on the geographical or social periphery of established cultural life; participation in the exchange of letters was a mark of citizenship in the *respublica litterarum*. Indeed, Anne Goldgar has argued that one of the widely shared expectations of the Republic of Letters was that one would make information from one's own locale available to far-flung colleagues.[20] Writing a letter to a prominent scholar was a rite of passage for a young learner who sought to become part of the Republic.

Figures like the French polymaths Marin Mersenne (1588–1648) and Nicolas-Claude Fabri de Peiresc (1580–1637) were at the center of vast and interlacing networks of correspondence and celebrated by contemporaries as clearing houses of information. Adrien Baillet (1649–1706), the scholar and biographer of Descartes, reckoned that Mersenne had contact with "all the savants of Europe ... he established himself as the center of the men of letters through the continuous commerce he maintained with everyone, and everyone with him."[21] Descartes used a biological analogy to situate Mersenne in the *respublica litterarum*: "he serves a function in the Republic of Letters similar to that of the heart in the circulation of blood within the human body."[22] Mersenne was the "letter box" of Europe and known in Italy as the *gran trafficante* of scholarly information. Peiresc used the term "midwife" to describe his own role in providing information and encouragement for the scholarship of colleagues. He had more than 500 attested correspondents, and at his death there were upwards of 14,000 registered copies of his letters.

---

[19] Ann Blair, "The 2016 Josephine Waters Bennett Lecture: Humanism and Printing in the Work of Conrad Gessner." *Renaissance Quarterly*, 70.1 (2017), 1–43; see also Laurent Pinon, "Conrad Gessner and the historical depth of Renaissance natural history." In Gianna Pomata and Nancy Siraisi, eds., Historia : *Empiricism and Erudition in Early Modern Europe* (Cambridge, MA: MIT Press, 2005), 242–267.

[20] Goldgar, *Impolite Learning*.

[21] "... tous les Sçavans et Curieux de l'"Europe ... il s'étoit rendu comme le centre de tous les Gens de Lettres par le commerce continuel qu'il entretoit avec tous, et tous avec luy." Quoted in Françoise Waquet, "Qu'est ce que la République des Lettres? Essai de semantique historique." *Bibliothèque de l'École des Chartes*, 147 (1989), 473–502 (here 473).

[22] Paul Dibon, "Communication in the Respublica literaria of the 17th century." *Res publica litterarum*, 1 (1978), 43–55 (here 50).

Claude Clerselier (1614–1684), who made an inventory of the manuscripts of Descartes shortly after the latter's death in 1650, recorded that seven of the philosopher's twenty-three boxes were full of correspondence.[23] The Jesuit Athanasius Kircher (1602–1680), who seemingly wrote about everything, has been called one of the "living monuments" of the Republic of Letters.[24] Daniel Stolzenberg has described Kircher's role as information broker as that of a "boundary spanner," one who connected the learning and global reach of the Society of Jesus with other webs of information sharing within Europe.[25]

Among natural philosophers, the exchange of information – both data and their interpretation – through correspondence was an essential element in the emergence of modern science. One of the most important features of modern scientific work is that it is almost always collaborative – this is a truism that has its origins in the real and virtual sodalities that formed among early modern natural philosophers. "Communication" was among the most important words of the Republic of Letters – it has a rich and varied semantic usage.[26] Personal interactions, travel, publication, and the exchange of letters were all components of the collaboration across distances, but the last of these assumed particular importance. There was not the same assumption of privacy attached to letters that there is today, and there was an expectation that they would be passed around. The familiar image of the scholar as eremitic, retreating to the seclusion of his study (his *solitarium*, as Montaigne called it) is belied by the way networks of correspondence and pathways of information flow. The world of early modern learning was a profoundly social space.

Correspondence offered an alternative to the time and expense of travel. For some, epistolary exchange was vital to becoming a natural historian with broad knowledge. Ulisse Aldrovandi (1522–1605), the great sixteenth-century naturalist, never left Italy, and his extensive network of correspondents was essential to his learning, as he once remarked, *non potendo l'huomo andare in tutti i luoghi* ('a man cannot go to every location.'). In a 1596 letter to a naturalist colleague, Aldrovandi wrote

---

[23] Charles Adam and Paul Tennery, eds., *Oeuvres de Descartes*, Vol. I: *Correspondance* (Paris: Léopold Cerf, 1897), xvii.
[24] Paula Findlen, "Scientific spectacle in Baroque Rome: Athanasius Kircher and the Roman College Museum." *Roma moderna e contemporanea*, 3 (1995), 625–665; Burke, "Erasmus and the Republic of Letters."
[25] Daniel Stolzenberg, "A spanner and is works: books, letters, and scholarly communications networks in early modern Europe." In Ann Blair and Anja-Silvia Goeing, eds., *For the Love of Learning: Essays in Honor of Anthony Grafton*, Vol. I (Leiden: Brill, 2016), 157–172.
[26] Paul Dibon, "Communication epistolaire et mouvement des idées au XVIIème siècle." In Guido Canziani and Gianni Paganini, eds., *Le edizioni dei testi filosofici e scientifici del' 500 e del' 600: problemi di metodo e prospettive di ricerca* (Milan: Angeli, 1986), 73 ff.

that, in order to have knowledge of nature, one had to have "friends in many places."[27] Such attitudes allowed what Steven Shapin and Simon Schaffer in their work on Boyle and Hobbes have described as "virtual witnessing."[28] The sharing of results of observation helped create in the mind's eye of those separated by great physical distance the impression of having been present at the act of observation itself; it multiplied the sets of eyes at one's disposal.

This commitment to collaboration created a sort of mutual support society that encompassed not only academic naturalists, but also physicians, astronomers, herbalists, antiquaries, as well as artisans, mariners, and travelers of many sorts. Such a virtual community of learning required the maintenance of what sociologists have termed "strong ties" and "weak ties."[29] Strong ties include traditional face-to-face encounters of a personal and institutional nature, where testimony can be shared directly. The information shared via these "strong ties," however, was unlikely to spread beyond those directly involved. "Weak ties," which were based on long-distance communication among early modern scholars and natural philosophers, sometimes between far-flung friends but just as often between colleagues who had rarely or perhaps never met, were essential for the learned sociability of the Scientific Revolution.[30] The currency of this genuinely international "philosophical commerce" (in the terminology of the day) was the testimony of others, and, like coinage, its worth depended on the trust that people placed in it. The establishment of trust in faraway individuals, often strangers, was a prerequisite for the collaborative pursuit of knowledge. Facts could not be disentangled from the person who provided them – weak ties had to be buttressed by credibility: letters of reference from trusted individuals were especially important in this regard. *Virtuosi* naturalists sought to establish and maintain correspondence with contacts who possessed such bona fides.

The scientific institutions that emerged in the course of the seventeenth century fully integrated correspondence and the testimony it contained into their pursuit of knowledge. The Royal Society of London in the 1660s instituted a Correspondence Committee, which collected

---

[27] Giuseppe Olmi, "'Molti amici in varij luoghi': studio della natura e rapporti epistolari nel secolo XVI." *Nuncius. Annali di Storia della Scienza*, 7.1 (1991), 3–31 (here 5, 9).
[28] *Leviathan and the Air-pump. Hobbes, Boyle and the Experimental Life* (Princeton: Princeton University Press, 1985).
[29] Mark Granovetter, "The strength of weak ties." *American Journal of Sociology*, 88 (1973), 1360–1380.
[30] On weak ties, see David Lux and Harold Cook, "Closed circles or open networks?: Communicating at a distance during the Scientific Revolution." *History of Science*, 36 (1998), 179–211.

information from foreigners and assessed published reports of voyages in order to establish matters of fact. It also drew up questions for members intending to travel abroad so that they could maximize the effectiveness of the information that they gathered, and establish reliable weak ties. The Society also composed "Letter Books" in which the most important contents of all the letters read at its meetings were recorded. Henry Oldenburg (1619–1677), the initial First Secretary of the Society, had long experience in the systematic organization of correspondence and, as tutor to Robert Boyle's nephew, had seen how the exchange of letters could jump-start scientific discovery. Oldenburg would himself frequently share the experimental findings established in the Society via handwritten correspondence with trusted correspondents. A catalog of prominent scientific figures from abroad (Huygens, Hevelius, Malpighi, Cassini, and Leibniz, among others) became regular correspondents with the Society, and the exchange of letters between trusted colleagues near and far "tied words to things with knots of civility."[31] The Society was an exchange for information, but also an arbiter and coordinator of that information, not only for scientists in Britain, but for many on the Continent as well.[32]

Early modern scholars and scientists were surprisingly mobile, and often sought affirmation of their weak ties through personal visits, or following up on their prior correspondence. In this desire for a hybrid connectivity that affirmed the viability of the weak ties through direct contact, the practitioners of early modern science and scholarship mirrored the informational practice of merchants and diplomats. They too gathered large volumes of information, generated by a dedication to observation and description, but then felt compelled to assess its reliability and trustworthiness.

Books, specimens, illustrations of specimens, and other gifts were also regularly objects of exchange.[33] These were means of currying favor and extending friendships, but they were also important means of sharing information. Many important European naturalists maintained collections, and the receipt of gifts was essential in seeding and building them. The exchange of specimens, especially a rare or marvelous one, could be doubly purposeful, serving as an exchange of information and an

---

[31] Adrian Johns, "Reading and experiment in the early Royal Society." In Kevin Sharpe and Steven Zwicker, eds., *Reading, Society, and Politics in Early Modern England* (Cambridge: Cambridge University Press, 2003), 244–271 (here 264).

[32] Marie Boas Hall, "The Royal Society's role in the diffusion of information in the 17th century." *Notes and Records of the Royal Society of London*, 29.2 (1975), 173–192.

[33] See Paula Findlen, "The economy of scientific exchange in early modern Italy." In Bruce Moran, ed., *Patronage and Institutions: Science, Technology and Medicine at the European Court* (Rochester, NY: Boydell Press, 1991), 5–24.

affirmation of the social ties between correspondents. Books served to condense information, offering a highly effective means of sharing opinions and information, and might also play a special role in confirming social connections, by including mentions, dedications, and acknowledgments of the recipient.

But it was not just the *virtuosi* who availed themselves of this infrastructure. Early modern systems of communications, the paper technologies disposable, and the availability of print meant that figures of relatively modest standing could participate in paper informational networks that extended well beyond their immediate environs. An example of such a figure is the subject of a fascinating recent study of the seventeenth-century Zwickau schoolmaster Christian Daum (d. 1687), who left one of the period's largest private libraries and collections of papers.[34] More than 5,000 letters to and from 490 correspondents, along with dozens of filled notebooks and drafts of letters, survive. Many of his correspondents were fellow teachers at other schools, as well as former and current students: these connections were essential for Daum to keep up his scholarly activities.

Daum also kept large numbers of textbooks, exams and essays that he graded, and matriculation records from the school that he served for several decades. His massive library numbered 10,000 volumes at his death – four times the size of the library of the region's closest university in Rostock – for which he composed a handwritten catalog, which he divided by size and then by discipline. Daum was systematic in his preservation of both his books and his correspondence – his record-keeping was directed toward both the present and the past.

As Ross describes it, "Daum did not merely collect letters – he collected people."[35] This was why, for example, he preserved the matriculation records for the school. Keeping tabs on former students was another means of cultivating connections and friendships within the broader Republic of Letters. His social knowledge allowed him to drop names, gain access to desirable books and knowledge, and target those who might be most useful for his own process of self-promotion. Daum's obsessive accumulation of paper is exceptional only in its size and almost complete survival. There must have been a great many individuals like Christian Daum: men and women who were members of informational networks constructed of a shared culture of printed books and manuscript

---

[34] Alan Ross, *Daum's Boys. Schools and the Republic of Letters in Early Modern Germany* (Manchester: Manchester University Press, 2015).
[35] Ross, *Daum's Boys*, 166.

communication, connected physically by networks of correspondence and trade in books, and virtually by the sharing of observations and ideas.

7.2 Paper Technologies of the Self

Daum was explicit in the purposes behind his commitment to ceaseless writing and record-keeping. He declared that his desire was that "his memory might be preserved in eternity." He wanted a version of himself, preserved in his writing, to survive him beyond the grave. Despite the recent claims of bestselling literary critics, the construction of selves and the practice of what has been described as "self-fashioning" were not novel to the early modern period. Any honest attempt to understand the medieval mind reveals that it regularly explored the ideas and languages of interiority and divided selves.[36] Europeans had long sought to represent themselves, and their selves, in writing. But there also can be little dispute that, from the late Middle Ages going forward, there was an explosion in what the Dutch historian of the Holocaust, Jacob Presser, termed "ego-documents," self-referential and reflective manuscript products in which the author writes about his or her personal life and feelings.[37] This label is a catchall for a wide range of paper technologies, including memoirs, diaries, wills, travel accounts, spiritual reflections, personal commonplace notebooks, family books, and even extended reflections written into the margins of printed books, almanacs, and calendars.[38] Some German diaries from the early sixteenth century began as personal annotations written on the blank areas of printed calendars that circulated as organizers and agendas.[39] Similarly, in England, printed almanacs sold in huge numbers served as matrices for the construction of impromptu autobiographical handwritten texts.[40] Madeleine Foisil has labeled such items "écrits du for privé."[41]

---

[36] See the convincing critique of the work of Stephen Greenblatt and others by David Aers. "A whisper in the ear of early modernists; or, reflections on literary critics writing the 'history of the subject.'" In Aers, ed., *Culture and History, 1350–1600: Essays on English Communities, Identities, and Writing* (Detroit: Wayne State University Press, 1992), 177–202.
[37] Jacob Presser, "Memoires als geschiedbron." In Presser, ed., *Uit het werk van J. Presser* (Amsterdam: Athenaeum – Polak & Van Gennep, 1966), 277–282. See also Rudolf Dekker, ed., *Egodocuments and History. Autobiographical Writing in its Social Context Since the Middle Ages* (Hilversum: Verloren, 2002).
[38] Sylvie Mouysset, *Papiers de famille: Introduction à l'étude des livres de raison* (Rennes: Presses Universitaires de Rennes, 2008), 238.
[39] Mouysset, *Papiers de famille*, 238.
[40] Adam Smyth, *Autobiography in Early Modern England* (Cambridge: Cambridge University Press, 2010), 15–56.
[41] Madeleine Foisil, "L'écriture du for privé." In Philippe Ariès and Georges Duby, eds., *Histoire de la vie privée*, Vol. 3: *De la Renaissance aux Lumières* (Paris, Éditions du Seuil, 1985), 319–359.

Such "writings of the private sphere" or "literature of personal experience" might be confined to a few pieces of scrap paper, or reach massive proportions, such as the 5,000-page diary of Rijklof Michael van Goens, now in the Koninklijke Bibliotheek in The Hague.[42] They were also authored by an extremely wide cross-section of early modern society: male and female, urban and rural, noble and commoner. Those who had regular occasion to use pen and paper were most likely to author such documents: clerics, professors and teachers, lawyers, and merchants, among others. But the recourse to ego-documents was not confined to such burghers and professionals. There are many examples, especially from the fifteenth century forward, of the creation of such material by the lower social classes.[43]

The stimuli to create such "technologies of the self" were multiple.[44] The printing press meant that there were many more *exampla* of first-person writing in circulation: narratives, family histories, chronicles, biographical literature, and collections of letters.[45] The availability of paper in households and the related emergence of quotidian writing helped create the material and mental circumstances that encouraged this sort of production. The domestication of regular writing exhibited many of the same sensibilities that we have seen in early modern institutional settings, chief among them being a desire to preserve: to record the past, account for the present, and plan for the future. The more intimate and reflective of them suggest an effort to convey an individual's spiritual reality after death. This concern became especially common with the advent of the Protestant and Catholic Reformations, both of which encouraged this sort of religious stocktaking. Protestants, in particular, pursued personal interfaces with God through writing, in the form of spiritual diaries, devotional notebooks, and theological commonplace books that bridged the personal and scholarly. It became a familiar practice for Christians to take "brief notes on the conditions of their souls" in their diaries and journals.[46] The association of salvation with both words and personal spiritual stories gave impetus to autobiographical religious

---

[42] Rudolf Dekker, "Ego-documents in the Netherlands, 1500–1814." *Dutch Crossings*, 39.13 (1989), 61–71 (here 64). The latter expression comes from James Amelang, *The Flight of Icarus. Artisan Autobiography in Early Modern Europe* (Stanford: Stanford University Press, 1998), 11.

[43] Amelang, *The Flight of Icarus*.

[44] "Technology of the self" is a term employed by Tom Webster: "Writing to redundancy: approaches to spiritual journals and early modern spirituality." *The Historical Journal*, 39.1 (1996), 33–46.

[45] Peter Burke, "Representations of the self from Petrarch to Descartes." In Roy Porter, ed., *Rewriting the Self from the Renaissance to the Present* (London: Routledge, 1997), 17–28.

[46] The words of a minister of St. Andrews, Scotland, Robert Blair, in 1616, quoted in Tom Webster, "Writing to redundancy," 37.

writing among reformed Protestants, and Puritans in particular.[47] Self-reflective spiritual first-person accounts were a Catholic genre as well: the remarkable autobiography composed by the sixteenth-century Milanese carpenter, Giambattista Casale (1554–1598), is an early example.[48] Casale's memoirs combine aspects of civic chronicle, family book, and spiritual reflection. His deep piety is brought to bear on the events of his own life and on the religious fervor of activist Archbishop Carlo Borromeo's Milan. These spiritual ego-documents took religious practice that was oral or active, such as sermons, prayer, fasting, meditation, and self-examination, and rendered it materially on the page. They turned what was fundamentally ephemeral and transformed it into written information, subject to subsequent reference and manipulation, not unlike what one would do to the accounts of one's business.

"Family books" have a lineage that extends back into the Middle Ages, among the most studied being the *ricordanze* produced by the families of the Italian towns, especially in the years after about 1350. Versions of these appeared in non-Italian contexts as well: *livres de raison* in French, *Tägebücher* and *Familienbücher* in German, *dietaris* and *llibres de pages* in Catalan.[49] Some originated as account books, with personal reflections and family information appended to financial details, while others resembled memoirs, designed to pass on the experiences of the writer to future generations. They also often acted as repositories for documentation regarding family legal and property rights, and might include lists of family officeholders, genealogies, and chronicles. The systematic maintenance of such records by families in late medieval Italy was reflective of the culture of writing that prevailed in the urban environment and extended into households, where the *libri di famiglia* were stored in the *scrittoio* or *studiolo*, the domestic equivalent of the civic archive.[50] Like the records of the urban administration, the *ricordanze* connected past, present, and future. This tripartite temporality can be seen in the remarks of the Florentine Giovanni di Andrea Pelli, who declared in his *ricordanza* that he had decided to "write everything that in truth I have been able to draw from the life and progress of my ancestors ... [and] also wanted to

---

[47] Owen Watkins, *The Puritan Experience: Studies in Spiritual Experience* (New York: Schocken Books, 1972).
[48] Carlo Marcara, "Il diario di Giambattista Casale (1554–1598)." *Memorie storiche della Diocesi di Milano*, 12 (1965), 209–437.
[49] Giovanni Ciapelli, "Introduction: memory, family and identity in early modern Italy and Europe." In Ciapelli, ed., *Memory, Family and Self. Tuscan Family Books and Other European Egodocuments (14th–18th Century)* (Leiden: Brill, 2014), 1–11.
[50] A parallel drawn by Dora Thornton in *The Scholar in His Study: Ownership and Experience in Renaissance Italy* (New Haven, CT: Yale University Press, 1997).

keep some memory of my actions."[51] Just as the maintenance of state papers was for regimes a means of legitimization, these family papers establishing ancestral status, and recounting the activities of the family and its scions, were a legitimizing force in their own right. In Florence in the fifteenth century, merchant families were expected to open up their books to the tax officials of the *Uffiziali*, the agents of the *catasto*. The remarkable documentary effluence of late medieval Tuscany was thus a product of both public and private writing.[52]

In Germany, *Familienbücher* generally contained autobiographical information without being strictly autobiographical, chronicling births, deaths, baptisms, and marriages, as well as records of officeholding and deeds of property ownership.[53] They often resembled the cartularies produced by political and ecclesiastical institutions. Karin Czaja has examined the massive family book kept by the Rieter family of Nuremberg, begun by Peter in 1401 and then continued by his descendants into the early sixteenth century. Running to more than 400 folio pages, it includes coats of arms; testaments and charters related to property divisions; rent documents; descriptions of fiefs; and details concerning births, marriages, and deaths. It also includes recounted pilgrimages undertaken by family members.[54] In its layout, its cross-references, and marginal notes, the collection resembles "official" documentation in multiple ways.

A quite remarkable example of the lengths to which an individual would go to encompass his life in written records is the massive, three-volume *Gedenkbuch* left by the sixteenth-century Cologne lawyer Hermann Weinsberg (1518–1597), a "fifty-year experiment with the possibilities of bourgeois writing and self-representation" and the subject of Matthew Lundin's *Paper Memory*.[55] In the pages of his sprawling family book, he repeatedly marveled at, and praised, the preservative power of

---

[51] Giovanni Ciapelli, "Family memory and individual memory: Florentine diaries and family books of the early modern period." In Ciapelli, ed., *Memory, Family and Self*, 241–259 (here 248).

[52] Paolo Cammarosano, *Italia medievale. Struttura e geografia delle fonti scritte* (Rome: Nuova Italia Scientifica, 1991), 284.

[53] The variety of these paper technologies is on display in the essays in Birgit Studt, *Haus- und Familienbücher in der städtischen Gesellschaft des Spätmittelalters und der Frühen Neuzeit* (Cologne: Böhlau, 2007). For a close study of one Frankfurt family book, see Pierre Monnet, *Les Rohrbach de Francfort. Pouvoirs, affaires, et parenté à l'aube de la Renaissance allemande* (Geneva: Droz, 1997).

[54] Karin Czaja, "The Nuremberg *Familienbücher*: archives of family identity." In Marco Mostert and Anna Adamska, eds., *Uses of the Written Word in Medieval Towns* (Turnhout, Belgium: Brepols, 2014), 325–338.

[55] Matthew Lundin, *Paper Memory. A Sixteenth-century Townsman Writes His World* (Cambridge, MA: Harvard University Press, 2013), 16. Comparable to the massive undertaking of Weinsberg to memorialize the history and deeds of his family, are the efforts of the Swiss Protestant Thomas Platter (1499–1582), who felt the need to record

pen and paper. He was a lawyer, a wine merchant, a churchwarden for his parish (for which he composed a detailed *Memorialbuch*), and family record-keeper, and in all these roles he generated paper records. Weinsberg's family book is a bewildering combination of essential documents, reminiscences, descriptions and observations, aimed both at posterity and at the social world of his present, to help secure his rank in urban society. Weinsberg was an obsessive scribbler, and his writings exemplify what German historians have called the *Verschriftlichung* ('textualization') of early modern secular life.[56] Weinsberg's efforts to secure his family's name and *gestae* in two temporal registers expanded into quixotic attempts to encompass his whole world. Lundin points out that in less than eight months, Weinsberg filled more than 700 folio pages with anecdotes from his earlier years; he described his own habit of daily writing as being like a fish in water.[57] His constant writing wrestled with the twin foes of disorder and forgetfulness. Like many who commit themselves to recording nearly everything, he found himself deluged by the results. He found it impossible to draw a bright line between what was essential and non-essential to record. Weinsberg remarked on the superiority of, and professed his love for, written record-keeping, but found the resulting information (as we would understand it) overwhelming.

In France, *livres de famille* ranged from the chiefly accounting-focused *livres de raison* to more personal journals and memoirs, as well as many hybrid forms.[58] Claude Mermet, in a 1583 treatise on the art of writing entitled *La pratique de l'orthographe françoise*, wrote that "[e]very man who wishes to set about/the proper upkeep of his house/in all things must learn/to keep a *livre de raison*."[59] As elsewhere in early modern Europe, those most likely to keep such family books came from among people with civic duties that required writing, like merchants, nobles, lawyers, and the

---

for his family his rise from goat herder to prominent scholar and teacher. This work is the subject of Emmanuel Le Roy Ladurie, *The Beggar and the Professor: A Sixteenth-Century Family Saga*. Trans. by Arthur Goldhammer (Chicago: University of Chicago Press, 1997). Generally on such autobiographical works, see Hans-Rudolf Velten, *Das selbst geschriebene Leben. Eine Studie zur deutschen Autobiographie im 16. Jahrhundert* (Heidelberg: Winter, 1995).

[56] See Horst Wenzel, Wilfried Seipel, and Gotthard Wunberg, eds., *Die Verschriftlichung der Welt: Text und Zahl in der Kultur des Mittelalters und der frühen Neuzeit* (Vienna: Kunsthistorisches Museum/Skira, 2000).

[57] Lundin, *Paper Memory*, 214.

[58] Focusing on texts from the south of France, Mouysset, *Papiers de famille*; also Jean-François Courouau and Sylvie Mouysset, "À la rececherche des écrits du for privé du Midi de la France et de Catalogne." *Annales du Midi: revue archéologique, historique et philologique de la France méridionale*, 122.270 (2010), 165–173.

[59] Claude Mermet, *La pratique de l'orthographe françoise* (Lyon: Basile Bouquet, 1583), 149: "Tout homme qui veut entreprendre/De bien conduire sa maison/Sur toute chose doit apprendre/A tenir livre de raison.".

occasional artisan. And they tended to be male heads of family, although there are plenty of examples of women maintaining such books, and the contents were invariably in the vernacular.

Many European families, therefore, shared the preservative instinct that took root in early modern European bureaucracies. One of the more famous examples is an English one: the Verney family of Buckinghamshire. For fourteen generations spanning the entire early modern period, the Verneys preserved a largely unbroken run of family papers, including well in excess of 30,000 personal letters from the period from 1643 to 1754 alone.[60] The commitment of the Verneys to saving every scrap of correspondence, keeping copies of every property transaction, and accumulating every piece of potentially relevant genealogical details culled from public records, the works of antiquaries, and the collections of members of the family, demonstrates an awareness that their pretensions to social importance had to rely on a documentary foundation. It was their database for family survival and thriving.

Unexceptional burghers like Weinsberg in Cologne and nobles like the Verneys in England, in their compulsion to write so many details down, to secure them on paper, generated their own informational challenges. The implication is that in the new world of paper, information overload was a preoccupation not just for chancery secretaries and scientific *virtuosi*, but for individuals and families who sought to encompass their lives in writing. These various ego-documents were thus archives, born of the same preservative, justificatory, and practical instincts one sees in administrative settings. They were meant to outlive their creators, provide a reservoir of precedent, and offer a deliberately selective picture of the individual or family. Like archivists for institutions, their compilers made deliberate choices about what to include and exclude. And like merchants representing their businesses on the pages of their ledgers, they offered an accounting of their lives and of their place in their world, a world in writing.

Daily inscription using paper technologies in the private sphere, in personal correspondence, in the wide array of ego-documents just discussed, and in more mundane scribbles, was an unprecedented feature of early modern life. The yield of resulting documents is almost certainly undercounted by historians, and any accurate measure of this material is nigh impossible. Nonetheless it is clear that for literate early modern Europeans, writing became habitual, resulting in a flow of written information that paralleled the commitment of institutions to documentation.

---

[60] Susan Whyman, *Sociability and Power in Late-Stuart England. The Cultural Worlds of the Verneys, 1660–1720* (Oxford: Oxford University Press, 1999).

What is more, the habits of writing and record-keeping penetrated beyond a narrow band of urban and noble elites. Artisans often perceived the benefits of the possession of written instruments to document their activities and support their claims. "Through the creation of new types of institutional town records, produced by the clerks of the urban chancery, a new section of society became aware of the importance of the written record."[61] The legal protections that were offered by urban courts and other institutions encouraged those in rural areas to safeguard their rights with written documents. Notaries, who, by the fifteenth century were in many towns the "priests of practical literacy" (a term coined by Edward Muir), were regularly enjoined by those in the countryside who, even if they themselves were only partially literate or nonliterate, recognized the value of participating in written culture.[62]

One celebrated case is that of the fifteenth-century Tuscan peasant Benedetto, who undertook lifelong efforts to maintain an account book of his affairs.[63] Employing some thirty different notaries over the course of his life to record the minutiae of his affairs, he generated two books of memoranda, revealing the expansion of an ethos of documentation and record-keeping that became so pervasive that even a semiliterate farmer felt compelled to participate. Benedetto aped the commercial and political writing practices of civic spaces, even if he was incapable of the requisite writing himself. :

> Written culture was not reserved exclusively for the ruling classes; and in both the city and the country there were people who could write and read; people who could not write but could read (representatives of a culture in which reading is far more important than writing); and semiliterate folk, as well as people who had once known, but now had forgotten their alphabet.[64]

It was a set of affairs that bears resemblance with today: while there are very few who genuinely understand how computers and cyberspace work, most participate in this digital culture, and all recognize how essential it is to social flourishing in our age.

The emergence of these ego-documents points toward three features of information management in this period. First, they are one indication of how pervasive practical, everyday literacy was. Writing was the chief

---

[61] Geertrui van Synghel, "The use of records in medieval towns: the case of 's-Hertogenbosch (Brabant)." In Marco Mostert and Anna Adamska, eds., *Writing and the Administration of Medieval Towns* (Turnhout: Brepols, 2014), 31–47 (here 39).

[62] From Muir's introduction to Duccio Balestracci, *The Renaissance in the Fields. Family Memoirs of a Fifteenth-century Tuscan Peasant*. Trans. by Paolo Squatriti and Betsy Merideth (University Park, PA: Penn State University Press, 1999), xiv.

[63] Balestracci, *The Renaissance in the Fields*.

[64] Balestracci, *The Renaissance in the Fields*, 2.

means of purposefully and systematically representing one's life and that of one's family, as they were lived. A broad swath of society had come to believe that preserving and managing information in ego-documents was desirable, even essential.

Second, many of these family books, with their roots in the techniques of merchants and financiers, evinced a new comfort with numeracy and with accounting (in the broadest sense) as means of demonstrating the state of health of business, family, and self.

Third, these documents reveal how the preservative instinct that drove the burgeoning culture of archives in Europe extended to the personal and familial level. Saving information for posterity, for the maintenance of unbroken memory, and for the creation of consultable precedent, was now an individual and not just an institutional concern.

Literacy, numeracy, and documentary preservation – these informational devices came together in the everyday commitment to maintain these instruments. Such devices remain essential to our informational landscape today: we continue to wish to preserve a record of ourselves. The construction of these technologies of the self through the systematic deployment of pen and paper permitted literate people to offer an accounting of themselves to multiple audiences: themselves, their peers, the state, and family members in the future. Memory and identity were thus secured in paper.

7.3 What News?

The Oxford scholar Robert Burton (1577–1640), in *Anatomy of Melancholy* (1628), cited in the opening chapter, complained of the flow of news that daily plagued English society : "I hear news every day, and those rumours of war, plagues, fires, inundations, thefts, murders, massacres, meteors, comets, spectrums, prodigies, apparitions, of towns taken, cities besieged in France, Germany, Turkey, Persia, Poland, etc." All this news was for him a source of confusion. Amid all of this information, Burton found it difficult to determine right and wrong: "Thus I daily hear, and such-like, both private and public news, amidst the gallantry and misery of the world – jollity, pride, perplexities and cares, simplicity and villainy; subtlety, knavery, candour and integrity, mutually mixed and offering themselves."[65]

---

[65] Quoted in C. John Somerville, *The News Revolution in England: Cultural Dynamics of Daily Information* (Oxford: Oxford University Press, 1996), 28–29.

Burton's discomfiture was the product of a transformed media landscape, again wrought by the circulation of paper instruments. Early modern Europe "invented" news as we understand it today, as Europeans came to expect timely specifics about events transpiring both near and far away. Information was collected and then copied, in writing or in print, into packets that were not intended for a specific individual, but rather for a base of consumers. The vehicles by which this transmission took place were varied: books, pamphlets, currantoes, newssheets, polemics, *avisi*, printed journals, and, eventually, by the end of the period, newspapers. Thus, Europeans were now learning unprecedented information about people whom they did not know personally; it was yet another stream of information coursing through early modern society. The culture of news connected more people regularly with a far more expansive world and set of characters than had ever before been possible, and introduced to a broader public the notion that information could be both timely and synchronous.

A combination of factors led to the emergence of the regular news services that proliferated in the early modern period: the regular, even daily, use of paper; the need of certain individuals, especially merchants and statesmen, to be kept up-to-date on events near and far; and the growing availability of planned and even timetabled postal services. There were very close links between news networks and trade routes, postal and courier services.

Many written instruments used by early modern Europeans were intended to be shared at a distance, and reliable systems for their conveyance became essential for the functioning of many commercial and political institutions. There was in the early modern period what Bruno Caizzi has called "a new type of post."[66] Both private and public courier services expanded greatly, especially after 1500, building on the systems employed by medieval merchants and diplomats. For a number of historians, this increase in the footprint, frequency, and reliability of postal services in early modern Europe was an important component of a "communications revolution."[67]

As in so many other areas relating to information and communication, Italian precursors appear to have been particularly important. The

---

[66] Bruno Caizzi, *Dalla posta dei re alla posta di tutti; territorio e comunicazioni in Italia dal XVI secolo all'Unità* (Milan: Franco Angeli, 1993), 13–68.

[67] This term has been used especially by German historians; for example Michael North, *Kommunikation, Handel, Geld und Banken in der Frühen Neuzeit* (Munich: R. Oldenbourg, 2000); Wolfgang Behringer, *Thurn und Taxis. Die Geschichte ihrer Post und ihrer Unternehmen* (Munich: Piper, 1990); Wolfgang Behringer, *Im Zeichen der Merkur. Reichspost und Kommunikationsrevolution in der Frühen Neuzeit* (Göttingen: Vandenhoeck and Ruprecht, 2003).

traditional vitality of Italian communication networks, the many outlets for the circulation of news in Italian towns (including the first handwritten newsletters), and local and regional postal services, all combined to create a model for the rest of Europe. In the fifteenth century, consortia of merchant companies created postal services called *scarselle*, using dedicated couriers and innkeepers whose establishments served as post offices. Pierre Sardella and Federigo Melis have described the creation in Renaissance Italy of an "information market."[68] The Sforza dukes in Milan, in order to support their commitment to stationing permanent resident ambassadors across Italy, in the second half of the fifteenth century established postal routes connecting Milan to the most important Italian cities. The Milan to Rome route consisted of a series of relays with horse-changing stations at forty-mile intervals.

It is not surprising then that among the most important protagonists in the expansion of European postal services were an Italian family, the Tasso, who were soon enjoined to reorganize the postal system of the papacy, and then the first imperial postal service in Innsbruck, in 1489.[69] In 1504, Gabriele Tasso was appointed the imperial postmaster.[70] In 1518, Charles V granted the Tasso a monopoly on the imperial postal services in Italy, France, and Germany.[71] The Tasso revolutionized the transit of the post north of the Alps, establishing postal stations along predetermined routes, between which couriers on horseback would relay, greatly reducing the uncertainty of postal traffic. When stationed as ambassador in Spain in 1513, Francesco Guicciardini remarked on the efficiencies of the royal post there: "the means of sending letters here is easy, because the King ordinarily receives every fifteen days the post from Rome, which brings not only the King's letters, but also those of merchants there. You only have to address your letters to someone in Rome and they will be given to the courier."[72] In 1517, the Tasso drew up

---

[68] Pierre Sardella, *Nouvelles et speculations à Venise au début du XVIe siècle* (Paris: A. Collin, 1948); Federigo Melis, *Intensità e regolarità nella diffusione dell'informazione economica generale nella Mediterraneo e in Occidente alla fine del Medioevo* (Prato: Istituto di studi storici postali, 1983).
[69] Tarcisio Bottani, *I Tasso e le poste pontifice, secoli XV–XVI* (Bergamo: Camerata Cornello, 2000).
[70] Martin Dallmeier, "Il casato principesco dei Thurn und Taxis e le poste in Europa (1490–1806)." In *Le poste di Tasso, un'impresa in Europa* (Bergamo: Comune di Bergamo, 1984) 1–32.
[71] The first sizable contract between Charles and Francesco and Battista Tasso, dated 12 November 1516, is reproduced in Martin Dallmeier, ed., *Quellen zur Geschichte des europäischen Postwesens 1501–1806*, Vol. II (Regensburg: Verlag Michael Lassleben Kallmunz, 1977).
[72] Francesco Guicciardini, *Le lettere*, Vol. I: *1499–1513*. Ed. by Pierre Jodogne (Rome: Instituto Storico per l'Età Moderna e Contemporaneana, 1986), 13 May 1513, 145–6.

a contract that stipulated the expected travel times for their deliveries from Brussels with some precision. Five and a half days to Innsbruck, twelve to Toledo, fifteen to Granada, ten and a half to Rome, fourteen to Naples, and thirty-six hours to Paris. The faster the couriers were, the more they were paid.[73]

Private mail services always existed alongside these "official" channels. In Philip II's Spain, numerous independent contractors operated out of multiple Spanish cities, alongside the royal postal network, which was known as the "ordinary" service. The latter, overseen by postmasters and with posthouses under the monarch's protection, increasingly operated according to a scheduled timetable. In 1560, the ordinary service ran fortnightly between Brussels and Madrid, as well as a similarly regular route to London, with a dedicated boat service between the port cities of Calais and Dover. Philip II, as a monarch who never left Spain after 1559, demanded regular correspondence from and among his agents and repeatedly expressed concern for the speed and security of the postal routes in his domains. The routes out of Madrid to specific locales were fixed. Mail service extended across the oceans, as well. Mail boats from Seville to New Spain became regular – correspondents could expect a letter to take thirty days to make the trip.

The trend across the continent in the early modern centuries was toward more dominant "official" posts.[74] In 1571, a consortium of merchants in Nuremberg petitioned for the creation of a regular public service to ferry correspondence to Antwerp, with stops at Frankfurt and Cologne. In 1572, the city of Cologne established a weekly service to Leipzig, known as *Ordinari-Boten*, operating on a set timetable. These were available for use to anyone who could afford them, with set routes and collection and delivery times. Emperor Rudolf II (r. 1576–1612) issued an edict in 1597 mandating wholesale reform of his postal system, proscribing many potential competitors to the official post.[75] The imperial postal system in Germany, by the turn of the seventeenth century connecting all of the major cities of the realm, boasted unprecedented breadth, reliability, and efficiency.[76]

---

[73] Cristina Borreguero Beltrán, "Philip of Spain, the Spider's Web of News and Information," in Brendan Dooley, ed., *The Dissemination of News and the Emergence of Contemporaneity in Early Modern Europe* (Farnham, Surrey. Ashgate, 2010), 23–49.

[74] See, for example, Onorato Pastine, "L'organizzazione postale della Repubblica di Genova." *Atti della società ligure di storia patria*, 53 (1926), 393–397; and Francesco Caracciolo, "Vie di comunicazione e servizio postale nel Regno di Napoli fra XVI e XII secolo." *Ricerche di storia sociale e religiosa*, 2 (1972), 213–228.

[75] Behringer, *Thurn und Taxis*, 70–71.

[76] Andrew Pettegree, *The Invention of News. How the World Came to Know about Itself* (New Haven, CT. Yale University Press, 2014), 179.

France and Britain, which for most of the sixteenth century had remained outside the European postal web, gradually developed their own postal infrastructures in the seventeenth century. Louis XI established a French national postal service in the fifteenth century, but this was a network reserved for the use of royal officials. With the end of the upheavals of the Wars of Religion, Henri IV (r. 1594–1610) set up postal stations at regular intervals along major road and river routes.[77] Louis XIV (r. 1643–1715) created the Superintendent General of the Posts in 1668 and the provinces were connected to Paris through *ordinaires*, biweekly deliveries of mail running on set schedules. Marie de Raburin-Chantal, Marquise de Sévigné (1626–1696), one of the seventeenth century's most famous letter writers, in 1671, expressed admiration for the way the French post had made regular communication with her correspondents feasible:

I am bent on admiring the goodness and decency of these postal messengers, who are incessantly on the roads, carrying our letters about. Not a day goes by that they are not carrying one letter or another to you and me; they are out and about at all times, at all hours. These kind men! They are so helpful! And what a lovely invention the postal system is.[78]

Developments unfolded more slowly in England. In 1657, the Commonwealth instituted the Settling the Postage for England, Scotland and Ireland Act, which created a single General Post Office in London, under the direction of a postmaster general. Upon the Restoration of the monarchy in 1660, legislation passed that largely duplicated these steps, and mandated the use of postal marks, an indication of increased systematization.[79]

This snapshot of postal systems in sixteenth-century Europe reveals an infrastructure of mail conveyance that is markedly different from the ad hoc services of the Middle Ages. After about 1500, the increase in the volume of traffic in written instruments, resulting from the needs of European diplomatic services, increased medium- and long-range commerce, and the growth in personal correspondence, led to public and private investment in a dedicated postal infrastructure. For those who wished to convey letters across distances, there were now permanent, structured, and readily available means of delivery. It was in the important hubs of Europe's postal systems, invariably locales of political and

---

[77] E. John B. Allen, *Post and Courier Service on the Diplomacy of Early Modern Europe* (Dordrecht: Springer, 2012), 8.
[78] Quoted in Roland Racevskis, *Time and Ways of Knowing Under Louis XIV: Molière, Sévigné, Lafayette* (Lewisburg, PA: Bucknell University Press, 2003), 91.
[79] Mark Brayshay, "Conveying correspondence: early modern letter bearers, carriers and posts." In Daybell and Gordon, eds., *Cultures of Correspondence*, 48–65 (here 63).

commercial importance, that news was gathered, aggregated, and disseminated.

The emergence of reliable postal systems was a necessary prerequisite in the rise of manuscript news services, the first steps toward the periodical press and public media, both of which were early modern inventions. The market for handwritten political information was highly variegated throughout the early modern period, involving a great many producers and products. This media format had its origins in a combination of concurrent trends: the regular circulation of news in the correspondence of merchants and diplomats and the emergence of scheduled private and then public postal services. Letters written by merchants and diplomats often contained extended sections detailing the news, and this informative section could easily be extracted from the body of the letter and made available to a broader audience. Multiple such sections might then be aggregated in a single place. Diplomatic dispatches were often larded with the latest news from near and far. In some Italian chanceries, the assorted news reported by ambassadors were assembled into *quaternetti*, global summaries that statesmen could then use at councils, in negotiations, and to facilitate policy-making.[80] One can find in the archives of the Este princes in Modena handwritten recapitulations of all the news from Bruges in 1464 and Rome in 1495, reflecting the information-gathering capabilities of their well-connected ambassadors.

The news-filled dispatches of ambassadors and the *quaternetti* derived from them were the precursors of the newsletters known as *avisi*. These began to circulate in large numbers, first in manuscript and then in print, in the sixteenth century (although there is evidence of them dating to the early fifteenth century[81]), meeting a demand for information on the latest political events among a clientele beyond diplomats. Some were individually produced and distributed as unsolicited favors to chosen recipients. Eventually, they were generated in multiple copies, speculatively without a specific recipient in mind. By the end of the fifteenth century, the creation, sale, and circulation of *avisi* were established practice.

The equivalent to the *aviso* in Germany was the *Briefzeitung*, literally a "letter-newspaper," a letter with a supplementary insert that furnished a summary of the latest news, compiled by an *Avisenschreiber*. It was a short step to extract the supplement and market it independently as a standalone

---

[80] Isabella Lazzarini, *Communication and Conflict. Italian Diplomacy in the Early Renaissance, 1350–1520* (Oxford: Oxford University Press, 2015), 81–82.
[81] Georg Christ, "A newsletter in 1419? Antonio Morosini's chronicle in the light of commercial correspondence between Venice and Alexandria." *Mediterranean Historical Review*, 20.1 (2005), 35–66.

news report.[82] In both contexts, the Italian and the German, we see a process whereby private correspondence morphs into public news, eventually becoming an information industry in its own right, subject to competition, professionalization, and innovation.

In Venice, handwritten newsletters were known as *reporti* and those who compiled them *reportisti*; these were the first "reporters" in the West. Similar items were produced in Rome, a city which had access to news from across Europe. By the mid-sixteenth century, the production of such news items, as well as their distribution via refined postal systems, were well established. In the mid-seventeenth century, Giovanni Quorli ran a *studio di reporti* out of Venice, from which he supplied more than sixty clients inside and outside of Italy with news from Venice, Paris, Rome, Milan, London, Vienna, and Cologne. Quorli fraternized with patricians, had access to ambassadorial *relazioni*, and incorporated information from manuscript and printed gazettes from all over Europe. It is clear that the audience for his newsletters was significantly larger than the number that he sold, as there were many secondary readers and those who heard them read out loud.[83]

A robust trade in manuscript news persisted well into the early eighteenth century. Handwritten newsletters retained an element of personalization that a printed newssheet or newspaper lacked, a sense that the news included was exclusive and for the eyes of the reader only. They retained a flexibility that was missing in printed *avisi* and gazettes, offering the capacity to adapt in short order to the specific demands of a client.

Handwritten newsletters were especially important in the supply of news in central and eastern Europe, where print was less pervasive. Massive collections of newsletters can be found in Budapest, Zurich, Vienna, and Graz. Hans Jacob Wick (1522–1588) in Zurich collected newsletters from 1560 to 1587, assembling them into twenty-four volumes that became known as the *Wickiana*. Wick was especially interested in news that recounted the spectacular and bizarre.[84] In Budapest, the Thurzo family also systematically gathered newsletters from the 1580s to the 1710s.[85]

---

[82] A point made in Johannes Weber, "Strassburg, 1605: the origins of the newspaper in Europe." *German History*, 24.3 (2006), 387–412.

[83] Mario Infelise, "News networks between Italy and Europe." In Dooley, ed., *The Dissemination of News*, 51–67.

[84] Matthias Senn, *Johann Jakob Wick (1522–1588) und seine Sammlung von Nachrichten zur Zeitgschichte* (Zurich: Leemann, 1974).

[85] Zsuzsa Barbarics and Renate Pieper, "Handwritten newsletters as means of communication in early modern Europe." In William Monter, ed., *Cultural Exchange in Early Modern Europe*, Vol. 3: *Correspondence and Cultural Exchange in Europe, 1400–1700* (Cambridge: Cambridge University Press, 2006), 53–79 (here 56–57).

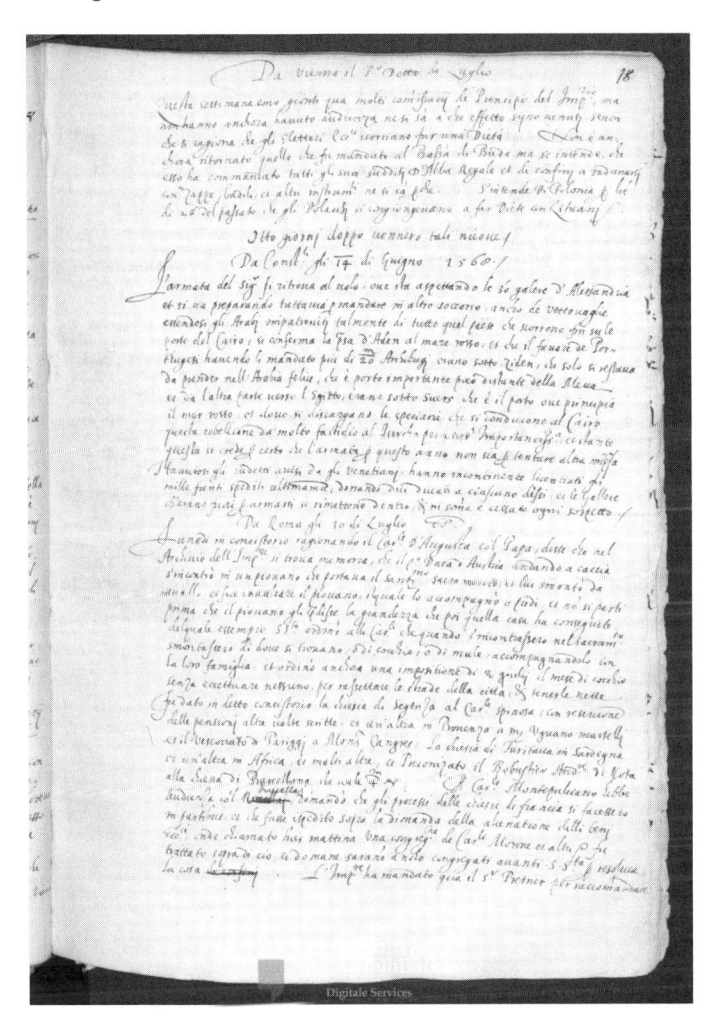

7.1 All the news that's fit to write: the Fugger banking family in Augsburg systematically amalgamated the latest news. A *Fuggerzeitung* from August 1568. National Library of Austria (reproduced with permission of the Library).

The compilation of these instruments was more than just an exercise in copying. It required discernment, selection, and excerpting. The authors of the newsletters had to determine that which was newsworthy, timely, and appealing to their audience. The abundance of news, like the abundance of books and of scientific observations, was subject to excerpting, with only the genuinely useful and interesting retained; it was a form of commonplacing reality.

Print was transformative for the circulation of news and information among the public. Gradually, in the course of the sixteenth century, especially north of the Alps, printed newsletters intended for a broader readership beyond statesmen and well-connected merchants emerged. By circulating international news as they did, these newsletters created social linkages beyond one's immediate community, and helped to shape and reflect the worldview of their readers. They were easy to produce, promised easy profits for printers, and were published in vast numbers.

These aggregations of "hard news," chiefly on political and military affairs, were paralleled in the sixteenth and seventeenth centuries by a bewildering array of occasional news pamphlets. These appeared in profusion in response to momentous events, such as the Reformation, the Ottoman threat in the East, and the Thirty Years' War. Newssheet producers would boast of the "freshness" of the news that they provided. They might also crow about the geographical scope of the news they included, essentially marketing it as "news from everywhere," as we can see in a *relación de sucesos* out of Seville that was entitled, *Relación de avisos de todo lo que ha sucedido en Roma, Napoles, Venecia, Genova, Sicilia, Francia, Alemania, Inglaterra, Malta y otras partes*.[86] Variously known as *Neue Zeitungen*, *occasionnels*, and *relaciones*, the subjects they covered ran the gamut. Most of them have vanished, but it is likely that they were produced in the millions in early modern Europe. By the seventeenth century, they were an important component of the public information nexus in many parts of Europe – after 1648, upwards of 300 a year were published in the Dutch Republic alone, with multiple print runs of more than 1,000 copies. Assuming that five people would read each pamphlet, this suggests a readership of at least 50,000. By the 1570s, more than 50,000 political pamphlets may have been in circulation in the Netherlands.[87]

---

[86] Henry Ettingshausen, "The news in Spain: *relaciones de sucesos* in the reigns of Philip III and IV." *European History Quarterly*, 14 (1984), 1–20 (here 10). In Spain, *relaciones de sucesos* were the only type of printed news produced in the period; Spain's relative backwardness in the provision of public printed news can be attributed largely to its geographic isolation from the most important crossroads of news and commerce. *Relaciones* tended to cover important military and political events, especially related to the Spanish crown, such as battles and royal marriages, but also church events and perceived miraculous occurrences.

[87] Craig Harline, *Pamphlets, Printing and Political Culture in the Early Dutch Republic* (Dordrecht: Martinus Nijhoff Publishers, 1987), 21.

Andrew Pettegree has examined surviving printed pamphlets from the Bibliothèque Méjanes in Aix-en-Provence, dating from as early as the 1530s. Between 1538 and 1544, the printer Jean l'Homme published dozens of cheap, crude pamphlets that focused on political and military affairs. Jean had royal sanction to print these items, and most assumed a patriotic tone. Many of them survive in a single copy, but there is reason to believe that they had received a wide and eager readership.[88] Pettegree's study suggests that printed news in France was already an important component in the circulation of information about current events.

Amid the advent of the political and religious controversies of the English Civil War, "Pamphlets," according to a 1642 polemic, "like wild geese, fly up and downe in flocks about the country. Never was more writing, or lesse matter."[89] Many betrayed a decidedly polemical perspective on the information that they furnished. Others sought to broadcast what we today would label "fake news." During the Dutch Revolt, a recurring trope in pamphlet literature was the bogus intercepted letter: the 1580 publication *A Lost or Intercepted Letter from the Prince of Orange* purported to present a missive which made clear that Orange and his ally, the Duke of Anjou, cared little for the Dutch people and were obsessed with their own narrow political ends.[90] Then, as now, an information-rich environment was populated by the true, the uncertain, and the deliberately deceptive. These printed news pamphlets generally provided accounts, often breathless ones, of single episodes. For example, Francesco Marcaldi over the course of a month in 1573, sent out six copies of his description of Cyprus and account of news there – each of which was fifty-six pages long.[91] Others were systematically published as a commercial ventures, generally located in important commercial entrepôts, and distributed to a network of subscribers.

As in the early years of the Reformation, the Thirty Years' War and the English Civil War saw a rash of printed media that competed for the attention of a public eager for the latest. Andrew Pettegree has highlighted the example of the Siege of Magdeburg in 1631, when the imperial forces of Count Tilly sacked the iconic Protestant town in an orgy of violence and fire. For Protestant publications, this was yet another sign of Catholic perfidy and bloodlust and an admonition to follow God's will. For

---

[88] Andrew Pettegree, "A provincial news community in sixteenth-century Europe." In Judith Pollmann and Andrew Spicer, eds., *Public Opinion and Changing Identities in the Early Modern Netherlands: Essays in Honour of Alastair Duke* (Leiden: Brill, 2007), 33–48.
[89] Dror Wahrman, *Mr. Collier's Letter Racks: A Tale of Art and Illusion at the Threshold of the Modern Information Age* (Oxford: Oxford University Press, 2012), 20.
[90] Harline, *Pamphlets*, 52.
[91] Brian Richardson, "A scribal publisher of political information: Francesco Marcaldi." *Italian Studies*, 64.2 (2009), 296–313.

publications sympathetic to the Catholic cause, like Munich's *Mercurii Ordinari Zeitung*, the fall of the city was a pious victory and a sign of God's favor.[92]

In the seventeenth century, news publications began to appear serially, signaling an attitude of expectation that regularity and timeliness should be features of the news. Serialization also allowed for the elaboration and amplification of stories over time.[93] The news therefore became a flow, rather than a series of distinct events.[94] The first printed periodical dedicated to political news appears to have been the *Mercurius gallobelgicus*, an aggregation of international news (compiled initially by a Catholic refugee from Holland, Michael ab Isselt (ca. 1530–1597)) published semiannually in Cologne and Frankfurt during the years 1592 to 1635. The format proved popular, and the *Mercurius* circulated widely.[95]

The best current argument is that the first real newspaper was published in Strasbourg in the first decade of seventeenth century. This was a weekly publication, and in it we see the marriage of supply, in an inexpensive and easily replicable format that produced numerous copies quickly, and demand, for news about the latest political developments within the Holy Roman Empire. Newspapers were essentially printed simulacra of manuscript precursors, which explains their initially unadorned appearance – they often did not even carry a masthead. Newspapers brought together in a single place multiple news reports. At first, newspapers were exclusively for news, and were consistently dry and serious, with little editorializing on the news itself. The German-speaking world had by far the most variegated newspaper landscape in the seventeenth century, driven by the political and religious crises associated with the Thirty Years' War. There were roughly 200 newspapers published in eighty different locales before 1700, meaning that all of Germany had access to up-to-date political information in serial format. One estimate is that 70 million individual newspapers had been produced in Germany by the end of the seventeenth century. The first European book on the subject of newspapers, Kaspar Stieler's *Zeitungs Lust und Nutz*, published in Hamburg in 1695, described the passion for the latest news among their readers:

---

[92] Pettegree, *The Invention of the News*, 213.
[93] Simon Davies and Puck Fletcher, "Introduction." In Davies and Fletcher, eds., *News in Early Modern Europe. Currents and Connections*. Library of the Written Word, Vol. 39. *The Handpress World* (Leiden: Brill, 2014), 1–18 (here 3).
[94] Jörg Jochen Berns, "*Parteylichkeit* and the periodical press." In Kathryn Murphy and Anita Traninger, eds., *The Emergence of Impartiality* (Leiden: Brill, 2013), 87–140.
[95] Joad Raymond, *Pamphlets and Pamphleteering in Early Modern Britain* (Cambridge: Cambridge University Press, 2003), 128–129.

They run after the new papers and can hardly wait for the day when these sheets are printed and put in circulation. For that reason, they hurry to the postal bureaus and newsstands, and time drags for them until they find out what the King of France, the Emperor, the Pope and the Sultan of Constantinople have done ... One learns such things out of the newspapers, and not out of books ... We honest men who are living in the world as it is today, need to understand the world of today, and neither Alexander, nor Caesar, nor Mohammed will help us if we want to be well-informed.[96]

Stieler's observations suggest a genuine appreciation of what today we would call "current affairs." This was altogether unprecedented.

The first newspaper published outside of Germany was the Amsterdam-based *Courante uyt italien, duytsland, etc.*, a single page, bearing no imprint of the publisher, printer, or date, although the stories themselves suggest a June 1618 publication.[97] In the years that followed, Amsterdam was also the site of publication for the first French- and English-language newspapers. The first newspaper in the Habsburg Netherlands, appearing regularly from 1620, was the *Nieuwe Tijdinghen*, published by Abraham Verhoeven (1575–1652) in Antwerp. It published two to three times a month in editions of about 2,000 copies. It was distributed across the Low Countries, but could also be found in Frankfurt, London, and other European cities. Verhoeven declared that his publication was "for the contentment of such as do not desire to be ignorant of the occasion of the public affairs of the world."[98] In the course of the seventeenth century, most of Western Europe witnessed the appearance of newspapers, with times of political upheaval, when people felt the need to be kept up-to-date particularly keenly, a spur to publication. In England, for example, the Civil Wars of mid-century saw many new titles appear.[99]

In France, a royal decree of 1631 granted the exclusive right to print, sell, and distribute newspapers in the kingdom to Théophraste Renaudot (1589–1653), a friend of Cardinal Richelieu who had been the personal physician to King Louis XIII. Renaudot's *Gazette* (later *Gazette de France*)

---

[96] Quoted in Jeremy Popkin, "New perspectives on the early modern European press." In Joop Koopmans, ed., *News and Politics in Early Modern Europe (1500–1800)* (Leuven: Peeters, 2005), 4.

[97] Stanley Morrison, "The origins of the newspaper." In David McKitterick, ed., *Selected Essays on the History of Letter-Forms in Manuscript and Print* (Cambridge: Cambridge University Press, 1980), 325–360.

[98] Paul Arblaster, "'Dat de Boecken Vrij Sullen Wesen.' Private profit, public utility and secrets of state in the seventeenth-century Habsburg Netherlands." In Koopmans, *News and Politics*, 79–95 (here 86).

[99] See Joseph Frank, *The Beginnings of the English Newspaper, 1620–1660* (Cambridge, MA: Harvard University Press, 1961); Joad Raymond, *The Invention of the Newspaper: English Newsbooks 1641–1649* (Oxford: Clarendon Press, 2005).

pledged to provide "[the] news, gossip and tales of everything that takes place inside and outside the kingdom." In fact, the news it contained was tightly controlled by the French government, and routinely included stories designed to cast the King in the best possible light. It was a weekly, appearing on Saturdays in runs of about 1,000 copies, each four to twelve pages, depending on the news of the week. Still, the demand was such that the *Gazette* was soon pirated in the provinces; Renaudot responded by franchising the production of the newspaper to local printers. As a result, there was a single newspaper for a country of more than twenty million. Apart from disruptions during the chaos of the Fronde, the newspaper continued to publish, under various titles, until the First World War.

The world's first daily newspaper was launched in 1650 in Leipzig, where Timothaeus Ritzsch (1614–1678) published the *Einkommende Zeitungen* (later *Leipziger Zeitung*) six days a week.[100] Its audience, as with many of earliest newspapers, was urban and middle-class, with a circulation of several hundred. Daily newspapers appeared outside of Germany only slowly. The first daily in English was *The Daily Courant*, which began publication in London in 1702.

Despite the advent of newspapers, manuscript newssheets continued to offer news that was customized and timely. William Trumbull, the English ambassador in Istanbul, received 160 European handwritten newsletters sent to him from London between September 1687 and September 1691, an average of one every seven to ten days. He received official ones issued from the British Secretary of State's office, as well as those from professional news writers and newsmongers who charged for their services.[101] Nor did the regular provision of news through the newspaper mean the end of one-off newssheets focusing on a single event or phenomenon: demand for these remained robust. It is telling that an English editor who, in 1696, finally acknowledged that he would have to change his handwritten news service from manuscript to print, to accord with the new mass-produced world, decided to call his new publication the *London News-Letter*, thus capturing the essence of his original product.[102]

Newspapers took well over a century to become a widespread component of everyday life. But their proliferation over the course of the seventeenth century was transformative for the circulation of information in a number of important ways. The speed and replicability of printed news

---

[100] Else Hauff, "Die 'Einkommenden Zeitungen' von 1650. Ein Beitrag zur Geschichte der Tageszeitung." *Gazette. International Journal for Mass Communications Studies*, 9 (1963), 227–235.
[101] John-Paul Ghobrial, *The Whispers of Cities: Information Flows in Istanbul, London and Paris in the Age of William Trumbull* (Oxford: Oxford University Press, 2013), 96.
[102] Wahrman, *Mr. Collier's Letter Racks*, 65.

sapped political news of its former exclusivity, as the same stories circulated across multiple publications and media platforms. Available for purchase, news became a commodity. Brought together in a single place, it became "information." Readers themselves had to determine what was genuinely important from among the mishmash of stories, from near and far. Political information became part of the everyday, grist for the mill of public conversation, and a shaper of public opinion. The availability of news led to the expectation of yet more news, with updates on ongoing stories, controversies, and conflicts. The "info-lust" that had afflicted diplomats and scholars across the early modern period now spread to a steadily growing reading public. In the eighteenth century, the news business would grow and diversify further, and begin to take on the role of opinion shaper, helping to give form to an increasingly well-informed *vox populi*.

The daily newspaper carried with it another important implication – that the timeliness of news was of the utmost importance. News was cumulative, and interest in stories was directed toward how they developed over time. They did not just happen; they unfolded, and readers waited expectantly for the "latest." The provision of news from afar also meant that there was more awareness of events taking place a long way from home. This confounding of distance helped generate a novel sense of simultaneity in political life, among the public as well as statesmen.[103] As Brian Dooley has suggested:

there is no denying that already in the early modern period people began to formulate in their minds a concept of the world shared with others, within the same time and space and within a basically secular context ... The new means of communication made possible the sharing of a perceived present across small, medium and large distances, at the various levels of family, neighborhood, village and wider world, encouraging a critical apprehension of events.[104]

The emphasis on receiving the most recent *novelle*, *nouvelles*, or *zeitungen*, which had been so important in the correspondence of merchants and

---

[103] "The fact that news was offered at regular increments ended up creating a degree of familiarity and interest in ongoing political events, both local and distant, regardless of whether or not they were particularly important. Thus, news from around the world became a part of many people's lives. Reading such news reduced distances and offered a means through which both interests and discussion could be broadened. Political events, like religious and military events, became subjects of discussions that evolved as an aspect of socializing with others, offering a chance to compare and contrast ideas, or to argue and disagree." Mario Infelise, "From merchants' letters to handwritten political *avvisi*: notes on the origins of public information." In Heinz Schilling and István György Tóth, eds., *Religion and Cultural Exchange in Europe, 1400–1700*, Vol. I of *Cultural Exchange in Early Modern Europe*, General ed. Robert Muchembled (Cambridge: Cambridge University Press, 2006), 33–52 (here 51).
[104] Brendan Dooley, "Introduction." In Dooley, ed., *The Dissemination of News*, 1–22 (here 2–3).

7.2 The emerging early modern culture of news depended on the literate reading to the illiterate and semi-literate. Adriaen van Ostade, *Reading the News at the Weavers' Cottage* (1673). Metropolitan Museum of Art, New York City (Getty Images).

diplomats, now extended to a broader public. The early modern public, therefore, became "consumers" of news. Asking "what news?" was, among other things, a declaration of intent to participate in political life.

This "culture of news" also saw the emergence of specific locales for information exchange. Filippo De Vivo has shown how pharmacies became "sheltered spaces for sociability" in Venice, locales that facilitated conversation and the exchange of news and gossip. The shop of the apothecary Angelo Cerutti, in the Campo di Do Pazzi, near the Arsenal, was, in the early seventeenth century, a spot for Venetian men to converse, gamble, and watch and listen to others do both. Those who gathered there also regularly exchanged *avisi* – it appears that Cerutti welcomed those who authored or wanted to read the newsletters, seeing them as a means of attracting people to his shop. Apothecaries like Cerutti, given the relatively exotic nature of their merchandise, necessarily engaged in long-distance commerce and correspondence, offering a connection with a broader world. Visiting shops like Cerutti's gave customers the opportunity to linger, read the latest news, and deepen social connections with those in the know.[105]

In seventeenth-century England, coffeehouses came to play similar roles. They were spaces for information exchange, often where the post was collected and delivered, and where newssheets, newspapers, and other periodical literature could be consulted. As early as 1659, the political philosopher James Harrington (1611–1677) organized debates about the history and philosophy of government at Miles' Coffee House in Westminster. The gathering became known as the Rota. In 1675, King Charles II (r. 1660–1685) sought to abolish coffeehouses because of their role in the circulation of materials, such as lampoons and satirical poems, perceived as seditious. In *The Athenian Gazette*, a twice-weekly periodical published in London in the 1690s, the editor, John Dunton (1659–1733), encouraged the coffeehouses that kept volumes of his publication to bind them together, so that they could be searched by the alphabetical index that he was to publish. Public readings of the latest news also regularly occurred within coffee-shop walls. The influence of such periodicals was magnified by the open access provided in the coffeehouse as well as the opportunities for discussion of their content.[106] Coffeehouses were also frequented by the *virtuosi* of English science, such as Robert Hooke (1635–1703), and assumed an important role in their learned sociability.[107] Adrian Johns has gone as far as to say that "experimental philosophy came to prominence on a wave of coffee."[108]

Coffeehouses were especially important social spaces for exchanges between businesspersons. In London, coffeehouses held auctions and posted lists of prices and stock offerings. In 1692, Edward Lloyd (1648–1713), the proprietor of Lloyds Coffee House on Lombard Street, started publishing a Marine List, which reported the arrival and departure of ships at ports in England and abroad, information compiled from the merchants who frequented his shop. Lloyds became the "centre of the London shipping world" and soon the unofficial headquarters of the emerging maritime insurance business. The current-day insurance

---

[105] Filippo DeVivo, "Pharmacies as centres of communication in early modern Venice." *Renaissance Studies*, 21.4 (2007), 505–521.

[106] Hazel Bell, ed., *Indexers and Indexes in Fact & Fiction* (Toronto: University of Toronto Press, 2001), 32; Helen Berry, "An early coffee house periodical and its readers: the *Athenian Mercury*, 1691–1697." *The London Journal*, 25.1 (2000), 14–33. On the earliest coffeehouses in London, see Markman Ellis, "Pasqua Rosee's coffee-house, 1652–1666." *The London Journal*, 29.1 (2004), 1–24.

[107] Robert Iliffe, "Material doubts: Hooke, artisan culture and the exchange of information in 1670s London." *The British Journal for the History of Science*, 28.3 (1995), 285–318.

[108] Adrian Johns, "Coffeehouses and print shops." In Katherine Park and Lorraine Daston, eds,. *The Cambridge History of Science*, Vol 3: *Early Modern Science* (Cambridge: Cambridge University Press, 2006), 320–340 (here 320).

giant thus has its origins in the exchange of information between merchants and sailors over cups of coffee.[109]

Public spaces such as taverns, apothecaries, and coffeehouses served as nuclei for an incipient public sphere and a locus of sociability that extended beyond family and close friends. It was Jürgen Habermas who suggested that eighteenth-century England saw the creation of a "bourgeois public sphere" that depended on the circulation of news and shared public conversations. Already in the seventeenth century, we see the requisite media and spaces for such information exchange in place.

This was not yet the world of the cable and internet news cycle, which seems to shorten month by month, and which presumes instantaneity and immediate updating. Early modern Europeans were aware of, and often complained about, the logistical constraints to which their provision of news was subject. But breathlessly seeking out (or demanding) the latest news became proverbial in early modern Europe. This was an important component of Pettegree's "invention of news," in the sense of publicly circulating information about the events of the day. The demand for timely information about the world around went from being the concern of a relatively narrow band of merchants, diplomats and statesmen, to a large swath of the literate public. In about 1550, many years before the first newspapers, the zeal for the latest news among the public became the object of satire for the Italian poet Matteo Franzesi who, in his *Sopra le nuove*, described the scenes in Rome as people await the courier arriving with the latest news:

> Right about now, Busino, everyone is bugging me
> > That I tell them about the News,
> > News from whom they don't know,
> Before it goes anywhere else,
> > I should tell them about this News on this piece of paper,
> > While it is still in my hand.
> They want to be informed before it leaves,
> > Before a courier arrives,
> > Before the news has traveled far and wide.
> And before they have even looked you in the eye,
> > After they have kissed both cheeks,
> > After a short greeting, a pat on the back, a chuckle,
> After the first or second word,
> > They confront you with a certain *What does it say?* ...
> These people then gather round in a circle,

---

[109] Markman Ellis, *The Coffee House: A Cultural History* (London: Weidenfeld and Nicolson, 2004), 166–168.

> They make a more raucous noise with their chatter
>> Than if they had a hornet in a flask.
> And with such discordant yakking,
>> They go about informing the whole world,
>> Like water flowing in a twisting (or wrong) river.
> And here comes someone on the side,
>> Who opens a letter of rumor (or noise)
>> Written by a great man in his own hand,
> So that every clumsy buffoon
>> Feasts on and is occupied by these fables,
>> Wallows in them, revels in them, and feasts on them.
> They discuss the Turks, Italy, Spain, France,
>> Armadas, liberty, wars, treaties,
>> And they weigh all of this in their balances,
> O how many charlatans and babblers
>> Go droning on! And if they go on and on,
>> They deafen us with so many little lies ...
> Certain folks are so curious,
>> That they are always in your ears, and ask of you,
>> And seek to discover the hidden News.
> Some come in person, and others send
>> To banks, to ambassadors, to chamberlains,
>> And demand that news be brought to them by others,
> Such that it appears to them that it is worse to be an animal than
>> To be without News, in whose company
>> They make such a racket.
> Each one tells you his fantasy;
>> What he had seen in a letter, and what by mouth
>> He had heard from a great man in Barbary.[110]

In a world before news tickers, before the refresh button on email, and before social media, Franzesi depicts anxieties with which we are familiar: the need to be the first to know, the worries over whether what one heard was the truth, and the obsession of some for knowing all.[111]

In the early modern period, individual writing (of outgoing letters, of account books, diaries, journals, and other ego-documents) and reading (of incoming letters, books acquired, and the latest news to arrive) became quotidian activities for a great many people in Europe. More and more of everyday life, not just for institutions but also for individuals, was mediated through the consultation of paper instruments. And, as a matter of course, more and more individual Europeans became managers of information in their own right.

---

[110] Pietro Fanfani, ed., *Rime Burlesche di eccelenti autori, raccolte, ordinate e postillate* (Florence: Felice le Monnier, 1856), 205–206.

[111] Andrew Pettegree, *The Invention of the News*, 131.

8 Conclusion
Information Revolutions, Past and Present

Every age is an age of information, in which systems of communication and knowledge exchange shape events and institutions in distinctive ways. The specific nature of these systems helps determine how individuals in an age made sense of themselves and the world around them. This book has shown that in early modern Europe approaches to information underwent profound change, resulting in new containers for the housing and conveyance of information; new institutions chiefly concerned with information flows; new jobs and social functions tasked primarily with information management; and new attitudes towards the importance of information, including the need to organize and taxonomize it systematically. Taken together, these phenomena constitute a revolution in information.

In this book, while I have sought to bind myself to the mast in the face of the sirens of anachronism, and taken pains throughout to address my early modern subjects on their own terms, I readily concede that my thinking about the early modern period has been conditioned by our present preoccupations and challenges; just as my understanding of the present is invariably shaped by awareness of the past. In this endeavour, I feel vindicated by the insight of Marc Bloch that humans both understand their present through the lens of the past in light of the present. "Misunderstanding of the present is the inevitable consequence of ignorance of the past. But a man may wear himself out just as fruitlessly in seeking to understand the past, if he is totally ignorant of the present ... This faculty of understanding the living is, in very truth, the master quality of the historian."[1]

This book has recounted the recombinant triumph of a technology of the intellect, writing, and its corresponding hardware, paper. In ways mostly implicit, I have presented an image of opposing bookends, where the late medieval embrace of paper in the West is reflected in the inverse

---

[1] Marc Bloch, *The Historian's Craft*. Trans. by Peter Putnam (New York: Vintage Books, 1953), 43.

by the present-day much talked-about close of the age of paper, brought about by the pervasive influence of digital media. In this sense, I have told the story of how the West entered into an information era from which we are now, we are told, emerging.

A good part of the discomfiture that early modern Europeans felt in the face of informational change (many expressions of which have appeared in the pages of this book) was rooted in fear of the unknown, expressed in dire predictions that never came to pass. The story of information in early modern Europe is, among other things, a lesson in the unintended consequences of technological change. The many worlds of paper which I have described in this book were not the ones envisioned by those who decided, in the late Middle Ages, to embrace the use of inexpensive, newly available paper. The virtuosity of paper meant that it insinuated itself into preexisting practices and, on account of its virtues, created altogether new ones.

As with these earlier changes in information, so it is with our current flurry of technologically induced transformations. The advent of the new communication technologies invariably results in the creation of novel practices and medial forms. Who, twenty years ago, had heard of a "selfie," a video of a kitten "going viral," or "virtual conferencing" (or indeed of "virtual" anything), let alone texting, Instagramming, or Googling? As Andrew Pettegree has written while reflecting on his own work on the impact of the printing press: "There is an added pleasure to be found in using the twenty-first-century information revolution to unlock the secrets of the last great technological breakthrough, the invention of printing. But that comparison should also give us pause. Technological innovation is frequently accompanied by excitable rhetoric and false prophecy. So it was with printing in the fifteenth century."[2]

This tale of informational change is thus also a story of resonances. In multiple sectors of early modern life – government and statecraft, finance and commerce, learning and scholarship, efforts to understand nature, news and communication – Europeans faced challenges in knowing what to do with the stacks of paper that their new practices generated. And, as with us, the primary challenge was how to mediate and manage the information. This was a challenge that was practical and logistical, to be sure; but it was also epistemological, even moral and ethical.

One of the notable transformations that accompanied the early modern information revolution was the validation of human curiosity, which had

---

[2] Andrew Pettegree, "'The Renaissance library and the challenge of print." In Alice Crawford, ed., *The Meaning of the Library. A Cultural History* (Princeton, NJ: Princeton University Press, 2015), 72–90 (here 89).

long carried associations of discord, waywardness, and heresy. As late as 1593, Cesare Ripa's emblematic book *Iconologia* depicted Curiosity as a woman with ears and wide-eyed frogs on her vestments, her hair standing on end and hands lifted high, "to know and hear news from every corner." All of these features are indications of someone who seeks to know "more than [she] should."[3] Gradually, if haltingly, curiosity began to shed such malign connotations. The proliferation of information, especially on paper instruments, abetted its investigation through the indulgence of curiosity. The avenues for the satisfaction of curiosity multiplied. The paper records of commercial concerns and bureaucratic institutions generated a sea of precedent and documentary justification to explore and exploit; the multiplication of books and other printed items created a ready repository of knowledge, news, and gossip; and the book of nature was increasingly regarded as an essentially endless trove of the unknown, awaiting discovery by the curious, rather than a storehouse of secrets to be pried out by the guileful. Curiosity might not have been universally regarded as an unalloyed good, but in the course of the early modern period, it was frequently acknowledged as a useful and valuable outlook, one aligned to a world that was awash in information. The collection of data via "experience" and "observation" became an essential step in many areas of early modern life. Today, of course, we largely accept such actions as the starting point for the process of discovery in the modern world.

Philip Ball, however, has pointed out that curiosity, when unrestrained, can become pathological.[4] There are hints that the early modern embrace of *observatio* and *historia* was already revealing this peril. In *Conversations on the Plurality of Worlds* (1686), Fontenelle's Marquise lamented: "here's a universe so large that I'm lost, I no longer know where I am, I'm nothing... This confounds me – troubles me – terrifies me... you'd scarcely know how to pick us out in the middle of so many worlds."[5] Like many others of his age, Fontenelle struggled to give shape and direction to the immense quantities of information available to him, issuing forth from multiple worlds. There are audible echoes of the Marquise's discomfiture with the data swamp we encounter in cyberspace. Astride this sea of information, there is the opportunity, and temptation, to indulge one's curiosity to

---

[3] Cesare Ripa, *Iconologia di Cesare Ripa Perugino* (Rome: Matteo Florimi), 152.
[4] Philip Ball, *Curiosity. How Science Became Interested in Everything* (Chicago: University of Chicago Press, 2012). See also Neil Kenny, *Curiosity in Early Modern Europe: Word Histories* (Wiesbaden: Harrassowitz, 1998).
[5] Bernard Le Bovier, Marquis de Fontenelle, *Entretiens sur la pluralité des mondes* (Lyon: Leroy, 1800, c1686), 113: 'Mais, reprit-elle, voilà l'univers si grand que je m'y perds, je ne sais plus où je suis, je ne suis plus rien... Cela me confond, me trouble, m'epouvante... avouëz que vous ne sçauriez presque plus nous démêler au milieu de tant de mondes."

the point of paralysis. The current world poses the risk of what Ball calls "the empty immediacy of a virtual view." Untrammeled curiosity, set loose on a bottomless pit of data, is liable to end up with ephemera, epistemological dead ends, and the collection of data as mere curios. Drawing meaningful connections and relationships between disassociated data that is now more accessible than ever before is among the great challenges of the digital age. Applying the necessary parsimony to the facts, already taxing for the contemporaries of Fontenelle, is today more difficult than ever. Early modern Europe gradually (if not entirely) left behind the ancient and medieval tendency to engage in observation with the intent of revealing occluded truths and fitting the resulting data into an established constellation of axioms. In the digital world, the scales of this duality have been imbalanced by the weight of data; we now, often in vain, search for the axioms. The Internet is a million miles wide and an inch deep. Information is easily accessed, but genuine knowledge and wisdom are illusive amid the visual and typographic cacophony. Curiosity amid *copia* might, then, lead us to aimless cognitive meandering.

Like our early modern forbears, we wonder at, and complain about, the abundance of information now available to us. Increases in information, combined with novelty in medial forms, have always in human history prompted unease, cognitive dissonance, and complaints of overload. Such discomfiture has each time prompted a set of responses, resulting in new practices, new institutions, and new forms of information processing. This book has largely focused on two related and simultaneous developments in early modern Europe: the great increase in information created and circulating in European society, largely rendered on paper, and the accompanying efforts to manage and make sense of it, also chiefly via paper. One of the reasons why humans have emerged as the dominant species on the planet is our capacity to filter, to reduce, and to organize the information before us. The world is complicated and confusing, and contains more particulars than our brains could ever encompass: a process of distillation is essential to our thriving. Knowledge is, in many regards, about shrinking what it is that we have to know. To some extent, there has always been too much to know, too much to read, too much to process, and humans have always drawn upon tools external to themselves to bolster the capacity of their brains. As Jeffrey Todd Knight has described it: "How we collate is how we think."[6] The anxiety that many feel regarding information is not strictly that there is too much of it, but that they are not getting enough of the *right sort* of information, and that they are not

---

[6] Jeffrey Todd Knight, *Bound to be Read. Compilations, Collections, and the Making of Renaissance Literature* (Philadelphia: University of Pennsylvania Press, 2013), 184.

receiving it in as timely a fashion as others are. With so much stuff out there, we are concerned that we are missing out on the most important stuff. What we need is the right sort of filters. Seen from this perspective, perhaps the operative challenge of our age is not necessarily information overload, but what Clay Shirky has called "acute filter failure."

This need for an effective filter was, as we have seen, already keenly felt in early modern Europe. Knowledge in the early modern period, also amid profound informational change, was created amid bonds of sociability, in libraries, in the Republic of Letters, in the circulation of news, and in the exchange of political paper. Plato famously worried in *Phaedrus* that the written word would mean the end of human memory. As it turned out, contrary to his fears, it served instead as a bulwark. The surge in early modern Europe of writing on paper, in manuscript and in print, meant that it became a supplement and a spur to memory. The great expansion in printed books (in libraries and in private hands) amplified the information available to individuals and institutions, paper records deepened institutional memories, and notes scrawled on loose paper and in notebooks allowed the owner to recall and expand on their previous thoughts and those of others. These various inscriptions registered information from specific moments in time and restored them for mobilization in the present. The technologies of script and paper together thus served as a preservative, the "conserved energy" which I discussed in the introductory chapter, available for subsequent recall and deployment.[7] They were tools for use by the human mind, employed for the abstraction, stowage, and then elaboration of ideas and information.

Europeans in the early modern period devised all sorts of tools and methods to circumvent extended, continuous reading and facilitate non-linear access to information. Expurgation, summarizing, listing and ranking, and taxonomy – all were among the tools of early modern bureaucrats, scholars, and scientists employed to maximize the utility of their reading. They were the filaments of the sifter that early modern Europeans sought to construct in order to make sorting through their information less arduous by facilitating nonlinear consultation. Many of these practices responded to a sense of dislocation and bewilderment in the face of an abundance of books and paperwork. Many early modern readers were, it turns out, information mining, reading to extract what they needed or wanted. This selective and targeted method of reading is, it appears, a feature of much reading in every age. Michel de Certeau, in his *L'invention du quotidien*, has described the reader as a poacher, a consumer who, in his encounter with the book, picks off only what he

---

[7] Aleida Assmann, *Erinnerungsräume: Formen und Wandlungen des kulturellen Gedächtnis* (Munich: C.H. Beck, 1999).

needs.[8] To some extent, the intensive early modern efforts to provide shortcuts to distill useful information from the mass of books and stacks of inscribed paper are merely an extension of forms of nonlinear reading prominent since at least the invention of the codex. A great many medial forms that emerged in early modern Europe – epitomes, commonplace books, encyclopedias, *relazioni*, account books – to some degree sought to miniaturize and paraphrase reality. They were paper instruments, reflecting the emergence of paper as the prevailing vehicle for encapsulating the world. Like so many of the most prized tools of cyberspace, they were promising shortcuts to knowledge and wisdom.

Today that information is abstracted a degree further, into digital form, and the shortcuts offered are instant. In order to render the location of the germane information instant, we subcontract the search to web applications, algorithms, and, ultimately, commercially conflicted internet companies. Usually left unsaid here is that these shortcuts are not only saving time and effort, they are also interdicting thinking, by farming it out to machines. We do not have to agree entirely with Méric Casaubon's seventeenth-century admonition that "the best method to learning is indefatigable (so far as the body will bear), industry, and assiduity, in reading good authors, such as have had the approbation of all learned ages," to fear that, by doing this, we risk impairing our own cognitive discernment.[9] While we must take care not to exaggerate the prevalence of deep reading, focused cognition, and layered, contemplative thinking in the pre-digital world, this is the intellectual equivalent of resolving to drive, rather than walk, the three blocks to the office.

Accompanying the many worlds of early modern paper, of course, was an enormous quantity of writing. The current ongoing digital revolution has brought into question the continuing relative importance of writing. Digital platforms have created something very different from a strictly documentary age, with an informational smorgasbord of text, video, image, and audio. These elements are designed to resemble as much as possible the spoken word, rather than traditional written compositions. They may not involve the physical proximity of face-to-face oral communication, but they do ape its informality, its two-way nature, and its capacity for near-instantaneous response. The digital Bacchanal of today's informational universe is a testament to just how incomplete, and contingent, the triumph of the written medium actually was, and to the enduring importance of oral and visual communication. Our current-day frenzied exchange of oral and visual data, as well as new textual hybrids, suggests that the human predisposition

---

[8] Michel de Certeau, *L'invention du quotidien 1. Arts de faire* (Paris: Gallimard, 1990), ch. 12.
[9] Quoted in Alan Jacobs, *The Pleasures of Reading in an Age of Distraction* (Oxford: Oxford University Press, 2011), 111.

to non-written forms of expression and communication remains predominant. A great majority of the data that we transmit and share in the digital age is image, audio, and video. As of 2021, YouTube had more than 2.2 billion users, and 98% of American internet users reported using YouTube monthly.[10] Astonishingly, more video content is added to the Internet every thirty days than the major American television networks have created in the past thirty years. The most recent estimates suggest that, in 2021, 80 percent of all internet traffic will be in video format.[11] It would take an individual 5 million years to watch the new video that crosses global IP networks in a single month. The Web is not chiefly a typographic communicative platform.

In many ways, the shape of the Internet demonstrates the resilience among human society of non-written forms of communication, and we might very well query whether the contemporary West remains "profoundly documentary." If anything, the current means of encasing and communicating information have seen text go into eclipse, as familiar forms of text are replaced with video reports or audio equivalents. In moving away from paper, we are moving away from writing – a reversal of the process of "learning to trust the written word" that I discussed in the introductory chapter.

In this sense, the digital information revolution, for all of its technology-driven innovation, condensing time and obliterating distance, has occasioned the return of paradigms that prevailed before paper and writing achieved their wholesale penetration of society. Like paper, written text (either in script or in print) is not going to disappear any time soon. But its role as a chief means of abstracting reality, so important to its rise in the early modern period, is likely to be progressively challenged. In the digital universe, it turns out, seeing and hearing, as much as reading, are believing. Under such conditions, the authority of the written word, the waxing of which is one of the important strands that this book has followed, will without doubt continue to wane. The long-standing marriage of paper and information, which, I hope I have shown, was such a formative relationship in the early modern world, has begun a process of separation. The age of paper was one that privileged a particular type of abstraction, one in which various realities – oral, visual, and natural – were depicted, and granted social, political, and intellectual authority by virtue of being inked on paper. Now that the age of paper is supposedly drawing to a close, our methods of abstraction are changing.

---

[10] These statistics come from https://www.statista.com/topics/2019/youtube/.
[11] These numbers come from www.wordstream.com/blog/ws/2017/03/08/video-marketing-statistics and https://www.cisco.com/c/dam/m/en_us/solutions/service-provider/vni-forecast-highlights/pdf/Global_2021_Forecast_Highlights.pdf.

We may very well be entering an informational landscape that in many ways resembles the world before the age of paper and print: one that privileges the oral and visual (or at least their digital simulacra), or at least reduces the authority that we have for several centuries invested in ink on paper. It thus resembles the ancient and medieval worlds, cultures in which the oral and visual were predominant and interfaced with the manuscript in layered ways. In this, we hear the echoes of an observation by Umberto Eco that current Western society is "neomedieval" – an anxious, post-literate age akin to that of the millennium post-Rome.[12] The capabilities of the Web and digital communication have unleashed a frenzied bout of experimentation in our traditional means of oral and visual exchanges, the latest expression of humankind's inclination toward the semiotics of images and the spoken word. We are, in the memorable term employed by Robbins Burling, the "talking ape," and, for all the power and potential of the written word, our most robust and enduring information systems are oral and visual.[13]

So is the age of paper over? If so, its undertakers are the ease, expanse, and ethereality of the digital milieu. The byte has displaced the sheet of paper. Progress is paperless. In the name of conservation, in the name of convenience, in the name of saving space, paper is deemed no longer necessary. What was deemed indispensable is now considered dispensable. The signs are everywhere, so it seems. The emergence of email and other forms of digital communication means that personal correspondence by letter has disappeared almost entirely. In the United States, nearly half of all schools in the United States have dropped handwriting from the elementary school curriculum altogether, deeming it an obsolete skill – the federal Common Core standards, for example, require keyboarding skills but no training in cursive.[14] Cash is still the most common form of exchange, but one in prolonged, steady, decline.[15] The use of paper checks, paper tickets, paper contracts, bound paper books and, of

---

[12] Umberto Eco, *Travels in Hyper Reality: Essays* Trans. by William Weaver (San Diego, CA: Harcourt Brace Jovanovich, 1986), 73.
[13] Robbins Burling, *The Talking Ape: How Language Evolved* (Oxford: Oxford University Press, 2007).
[14] www.today.com/parents/cursive-comeback-handwriting-lessons-return-some-schools-t41081; for a view that cursive should go the way of the dodo, see www.nytimes.com/roomfordebate/2013/04/30/should-schools-require-children-to-learn-cursive/let-cursive-handwriting-die.
[15] www.cnbc.com/2018/08/06/spike-the-dollars-obit-cash-is-still-a-growth-business.html In 2018, 31 percent of all transactions in the United States were carried out in cash, that is, sales with paper money. The consensus of experts, however, is that it will take several generations before cash disappears completely.

course, newspapers, are all in decline, replaced by (forgive the tautology) digital analogs.

And yet there are reasons to think that reports of paper's demise (like those of Mark Twain) are greatly exaggerated, even as paper is gradually displaced from milieus where its place has long been central. Paper doggedly hangs on as a vessel of information storage and exchange and as a medium of social interface.[16] If this represents the end of our love affair with paper, it is proving hard to let go. The availability of digital platforms has not fundamentally detracted from the practical advantages of paper, admirably summarized by Andrea Pellegram: "Paper is the filing method of preference because of its practical qualities. Five hundred sheets can take up a space as small as nine inches by eleven by three. So many words stored in so little space; and it can all be seen, smelled, touched and leaved through, photocopied and saved for later, just in case."[17] We also continue to endow paper with trust that we do not necessarily place in digital forms. We still require, for example, physical signatures, in ink, on paper copies of mortgages that are generated, shared, and reviewed in digital form among the stakeholders. The long-won trust in writing has not yet eroded entirely. That paper is likely to retain enduring utility and appeal is rooted in large part by the increasingly evident ephemeral nature of its putative replacements.

The tenacious hold of the world of paper is also revealed in the words we use to describe our new environment. We still "browse" web "pages" and save computer "files" in "folders" that enclose "documents" in "libraries," where we can retrieve them if we wish to "copy" them. Rhetorically, at least, it is evident that we remain tethered to the world of paper. When it comes to text, we desire fonts and formats that most closely approximate the experience of encountering words on paper. We desire similar fonts and pagination; we wish to retain table of contents and indices, even though the text is now searchable. Manufacturers of e-book readers still seek to make their backlit products resemble their paper, glue, and binding predecessors as much as possible, even to the point of generating noises akin to paper pages turning. In these choices we

---

[16] Americans still consume an average of 222 kg of paper per capita each year, the equivalent of more than five 40-ft trees per year. The global production of graphic paper is flat, or in very slight decline, but overall paper consumption is at an all-time high, much of it for use in packaging, and in the last decade production levels have risen by an average of about 1 percent per year. The bulk of the increase, predictably, came from demand in Asia and production levels in North America and Europe continued what are now persistent declines, some of which is explained by the increasing use of repurposed paper. www.statista.com/topics/1701/paper-industry/.

[17] Andrea Pellegram, "The message in paper." In Daniel Miller, ed., *Material Cultures. Why Some Things Matter* (Chicago: Chicago University Press, 1997), 103–120 (here 118).

make, we resemble the early printers, who left spaces in their books for illuminated capitals – the comfort of familiarity eased the jarring discontinuities of technological change. Today, as in the early modern period, we live in a hybridized era of technology overlap. Although the physical book is no longer the best format for the type of knowledge that prevails in the digital environment, it is still unlikely to disappear any time soon. It is true that books offer a brand of knowledge that is univocal, presented in a single, progressing pathway, and bound by the pages on which it appears, and are thus marginally compatible with the digitally networked knowledge of the Web. But that is far from the sum of the appeal of the book, as any booklover will tell you.

The virtues and familiarity of paper have also pushed the much prognosticated paperless office farther and farther into the future. In any case, the various electronic tools that have been presented as remedies to the ills of paperwork have offered only imaginary solutions. The environmental imperatives for a paperless office are compelling, but these remedies do not effectively reduce the amount of paperwork required, just the amount of material paper that the office consumes. Many find themselves missing the features that made paper indispensable in the first place, while struggling to perceive in meaningful ways how their lives have been made easier by machines. It is telling that printers, which exist to render digital information on paper, remain a staple in every office, a machine whose very presence repudiates the idea of the paperless office.

I could cite here many other examples that suggest that writing an obituary for the age of paper is at best premature. There are plenty of reasons to believe that paper is here to stay, in certain forms and in large volumes. As Lothar Müller has pointed out, paper has managed to exist symbiotically with a large array of different technologies.[18] It has insinuated itself into myriad routines, and also by its very nature generated altogether new ones. It has combined with a great many cultural settings and institutions, fulfilling existing and creating new functionalities. Advances in digital technology do not sap paper of this virtuosity. It is likely that it will retain its place alongside other virtual representations of reality, both in competition and in collaboration. While the many, well-advertised endeavors to render operations paperless seek to circumvent the accumulation of paper that so vexed early modern secretaries, merchants, and scholars, the material appeal of paper remains real.

The challenges (and dangers) of abundance were expressed before the early modern information revolution – there was already too much to know. For a medieval mind like that of Francesco Petrarch (1304–1374),

---

[18] Lothar Müller, *Weisse Magie: Die Epoche des Papiers* (Munich: Carl Hanser Verlag, 2012).

an abundance of books was an obstacle to learning, instead of a gateway. In his treatise *De remediis utriusque fortunae*, Petrarch imagines a conversation between his genius and his critical reason in which they discuss the various implications of his having accumulated a great quantity of books:

PETRARCH: I have a great abundance of books.
CRITICAL REASON: Yes, and a great abundance of hard work and a great lack of repose. You have to keep your mind marching in all directions, and to overload your memory. Books have led some to learning, and others to madness, when they swallow more than they can digest. In the mind, as in the body, indigestion does more harm than hunger; food and books alike must be used according to the constitution, and what is little enough for one is too much for another ...
...PET: *I* have books which help me in my studies.
CRIT: Take care that they do not prove a hindrance. Many a general has been beaten by having too many troops. If books came in like recruits one would not turn them away, but would stow them in proper quarters, and use the best of them, taking care not to bring up a force too soon which would be more useful on another occasion.
PET: I have a great variety of books.
CRIT: A variety of paths will often deceive the traveller.
PET: I have collected a number of fine books.
CRIT: To gain glory by means of books you must not only possess them but know them; their lodging must be in your brain and not on the bookshelf.[19]

Petrarch was expressing the fear that, given the number of books he had acquired (in a pre-print world), their abundance would prove a burden and preclude him from getting to know them intimately. With the advent of the printing press, such sentiments were heard even more widely, but the calculus underlying the use of books gradually changed. As we have seen, the early modern availability of printed books and written material of all sorts effected a shift toward extensive, rather than intensive, reading. All serious scholars in the early modern period had to become bibliophiles, familiar with a great number and variety of books, rather than a select few to which they could assume regular access. The flip side of this is that the sheer number of books could make the task seem thoroughly unmanageable. The Spanish philosopher Francisco Sanchez estimated as early as 1581 that it would take ten million years to read all the books in the world.[20]

And that was just the books. Those figures who embraced the manifold components of the early modern information culture found themselves

---

[19] This translation from Charles Isaac Elton and Mary Augusta Elton, *The Great Book-Collectors* (London: Kegan Paul, 1893), 44–47.
[20] Ann Blair, *Too Much to Know: Managing Scholarly Information Before the Modern Age* (New Haven, CT: Yale University Press, 2010), 57.

8.1 Heinrich Bullinger (1504–75) generated multiple paper flows in his roles as pastor, theologian, author, news aggregator, and international advocate for Reformed Christianity. Jacob Verheiden, *Imagines et elogia praestantium aliquot theologorum* ... (The Hague, 1725) (Getty Images).

producing, and surrounded by, multiple worlds of paper. Heinrich Bullinger (1504–1575), whose glossing practices I described in Chapter 5, was a Christian humanist who succeeded Huldrych Zwingli (1484–1531) as the head of the city's Großmünster. In his role, Bullinger turned Zürich into an important bulwark in support of international reformed Christianity. His chief means in doing so was many reams of paper, employed in his sustained, expansive, and voluminous correspondence; in his gathering, aggregation, and dispersal of news and information; and in his prolific scholarship and publication. Inscribed paper, received, sent, and printed, connected Bullinger, residing in a relatively small, isolated city in Switzerland, with a far broader world, and with the interlaced fate of confessional fellow travelers across Europe.

It was said of Bullinger that he would sit and await the latest news coming in from abroad. In support and encouragement of the new Protestant churches and in pursuit of his own scholarly interests, Bullinger maintained a prodigious rate of letter writing. In Bullinger, we see considerable support for the notion that the confessional conflicts of the period led to an overall increase in the volume of correspondence, as co-religionists wrote to inform, cajole, and encourage one another, often across long distances. There was also a sense that exchanging correspondence could serve to support vulnerable co-religionists by providing advice, spiritual succor, and vital news that might prove helpful. The ongoing project to publish the correspondence of his long life is currently at fourteen volumes comprising some 15,000 letters; about 2,000 of his autograph letters remain extant.[21] Bullinger's correspondence is bigger than the combined output of Luther, Zwingli, and Calvin. His correspondents, numbering some 1,000 separate individuals, ran the gamut, from the most prominent religious and political leaders to obscure village pastors and schoolmasters. The subjects included in these letters were equally wide-ranging, from high politics, disputes about theology and doctrine, pedagogical questions, advice for pastoral care, and the personal concerns of friendship. The letters also served as means of exchanging news. Bullinger routinely encouraged his correspondents to share whatever news they had heard or read at their end. The letters he received in return often betrayed a division seen in diplomatic dispatches of the period, whereby the section of the letters dedicated to reporting news would assume a separate rubric, sometimes even transitioning into the vernacular from Latin when providing the latest updates. Some of his correspondents penned letters that were almost entirely news, while some apologized that they had nothing novel or of interest to share. In 1569, late in Bullinger's life, he expressed surprise that he had recently consumed a full ream of paper, some 1,000 sheets, for use in his correspondence![22]

But letters exhausted only some of the many quires of paper that Bullinger consumed. Bullinger was also a prolific writer of books, treatises, and pamphlets – more than one hundred were published in his lifetime, at a prodigious rate of publication throughout his life. The range of his published work reflected his broad training as a Christian humanist. He wrote histories of Zürich and of the Protestant

---

[21] See the index, and details on the ongoing project at the University of Zürich, at www.irg.uzh.ch/de/bullinger-edition.html; Also on Bullinger's correspondence: Traugott Schiess, "Der Briefwechsel Heinrich Bullingers." *Zwingliana*, 5 (1933), 396–408; Schiess, "Ein Jahr aus Bullingers Briefwechsel (1559)." *Zwingliana*, 6 (1934), 16–33; and Oskar Farner, "Die Bullinger-Briefe." *Zwingliana*, 10 (1954), 103–108.

[22] Rainer Henrich, "Bullinger's correspondence: an international news network." In Bruce Gordon and Emilio Campi, eds., *Architect of Reformation: an Introduction to Heinrich Bullinger, 1504–1575* (Grand Rapids, MI: Baker Academic, 2004), 231–241 (here 233).

Reformation, as well as a curious tract on the chronology of the Bible. For these he assiduously sought out relevant records and conducted research in the relevant documentary depositories. Bullinger was also one of the most influential theologians of the second wave of the Protestant Reformation, and he saw numerous volumes of his sermons printed during his lifetime. Perhaps the most important of these was the *Decades*, a collection of sermons chiefly on pastoral theology that was translated into several vernaculars, including into English, in which it was widely read, more widely perhaps even than Calvin's *Institutes*. And, like many sixteenth-century intellectuals, he accumulated a large personal library of printed books as well, numbering in the hundreds of volumes. In amassing such a large collection, Bullinger was a typical citizen of the early modern Republic of Letters, gathering around him a reference library of his own. Much of Bullinger's collection is now housed at the Zentralbibliothek Zürich, often covered in the marginal comments he added in his reading.[23] Bullinger was thus responsible for producing, and acquiring, a great deal of printed paper as well.

Bullinger's love affair with paper involved one more tryst. Over the years, Bullinger regularly compiled summaries of religious and political events about which he had seen letters or heard reports. Frequently, in response to his requests for news, his correspondents would include separate *cedulae* along with their personal missives. Sometimes these were not in the same hand as the letter itself and of uncertain authorship. In some cases, he received from his correspondents copies of the manuscript newsletters in circulation in their locales. He also consulted news and newsletters that he received from his network of friends: Theodore Beza (1519–1605) in Geneva, Ambrosius Blarer (1492–1564) in Constance, Rudolf Gwalther (1519–1586) and Wolfgang Haller (1525–1601) (both pastors in Zürich), Joachim Vadian (1484–1551) in St. Gallen, Johannes Fabricius Montanus (1527–1566) and Tobias Egli Iconius (fl. 1560/70) (both pastors in Chur), and Johannes Haller (1523–1575) in Berne. Beza had access to French material, Egli from Italy and elsewhere.[24] Bullinger also managed to acquire news from places where he had no regular correspondents, such as Rome and Antwerp. The *Flugschriften* and *Gründlicherelationen*, the newssheets recounting important events published in numerous German cities,

---

[23] Paul Dover, "How Heinrich Bullinger read his Solinus: reading ancient geography in 16th-century Switzerland." In Kai Brodersen, ed., *Solinus: New Studies* (Heidelberg: Verlag Antike, 2014), 171–195.

[24] Zsuzsa Barbarics Hermanik, "Handwritten newsletters as interregional information sources in central and southeastern Europe." In Dooley, *The Dissemination of News*, 155–178 (here 172–173).

were not available in provincial Zürich, so he had them sent from elsewhere.[25] While his appetite for news was omnivorous, he was particularly interested in gathering and synthesizing information that reflected on the progress or setbacks of the Protestant Reformation.

Bullinger's unremitting zeal for the latest news made him "one of the best-informed men of his time."[26] He systematically worked his way through the news that he received from these manifold sources, determining what was trustworthy and important, and then composed newsletters of his own. These ersatz news bulletins, later called *Bullinger-Zeitungen*, were a sort of sixteenth-century selective news blog. He applied to the task of composing his *Zeitungen* the same sort of critical excerpting that he applied to his humanistic pursuits.[27] The items included were identified by date and place, and only occasionally by the source. The bulletins were completely without personal greetings and focused on the hard news that he deemed significant. Their impersonal nature indicated that they were standard items, duplicated for distribution to a range of friends, relatives, and acquaintances. The *Bullinger-Zeitungen* are reminiscent of the *Fugger-Zeitungen* being produced concurrently in Augsburg in much the same fashion.

There are many documents, including *Bullinger-Zeitungen*, today in the Zürich city archives, that appear to have been provided by Bullinger; this suggests that one of the implicit duties of the chief Protestant minister in a town like Zürich was to collect information and supply news in support of the civic authority. In assuming his role as an information clearinghouse for his municipality, Bullinger was by no means alone among partisans of the Reformation. Christoph Scheurl (1481–1542) in Nuremberg, Joachim Camerarius (1500–1574) in Leipzig, and Jacob (1489–1553) and Johannes (1507–1589) Sturm in Strasbourg, all gathered news and produced their own news reports for their locales. And so too did Philip Melanchthon, whose extensive network of correspondents and information sources helped turn Wittenberg into a major communications hub. These sixteenth-century figures, aware of the acute vulnerability of their newly reformed cities, recognized the importance of being well-informed about the latest regional and international events. The letters, books, and newsletters that passed between them created an interlocking network of information exchange, of which the masses of

---

[25] Henrich, "Bullinger's correspondence," 238.
[26] Henrich, "Bullinger's correspondence," 235.
[27] Carrie Euer in *Couriers of the Gospel: England and Zurich, 1531–1558* (Zürich: Theologischer Verlag, 2006), 66–67. See also *Die Bullinger Zeitungen: zur Halbjahrhundertfeier des Vereins der Schweizerischen Presse dargebracht vom Journalistischen Seminar der Universität Zürich* (Zürich: Buchdruckerei Berichthaus, 1933).

paper that gathered around Heinrich Bullinger in provincial Zürich were the by-product.

Bullinger was an international figure, with paper connections extending far beyond his provincial base, and a major intellectual and theological force, whose works and thoughts were recorded in script and print on more paper still. Bullinger was, by very few measures, typical. But the various categories of information that flowed to, from, and around Bullinger also caused paper to accumulate around individuals of far lesser prominence. Given his profile, role, and circumstances, his was a life that was especially mediated through abundances of paper. In this regard, his was not a singular life.

In his 1680 essay, "Precepts for Advancing the Sciences and Arts", Gottfried Leibniz bemoaned "that horrible mass of books which keeps on growing" and lamented that the "disorder will become nearly insurmountable."[28] As we have seen, such bibliophilia required new tools and technologies to handle the *copia*. More than ever before, scholars were textual travelers rather than spelunkers, moving across and between numerous texts rather than burrowing into a select, authoritative few. A new premium was placed on selection, navigation, and excerption. These are skills that sound familiar in the current information-saturated environment.

Leibniz's informational struggles went well beyond his books, and, in many ways, he embodies the promises and pitfalls of having daily life mediated by paper. Leibniz was one of the great letter writers of his age, keeping up a stream of epistolary communication with hundreds of correspondents. He frequently complained that his dedication to other interests was inhibited by the volume of letters to which he had to respond. In addition to his systematic pursuit of communication via paper, Leibniz tells us that when ideas came to him he would write them down on whatever piece of paper was at hand. But he would often have trouble relocating this information, because he did not have the opportunity to engage in real-time organizing. The resulting confusion of his papers had epistemic repercussions:

I believe that at present I have more than thirty letters waiting for a reply, in which it is always necessary to write something more than just compliments. And beyond the duties of my offices, one owes time to the court and to one's friends. Moreover, thoughts sometimes occur to me that I am pleased to preserve, new books need to be looked at, it is necessary to have some information on current affairs. And apart from the learned, if those who know me knew that on top of all

---

[28] Blair, *Too Much to Know*, 58.

this I also indulged in algebra, they would find it strange. After having done something, I forget it almost entirely within a few months, and rather than searching for it amid a chaos of jottings that I do not have the leisure to arrange and mark with headings, I am obliged to do the work all over again.[29]

Although he would become one the founders of library science and classification, there is no evidence that Leibniz was able to give his papers any archival structure during his lifetime.[30] He was often traveling, and it appears that he kept copies of nearly everything: not only nearly all of the letters he sent to and received from his many correspondents, but also memos, finished and unfinished papers, notes from his reading, and countless administrative documents, such as expense accounts, bills, prescriptions for medicine, and other records. He appears to have been loath to dispense with any piece of paper that documented his life in any way and might serve some purpose moving forward. Today, his papers total more than 200,000 pages of manuscript. All of this handwritten text is exclusive of the printed texts in his library, which had been seeded by his father, a professor of moral philosophy at the University of Leipzig. This personal collection would eventually grow to number several thousand volumes, although, ironically, as with his manuscript papers, Leibniz never furnished it with a catalog or any other finding aids.

Leibniz, across his life, demonstrated the "mania for inscription" shared by many in early modern Europe, and this was wedded to an instinct to preserve what he wrote. At every stage of his search for knowledge, from taking notes from reading to exchanging insights with acquaintances via letter, he generated writing on paper. As a result, he was faced with challenges of storing, sorting, and organizing. Even for one who was fundamentally interested in, and committed to, the speciation of books and the knowledge that they contained, the abundance of paper generated in his daily praxis proved a source of challenge and vexation. The man who invented calculus found himself confounded by challenges of information management. Like Bullinger a century earlier, Leibniz was creating his *copiae* through informational practices that were by his time widespread. Individual writing (of outgoing letters, of account books, diaries, journals, and other ego-documents) and reading (of incoming

---

[29] This from a letter of 24 February 1693 to Guillaume François de l'Hospital, quoted in James O'Hara, "'A chaos of jottings that I do not have the leisure to arrange and mark with headings': Leibniz's manuscript papers and their repository." In Michael Hunter, ed., *Archives of the Scientific Revolution: the Formation and Exchange of Ideas in Seventeenth-Century Europe* (Woodbridge, UK: Boydell and Brewer, 1998), 159–170 (here 160).
[30] Hans Schulte-Albert, "Gottfried Wilhelm Leibniz and library classification." *The Journal of Library History*, 2 (1971), 133–152.

letters, books acquired, and the latest news to arrive) became quotidian activities for a great many people in Europe. There were few, if any, lives ca. 1500 that were as well documented as that of Leibniz, but over the next two centuries the proliferation of practices of pen and paper provides us with well-documented profiles of lives such as his. More and more of everyday life, not just for institutions but also for individuals, was navigated through the consultation of paper instruments. And, as a matter of course, more and more individual Europeans became managers of information in their own right.

Leibniz's expressions of dismay about the abundance of books and correspondence might sound quaint today, given the fathomless depths of our information. Today, education is focused less on the acquisition of knowledge, that is, what we would call "learning," and more on where to find things. Ours is increasingly a look-it-up culture, where what is prized is the capacity for speedy and effective location of relevant material from amidst an ever-expanding sea of information. Rather than farmers, we are foragers, focused on finding the desired nuts rather than carefully cultivating the crop. The starting point for learning in the current day, it often seems, is an internet search engine, an imperfect and commercially conflicted route to what we "need" to know. Early modern Europeans could not possibly imagine the oceanic dimensions of information available to us in the digital age, nor a Boolean search by which to navigate these waters. But, as we have seen, they did already value methods and tools that could facilitate their own pursuit of knowledge by sorting through and refining the sheaves of paper around them. Then, as now, scholars, bureaucrats, secretaries, businessmen, bankers, and shopkeepers all appreciated such shortcuts. In *The Life of Samuel Johnson* (1791), James Boswell recalls Johnson saying: "Knowledge is of two kinds. We know a subject ourselves, or we know where we can find information upon it. When we enquire into any subject, the first thing we have to do is to know what books have treated of it. This leads us to look at catalogues, and at the backs of books in libraries."[31] He was at the time (1775) in the company of Boswell and the painter Joshua Reynolds, visiting the extensive library of Richard Owen in Cambridge. Johnson's reflection, while in a place of learning, reflects how, by the end of the eighteenth century, three hundred years of intensive deployment of paper technologies had shaped how one comes to know something. One's own studies and experience equipped one with knowledge of a subject but, just as important, in a world full of books, papers, and opinions, was an awareness of where and how to look for additional relevant information. And, Johnson

---

[31] James Boswell, *The Life of Samuel Johnson, LL.D.* (London: MacMillan, 1900), 128.

stresses, those locales are genuinely fruitful only if they are equipped with tools (such as indices and catalogs) to search for and identify precisely what one is looking for. Recourse to one's own memory, access to reservoirs of information, and tools to navigate those depths: these were the essentials of learning at the tail end of the early modern information revolution.

In a popular eighteenth-century work on how to excerpt useful and valuable knowledge from the abundance of available books, *De modo legendi et excerpendi* (1775), Ignatius Weitenauer wrote that a collection of disordered extracts taken from one's reading was akin to an army without ranks, a disordered confusion unsuitable for deployment for any meaningful end.[32] Hence the importance in organizing the information that one had garnered from one's studies. Without these efforts at information management, Weitenauer declared, *copia impedimento erit*: abundance ended up being an impediment.

Copia impedimento erit: this could be a byline for our time. One of the inescapable realities of our current age is that we are floundering to cope with a surfeit of information. We are beset with "big data," "information overload," and the "cloud" – a cloud, we should remind ourselves, for all its pretensions to unity and sharing, is composed of billions of individual water droplets with diameters as small as a single micron. In today's marketplace, enormous resources are channeled toward individuals, institutions, and applications that can manage these oceans of information, and present us with digestible portions or canned summaries, providing shortcuts to information desired by the user. The current "information age" demands the creation of discerning filters, ones that can distinguish the wheat from the chaff. Metadata, information about information, are more important than ever and their selling point is that they do a sequence of laborious tasks for you, that they save you time. And yet these tools easily become time sinks in their own right, leading us down all sorts of alternate avenues, and directing us toward information only tangentially related to our task. It turns out that this provision of metadata and then making effective use of the results can prove enormously arduous and time-consuming: this is something that early modern secretaries, chancery notaries, and archivists knew all too well. We struggle to cope with our own *copiae*, and it is increasingly evident that we do so at best partially, leaving us uncertain that we can ascertain genuine truth and actionable knowledge from among the swirl of information.

---

[32] Ignatius Weitenauer, *De modo legendi et excerpendi libri II* (Augsburg: Ignatius Eagner, 1775), 397.

Early modern Europeans might not have had to confront the gargantuan quantities of information with which one struggles in the digital age. Nonetheless, the discomfiture and disjunctures experienced in this earlier age of informational transformation were real, and the efforts and energies dedicated to their resolution a major theme of the period's history. As he penned *De copia verborum*, Erasmus was becoming aware that his world of scholarship and learning was indeed entering an *aetas nova*, in part because of the varied impacts of print, but also because of the paper sodalities created by networks of correspondence and scholarly exchange. Erasmus could scarcely have imagined the worlds of paper, scholarly and otherwise, that would come into being across Europe in the centuries to follow: *copiae* beyond his imagination. Erasmus's recommendations to readers and students for choosing words and phrases with which to bolster their rhetoric from amid the plethora of books were but a modest example of the broad array of mechanisms that Europeans would develop, adopt, and refine to cope with abundance and variety in their own areas of endeavor. Thus the account registers, commonplace notebooks, encyclopedias, almanacs, library catalogs, censuses, archives, newspapers, and indices, described in the preceding pages, all had at the core of their functionality the management of an unprecedented amount of information.

Welcome to the future, welcome to the past. But we historians are not in the future business; nor should we be in the nostalgia business. As one writer, Cathy Davidson, who enthusiastically embraces our brave new digital world, puts it: "to believe that the new totally and positively puts an end to the old is a mistaken idea that gets us nowhere, neither out of old habits nor finding new ones better suited to the demands of that which has changed."[33] This mistaken outlook that changes in information exchange will invariably result in the end of familiar practices, habits of mind, and institutions, John Seely Brown and Paul Duguid deride as "endism."[34] Well, I am no endist, and I fully expect to be living under the reign of paper for some time to come. As a historian, however, I do believe that the study of the past reveals patterns that can equip us for what is to come and, in that spirit, I hope that this treatment of the experience of Europeans amid informational change can give cause for reflection in our own age of transition.

The attempts of early modern Europeans to achieve mastery over information failed, as they were bound to do. It was impossible to keep

---

[33] Cathy Davidson, *Now You See It. How the Brain Science of Attention Will Transform the Way We Live, Work and Learn* (New York: Viking, 2011), 290.
[34] John Seely Brown and Paul Duguid, *The Social Life of Information* (Boston: Harvard Business School Press, 2000).

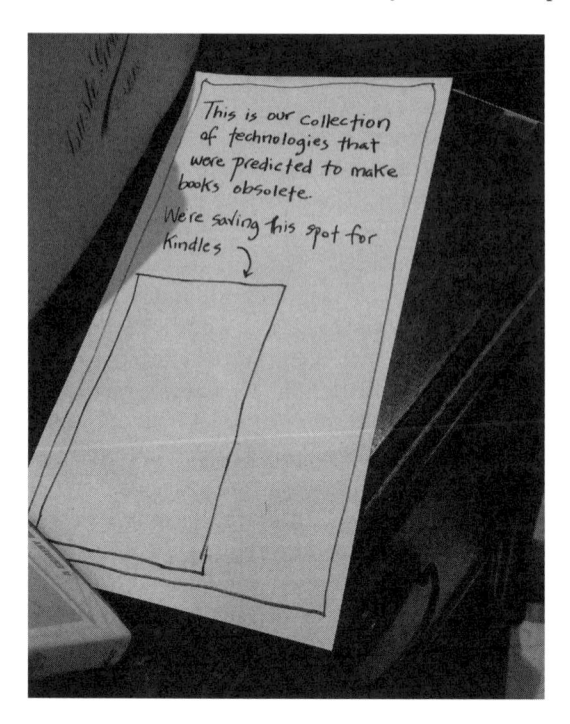

282   The Information Revolution in Early Modern Europe

8.2 Riverby Bookstore, Fredericksburg, Virginia.

up, for the forces that compelled Europeans to create practices and adopt sensibilities in pursuit of information management were the same forces that were simultaneously generating ever more information. It is a paradox familiar to those in the digital age. For them it was slips and sheets and piles of paper, for us it is gigabytes. Like those in the first age of paper, in our efforts to get on top of all the information and secure all that is relevant, we are like the figure of Tantalus. Condemned by the gods for stealing ambrosia and nectar in search of immortality, he is condemned forever to reach for fruit from a tree whose branches are always receding and seek water from a lake that is always sinking away from him.[35]

---

[35] Iolanda Ventura also invokes the figure of Tantalus in describing early modern botany in "Changing Representations of Botany in Encyclopaedias from the Middle Ages to the Renaissance." In Anja-Silvia Goeing, Anthony Grafton, and Paul Michel, eds., *Collector's Knowledge: What is Kept, What is Discarded = Aufbewahren oder wegwerfen – Wie Sammler entscheiden* (Leiden: Brill, 2013), 97–143.

Their *copiae* were not our *copiae*, but their successes and failures in coping with them surely hold lessons for us today. The digital age has made archivists and information managers out of us all, as we routinely engage in processes of storage, organization, and retrieval in the face of unfathomable deeps of information at our fingertips. Understanding the challenges and responses of early modern Europeans in their own *nova aetas* of information might make us feel a little less alone.

Bibliography

Aers, David. "A whisper in the ear of early modernists; or, reflections on literary critics writing the 'History of the Subject.'" In Aers, ed. *Culture and History, 1350–1600: Essays on English Communities, Identities, and Writing*. Detroit: Wayne State University Press, 1992, 177–202.
Aho, James. "Rhetoric and the invention of double-entry bookkeeping." *Rhetorica*, 3.3 (1985), 21–43.
Albèri, Eugenio, ed. *Relazioni degli ambasciatori veneti al Senato*, Series II, Vol. III. Florence: Società editrice fiorentina, 1846.
Alberti, Leon Battista. *I tre libri della famiglia (1434)*. Ed. by Francesco Carlo Pellegrini. Florence: Sansoni, 1911.
Al-Nuwayri, Shihab al-Din. *The Ultimate Ambition in the Arts of Erudition. A Compendium of Knowledge from the Classical Islamic World*. Trans. and ed. by Elias Muhanna. New York: Penguin, 2016.
Allen, E. J. B. *Post and Courier Service on the Diplomacy of Early Modern Europe*. Dordrecht: Springer, 2012.
Allinson, Rayne. *A Monarchy of Letters: Royal Correspondence and English Diplomacy in the Reign of Elizabeth I*. Basingstoke, UK: Palgrave Macmillan, 2012.
Amelang, James. *The Flight of Icarus. Artisan Autobiography in Early Modern Europe*. Stanford: Stanford University Press, 1998.
Anagnostou, Sabine. *Missionspharmazie: Konzepte, Praxis, Organisation und wissenschaftliche Ausstrahlung*. Stuttgart: Steiner Verlag, 2011.
Andreani, Angela. *The Elizabethan Secretariat and the Signet Office*. New York: Routledge, 2017.
Antenhoffer, Christina and Mario Müller, "Briefe in politischer Kommunikation. Einführung." In Antenhoffer and Müller, eds. *Briefe in politischer Kommunikation vom Alten Orient bis ins 20. Jahrhundert*. Göttingen: V&R Unipress, 2008, 9–30.
Antsey, Peter. "Locke, Bacon and natural history." *Early Science and Medicine*, 7 (2002), 65–92.
Appuhn, Karl. "Tools for the development of the European economy." In Guido Ruggiero, ed. *A Companion to the Worlds of the Renaissance*. London: Blackwell, 2002, 259–278.
Aquilon, Pierre. "Petites et moyennes bibliothèques 1530–1660." In *Histoires des bibliothèques françaises*, Vol. 1: *Les bibliothèques sous l'Ancien regime 1530–1789*. Paris: Editions du Cercle de la Librairie, 1998, 180–205.

Aquilon, Pierre. "Quatre avocats angevins dans leurs librairies (1586–1592)." In Aquilon and Henri-Jean Martin, eds. *Le livre dans l'Europe de la Renaissance: actes du XXVIIIe Colloque international d'études humanistes de Tours*. Paris: Promodis/Editions du Cercle de la Librairie, 1998, 503–549.

Arblaster, Paul. "'Dat de Boecken Vrij Sullen Wesen.' Private profit, public utility and secrets of state in the seventeenth-century Habsburg Netherlands." In Joop Koopmans, ed. *News and Politics in Early Modern Europe (1500–1800)*. Leuven: Peeters, 2005, 79–95.

Arlinghaus, F. J. "Account books." In Arlinghaus, ed. *Transforming the Medieval World: Uses of Pragmatic Literacy in the Middle Ages*. Turnhout: Brepols, 2006, 43–69.

Artifoni, Enrico. "Podestà professionali e la fondazione retorica della politica communale." *Quaderni storici*, 63 (1986), 687–719.

Ashworth, William. "Natural history and the emblematic world view." In David Lindberg and Robert Westman, eds. *Reappraisals of the Scientific Revolution*. Cambridge: Cambridge University Press, 1990, 303–332.

Assmann, Aleida. *Erinnerungsräume: Formen und Wandlungen des kulturellen Gedächtnisses*. Munich: C.H. Beck, 1999.

Assmann, Aleida. *Cultural Memory and Western Civilization. Functions, Media, Archives*. Cambridge: Cambridge University Press, 2011.

Aston, Margaret. "Epilogue." In Julia Crick and Alexandra Walsham, eds. *The Uses of Script and Print 1300–1700*. Cambridge: Cambridge University Press, 2004.

Bacchi, Teresa. "Cancelleria e segretari estensi nella seconda metà del secolo XV. Prime ricerche." In Franca Leverotti, ed. *Cancellerie e amministrazione negli stati italiani del Rinascimento*. Special issue of *Ricerche storiche*, 24.2 (1994), 351–359.

Bacon, Francis. *The New Organon*. Trans. and ed. by Lisa Jardine. Cambridge: Cambridge University Press, 2000.

Bacon, Francis. *Novum Organum*. Trans. and ed. by Peter Urbach and John Gibson. Chicago: Open Court, 1994.

Balestracci, Duccio. *The Renaissance in the Fields. Family Memoirs of a Fifteenth-century Tuscan Peasant*. Trans. by Paolo Squatriti and Betsy Merideth. University Park, PA: Penn State University Press, 1999.

Ball, Philip. *Curiosity. How Science Became Interested in Everything*. Chicago: University of Chicago Press, 2012.

Barbarics-Hermanik, Zsuzsa. "Handwritten newsletters as interregional information sources in central and southeastern Europe." In Brendan Dooley, ed. *The Dissemination of News and the Emergence of Contemporaneity in Early Modern Europe*. Farnham, Surrey: Ashgate, 2010, 155–178.

Barbarics, Zsuzsa and Renate Pieper. "Handwritten newsletters as means of communication in early modern Europe." In Francisco Bethencourt and Florike Egmond, eds. *Correspondence and Cultural Exchange in Europe 1400–1700*, Vol. III of *Cultural Exchange in Early Modern Europe*, General ed. Robert Muchembled. Cambridge: Cambridge University Press, 2006, 53–79.

Baron, Sabrina Alcorn, Eric Lindquist, and Eleanor Shevlin, eds. *Agent of Change. Print Culture Studies after Elizabeth L. Eisenstein*. Amherst, MA: University of Massachusetts Press, 2007.

Barrera-Osorio, Antonio. *Experiencing Nature: The Spanish-American Empire and the Early Scientific Revolution*. Austin, TX: University of Texas Press, 2006.

Bartlett, Beatrice. "Qing statesmen, archivists and the question of memory." In Francis X. Blouin Jr. and William Rosenberg, eds. *Archives, Documentation and Institutions of Social Memory (the Sawyer Seminar)*. Ann Arbor, MI: University of Michigan Press, 2006, 417–426.

Bartoli Langeli, Attilio, Andrea Giorgi, and Stefano Moscadelli, eds. *Archivi e communità tra medioevo ed età moderna*. Rome: Ministero per i beni e le attività culturali, 2009.

Basbanes, Nicholas. *On Paper. The Everything of its Two-Thousand-Year History*. New York: Knopf, 2013.

Bautier, R. H. "La phase cruciale de l'histoire des archives. La construction des dépôts d'archives et la naissance de l'archivistique (XVIe – début du XIXe siècle)." *Archivum*, 18 (1968), 139–149.

Bayerl, Günter. *Die Papiermühle. Vorindustrielle Papiermacherei auf dem Gebiet des alten deutschen Reiches – Technologie, Arbeitsverhältnisse, Umwelt. Teil I und II*. Frankfurt: Lang, 1987.

Bayly, C. A. *Empire and Information: Intelligence Gathering and Social Communication in India, 1780–1870*. Cambridge: Cambridge University Press, 1996.

Beal, Peter. *In Praise of Scribes. Manuscripts and Their Makers in Seventeenth-century England*. Oxford: Clarendon Press, 1998.

Becker Peter and William Clark, eds. *Little Tools of Knowledge: Historical Essays on Academic and Bureaucratic Practices*. Ann Arbor, MI: University of Michigan Press, 2001.

Behne, Axel. "Archivordnung und Staatsurdnung im Mailand der Sforza-Zeit." *Nuovi Annali della Scuola per Archivisti e Bibliotecari*, 2 (1988), 93–102.

Behne, Axel. *Antichi inventari dell'Archivio Gonzaga*. Rome: Ministero per i beni culturali e ambientali, Ufficio centrale per i beni archivistici, 1993.

Behre, Otto. *Geschichte der Statistik in Brandenburg-Preussen bis zur Gründung des Königlichen Statistischen Bureaus*. Berlin: Topos, 1905.

Behringer, Wolfgang. *Thurn und Taxis. Die Geschichte ihrer Post und ihrer Unternehmen*. Munich: Piper, 1990.

Behringer, Wolfgang. *Im Zeichen der Merkur. Reichspost und Kommunikationsrevolution in der Frühen Neuzeit*. Göttingen: Vandenhoeck and Ruprecht, 2003.

Behringer, Wolfgang. "Communications revolutions: a historiographical concept." *German History*, 24.3 (2006), 333–374.

Behrmann, Thomas. "Einleitung: Ein neuer Zugang zum Schriftgut der oberitalienischen Kommunen." In H. Keller and Behrmann, eds. *Kommunales Schriftgut in Oberitalien: Formen, Funktioneen, Überlieferung*. Munich: W. Fink, 1995, 1–16.

Bell, Hazel, ed. *Indexers and Indexes in Fact & Fiction*. Toronto: University of Toronto Press, 2001.

Bellingradt, Daniel, and Anna Reynolds, eds. *The Paper Trade in Early Modern Europe*. Leiden: Brill, 2021.

Beltrán, Cristina Borreguero. "Philip of Spain: the spider's web of news and information." In Brendan Dooley, ed. *The Dissemination of News and the Emergence of Contemporaneity in Early Modern Europe*. Farnham, Surrey: Ashgate, 2010, 23–49.

Belussi, Fiorenza and Katia Caldari, "At the origin of the industrial district: Alfred Marshall and the Cambridge School." *Cambridge Journal of Economics*, 33.2 (2009), 335–355.
Bentley, Jerry. *Politics and Culture in Renaissance Naples*. Princeton: Princeton University Press, 1987.
Berns, Jörg Jochen. "*Parteylichkeit* and the periodical press." In Kathryn Murphy and Anita Traninger, eds. *The Emergence of Impartiality*. Leiden: Brill, 2013, 87–140.
Berry, Helen. "An early coffee house periodical and its readers: the *Athenian Mercury*, 1691–1697." *The London Journal. A Review of Metropolitan Society Past and Present*, 25.1 (2000), 14–33.
Bethencourt, Francisco, and Florike Egmond. "Introduction." In Bethencourt and Egmond, eds. *Correspondence and Cultural Exchange in Europe 1400–1700*, Vol. III of *Cultural Exchange in Early Modern Europe*, General ed. Robert Muchembled. Cambridge: Cambridge University Press, 2007, 1–30.
Bidwell, John. "The study of paper as evidence, artefact and commodity." In Peter Davison, ed. *The Book Encompassed. Studies in Twentieth-Century Bibliography*. Winchester, DE: Oak Knoll Press, 1998, 69–82.
Birrell, Thomas Anthony. "The reconstruction of the library of Isaac Casaubon." In Arnold Croiset van Uchelen, ed. *Hellinga Festschrift. Feestbundel: Forty-Three Studies in Bibliography to Prof. Wytze Hellinga on the occasion of his retirement from the Chair of Neophilology in the University of Amsterdam at the end of the Year 1978*. Amsterdam: Nico Israël, 1980, 56–69.
Bischoff, Bernhard. *Latin Paleography: Antiquity and the Middle Ages*. Cambridge: Cambridge University Press, 1990.
Black, Jeremy. *The Power of Knowledge: How Information and Technology Made the Modern World*. New Haven, CT: Yale University Press, 2014.
Blair, Ann. "*Ovidius Methodizatus*: the *Metamorphoses* of Ovid in a sixteenth-century Paris college." *History of Universities*, 9 (1990), 73–118.
Blair, Ann. *The Theater of Nature: Jean Bodin and Renaissance Science*. Princeton: Princeton University Press, 1997.
Blair, Ann. "An early modernist's perspective." *Isis*, 95.3 (2004), 420–430.
Blair, Ann. "Note taking as an art of transmission." *Critical Inquiry*, 31.3 (2004), 85–107.
Blair, Ann. "Organizations of knowledge." In James Hankins, ed. *The Cambridge Companion to Renaissance Philosophy*. Cambridge: Cambridge University Press, 2007, 287–305.
Blair, Ann. *Too Much to Know: Managing Scholarly Information before the Modern Age*. New Haven, CT: Yale University Press, 2010.
Blair, Ann. "The rise of note-taking in early modern Europe." *Intellectual History Review*, 20.3 (2010), 303–316.
Blair, Ann. "The 2016 Josephine Waters Bennett Lecture: Humanism and printing in the work of Conrad Gessner." *Renaissance Quarterly*, 70.1 (2017), 1–43.
Blair, Ann and Anthony Grafton. "Reassessing humanism and science." *Journal of the History of Ideas*, 53.4 (1992), 535–540.
Blair, Ann and Peter Stallybrass. "Mediating information 1450–1800." In Clifford Siskin and William Warner, eds. *This is Enlightenment*. Chicago: University of Chicago Press, 2010.

Bland, Mark. "Italian paper in early seventeenth-century England." In Rosella Graziaplena and Mark Livesey, eds. *Paper as a Medium of Cultural Heritage: Archaeology and Conservation.* Milan: Istituto centrale per la patologia del libro, 2004.
Bloch, Marc. *The Historian's Craft.* Trans. by Peter Putnam. New York: Vintage Books, 1953.
Blockmans, Wim. *Emperor Charles V 1500–1558.* London: Arnold, 2002.
Bloom, Jonathan. *Paper Before Print. The History and Impact of Paper in the Islamic World.* New Haven: Yale University Press, 2001.
Boas Hall, Marie. "The Royal Society's role in the diffusion of information in the 17th century." *Notes and Records of the Royal Society of London,* 29.2 (1975), 173–192.
Boeuf, Estelle. *La bibliothèque parisienne de Gabriel Naudé en 1630.* Geneva: Droz, 2007.
Boone, Rebecca Ard. "Empire and medieval simulacrum. A political project of Mercurino Arborio di Gattinara, Grand Chancellor of Charles V." *Sixteenth-century Journal,* 42.4 (2011), 1027–1049.
Borkenau, Franz. *Der Übergang von feudalen zum bürglerichen Weltbild.* Darmstadt, Wissenschaftliche Buchgesellschaft, 1971, c1934.
Born, Lester. "Baldassare Bonifacio and his essay *de Archivis.*" *The American Archivist,* 4 (1941), 221–237.
Born, Lester. "The *De archivis commentarius* of Albertino Barisoni (1587–1667)." *Archivalische Zeitschrift,* 50/51 (1955), 13–22.
Boswell, James. *The Life of Samuel Johnson, LL.D.* London: MacMillan, 1900.
Bot, Hans and Françoise Waquet. *La République des Lettres.* Berlin: De Boeck, 1997.
Bottani, Tarcisio. *I Tasso e le poste pontifice, secoli XV–XVI.* Bergamo: Camerata Cornello, 2000.
Boudreau, Claire, Kouky Fianu, Claude Gauvard, and Michel Hébert, eds. *Information et societé en Occident à la fin du Moyen Âge. Actes du colloque international tenu à l'Université du Québec à Montréal et a l'Université d'ottowa (9–11 mai 2002).* Paris: Publications de la Sorbonne, 2004.
Bougard, François, Laurent Feller, and Régine LeJan, eds. *Dots et douaires dans le haut Moyen Âge.* Rome: École française de Rome, 2002.
Bougard, François, Cristina LaRocca, and Régine LeJan, eds. *Sauver son âme et se perpétuer: La transmission du patrimonie au haut Moyen Âge.* Rome: École française de Rome, 2005.
Boureau, Alain. "La norme épistolaire, une invention medieval." In Roger Chartier, ed. *La correspondance: les usages de la lettre au XIXe siècle.* Paris: Fayard, 1991, 127–157.
Boutier, Jean, Alain Dewerpe, and Daniel Nordman. *Un tour de France royal: le voyage de Charles IX, 1564–1566.* Paris: Aubier, 1984.
Boutier, Jean, Sandro Landi, and Olivier Rouchon. *Politique par correspondence. Les usages politiques de la lettre en Italie (XIVe–XVIIIe siècle).* Rennes: Presses universitaires de Rennes, 2009.

Bouza, Fernando. *Corre manuscrito: Una historia cultural del Siglo del Oro*. Madrid: Marcial Pons, 2001.
Bouza, Fernando. "Felipe II sube a los cielos. Cartapacios, pliegos, papeles y visions." In Miguel Rodríguez Cancho, ed. *Historia y perspectivas de investigación estudios en memoria del profesor Angel Rodríguez Sánchez*. Merida, Badajoz: Editora Regional de Extremadura, 2002, 301–306.
Bouza, Fernando. *Communication, Knowledge and Memory in Early Modern Spain*. Trans. by Sonia López and Michael Agnew. Philadelphia: University of Pennsylvania Press, 2004.
Boyd, Robert and Peter Richerson. *Not by Genes Alone: How Culture Transformed Human Evolution*. Chicago: University of Chicago Press, 2005.
Boyle, Robert. *The Works of Robert Boyle*, Vol. III. Ed. by Michael Hunter and Robert Davis. London: Pickering and Chatto, 1999.
Bozzolo, Carla and Etio Ornato. *Pour une histoire du livre manuscrit au Moyen Âge: trois essais de codicologie quantitative*. Paris: Éditions du Centre national de la recherche scientifique, 1983.
Branca, Vittore, ed. *Merchant Writers of the Italian Renaissance*. Trans. by Martha Baca. New York: Mursilio, 1999.
Braudel, Fernand. *Civilization and Capitalism, 15th–18th Century*, Vol. II: *The Wheels of Commerce*. Trans. by Sian Reynolds. Berkeley, CA: University of California Press, 1982.
Brayshay, Mark. "Conveying correspondence: early modern letter bearers, carriers and posts." In James Daybell and Andrew Gordon, eds. *Cultures of Correspondence in Early Modern Britain*. Philadelphia: University of Pennsylvania Press, 2016, 48–65.
Bréhier, Émile. *Histoire de la philosophie*, Vol. II: *La philosophie moderne*. Paris: Librairie Félix Alcan, 1928.
Brendecke, Arndt. ""Diese Teufel, meine Papiere ... " Philipp II von Spanien und das Anwachsen administrativer Schriftlichkeit." *Aventinus. Die Historische Internetzeitschrift von Studenten für Studenten*, 5 (2006), n.p.
Brendecke, Arndt. "Papierfluten. Anwachsende Schriftlichkeit als Pluralisierungsfaktor in der Frühen Neuzeit." *Mitteilungen des Sonderforschungsbereiches*, 573.1 (2006), 21–30.
Brendecke, Arndt. "Papierbarrieren. Über Ambivalenzen des Mediengebrauchs in der Vormoderne." *Mitteilungen des Sonderforschungsbereiches, 573. Pluralisierung und Autorität in der Frühen Neuzeit*, 2 (2009), 7–15.
Brendecke, Arndt. *Imperium und Empirie. Funktionen des Wissens in der spanischen Kolonialherrschaft*. Cologne: Böhlau Verlag, 2015.
Brendecke, Arndt. *The Empirical Empire. Spanish Colonial Rule and the Politics of Knowledge*. Berlin: De Gruyter Oldenbourg, 2016. Abridged translation of *Imperium und Empirie*.
Brendecke, Arndt. "Knowledge, oblivion, and concealment in early modern Spain: the ambiguous agenda of the Archive of Simancas." In Liesbeth Corens, Kate Peters, and Alexandra Walsham, eds. *Archives and Information in the Early Modern World. Proceedings of the British Academy 212*. Oxford: Oxford University Press, 2018, 131–149.

Brendecke, Arndt, Markus Friedrich, and Susanne Friedrich, eds. *Information in der Frühen Neuzeit: Status, Bestände, Strategien*. Berlin: LIT Verlag, 2008.
Briggs, Asa and Peter Burke. *A Social History of the Media: Gutenberg to the Internet*. Cambridge: Polity, 2005.
Briquet, Charles Moïse. *Les Filigranes. Dictionnaire historique des marques du papier dès leur apparition vers 1282 jusqu'en 1600*. Paris: Alfonse Picard, 1907–.
Brooks, Christopher W. *Pettyfoggers and Vipers of the Commonwealth*. Cambridge: Cambridge University Press, 1986.
Brown, Alison. *Bartolomeo Scala, 1430–1497, Chancellor of Florence*. Princeton: Princeton University Press, 1979, 161–395.
Brown, Piers. "'Hac ex consilio meo via progredieris': courtly reading and secretarial mediation in Donne's *The Courtier's Library*." *Renaissance Quarterly*, 61.3 (2008), 833–866.
Brown, Warren, Marius Costambeys, Matthew Innes, and Adam Kosto, eds. *Documentary Culture and the Laity in the Early Middle Ages*. Cambridge: Cambridge University Press, 2013.
Brunetti, Mario. "Tre ambasciate annonarie veneziane. Marino e Sigismondo Cavalli (1559–60) in Baviera; Marco Ottoboni (1590) in Danzica." *Archivio Veneto*, 5.86 (1956), 88–115.
Bucciantini, Massimo. "Celebration and conservation: the Galilean Collection of the National Library of Florence." In Michael Hunter, ed. *Archives of the Scientific Revolution. The Formation and Exchange of Ideas in Seventeenth-Century Europe*. Woodbridge: Boydell Press, 1998, 21–34.
Bullard, Melissa Meriam. "The language of diplomacy in the Renaissance." In Bernard Toscani, ed. *Lorenzo de' Medici: New Perspectives*. New York: Peter Lang, 1993, 263–278.
Bullard, Melissa Meriam. *Lorenzo il Magnifico: Image and Anxiety, Politics and Finance*. Florence: Olschki, 1994.
Die Bullinger Zeitungen: zur Halbjahrhundertfeier des Vereins der Schweizerischen Presse dargebracht vom Journalistischen Seminar der Universität Zürich. Zurich: Buchdruckerei Berichthaus, 1933.
Buono, Benedict. "La trattatistica sul 'segretario' e la codificazione linguistica in Italia fra Cinque e Seicento." *Verba*, 37 (2010), 301–312.
Buringh, Eltjo. "The role of cities in medieval book production: quantitative analyses." In Marco Mostert and Anna Adamska, eds. *Uses of the Written Word in Medieval Towns*. Turnhout, Belgium: Brepols, 2014, 119–177.
Buringh, Eltjo and Jan Luiten Van Zanden. "Charting the 'rise of the West': manuscripts and printed books in Europe, a long-term perspective from the sixth through eighteenth centuries." *Journal of Economic History*, 69.2 (2009), 409–445.
Burke, Peter. "Classifying the people: the census as collective representation." In Burke, *The Historical Anthropology of Early Modern Italy*. Cambridge: Cambridge University Press, 1987, 27–39.
Burke, Peter. "Representations of the self from Petrarch to Descartes." In Roy Porter, ed. *Rewriting the Self from the Renaissance to the Present*. London: Routledge, 1997, 17–28.
Burke, Peter. "Erasmus and the Republic of Letters." *European Review*, 7.1 (1999), 5–17.

Burke, Peter. *The Social History of Knowledge: From Gutenberg to Diderot.* Cambridge: Polity, 2000.
Burke, Peter. "The circulation of knowledge." In John Jeffries Martin, ed. *The Renaissance World.* London: Routledge, 2007, 191–207.
Burke, Peter. "Communication." In Ulinka Rublack, ed. *A Concise Companion to History.* Oxford: Oxford University Press, 2011, 157–176.
Burke, Peter. *The Social History of Knowledge II: From the Encyclopedia to Wikipedia.* Cambridge: Polity, 2011.
Burke, Peter. "Postfazione: Che cos'è la storia degli archivi?" In Filippo de Vivo, Andrea Guidi, and Alessandro Silvestri, eds. *Archivi e archivisti in Italia tra medioevo ed età moderna.* Rome: Viella, 2015, 359–372.
Burling, Robbins. *The Talking Ape: How Language Evolved.* Oxford: Oxford University Press, 2007.
Burns, Robert. "The paper revolution in Europe: crusader Valencia's paper industry – a technological and behavioral breakthrough." *Pacific Historical Review*, 50 (1981), 1–30.
Burton, Richard, *The Anatomy of Melancholy* (1628). London: E.P. Dutton. 1961 ed.
Bywater, M. F. and Basil Yamey. *Historic Accounting Literature: A Companion Guide.* London: Scholars Press, 1982.
Caizzi, Bruno. *Dalla posta dei re alla posta di tutti: territorio e comunicazioni in Italia dal XVI secolo all'Unità.* Milan: Franco Angeli, 1993.
Calabi, Donatella and Derek Keene. "Exchanges and cultural transfer on European cities." In Donatella Calabi and Stephen Turk Christensen, eds. *Cities and Cultural Exchange in Europe, 1400–1700*, Vol. II of *Cultural Exchange on Early Modern Europe*, General ed. Robert Muchembled. Cambridge: Cambridge University Press, 2006, 286–314.
Cammarosano, Paolo. *Tradizione documentaria e storia cittadina. Introduzione al "Caleffo Vecchio" del Comune di Siena.* Siena: Accademia senese degli Intronati, 1988.
Cammarosano, Paolo. *Italia medievale: struttura e geografia delle fonti scritte.* Rome: La Nuova Italia Scientifica, 1991.
Capaccio, Giulio Cesare. *Il Secretario. Opera di Giulio Cesare Capaccio Napolitano. Ove quanto conviene allo scriver Familiare. Cioè All'ornato del dire. All'ortograifa. Alla materia dei Titoli, delle Cifre, dello scriver Latino, brevemente si espone.* Venice: Niccolò Moretti, 1599.
Capra, Carlo. "Governance." In Hamish Scott, ed. *Oxford Handbook of Early Modern European History*, Vol. II. Oxford: Oxford University Press, 2015.
Caracciolo, Francesco. "Vie di comunicazione e servizio postale nel Regno di Napoli fra XVI e XII secolo." *Ricerche di storia sociale e religiosa*, 2 (1972), 213–228.
Carlson, David. *English Humanist Books; Writers and Patrons, Manuscript and Print, 1475–1525.* Toronto: University of Toronto Press, 1993.
Carr, Nicholas. *The Shallows. What the Internet is Doing to Our Brains.* New York: Norton, 2011.
Carrara, Daniela Mugnai. *La Biblioteca di Nicolò Leoniceno. Tra Aristotele e Galeno: Cultura e Libri di un medico umanista.* Florence. Olschki, 1991.

Carruthers, Mary. *The Book of Memory: a Study of Memory in Medieval Culture*, 2nd ed. Cambridge: Cambridge University Press, 2008.
Carter, Thomas Francis. *The Invention of Printing in China and its Spread Westward*. New York: Columbia University Press, 1925.
Cassan, Michel, Jean-Pierre Bardet, and François-Joseph Ruggiu, eds. *Les écrits du for privé. Objets matériels, objets edités*. Limoges: Presses universitaires de Limoges, 2007.
Castelnuovo, Guido. "Offices and officials." In Andrea Gamberini and Isabella Lazzarini, eds. *The Italian Renaissance State*. Oxford: Oxford University Press, 2012, 368–385.
Cavalli, Marino. *Informatione dell'offitio dell'ambasciatore di Marino de Cavalli il Vecchio.* (1550). Ed. by Tommaso Bertelè. Florence: Olschki, 1935.
Cave, Terence. *The Cornucopian Text: Problems of Writing in Renaissance France*. Oxford: Clarendon Press, 1979.
Cecchi, Elena. *Le lettere di Francesco Datini alla moglie Margherita (1385–1410)*. Prato: Società Pratese di Storia Patria, 1992.
Celenza, Christopher. "Poliziano's *Lamia* in context." In Celenza, ed. *Angelo Poliziano's* Lamia: *Text, Translation, and Introductory Studies*. Leiden: Brill, 2010, 1–46.
Certeau, Michel de. *L'invention du Quotidien 1. Arts de Faire*. Paris: Gallimard, 1990.
Cevolini, Alberto. *De arte excerpendi. Imparare a dimenticare nella modernità*. Florence: Olschki, 2006.
Cevolini, Alberto, ed. *Forgetting Machines: Knowledge Management Evolution in Early Modern Europe*. Leiden: Brill, 2016.
Charmantier, Isabelle and Staffan Müller-Wille. "Natural history and information overload." *Studies in History and Philosophy of Biological and Biomedical Sciences*, 43 (2012), 4–15.
Charmantier, Isabelle and Staffan Müller-Wille. "Worlds of paper: an introduction." *Early Science and Medicine*, 19 (2014), 379–397.
Chartier, Roger. "Texts, printings, readings." In Lynn Hunt, ed. *The New Cultural History*. Berkeley, CA: University of California Press, 1989, 154–175.
Chartier, Roger. "Avant-propos." In Chartier, Alain Boureau, Cécile Dauphin, and Michel Demonet, eds. *La correspondance. Les usages de la lettre au XIXe siècle*. Paris: Fayard, 1991, 7–13.
Chartier, Roger. *The Order of Books*. Stanford, CA: Stanford University Press, 1994.
Chartier, Roger. "Languages, books, and reading from the printed word to the digital text." *Critical Inquiry*, 31 (2004), 133–152.
Chartier, Roger. *Inscription and Erasure: Literature and Written Culture from the Eleventh to the Eighteenth Century*. Trans. by Arthur Goldhammer. Philadelphia: University of Pennsylvania Press, 2007.
Chartier, Roger. "The printing revolution: a reappraisal." In Sabrina Alcorn Baron, Eric Lindquist, and Eleanor Shevlin, eds. *Agent of Change. Print Culture Studies after Elizabeth L. Eisenstein*. Amherst, MA: University of Massachusetts Press, 2007, 397–408.

Christ, Georg. "A newsletter in 1419? Antonio Morosini's chronicle in the light of commercial correspondence between Venice and Alexandria." *Mediterranean Historical Review*, 20.1 (2005), 35–66

Ciapelli, Giovanni. "Introduction: memory, family and identity in early modern Italy and Europe." In Ciapelli, ed. *Memory, Family and Self. Tuscan Family Books and Other European Egodocuments (14th–18th Century)*. Leiden: Brill, 2014, 1–11.

Ciapelli, Giovanni. "Family memory and individual memory: Florentine diaries and family books of the early modern period." In Ciapelli, ed. *Memory, Family and Self. Tuscan Family Books and Other European Egodocuments (14th–18th Century)*. Leiden: Brill, 2014, 241–259.

Clanchy, Michael. "Literacy, law and the power of the state." In *Culture et idéologie dans la genèse de l'État moderne. Actes de la table ronde de Rome (15–17 octobre 1984)*. Rome: École Française de Rome, 1985, 25–34.

Clanchy, Michael. "Does writing construct the state?" *Journal of Historical Sociology*, 15.1 (2002), 68–70.

Clanchy, Michael. "Parchment and paper: manuscript culture, 1100–1500." In Simon Eliot and Jonathan Rose, eds. *A Companion to the History of the Book*. Oxford: Blackwell, 2003, 194–206.

Clanchy, Michael. *From Memory to Written Record. England, 1066–1307*, 3rd ed. Oxford: Blackwell, 2013.

Cline, Howard. "The Relaciones Geograficas of the Spanish Indies, 1577–1648." *Handbook of Middle American Indians*, 12 (1972), 183–242.

Clossey, Luke. *Salvation and Globalization in the Early Jesuit Missions*. Cambridge: Cambridge University Press, 2008.

Codogno, Ottavio. *Nuovo itinerario delle Poste per tutto il mondo di Ottavio Codogno. Aggiountovi il modo di scrivere à tutte le parti. Utilissimo non solo Segretarij, ma à Religiosi, & à Mercanti. Con licenza de'Superiori, & Privilegio*. Venice: Lucio Spineda, 1620.

Coleman, Olive. "What figures? Some thoughts on the use of information by medieval governments." In Donald C. Coleman and Arthur H. John, eds. *Trade, Government and Economy in Pre-Industrial England: Essays Presented to F. J. Fisher*. London: Weidenfeld and Nicolson, 1976, 96–112.

Columbus, Hernando. *The History of the Life and Deeds of the Admiral Don Christopher Columbus*. Repertorium Columbianum, Vol. XIII. Ed. by Ilaria Caraci Luzzana and trans. by Geoffrey Symcox. Turnhout, Belgium: Brepols, 2014.

Compagni, Dino. *La cronica delle cose occorrenti ne' tempi suoi; e la canzone morale del pregio*. Ed. by Isidoro del Lungo. Florence: Successori Le Monnier, 1908.

Contamine, Philippe. "Conclusion." In Claire Boudreau, Kouky Fianu, Claude Gauvard, and Michel Hébert, eds. *Information et société en Occident à la fin du Moyen Âge. Actes du colloque international tenu à l'Université du Québec à Montréal et à l'Université d'Ottawa (9–11 mai 2002)*. Paris: Publications de la Sorbonne, 2004.

Conte, Maria Antonietta. "La biblioteca di Giovanni Battista Bianchini (1613–1699): fra i Cisterciensi di S. Ambrogio e il collegio dei notai di Milano." *Archivio storico Lombardo*, 118 (1992), 405–470.

Contini, Alessandra. "L'informazione politica sugli stati italiani non spagnoli nelle relazioni veneziane a metà cinquecento (1558-1566)." In Elena Fasano Guarini and Maria Rosa, eds. *L'informazione politica in Italia (secoli xvi-xviii)*. Pisa: Scuola Normale Superiore, 2001, 1-57.

Cook, Harold. *Matters of Exchange: Commerce, Medicine and Science in the Dutch Golden Age*. New Haven, CT: Yale University Press, 2007.

Cooper, Alix. *Inventing the Indigenous: Local Knowledge and Natural History in Early Modern Europe*. Cambridge: Cambridge University Press, 2007.

Copernicus, Nicolaus. *De revolutionibus orbium coelestium*. Nuremberg: Johann Petreius, 1543.

Coron, Antoine. "*Ut posint aliis*: Jacque-Auguste de Thou et sa Bibliothèque." In *Histoire des bibliothèques françaises*, Vol. II: *Les bibliothèques sous l'Ancien Regime, 1530-1789*. Paris: Promodis – Éditions du Cercle, 1988, 100-125.

Cortada, James. "Shaping information as an intellectual discipline." *Information & Culture*, 47.2 (2012), 119-144.

Corti, Gino. "Consiglio sulla mercatura di un anonimo trecentista." *Archivio storico italiano*, 110 (1952), 114-119.

Cotrugli, Benedetto, *Il libro dell'arte di mercatura* (1459). Ed. by Vera Ribaudo. Venice: Edizioni Ca' Foscari, 2016.

Courouau, Jean-François and Sylvie Mouysset. "À la recherche des écrits du for privé du Midi de la France et de Catalogne." *Annales du Midi: revue archéologique, historique et philologique de la France méridionale*, 122.270 (2010), 165-173.

Couvée, Dirk. "The first coranteers – the flow of the news in the 1620s." *Gazette: International Journal of the Science of the Press*, 8.2 (1962), 22-36.

Cressy, David. *Literacy and the Social Order, Reading and Writing in Tudor and Stuart England*. Cambridge: Cambridge University Press, 1980.

Cressy, David. "Literacy in context: meaning and measurement in early modern England." In John Brewer and Roy Porter, eds. *Consumption and the World of Goods*. London: Routledge, 1994, 305-319.

Julia Crick and Alexandra Walsham. "Introduction: script, print and history." In Crick and Walsham, eds. *The Uses of Script and Print 1300-1700*. Cambridge: Cambridge University Press, 2004, 1-26.

Croce, Benedetto. *History, its Theory and Practice*. Trans. by Douglas Ainslie. New York: Harcourt Brace, 1921.

Crosby, Alfred. *The Measure of Reality: Quantification and Western Society, 1250-1600*. Cambridge: Cambridge University Press, 1997.

Czaja, Karin. "The Nuremberg *Familienbücher*: archives of family identity." In Marco Mostert and Anna Adamska, eds. *Uses of the Written Word in Medieval Towns*. Turnhout, Belgium: Brepols, 2014, 325-338.

Daillon, Jacqueline. "Jean Grüninger, imprimeur-éditeur à Strasbourg." *Arts et métiers graphiques*, 65 (1938), 41-46.

Dallmeier, Martin, ed. *Quellen zur Geschichte des europäischen Postwesens 1501-1806*, Vol. II. Regensburg: Verlag Michael Lassleben Kallmunz, 1977.

Dallmeier, Martin. "Il casato principesco dei Thurn und Taxis e le poste in Europa (1490-1806)." In *Le poste di Tasso, un'impresa in Europa*. Bergamo: Comune di Bergamo, 1984, 1-32.

Dane, Joseph. *The Myth of Print Culture. Essays on Evidence, Textuality, and Bibliographical Method.* Toronto: University of Toronto Press, 2003.

Darnton, Robert. "An early information society: news and the media in eighteenth-century Paris." *American Historical Review*, 105.1 (2000), 1–35.

Daston, Lorraine. "Curiosity in early modern science." *Word & Image*, 11.4 (1995), 391–404.

Daston, Lorraine. "Strange facts, plain facts, and the texture of scientific experience in the Enlightenment." In Suzanne Marchand and Elizabeth Lunbeck, eds. *Proof and Persuasion: Essays on Authority, Objectivity and Evidence.* Turnhout: Brepols, 1996, 42–59.

Daston, Lorraine. "The cold light of facts and the facts of cold light: luminescence and the transformation of the scientific fact." *Early Modern France*, 3 (1997), 17–44.

Daston, Lorraine. "Taking note(s)." *Isis*, 95 (2004), 443–448.

Daston, Lorraine. "Perché sono i fatti brevi?" *Quaderni storici*. New series 36 108.3 (2011), 745–770.

Daston, Lorraine and Katharine Park, *Wonders and the Order of Nature.* New York: Zone Books, 1998.

Davidson, Cathy. *Now You See It. How the Brain Science of Attention Will Transform the Way We Live, Work and Learn.* New York: Viking, 2011.

Davies, Joan. "Student libraries in sixteenth-century Toulouse." *History of Universities*, 3 (1983), 61–86.

Davies, Simon and Puck Fletcher. "Introduction." In Davies and Fletcher, eds. *News in Early Modern Europe. Currents and Connections.* Library of the Written Word, Vol. 39: *The Handpress World*. Leiden: Brill, 2014, 1–18.

Daybell, James. *The Material Letter in Early Modern England: Manuscript Letters and the Culture and Practices of Letter-Writing, 1512–1635.* Basingstoke, UK: Palgrave Macmillan, 2012.

Daybell, James and Peter Hinds. "Introduction: material matters" In Daybell and Hinds, eds. *Material Readings of Early Modern Culture: Texts and Social Practices, 1580–1730.* Basingstoke, UK: Palgrave Macmillan, 2010, 1–10.

De Andrés, Gregorio. *La real Biblioteca de El Escorial.* Madrid: Aldus, 1970.

Dear, Peter. *Revolutionizing the Sciences. European Knowledge and its Ambitions*, 2nd ed. Princeton: Princeton University Press, 2009.

De Biasi, Pierre Marc. "Le papier, fragile support de l'essentiel." *Les cahiers de médiologie*, 2 (1997), 7–17.

De Certeau, Michel. *The Practices of Everyday Life.* Berkeley, CA: University of California Press, 1984.

Degl'Innocenti, Luca, Brian Richardson, and Chiara Sbordoni, *Interactions between Orality and Writing in Early Modern Italian Culture.* London: Routledge, 2016.

De Hamel, Christopher. *Scribes and Illuminators. Medieval Craftsmen.* Toronto: University of Toronto Press, 1993.

Dekker, Rudolf. "Ego-documents in the Netherlands, 1500–1814." *Dutch Crossings*, 39.13 (1989), 61–71.

Dekker, Rudolf, ed. *Egodocuments and History. Autobiographical Writing in its Social Context Since the Middle Ages.* Hilversum: Verloren, 2002.

Delaunay, Paul. *La zoologie au seizième siècle*. Paris: Hermann, 1962.
Derrida, Jacques. *Archive Fever: a Freudian Impression*. Trans. by Eric Prenowitz. Chicago: University of Chicago Press, 1996.
De Rijk, Elisabeth. "Thomas Hyde, Julia Pettee and the development of cataloging principles; with a translation of Hyde's 1674 Preface to the Reader." *Cataloging & Classification Quarterly*, 14.2 (2010), 31–62.
Dery, David. "'Papereality' and learning in bureaucratic organizations." *Administration and Society*, 29.6 (1998), 277–289.
Descartes, René. *Oeuvres de Descartes*, Vol. I: *Correspondance*. Ed. by Charles Adam and Paul Tennery. Paris: Léopold Cerf, 1897.
De Roover, Raymond. "Aux origines d'une technique intellectuelle: la formation et l'expansion de la comptabilité à partie double." *Annales d'histoire économique et sociale*, 9 (1937), 171–193 and 270–293.
De Roover, Raymond. "New perspectives on the history of accounting." *The Accounting Review*, 30 (1955), 405–420.
De Vera, Juan Antonio. *El Anbaxador*. Seville: Francisco de Lyra, 1620.
De Vincentiis, Amedeo. "Memorie bruciate. Conflitti, documenti, oblio nelle città italiane del tardo medioevo." *Bullettino dell'Istituto storico Italiano per il medio Evo e archivio muratoriano*, 106 (2004), 167–198.
De Vivo, Filippo. *Information and Communication in Venice. Rethinking Early Modern Politics*. Oxford: Oxford University Press, 2007.
DeVivo, Filippo. "Pharmacies as centres of communication in early modern Venice." *Renaissance Studies*, 21.4 (2007), 505–521.
De Vivo, Filippo. "Ordering the archive in early modern Venice (1400–1650)." *Archival Science*, 10 (2010), 231–248.
De Vivo, Filippo. "Archival intelligence: diplomatic correspondence, information overload, and information management in Italy, 1450–1650." In Liesbeth Corens, Kate Peters, and Alexandra Walsham, eds. *Archives and Information in the Early Modern World*. Proceedings of the British Academy 212. Oxford: Oxford University Press, 2018, 53–85.
De Vivo, Filippo and Brian Richardson. "Preface." *Italian Studies*, 66.2. Special issue on cultural transmission in early modern Italy (2011), 157–160.
De Vivo, Filippo, Andrea Guidi, and Alessandro Silvestri, eds. *Archivi e archivisti in Italia tra medioevo ed età moderna*. Rome: Viella, 2015.
De Vivo, Filippo, Andrea Guidi, and Alessandro Silvestri. "Archival transformations in early modern European history." *European History Quarterly*, 46.3 (2016), 421–434.
De Vries, Jan. *Industrious Revolution: Consumer Behavior and the Household Economy, 1650 to the Present*. Cambridge: Cambridge University Press. 2008.
De Vries, Jan and Ad van der Woude. *The first modern economy: success, failure, and perseverance of the Dutch economy, 1500–1815*. Cambridge: Cambridge University Press, 1997.
D'Haensens, Albert. "Un exemple d'utilisation du papier á Tournai peu avant 1350." *Scriptorium*, 16 (1962), 89–92.
Dibon, Paul. "Communication in the Respublica literaria of the 17th century." *Res publica litterarum*, 1 (1978), 43–55.

Dibon, Paul. "Communication epistolaire et mouvement des idées au XVIIème siècle." In Guido Canziani and Gianni Paganini, eds. *Le edizioni dei testi filosofici e scientifici del' 500 e del' 600: problema di metodo e prospettive di ricerca*. Milan: Angeli, 1986, 73–88.

Dierks, Konstantin. "Letter writing, stationery supplies, and consumer modernity in the eighteenth-century Atlantic world." *Early American Literature*, 41.3 (2006), 473–494.

Digges, Leonard. *A Progostication Everlastinge of Right Good Effecte*. London: Thomas Marsh, 1576.

Dini, Bruno. "L'archivio Datini." In Simonetta Cavaciocchi, ed. *L'impresa, industria, commercio, banca secc. XIII–XVIII*. Florence: Le Monnier, 1991, 45–58.

Dittmar, Jeremiah. "Information technology and economic change: the impact of the printing press." *Quarterly Journal of Economics*, 126.3 (2011), 1133–1172.

Donoso Anes, Rafael. *Una contribución a la historia de la contabilidad: análisis de la prácticas contables desarolladas por la tesorería de la Casa de la Contratación de las Indias de Sevilla (1503–1717)*. Seville: Universidad de Sevilla, 1996.

Dooley, Brendan. *The Social History of Skepticism. Experience and Doubt in Early Modern Culture*. Baltimore, MD: Johns Hopkins University Press, 1999.

Dooley, Brendan. "The public sphere and the organization of knowledge." In John Martin, ed., *Early Modern Italy, 1550–1776*. Oxford: Oxford University Press, 2002, 209–228.

Dooley, Brendan. "Introduction." In Dooley, ed. *The Dissemination of News and the Emergence of Contemporaneity in Early Modern Europe*. Farnham, Surrey: Ashgate, 2010, 1–22.

Doria, Giorgio. "Conoscenza del mercato e sistema informativo: il know-how dei Mercanti-finanzieri genovesi nei secoli XVI et XVII." In Aldo De Maddalena and Hermann Kellenbenz, eds. *La Repubblica internazionale del denaro tra XV e XVII secolo*. Bologna: il Mulino, 1986, 57–115.

Dosio, G. Bonfiglio. *La politica archivistica del comune di Padova dal XIII al XIX secolo con l'inventario analitico del fondo Costituzione e ordinamento dell'archivio*. Rome: Viella, 2002.

Douglas, Jennifer. "'Kepe wysly youre wrytyngs': Margaret Paston's fifteenth-century letters." *Libraries and the Cultural Record*, 44.1 (2009), 29–49.

Dover, Paul. "Good information, bad information and misinformation in fifteenth-century Italian diplomacy." In Mark Crane, Richard Raiswell, and Margaret Reeves, eds. *Shell Games. Studies in Scams, Frauds, and Deceits (1300–1650)*. Toronto: Centre for Reformation and Renaissance Studies, 2004, 81–102.

Dover, Paul. "Royal diplomacy in Renaissance Italy: Ferrante d'Aragona (1458–1494) and his ambassadors." *Mediterranean Studies*, 14 (2005), 57–94.

Dover, Paul. "The resident ambassador and the transformation of intelligence gathering in Renaissance Italy." In Eunan O'Halpin, Robert Armstrong, and Jane Ohlmeyer, eds. *Intelligence, Statecraft and International Power: Papers read before the 27th Irish Conference of Historians held at Trinity College, Dublin, 19–21 May 2005*. Dublin: Irish Academic Press, 2006, 18–34.

Dover, Paul. "Deciphering the diplomatic archives of fifteenth-century Italy." *Archival Science*, 7.4 (2007), 297–316.
Dover, Paul. "'Saper la mente della soa Beatitudine': Pope Paul II and the ambassadorial community in Rome (1464–71)." *Renaissance and Reformation*, 31.3 (2008), 3–34.
Dover, Paul. "Philip II, information overload, and the early modern moment." In Tonio Andrade and William Reger, eds. *The Limits of Empire: European Imperial Formations in Early Modern World History*. Farnham, Surrey: Ashgate, 2012.
Dover, Paul. "How Heinrich Bullinger read his Solinus: reading ancient geography in 16th-century Switzerland." In Kai Brodersen, ed. *Solinus: New Studies*. Heidelberg: Verlag Antike, 2014, 171–195.
Dover, Paul. "Introduction: the age of secretaries." In Dover, ed. *Secretaries and Statecraft in the Early Modern World*. Edinburgh: Edinburgh University Press, 2016, 1–15.
Dover, Paul, ed. *Secretaries and Statecraft in the Early Modern World*. Edinburgh: Edinburgh University Press, 2016.
Dover, Paul. "Reading Dante in the sixteenth century: the Bentley Aldine Divine Comedy and its marginalia." *Studies in Medieval and Renaissance History*, 3.14 (2017).
Drexel, Jeremias. *Aurifodina artium et scientiarum omnium: Excerpendi sollertia, omnibus litterarum amantibus monstrata*. Antwerp: Ioannis Cnobbari, 1638.
Droste, Heiko. *Im Dienst der Krone: schwedische Diplomaten in 17. Jahrundert*. Berlin: LIT Verlag, 2006.
Dry, Sarah. *The Newton Papers*. Oxford: Oxford University Press, 2014.
Dufour, Jean. *La bibliothèque et le scriptorium de Moissac*. Geneva: Librairie Droz, 1972.
Duguid, Paul. "The ageing of information: from particular to particulate." *Journal of the History of Ideas*, 76.3 (2015), 347–368.
Dupré, Sven and Christoph Lüthy. "Introduction." In Dupré and Lüthy, eds. *Silent Messengers: The Circulation of Material Knowledge in the Early Modern Low Countries*. Münster: LIT Verlag, 2011.
Dupuy, Christophe. *Humanisme et politique. Lettres romaines de Christophe Dupuy à ses frères (1636–1645)*. Ed. by Kathryn Willis Wolfe and Philip Wolfe. Paris and Seattle: Papers on French Seventeenth Century Literature, 1988.
Durling, Richard. "Girolamo Mercuriale's *De modo studendi*." *Osiris*, 2.6 (1990), 181–195.
Eamon, William. "Markets, piazzas and villages." In Katherine Park and Lorraine Daston, eds. *The Cambridge History of Science*, Vol. 3. Cambridge: Cambridge University Press, 2006, 206–223.
Eco, Umberto. *Travels in Hyper Reality: Essays*. Trans. by William Weaver. San Diego: Harcourt Brace Jovanovich, 1986.
Edelstein, Dan, Paula Findlen, Giovanni Ceserani, Caroline Winterer, and Nicole Coleman. "Historical research in a digital age: reflections from the mapping the Republic of Letters project." *American Historical Review*, 122.2 (2017), 400–424.

Edwards, Clinton. "Mapping by questionnaire: an early Spanish attempt to determine New World geographical position." *Imago Mundi*, 23 (1969), 17–28.
Edwards, Mark. *Printing, Propaganda and Martin Luther*. Berkeley, CA: University of California Press, 1994.
Edwards, Paul, Lisa Gitelman, Gabrielle Hecht, Adrian Johns, Brian Larkin, and Neil Safier. "*AHR* Conversation: historical perspectives on the circulation of information." *American Historical Review*, 116.4 (2011), 1393–1435.
Egmond, Florike. *The World of Carolus Clusius: Natural History on the Making, 1550–1610*. London: Pickering and Chatto, 2010.
Eisenstein, Elizabeth. *The Printing Press as an Agent of Change: Communications and Cultural Transformations in Early Modern Europe*, 2 vols. Cambridge: Cambridge University Press, 1979.
Eisenstein, Elizabeth. *The Printing Revolution in Early Modern Europe*. Cambridge: Cambridge University Press, 2005.
Eisenstein, Elizabeth. *Divine Art, Infernal Machine: the Reception of Printing in the West from First Impressions to the Sense of Ending*. Philadelphia: University of Pennsylvania Press, 2012.
Eisermann, Falk. "Der Ablass als Medienereignis: Kommunikationswandel durch Einblattdrucke im 15. Jahrhundert; Mit einer Auswahlbibliographie." In Rudolf Suntrup and Jan Veenstra, eds. *Tradition and Innovation in an Era of Change*, Vol. 1 of *Medieval to Early Modern Culture*. Frankfurt: Peter Lang, 2001, 99–128.
Eisermann, Falk. "The indulgence as a media event." In Robert Swanson, ed. *Promissory Notes on the Treasury of Merits: Indulgences in Late Medieval Europe*. Leiden: Brill, 2006, 309–330. An abridged translation of "Der Ablass als Medienereignis."
Ekedahl, Nils. "Linnean method and the humanist art of reading." *Symbolae Botanicae Upsalienses*, 33.3 (2005), 47–59.
Elliott, John Huxtable. *Imperial Spain, 1469–1716*. New York: St. Martin's Press, 1964.
Ellis, Markman. "Pasqua Rosee's coffee-house, 1652–1666." *The London Journal*, 29.1 (2004), 1–24.
Ellis, Markman. *The Coffee House: A Cultural History*. London: Weidenfeld and Nicolson, 2004.
Elton, Charles Isaac and Mary Augusta Elton. *The Great Book-Collectors*. London: Kegan Paul, 1893.
Elton, Geoffrey. *The Tudor Revolution in Government: Administrative Changes in the Reign of Henry VIII*. Cambridge: Cambridge University Press, 1953.
Erasmus, Desiderius. *On Copia of Words and Ideas* (De Utraque Verborum ac Rerum Copia). Trans. by Donald King and H. David Rix. Milwaukee, WI: Marquette University Press, 1999.
Ertman, Thomas. *Birth of the Leviathan. Building States and Regimes in Medieval and Early Modern Europe*. Cambridge: Cambridge University Press, 1997.
Esch, Arnold. "Überlieferungs-Chance und Überlieferungs-Zufall als methodisches Problem des Historikers." *Historische Zeitschrift*, 240.3 (1985), 529–570.

Estienne, Henri. *The Frankfort Book Fair: The* Francofordiense Emporium *of Henri Estienne.* Ed. by James Westfall Thompson. Chicago: The Caxton Club, 1911.
Ettingshausen, Henry. "The news in Spain: *relaciones de sucesos* in the reigns of Philip III and IV." *European History Quarterly*, 14 (1984), 1–20.
Euer, Carrie. *Couriers of the Gospel: England and Zurich, 1531–1558*. Zurich: Theologischer Verlag, 2006.
Evelyn, John. *The Letterbooks of John Evelyn*, Vol. 2. Ed. by Douglas Chambers and David Galbraith. Toronto: University of Toronto Press, 2014.
Fahy, Conor. "Paper making in seventeenth-century Genoa: the account of Giovanni Domenico Peri (1651)." *Studies in Bibliography*, 56 (2003/4), 243–259.
Fanfani, Pietro, ed. *Rime Burlesche di eccelenti autori, raccolte, ordinate e postillate.* Florence: Felice le Monnier, 1856.
Farner, Oskar. "Die Bullinger-Briefe." *Zwingliana*, 10 (1954), 103–108.
Febvre, Lucien. *Philippe II et le Franche-Comté: la crise de 1567, ses origines et ses conséquences: étude d'histoire politique, religieuse et sociale.* Paris: H. Champion, 1912.
Febvre, Lucien. *The Problem of Unbelief in the Sixteenth Century.* Cambridge, MA: Harvard University Press, 1982.
Feingold, Mordechai. "Of records and grandeur: the archive of the Royal Society." In Michael Hunter, ed. *Archives of the Scientific Revolution: the Formation and Exchange of Ideas in Seventeenth-Century Europe.* Woodbridge, UK: Boydell and Brewer, 1998, 171–184.
Felix, D. A. "What is the oldest dated paper in Europe?" *Papiergeschichte*, 2.6 (1952), 73–75.
Findlen, Paula. "The economy of scientific exchange in early modern Italy." In Bruce Moran, ed. *Patronage and Institutions: Science, Technology and Medicine at the European Court.* Rochester, NY: Boydell Press, 1991, 5–24.
Findlen, Paula. "Scientific spectacle in Baroque Rome: Athanasius Kircher and the Roman College Museum." *Roma moderna e contemporanea*, 3 (1995), 625–665.
Findlen, Paula. *Possessing Nature: Museums, Collecting, and Scientific Culture in Early Modern Italy.* Berkeley: University of California Press, 1996.
Findlen, Paula. "Anatomy theaters, botanical gardens, and natural history collections." In Katherine Park and Lorraine Daston, eds. *The Cambridge History of Science*, Vol. 3. Cambridge: Cambridge University Press, 2006, 272–289.
Finnegan, Ruth. *Literacy and Orality.* Oxford: Blackwell, 1988.
Fletcher, Catherine. *Diplomacy in Renaissance Rome. The Rise of the Resident Ambassador.* Cambridge: Cambridge University Press, 2015.
Flood, John. "The book in Reformation Germany." In Jean-François Gilmont and Karin Maag, eds. *The Reformation and the Book.* Aldershot: Ashgate, 1998, 21–103.
Flood, John. "The printed book as a commercial commodity' in the fifteenth and early sixteenth centuries." *Gutenberg Jahrbuch*, 76 (2001), 172–182.
Flori, Ludovico. *Trattato del modo di tenere il libro doppio domestico col suo essemplare.* Palermo: Per Decio Cirillo, 1636.

Foisil, Madeleine. "L'écriture du for privé." In Philippe Ariès and Georges Duby, eds. *Histoire de la vie privée*, Vol. 3: *De la Renaissance aux Lumières*. Paris, Éditions du Seuil, 1985, 319–359.
Folli, Irene Ventura. "La natura 'scritta', la 'libraria' di Ulisse Aldrovandi (1522–1605)." In Eugenio Canone, ed. *Bibliothecae selectae: da Cusano a Leopardi*. Florence: Olschki, 1993, 496–506.
Fontenelle, Bernard Le Bovier, Marquis de. *Entretiens sur la pluralité des mondes*. Lyon: Leroy, 1800, c1686.
Fontes de Costa, Palmira. *The Singular and the Making of Knowledge at the Royal Society of London in the Eighteenth Century*. Newcastle: Cambridge Scholars Publishing, 2009.
Foucault, Michel. *The Archaeology of Knowledge*. Trans. by A. M. Sheridan Smith. New York: Pantheon Books, 1972.
Fox, Adam. *Oral and Literate Culture in England 1500–1700*. Oxford: Clarendon, 2000.
Frank, Joseph. *The Beginnings of the English Newspaper, 1620–1660*. Cambridge, MA: Harvard University Press, 1961.
Freedberg, David. *The Eye of the Lynx: Galileo, His Friends, and the Beginnings of Modern Natural History*. Chicago: University of Chicago Press, 2002.
Friedrich, Markus. "Government and information-management in early modern Europe. The case of the Society of Jesus (1540–1773)." *Journal of Early Modern History*, 12 (2008), 539–563.
Friedrich, Markus. "Governance in the Society of Jesus: 1540–1773. Its Methods, Critics, and Legacy Today." *Studies in the Spirituality of the Jesuits*, 41.1 (2009), 1–42.
Friedrich, Markus. "Archives as networks: the geography of record-keeping in the Society of Jesus (1540–1773)." *Archival Science*, 10 (2010), 285–329.
Friedrich, Markus. *Der lange Arm Roms? Globale Verwaltung und Kommunikation im Jesuiten orden 1540–1773*. Frankfurt: Campus Verlag, 2011.
Friedrich, Markus. *Die Geburt des Archivs. Ein Wissensgeschichte*. Munich: Oldenbourg Verlag, 2013.
Friedrich, Markus. "The rise of archival consciousness in provincial France: French feudal records and eighteenth-century seigneurial society." *Past and Present*, 230 (2016), Supplement 11. *The Social History of the Archive: Record-Keeping in Early Modern Europe*. Ed. by Alexandra Walsham, Liesbeth Corens, and Kate Peters, 49–70.
Friedrich, Markus. "How to make an archival inventory in early modern Europe: carrying documents, gluing paper and transforming archival chaos into well-ordered knowledge." *Manuscript Cultures*, 10.10 (2017), 160–173.
Frigo, Daniela. "Corte, honore et ragion di stato: il ruolo dell'ambasciatore in età moderna." In Frigo, ed. *Ambasciatori e nunzi. Figure della diplomazia in età moderna*. Special issue of *Chieron. Materiali e strumento di aggiornamento storiografico* (1999), 13–55.
Fubini, Riccardo. "La figura politica dell'ambasciatore negli sviluppi dei regimi oligarchici quattrocenteschi." In Sergio Bertelli, ed. *Forme e tecniche del potere nella citta (secolo XIV–XVII). Annuario della Facoltà di Scienze Politiche dell'Università di Perugia*. 16 (1979–1980). Perugia: Università di Perugia, 1982, 33–59.

Fubini, Riccardo. "Classe dirigente ed esercizio della diplomazia nella Firenze quattrocentesca." In Donatella Rugiadini, ed. *I ceti dirigenti nella Toscana nel XV secolo.* Monte Oriolo, Impruneta: F. Papafava, 1987, 117–189.

Fubini, Riccardo. "La 'résidentialité' de l'ambassadeur dans le mythe et dans la réalité: une enquête sur les origines." In Lucien Bély, ed. *L'invention de la diplomatie.* Paris: Presses universitaires de Paris, 1998, 27–35.

Fubini, Riccardo. "Diplomacy and government in the Italian city-states of the fifteenth century (Florence and Venice)." In Daniela Frigo, ed. *Politics and Diplomacy in Early Modern Italy. The Structure of Diplomatic Practice, 1450–1800.* Cambridge: Cambridge University Press, 2000, 25–48.

Garberson, Eric. "Libraries, memory and the space of knowledge." *Journal of the History of Collections*, 18 (2006), 105–136.

Garin, Eugenio. *L'educazione in Europa, 1400–1600: Problemi e Programmi.* Bari: Laterza, 1957.

Garzoni, Tomaso. *La piazza universale di tutte le professioni del mondo, e nobili et ignobili.* Venice: Giovan Battista Somascho, 1586.

Gavard, Claude. "Conclusion." In Kouky Fianu and DeLloyd J. Guth, eds. *Écrit et pouvoir dans les chancelleries médiévales: espace français, espace anglais.* Turnhout: Brepols, 1997, 333–342.

Geüsbeek, J. B. *Ancient Double-Entry Bookkeeping.* Houston: Scholars Book, 1974.

Geyer-Kordesch, Johanna. "Medizinische Fallbeschreibungen und ihre Bedeutung in der Wissensreform des 17. und 18. Jahrhunderts." *Medizin, Gesellschaft und Geschichte*, 9 (1990), 7–19.

Ghobrial, John-Paul. *The Whispers of Cities: Information Flows in Istanbul, London and Paris in the Age of William Trumbull.* Oxford: Oxford University Press, 2013.

Giard, Luce and Antonella Romano. "L'usage jésuite de la correspondance. Sa mise en pratique par le mathématicien Christoph Clavius (1570–1611)." In Romano, ed. *Rome et la science moderne: entre Renaissance et Lumières.* Rome: École française de Rome, 2009, 65–119.

Giesecke, Michael. "Als die alten Medien neu waren. Medienrevolutionen in der Geschichte." In Rüdiger Weingarten, ed. *Information ohne Kommunikation?: die Loslösung der Sprache vom Sprecher.* Frankfurt: Fischer, 1990, 75–98.

Giesecke, Michael. *Der Buchdruck in der frühen Neuzeit. Eine historische Fallstudie über die Durchsetzung neuer Informations- und Kommunikationstechnologien.* Frankfurt: Suhrkamp, 1991.

Gilbert, William. *De magnete, magnetisque corporibus, et de magno magnete tellure.* London: Peter Short, 1600.

Gillespie, Vincent. "Vernacular books of religion." In Jocelyn Wogan-Brown, Nicholas Watson, Andrew Taylor, and Ruth Evans, eds. *The Idea of the Vernacular: An Anthology of Middle English Literary Theory, 1280–1520.* University Park, PA: Penn State University Press, 1999, 353–365.

Gilliodts-Van Severen, Louis. *Inventaire des archives de la ville de Bruges: Introduction.* Bruges: Gaillard, 1878.

Gingerich, Owen. *The Book Nobody Read: Chasing the Revolutions of Nicolaus Copernicus.* New York: Walker and Company, 2004.

Bibliography

Gleick, James. *The Information. A History, a Theory, A Flood.* New York: Vintage, 2011.

Godenne, Willy. "Le Papier des comptes communaux de Malines datant au Moyen Âge." *Handelingen van de Koninklijke Kring voor Oudheidkunde, Letteren en Kunst van Mechelen,* 64 (1960), 36–53.

Goeing, Anja-Silvia. "Storing to know: Konrad Gessner's *De Anima* and the relationship between textbooks and citation collections in sixteenth-century Europe." In Anja-Silvia Goeing, Anthony Grafton, and Paul Michel, eds. *Collector's Knowledge: What is Kept, What is Discarded = Aufbewahren oder wegwerfen – Wie Sammler entscheiden.* Leiden: Brill, 2013, 209–242.

Goeing, Anja-Silvia. *Storing, Archiving, Organizing. The Changing Dynamics of Scholarly Information Management in Post-Reformation Zurich.* Leiden: Brill, 2017.

Goitein, Shelomo Dov. *A Mediterranean Society: An Abridgement in One Volume.* Berkeley, CA: University of California Press, 1999.

Goldgar, Ann. *Impolite Learning: Conduct and Community in the Republic of Letters, 1680–1750.* New Haven, CT: Yale University Press, 1995.

Gómez, Antonio Castillo. *Entre la pluma y la pared: una historia social de la escritura en los siglos de oro.* Madrid: AKAL, 2006.

Gómez, Antonio Castillo. "The new culture of archives in early modern Spain." *European History Quarterly,* 46.3 (2016), 545–567.

Goodman, David. *Power and Penury. Government, Technology and Science in Philip II's Spain.* Cambridge: Cambridge University Press, 1988.

Goody, Jack. *The Logic of Writing and the Organization of Society.* Cambridge: Cambridge University Press, 1986.

Goody, Jack. *The Interface between the Written and the Oral* Cambridge: Cambridge University Press, 1988.

Grafton, Anthony. "Teacher, text and pupil in the Renaissance classroom: a case study from a Parisian classroom." *History of Universities,* 1 (1981), 37–70.

Grafton, Anthony. "*Discitur ut agatur*: how Gabriel Harvey read his Livy." In Stephen Barney, ed. *Annotation and Its Texts.* Oxford: Oxford University Press, 1991, 108–129.

Grafton, Anthony. "Kepler as a reader." *The Journal of the History of Ideas,* 53.4 (1992), 561–572.

Grafton, Anthony. *Commerce with the Classics: Ancient Books and Renaissance Readers.* Ann Arbor, MI: University of Michigan Press, 1997.

Grafton, Anthony. "A sketch of a lost continent: the Republic of Letters." *Republic of Letters: A Journal for the Study of Knowledge, Politics and the Arts* 1.1 (2009). Online at https://arcade.stanford.edu/rofl/sketch-map-lost-continent-republic-letters. Also in *Worlds Made by Words: Scholarship and Community in the Modern West.* Cambridge, MA: Harvard University Press, 2009, 9–34.

Grafton, Anthony. *The Culture of Correction in Renaissance Europe.* London: British Library, 2011.

Grafton, Anthony and Ann Blair, eds. *The Transmission of Culture in Early Modern Europe.* Philadelphia: University of Pennsylvania Press, 1990.

Grafton, Anthony and Lisa Jardine. *From Humanism to the Humanities: Education and the Liberal Arts in Fifteenth and Sixteenth-Century Europe.* Cambridge, MA: Harvard University Press, 1986.

Grafton Anthony, and Joanna Weinberg, "*I Have Always Loved the Holy Tongue*": *Isaac Casaubon, the Jews and a Forgotten Chapter in Renaissance Scholarship.* Cambridge, MA: Harvard University Press, 2011.

Grafton, Anthony, Elizabeth Eisenstein, and Adrian Johns. "How revolutionary was the print revolution? *American Historical Review*, 107.1 (2002), 84–128.

Grafton, Anthony, Nancy Siraisi, and April Shelford. *New Worlds, Ancient Texts: the Power of Tradition and the Shock of Discovery.* Cambridge: Cambridge University Press, 1992.

Gramigna, Vincenzo. *Opuscoli del signor Vincenzo Gramigna segretario.* Florence: Pietro Cecconcelli, 1620.

Granovetter, Mark. "The strength of weak ties." *American Journal of Sociology*, 88 (1973), 1360–1380.

Graziaplena, Rosella. "Paper trade and diffusion in late medieval Europe." In Graziaplena and Mark Livesey, eds. *Paper as a Medium of Cultural Heritage. Archaeology and Conservation. 26th Congress – International Association of Paper Historians* (Rome-Verona, August 30–September 6, 2002). Rome: Istituto centrale per la patologia del libro, 2004.

Graziaplena, Rosella and Mark Livesey, eds. *Paper as a Medium of Cultural Heritage: Archaeology and Conservation.* Milan: Istituto centrale per la patologia del libro, 2004.

Greengrass, Mark. "Archive refractions: Hartlib's papers and the workings of an intelligencer." In Michael Hunter, ed. *Archives of the Scientific Revolution: the Formation and Exchange of Ideas in Seventeenth-Century Europe.* Woodbridge, UK: Boydell and Brewer, 1998, 35–47.

Greengrass, Mark. "Mapping structures of the intellectual field using citation and co-citation analysis of correspondences." *History of European Ideas*, 36 (2010), 330–339.

Grendler, Marcella. "Book collecting in Counter-Reformation Italy: the library of Gian Vincenzo Pinelli (1535–1601)." *Journal of Library History*, 16.1 (1981), 143–151.

Grendler, Paul. "Italian Biblical humanism and the papacy, 1515-1535." In Erika Rummell, ed., *Biblical Humanism and Scholasticism in the Age of Erasmus.* Leiden: Brill, 2008, 227–276.

Guarini, Battista. *Il secretario. Dialogo di Battista Guarini. Nel qual non sol si tratta dell'ufficio del Segretario, et el modo del compor Lettere.* Venice: Ruberto Megietti, 1594.

Guarini, Elena Fasano and Maria Rosa, eds. *L'informazione politica in Italia (secoli xvi–xviii).* Pisa: Scuola Normale Superiore, 2001.

Guicciardini, Francesco. *Le lettere*, Vol. I: *1499–1513*. Ed. by Pierre Jodogne. Rome: Instituto Storico per l'Età Moderna e Contemporaneana, 1986.

Guidi, Andrea. *Un segretario militante. Politica, diplomazia e armi nel Cancelliere Machiavelli.* Milan: Mulino, 2009.

Guidi, Andrea. "The Florentine archives in transition: government, warfare and communication (1289–1530 ca.)." *European History Quarterly*, 46.3 (2016), 458–479.

Guilmartin, John. *A Very Short War: The Mayaguez and the Battle of Koh Tang.* College Station, TX: Texas A&M Press, 1995.

Gullick, Michael. "How fast did scribes write? Evidence from Romanesque scripts." In Linda Brownrigg, ed. *Making the Medieval Book: Techniques of Production: Proceedings of the Fourth Conference of the Seminar in the History of the Book to 1500*. Los Altos Hills, CA: Anderson Lovelace, 1995, 39–58.

Gumbert, J. P. "The Speed of Scribes." In Emma Conello and Giuseppe de Gregorio, eds. *Scribi e colofoni: le sottoscrizioni di copisti dalle origini all'avento della stampa*. Spoleto: Centro Italiano di Studi sull'Alto Medievo, 1995, 57–69.

Gwynn, Lucy. "The design of the English domestic library in the seventeenth century: readers and their book rooms." *Library Trends*, 60.1 (2011), 45–53.

Hadden, Richard. *On the Shoulders of Merchants. Exchange and the Mathematical Conception of Nature in Early Modern Europe*. Albany: State University of New York Press, 1994.

Hall, Christopher. *Materials. A Very Short Introduction*. Oxford: Oxford University Press, 2014.

Hall, Marie Boas. "The Royal Society's role in the diffusion of information in the 17th century." *Notes and Records of the Royal Society of London*, 29.2 (1975), 173–192.

Halpoer, Barbara. "Libraries and printers in the fifteenth century." *The Journal of Library History*, 16.1 (1981), 134–142.

Hamm, Berndt. "Die Reformation als Medienreignis." *Jahrbuch für biblische Theologie*, 11 (1996), 137–166.

Harding, Vanessa. "Monastic records and the dissolution: a Tudor revolution in the archives?" *European History Quarterly*, 46.3 (2016), 480–497.

Harkness, Deborah. *The Jewel House: Elizabethan London and the Scientific Revolution*. New Haven, CT: Yale University Press, 2008.

Harline, Craig. *Pamphlets, Printing and Political Culture in the Early Dutch Republic* Dordrecht: Martinus Nijhoff Publishers, 1987.

Harms, Roeland, Joad Raymond, and Jeroen Salman. "Introduction: the distribution and dissemination of popular print." In Harms, Raymond, and Salman, eds. *Not Dead Things. The Dissemination of Popular Print in England and Wales, Italy and the Low Countries, 1500–1820*. Leiden: Brill, 2013, 1–30.

Harris, Steven. "Confession-building, long-distance networks and the organization of Jesuit science." *Early Science and Medicine*, 1.3 (1996), 287–318.

Harris, Steven. "Networks of travel, correspondence and exchange." In Katherine Park and Lorraine Daston, eds. *The Cambridge History of Science*, Vol. 3. Cambridge: Cambridge University Press, 2006, 341–362.

Hartig, Otto. *Die Gründung der Münchener Hofbiblothek durch Albrecht V. und Johann Jakob Fugger*. Munich: Verlag der Königlich-Bayerischen Akademie der Wissenschaften, 1917.

Hauff, Else. "Die 'Einkommenden Zeitungen' von 1650. Ein Beitrag zur Geschichte der Tageszeitung." *Gazette. International Journal for Mass Communications Studies*, 9 (1963), 227–235.

Head, Randolph. "Knowing like a state: the transformation of political knowledge in Swiss Archives, 1450–1770." *The Journal of Modern History*, 75.4 (2003), 745–782.

Head, Randolph. *Making Archives in Early Modern Europe*. Cambridge: Cambridge University Press, 2019.
Headley, John. *The Emperor and his Chancellor: A Study of the Imperial Chancellery under Gattinara*. Cambridge: Cambridge University Press, 1983.
Headrick, Daniel. *When Information Came of Age. Technologies of Knowledge in the Age of Reason and Revolution, 1700–1850*. Oxford: Oxford University Press, 2000.
Heimann, Heinz-Dieter and Ivan Hlaváček, eds. *Kommunikationspraxis und Korrespondenzwesen im Mittelalter und in der Renaissance*. Paderborn: F. Schöningh, 1998.
Hellinga, Lotte. "The Gutenberg Revolutions." In Simon Eliot and Jonathan Rose, eds. *A Companion to the History of the Book*. Oxford: Blackwell, 2003.
Henderson, Felicity. "Robert Hooke's archive." *Script & Print*, 33 (2009), 92–108.
Henderson, Judith Rice. "Erasmus on the Art of Letter-writing." In James Murphy, ed. *Renaissance Eloquence: Studies in the Theory and Practice of Renaissance Rhetoric*. Berkeley, CA: University of California Press, 1983, 331–355.
Henderson, Judith Rice. "Erasmus's *Opus de Conscribendis Epistolis* in sixteenth-century schools." In Carol Poster, ed. *Letter-writing Manuals and Instruction from Antiquity to the Present*. Columbia, SC: University of South Carolina Press, 2007, 141–177.
Henrich, Rainer. "Bullinger's correspondence: an international news network." In Bruce Gordon and Emilio Campi, eds. *Architect of Reformation: an Introduction to Heinrich Bullinger, 1504–1575*. Grand Rapids, MI: Baker Academic, 2004, 231–241.
Herlihy, David and Christiane Klapisch-Zuber. *Tuscans and Their Families: A Study of the Florentine Catasto of 1427*. New Haven, CT: Yale University Press, 1985.
Herold, Jürgen. "Von der "tertialitas" zum "sermo scriptus". Diskurswandel im mittelalterlichen Briefwesen und die Entstehung einer neuen Briefform von der Mitte des 13. bis zum Ende des 15. Jahrhunderts." In Christina Antenhoffer and Mario Müller, *Briefe in politischer Kommunikation vom Alten Orient bis ins 20. Jahrhundert*. Göttingen: V&R Unipress, 2008, 83–113.
Hess, Volker and J. Andrew Mendelsohn. "Case and series: medical knowledge and paper technology, 1600–1900." *History of Science*, 48 (2010), 287–314.
Higgs, Edward. "The rise of the information state: the development of central state surveillance of the citizen in England, 1500–2000." *The Journal of Historical Sociology*, 14.2 (2001), 175–195.
Hill, Roscoe. "Reforms in shelving and numbering in the Archivio de las Indias." *Hispanic American Historical Review* 10 (1930), 520–524.
Hindman, Sandra, ed. *Printing the Written Word: the Social History of Books, c. 1450–1520*. Ithaca, NY: Cornell University Press, 1991.
Hirsch, Rudolf. *Printing, Selling and Reading, 1450–1550*. Wiesbaden: Harrasowitz, 1974.

Hiscock, Andrew. *Reading Memory in Early Modern Literature*. Cambridge: Cambridge University Press, 2011.
Hobart, Michael and Zachary Schiffman. *Information Ages: Literacy, Numeracy and the Computer Revolution*. Baltimore, MD: Johns Hopkins University Press, 1998.
Hoffmann, Christophe. "Processes on paper: writing procedures as non-material research devices." *Science in Context*, 26.2 (2013), 279–303.
Holmes, Frederic Lawrence. *Investigative Pathways: Patterns and Stages in the Careers of Experimental Scientists*. New Haven, CT: Yale University Press, 2004.
Hooykaas, Reijer. *Humanisme, science et réforme: Pierre de la Ramée (1515–1572)*. Leiden: Brill, 1958.
Hornschuch, Hieronymus. *Hornschuch's Orthotypographia*. Trans. and ed. by Philip Gaskell and Patricia Bradford. Cambridge: The University Library, 1972.
Horodowich, Elizabeth. *Language and Statecraft in Early Modern Venice*. Cambridge: Cambridge University Press, 2008.
Hotman, Jean, Sieur de Villiers. *De la charge et dignité de l'ambassadeur*. Paris: J. Périer, 1603.
Hotson, Howard. *Commonplace Learning: Ramism and its German Ramifications, 1543–1630*. Oxford: Oxford University Press, 2007.
Houston, Keith. *The Book. A Cover-to-Cover Exploration of the Most Powerful Object of Our Time*. New York: Norton, 2016.
Houston, Robert Allan. *Literacy in Early Modern Europe. Culture and Education 1500–1800*. Harlow. Longman, 2002.
Howard, Nicole. *The Book. The Little Story of a Technology*. Baltimore, MD: Johns Hopkins University Press, 2009.
Hughes, Charles, ed. "Nicholas Faunt's discourse touching the office of the Principal Secretary of Estate." *English Historical Review*, 20 (1905), 499–508.
Hughes, Jane. *The Pepys Library and the Historic Collections of Magdalene College Cambridge*. New York: Scala, 2015.
Hugon, Alain. *Au service du roi catholique: honorables ambassadeurs et divins espions. Représentation diplomatique et service secret dans les relations hispano-françaises de 1598 à 1635*. Madrid: Casa de Velazquez, 2004.
Huguet-Termes, Teresa. "New World *materia medica* in Spanish Renaissance medicine: from scholarly reception to practical impact." *Medical History*, 45 (2001), 359–376.
Hull, Matthew. "Documents and bureaucracy." *Annual Review of Anthropology*, 41 (2012), 251–267.
Hull, Matthew. *Government of Paper. The Materiality of Bureaucracy in Urban Pakistan*. Berkeley, CA: University of California Press, 2012.
Hunt, Arnold. "Sloane as a collector of manuscripts." In Alison Walker and Michael Hunter, eds. *From Books to Bezoars: Sir Hans Sloane and his Collections*. London: The British Library, 2012.
Hunt, Arnold. "'Burn this letter': preservation and destruction in the early modern archive." In James Daybell and Andrew Gordon, eds. *Cultures of Correspondence in Early Modern Britain*. Philadelphia: University of Pennsylvania Press, 2016, 189–209.

Hunter, Michael. "The importance of being institutionalised." In Hunter, ed. *Establishing the New Science. The Experience of the Early Royal Society.* Woodbridge, UK: Boydell Press, 1989, 1–14.

Hunter, Michael, ed. *Archives of the Scientific Revolution: the Formation and Exchange of Ideas in Seventeenth-Century Europe.* Woodbridge, UK: Boydell and Brewer, 1998.

Hunter, Michael. *The Boyle Papers: Understanding the Manuscripts of Robert Boyle.* Aldershot: Ashgate, 2007.

Hutchinson, Terrence. *Before Adam Smith: The Emergence of Political Economy, 1662–1776.* Oxford: Blackwell, 1988.

Ihri, Yuri. "The beauty of double-entry bookkeeping and its impact on the nature of accounting information." *Economic Notes,* 22.2 (1993), 265–285.

Ilardi, Vincent. "The first permanent embassy outside Italy: the Milanese Embassy at the French Court, 1464–1483." In Malcolm R. Thorp and Arthur J. Slavin, eds. *Politics, Religion and Diplomacy in Early Modern Europe: Essays in Honor of Delamar Jensen.* Kirksville, MO: Sixteenth Century Journal Publishers, 1994, 1–18.

Iliffe, Robert. "Material doubts: Hooke, artisan culture and the exchange of information in 1670s London." *The British Journal for the History of Science,* 28.3 (1995), 285–318.

Illich, Ivan. *In the Vineyard of the Text. A Commentary to Hugh's* Didascalicon. Chicago: University of Chicago Press, 1993.

Infelise, Mario. "From merchants' letters to handwritten political *avvisi*: notes on the origins of public information." In Heinz Schilling and István György Tóth, eds. *Religion and Cultural Exchange in Europe, 1400–1700,* Vol. I of *Cultural Exchange in Early Modern Europe,* General ed. Robert Muchembled. Cambridge: Cambridge University Press, 2006, 33–52.

Infelise, Mario. "News networks between Italy and Europe." In Brendan Dooley, ed. *The Dissemination of News and the Emergence of Contemporaneity in Early Modern Europe.* Farnham, Surrey: Ashgate, 2010, 51–67.

Ingegneri, Angelo. *Del Buon Segretario Libri Tre di Angelo Ingegneri.* Rome: Guglielmo Faciotto, 1594.

Innis, Harold. "The Coming of Paper." In William Buxton, Michael Cheney, and Paul Heyer, eds. *Harold Innis' History of Communications: Paper and Printing.* Lanham: Rowman and Littlefield, 2015, 15–56.

Irigoin, Jean. "Les origines de la fabrication du papier en Italie." *Papiergeschichte,* 13.5–6 (1963), 62–67.

Irving, Sarah. *Natural Science and the Origins of the British Empire.* London: Routledge, 2015.

Jackson, Heather. *Marginalia: Readers Writing in Books.* New Haven, CT: Yale University Press, 2001.

Jackson, Maggie. *Distracted: The Erosion of Attention and the Coming Dark Age.* Amherst, MA: Prometheus Books, 2008.

Jacobs, Alan. *The Pleasures of Reading in an Age of Distraction.* Oxford: Oxford University Press, 2011.

Jacobs, Alan. "We can't teach students to love reading." *The Chronicle of Higher Education.* July 31, 2011.

Jardine, Nick. "Uses and abuses of anachronism in the history of the sciences." *History of Science*, 38 (2000), 251–270.
Jensen, Delamar. "French diplomacy and the wars of religion." *Sixteenth-century Studies Journal*, 5.2 (1974), 23–46.
Johns, Adrian. *The Nature of the Book. Print and Knowledge in the Making*. Chicago: University of Chicago Press, 1998.
Johns, Adrian. "Reading and experiment in the early Royal Society." In Kevin Sharpe and Steven Zwicker, eds. *Reading, Society, and Politics in Early Modern England*. Cambridge: Cambridge University Press, 2003, 244–271.
Johns, Adrian. "Coffeehouses and print shops." In Katherine Park and Lorraine Daston, eds. *The Cambridge History of Science*, Vol. 3: *Early Modern Science*. Cambridge: Cambridge University Press, 2006, 320–340.
Jones, Peter Murray. "Reading medicine in Tudor Cambridge." In Vivian Nutton and Roy Porter, eds. *The History of Medical Education in Britain*. Amsterdam: Rodopi, 1995, 153–183.
Kafka, Ben. *The Demon of Writing. Powers and Failures of Paperwork*. New York: Zone Books, 2012.
Keene, Derek. "Cities and cultural exchange." In Donatella Calabi and Stephen Turk Christensen, eds. *Cities and Cultural Exchange in Europe, 1400–1700*, Vol. II of *Cultural Exchange on Early Modern Europe*, General ed. Robert Muchembled. Cambridge: Cambridge University Press, 2006, 3–27.
Keller, Hagen, Klaus Grubmüller, und Nikolaus Staubach, eds. *Pragmatische Schriftlichkeit im Mittelalter: Erscheinungsformen und Entwicklungsstufen*. Munich: Fink, 1992.
Keller, Vera. "Nero and the last stalk of *Silphion*: collecting extinct nature in early modern Europe." *Early Science and Medicine*, 19 (2014), 424–447.
Keller, Vera, Anna Marie Roos, and Elizabeth Yale, eds. *Archival Afterlives: Life, Death and Knowledge-Making in Early Modern British Scientific and Medical Archives*. Leiden: Brill, 2018.
Kelley, Donald. "Jean du Tiller, archivist and antiquary." *Journal of Modern History*, 38 (1966), 337–354.
Kenny, Neil. *Curiosity in Early Modern Europe. Word Histories*. Wiesbaden: Harrassowitz, 1998.
Kenniston, Howard. *Francisco de los Cobos: Secretary of Emperor Charles V*. Pittsburgh: University of Pittsburgh Press, 1958.
Ketelaar, Eric. "The genealogical gaze: family identities and family archives in the fourteenth to seventeenth centuries." *Libraries & the Cultural Record*, 44.1 (2009), 9–28.
Ketelaar, Eric. "Records out and archives in: early modern cities as creators of records and as communities of archives." *Archival Science*, 10 (2010), 201–210.
Kilgour, Frederick. *The Evolution of the Book*. Oxford: Oxford University Press, 1998.
Kingdon, Robert. "Christophe Plantin and his backers. a study in the problems of financing business during war." In *Melange d'histoire économique et sociale en*

hommage au professeur Antony Babel à l'occasion de son soixante-quinzième anniversaire, Vol. 1. Geneva: Tribune de Genève, 1963, 303–316.
Knight, Jeffrey Todd. *Bound to Be Read. Compilations, Collections, and the Making of Renaissance Literature*. Philadelphia: University of Pennsylvania Press, 2013.
Knowles, David. *The Monastic Order in England*. Cambridge: Cambridge University Press, 1950.
Kraemer, Fabian. "Ulisse Aldrovandi's *Pandechion Epistemonicon* and the use of paper technology in Renaissance natural history." *Early Science and Medicine*, 19 (2014), 398–423.
Krajewski, Markus. *Paper Machines. About Cards and Catalogs, 1548–1929*. Trans. by Peter Krapp. Cambridge, MA: MIT Press, 2011.
Krugman, Paul. *Geography and Trade*. Cambridge, MA: MIT Press, 1991.
Kusukawa, Sachiko. *Picturing the Book of Nature. Image, Text and Argument in Sixteenth-Century Human Anatomy and Medical Botany*. Chicago: University of Chicago Press, 2012.
Kwakkel, Erik. "A new type of book for a new type of reader: the emergence of paper in vernacular book production." *Library*, 7.4 (2003), 219–248.
Lach, Donald and Edwin van Kley, *Asia in the Making of Europe*, Vol. I: *The Century of Discovery*. Chicago: University of Chicago Press, 1965.
Lapeyre, Henri. *Une famille de marchands: Les Ruiz*. Paris: Librairie Armand Colin, 1955.
Latour, Bruno. "Drawing things together." In Michael Lynch and Steve Woolgar, eds. *Representation in Scientific Practice*. Cambridge, MA: MIT Press, 1990.
Latour, Bruno. *Reassembling the Social: An Introduction to Actor-Network-Theory*. Oxford: Oxford University Press, 2007.
Latour, Bruno and Steve Woolgar, *Laboratory Life: the Construction of Scientific Facts*, 2nd ed. Princeton: Princeton University Press, 1986.
Lazzarini, Isabella. "*Peculiaris magistratus*: la cancelleria gonzhagesca nel Quattrocento (1407–1478)." In Franca Leverotti, ed. *Cancellerie e amministrazione negli stati italiani del Rinascimento*. Special issue of *Ricerche storiche* 24.2 (1994), 336–349.
Lazzarini, Isabella. "L'informazione politico-diplomatica nell'età della pace di Lodi: raccolta, selezione, trasmissione. Spunti di ricerca dal carteggio Milano-Mantova nella prima età sforzesca (1450–1466)." *Nuova Rivista Storica*, 83 (1999), 247–280.
Lazzarini, Isabella, ed. *Carteggio degli oratori mantovani alla corte sforzesca (1450–1500)*, Vol. III *(1461)*. Rome: Ministero per i beni e le attività culturali, 2000.
Lazzarini, Isabella, ed. "Scritture e potere. Pratiche documentarie e forme di governo nell'Italia tardomedievale (XIV–XV secolo)." Special issue of *Reti medievali*, 9 (2008).
Lazzarini, Isabella. "La nomination d'un cardinal de famille entre l'empire et la papauté: les pratiques de négociation de Bartolomeo Bonatti, orateur de Ludovico Gonzaga (Rome, 1461)." In Stefano Andreta, Stéphane Péquignot, Marie-Karine Schaub, Jean-Claude Waquet, and Christian Wilder, eds. *Parole des Négociateurs. l'entretien dans la pratique diplomatique de la fin du Moyen Âge à la fin du XIXe siècle*. Rome: École Française de Rome, 2010, 51–69.

Lazzarini, Isabella. *Communication and Conflict: Italian Diplomacy in the Early Renaissance, 1350–1520*. Oxford: Oxford University Press, 2015.

Leng, Thomas. "Epistemology. Expertise and knowledge in the world of commerce." In Philip Stern and Carl Wennerlind, eds. *Mercantilism Reimagined: Political Economy in Early Modern Britain and Its Empire*. Cambridge: Cambridge University Press, 2014, 97–116.

Le Roy, Louis. *De la vicissitude ou variété des choses en l'univers*. Paris: Pierre l'Huilier, 1576.

Le Roy Ladurie, Emmanuel. *The Beggar and the Professor: A Sixteenth-Century Family Saga*. Trans. by Arthur Goldhammer. Chicago: University of Chicago Press, 1997.

Letwin, William. *The Origins of Scientific Economics: English Economic Thought 1660–1776*. London: Methuen, 1963.

Leu, Urs. "Aneignung und Speicherung enzyklopädischen Wissens. Die Loci-Methode." In Christine Christ von Wedel and Leu, eds. *Erasmus in Zürich: eine verschwiegene Autorität*. Zurich: Verlag Neue Zürcher Zeitung, 2007, 327–342.

Leu, Urs and Sandra Weidmann. *Conrad Gessner's Private Library*. Leiden: Brill, 2008.

Leu, Urs and Sandra Weidmann. *Huldrych Zwingli's Private Library*. Leiden: Brill, 2019.

Leverotti, Franca. *Diplomazia e governo: i "famigli cavalcanti" di Francesco Sforza (1450–1466)*. Pisa: GISEM-ETS Editrice, 1992.

Levy, F. J. "How information spread among the gentry, 1550–1640." *Journal of British Studies*, 21.2 (1982), 11–34.

Licklider, J. C. R. "Man-computer symbiosis." *IRE Transactions on Human Factors in Electronics HFE*, 1.1 (1960), 4–11.

Licklider, J. C. R. *Libraries of the Future*. Cambridge, MA: MIT Press, 1965.

Lindemann, Mary. *Medicine and Society in Early Modern Europe*. Cambridge: Cambridge University Press, 2010.

Litschel, Andrea. "Writing and social evidence 'before the archives': revealing and concealing the written in late medieval Lüneberg." In Marco Mostert and Anna Adamska, eds. *Writing and the Administration of Medieval Towns*. Turnhout: Brepols, 2014.

Lorenz, Bernd. *Allgemeinbildung und Fachwissen. Deutsche Ärzte und ihre Privatbibliotheken*. Herzogenrath: Verlag Murken-Altrogge, 1992.

Love, Harold. *Scribal Publication in Seventeenth-Century England*. Oxford: Oxford University Press, 1993.

Love, Harold. *The Culture and Commerce of Texts. Scribal Publication in Seventeenth-Century England*. Amherst, MA: University of Massachusetts Press, 1998.

Loveman, Kate. *Samuel Pepys and His Books: Reading, Newsgathering, and Sociability, 1660–1703*. Oxford: Oxford University Press, 2015.

Lowood, Henry. "The new world and the European catalog of nature." In Karen Ordahl Kupperman, ed. *America in European Consciousness, 1493–1750*. Chapel Hill, NC: University of North Carolina Press, 1995, 295–323.

Lumsden, Charles and Edward O. Wilson. *Genes, Mind and Culture: the Coevolutionary Process*. Cambridge, MA: Harvard University Press, 1981.
Lundin, Matthew. *Paper Memory. A Sixteenth-century Townsman Writes His World*. Cambridge, MA: Harvard University Press, 2013.
Luther, Martin. *The Letters of Martin Luther*. Trans. and ed. by Margaret Currie. New York: Macmillan, 1908.
Lux, David and Harold Cook. "Closed circles or open networks? Communicating at a distance during the Scientific Revolution." *History of Science*, 36 (1998), 179–211.
Lyall, Roderick. "Materials: the paper revolution." In Jeremy Griffiths and Derek Pearsall, eds. *Book Publishing in Britain 1375–1475*. Cambridge: Cambridge University Press, 1989, 11–30.
Lyons, Martyn. *A History of Reading and Writing in the Western World*. Basingstoke, UK: Palgrave Macmillan, 2010.
Mackenzie, D. F. "Speech-manuscript-print." In Dave Oliphant and Robin Bradford, eds. *New Directions in Textual Studies*. Austin, TX: Harry Ransom Humanities Research Center, 1990, 86–109.
Maclean, Ian. "The market for scholarly books and conceptions of genre in Northern Europe, 1570–1630." In Georg Kaufmann, ed. *Die Renaissance im Blick der Nationen Europas*. Wiesbaden: Harrassowitz, 1991, 17–31.
MacNeil, Heather. *Trusting Records: Legal, Historical and Diplomatic Perspectives*. Dordrecht: Kluwer Academic Publishers, 2000
Magnusson, Lars. *Mercantilism: The Shaping of an Economic Language*. London: Routledge, 1994.
Maïer, Ida. "Un inédit de Politien: la classification des 'arts.'" *Bibliothèque d'humanisme et Renaissance*, 22 (1960), 338–355.
Maire Vigueur, Jean-Claude. "Révolution documentaire et révolution scripturaire: le cas de l'Italie médiévale." *Bibliothèque de l'École des Chartes*, 153.1 (1995), 177–185.
Mallett, Michael. "Ambassadors and their audiences in Renaissance Italy." *Renaissance Studies*, 8.3 (1994), 229–243.
Mallett, Michael. "Italian Renaissance diplomacy." *Diplomacy and Statecraft*, 12.1 (2001), 61–70.
Malynes, Gerald. *England's View in the Unmasking of Two Paradoxes*. London: Richard Field, 1603
Man, John. *The Gutenberg Revolution. How Printing Changed the Course of History*. New York: Random House, 2010.
Mandosio, J. M. "La fortune du Panepistemon d'Ange Politien en France au XVIe siècle." In Alfredo Perifano, ed. *La réception des écrits italiens en France à la Renaissance: ouvrages philosophiques, scientifiques, et techniques*. Paris: Sorbonne, 2000, 49–71.
Marcara, Carlo. "Il diario di Giambattista Casale (1554–1598)." *Memorie storiche della Diocesi di Milano*, 12 (1965), 209–437.
Margócsy, Dániel. *Commercial Visions. Science, Trade and Visual Culture in the Dutch Golden Age*. Chicago: University of Chicago Press, 2014.
Marks, Steven. *The Information Nexus. Global Capitalism from the Renaissance to the Present*. Cambridge: Cambridge University Press, 2016.

Marotti, Arthur and Michael Bristol, eds. *Print, Manuscript, and Performance: the Changing Relations of the Media in Early Modern England*. Columbus, OH: Ohio State University Press, 2000.
Marr, Alexander. "A Renaissance library rediscovered: the 'Repertorium librorum Mathematica' of Jean I du Temps." *The Library: the Transactions of the Bibliographical Society*, 9.4 (2008), 428–470.
Martin, Felipe Ruiz. *Pequeño capitalismo, gran capitalismo: Simón Ruiz y sus negocios en Florencia*. Barcelona: Critica, 1990.
Martin, Henri-Jean. "Classements et conjonctures." In Roger Chartier and Martin, eds. *Histoire de l'édition française*, Vol. I: *Le livre conquérant. Du Moyen Âge au milieu du XVII siècle*. Paris: Fayard, 1989, 429–457.
Martin, Henri-Jean. *The History and Power of Writing*. Chicago: Chicago University Press, 1994.
Marwick, Donna. *Death of a Notary: Conquest and Change in Colonial New York*. Ithaca, NY: Cornell University Press, 2002.
Mathison, Hamish. "Robert Hepburn and the Edinburgh *Tatler*: a study in an early British periodical." In Joad Raymond, ed. *News Networks in Seventeenth Century Britain and Europe*. London: Routledge, 2013, 145–160.
Mattingly, Garrett. *Renaissance Diplomacy*. London: Cape, 1955.
Mayr, Ernst. *The Growth of Biological Thought: Diversity, Evolution and Inheritance*. Cambridge, MA: Harvard University Press, 1982.
McCusker, John. "Information and transaction costs in early modern Europe." In Rainer Gömmel and Markus A. Denzel, eds. *Weltwirtschaft und Wirtschaftsordnung: Festschrift für Jürgen Schneider zum 65. Geburtstag. Vierteljahrschrift für Sozial- und Wirtschaftsgeschichte, Beihefte*, 159. Stuttgart: Steiner, 2002, 69–83.
McCusker, John. "The demise of distance: the business press and the origins of the information revolution in the early modern Atlantic world." *American Historical Review*, 110.2 (2005), 295–321.
McFarlane, K. B. *The Nobility of Later Medieval England*. Oxford: Clarendon Press, 1973.
McKie, Elsie. "A month in the life of John Calvin." In Murray Rae, Peter Matheson, and Brett Knowles, eds. *Calvin: The Man and the Legacy*. Hindmarsh, Australia: ATF Theology, 2014, 61–77.
McKitterick, David. *A History of Cambridge University Press*, Vol. 1: *Printing and the Book Trade in Cambridge 1534–1698*. Cambridge: Cambridge University Press, 1992.
McKitterick, David. *Print, Manuscript and the Search for Order, 1450–1830*. Cambridge: Cambridge University Press, 2003.
McKitterick, Rosamond. *The Carolingians and the Written Word*. Cambridge: Cambridge University Press, 1989.
McNeely, Ian and Lisa Wolverton. *Reinventing Knowledge. From Alexandria to the Internet*. New York: Norton, 2008.
Meinel, C. "Enzyklopädie der Welt und Verzettelung des Wissens: Aporien der Empirie bei Joachim Jungius." In Franz Eybl, Wolfgang Harms, Hans-Henrik Krummacher, and Werner Welzig, eds. *Enzyklopädien der frühen Neuzeit. Beiträge zu ihrer Forschung*. Tübingen: Niemeyer, 1995, 162–87.

Meli, D. B. "Authorship and teamwork around the Cimento Academy: mathematics, anatomy, experimental philosophy." *Early Science and Medicine*, 6 (2001), 65–95.

Melis, Federigo. *Intensità e regolarità nella diffusione dell'informazione economica generale nella Mediterraneo e in Occidente alla fine del Medioevo*. Prato: Istituto di studi storici postali, 1983.

Menne, Mareike. "Confession, confusion and rule in a box? Archival accumulation in Northwest Germany in the age of confessionalization." *Archival Science*, 10 (2010), 299–314.

Mermet, Claude. *La pratique de l'orthographe Françoise*. Lyon: Basile Bouquet, 1583.

Michon, Cédric, ed. *Conseils et conseillers dans l'Europe de la Renaissance v. 1450 – v. 1550*. Tours: Presses universitaires François Rabelais de Tours; Rennes: Presses universitaires de Rennes, 2012.

Miglio, Massimo ed. *Giovanni Andrea Bussi: Prefazioni alle edizioni de Swenheym e Pannartz, prototipografi romani*. Milan: Edizioni il Polifilo, 1978.

Miller, Peter. *Peiresc's Europe*. New Haven, CT: Yale University Press, 2000.

Miller, Peter. "Description terminable and interminable: looking at the past, nature and peoples in Peiresc's Archive." In Gianna Pomata and Nancy Siraisi, eds. Historia: *Empiricism and Erudition in Early Modern Europe*. Cambridge, MA: MIT Press, 2005, 355–397.

Miller, Peter. *Peiresc's Mediterranean World*. Cambridge, MA: Harvard University Press, 2015.

Millstone, Noah. *Manuscript Publishing and the Invention of Politics in Early Stuart England*. Cambridge: Cambridge University Press, 2016.

Mohlo, Anthony, ed. *Social and Economic Foundations of the Italian Renaissance*. New York: Wiley, 1969.

Mokyr, John. "The riddle of 'The Great Divergence': intellectual and economic factors in the growth of the West." *Historically Speaking*, 5.1 (2003), 2–6.

Monnet, Pierre. *Les Rohrbach de Francfort. Pouvoirs, affaires, et parenté à l'aube de la Renaissance allemande*. Geneva: Droz, 1997.

Monro, Alexander. *The Paper Trail. The Unexpected History of the World's Greatest Invention*. London: Allen Lane, 2014.

Montaigne, Michel de. *The Essays: A Selection*. Trans. and ed. by M. A. Screech. London: Penguin, 1991.

Moore, R. I. *The First European Revolution, c. 970–1215*. Oxford: Blackwell, 2000.

Moreni, Alberto. "La bibliotheca universalis de Konrad Gessner e gli Indici dei libri proibiti." *La Bibliofilia*, 88 (1986), 131–150.

Morrison, Stanley. "The origins of the newspaper." In David McKitterick, ed. *Selected Essays on the History of Letter-Forms in Manuscript and Print*. Cambridge: Cambridge University Press, 1980, 325–360.

Moss, Ann. *Printed Commonplace Books and the Structuring of Renaissance Thought*. Oxford: Clarendon, 1996.

Moss, Ann. "Power and persuasion: commonplace culture in early modern Europe." In David Cowling and Mette Bruun, eds. *Commonplace Culture in Western Europe in the Early Modern Period*. Leuven: Peeters, 2011, 1–18.

Mouysset, Sylvie. *Papiers de famille: Introduction à l'étude des livres de raison.* Rennes: Presses universitaires de Rennes, 2008.
Muldrew, Craig. *The Economy of Obligation. The Culture of Credit and Social Relations in Early Modern England.* Basingstoke, UK: Palgrave, 1998.
Müller, Ernst. "Transferences in the concept of information." In Jutta Weber, ed. *Interdisziplinierung? Zum Wissenschaft zwischen Geistes-, Sozial- und Technowissenschaften.* Bielefeld: Transcript, 2010, 143–163.
Müller, Lothar. *Weiße Magie. Die Epoche des Papiers.* Munich: Carl Hanser Verlag, 2012.
Müller, Lothar. *White Magic. The Age of Paper.* Trans. by Jessica Spengler. Cambridge: Polity, 2014. Translation of *Weiße Magie.*
Müller, Reinhold. *The Venetian Money Market. Banks, Panics and the Public Debt, 1200–1500.* Baltimore: Johns Hopkins University Press, 1997.
Müller-Wille, Staffan and Isabelle Charmantier, "Natural history and information overload: the case of Linnaeus." *Studies in History and Philosophy of Biological and Biomedical Sciences*, 43 (2012), 4–15.
Muratori, Ludovico Antonio. *Dei difetti della giurisprudenza.* Naples: Stamperia Muziana, 1743.
Murphy, Hannah. "Common place and private spaces. libraries, record-keeping and orders of information in sixteenth-century medicine." *Past and Present*, 230. (2016), Supplement 11. *The Social History of the Archive: Record-Keeping in Early Modern Europe.* Ed. by Alexandra Walsham, Liesbeth Corens, and Kate Peters, 253–268.
Nalle, Sara. "Literacy and culture in early modern Castile." *Past and Present*, 25 (1989), 74–98.
Natale, Alfio Rosario, ed. *Acta in Consilio Secreto in castello Portae Jovis Mediolani.* 3 Vols. Milan: A. Giuffre, 1963–1969.
Naudé, Gabriel. *Advis pour dresser une bibliothèque.* Paris: Rolet le Duc, 1644.
Naudé, Gabriel. *Instructions Concerning Erecting a Library.* Cambridge: Houghton, Mifflin and Company, 1903.
Naudé, Gabriel. *Two Tracts Written by Gabriel Naudé.* Trans. and ed. by John Cotton Dana and Henry W. Kent. Chicago: McClurg, 1907.
Neddermeyer, Uwe. *Von der Handschrift zum gedruckten Buch. Schriftlichkeit und Leseinteresse im Mittelalter und in der frühen Neuzeit. Quantitative und qualitative Aspekte.* Wiesbaden: Harrassowitz Verlag, 1998.
Needham, Paul. *The Printer and the Pardoner: an Unrecorded Indulgence Printed by William Caxton for the Hospital of St. Mary Rouneval, Charing Cross.* Washington, DC: Library of Congress, 1986.
Needham, Paul. "Res papirea: sizes and formats of the late medieval book." In Peter Rück and Martin Boghardt, eds. *Rationalisierung der Buchherstellung im Mittelalter und in der frühen Neuzeit.* Marburg: Philipps-Universität Marburg/Institut für Historische Hilfswissenschaften, 1994, 123–145.
Nelles, Paul. "The library as an instrument of discovery. Gabriel Naudé and the uses of history." In Donald Kelley, ed. *History and the Disciplines: The Reclassification of Knowledge in Early Modern Europe.* Rochester, NY: University of Rochester Press, 1997, 41–57.

Nelles, Paul. "Reading and memory in the universal library: Conrad Gessner and the Renaissance book." In Donald Beecher and Grant Williams, eds. *Ars reminiscendi: Mind and Memory in Renaissance Culture*. Toronto: Centre for Reformation and Renaissance Studies, 2009, 147–169.

Nelles, Paul. "Conrad Gessner and the mobility of the book: Zurich, Frankfurt and Venice (1543)." In Daniel Bellingradt, Paul Nelles, and Jeroen Salman, eds. *Books in Motion in Early Modern Europe. Beyond Production, Circulation and Consumption*. Basingstoke, UK: Palgrave Macmillan, 2017, 39–66.

Nickisch, Reinhard. *Brief*. Stuttgart: Metzler, 1991.

Nieto, Philippe. "Géographie des impressions européennes du XVe siècle." *Revue française d'histoire du livre*, 118–121 (2003), 125–173.

Nigro, Salvatore. "The secretary." In Rosario Villari, ed. *Baroque Personae*. Trans. by Lydia Cochrane. Chicago: University of Chicago Press, 1995, 82–99.

Nigro, Salvatore. "Il segretario: precetti e pratiche dell'epistolografia barocca." In Nino Borsellino and Walter Pedullà, eds. *Storia generale della letteratura italiana*, Vol. VI: *Il secolo barocco. Arte e scienza nel Seicento*. Milan: Federico Motta Editore, 1999, 507–530.

North, Michael. *Kommunikation, Handel, Geld und Banken in der Frühen Neuzeit*. Munich: R. Oldenbourg, 2000.

Nunberg, Geoffrey. "Farewell to the information age." In Nunberg, ed. *The Future of the Book*. Berkeley, University of California Press, 2002.

Nuovo, Angela. "*Et amicorum*: costruzione e circolazione del sapere nelle biblioteche private nel Cinquecento." In Rosa Maria Boraccini and Roberto Ruscon, eds. *Libri, biblioteche e cultura degli ordini regolari nell'Italia moderna attraverso la documentazione della Congregazione dell'indice*. Vatican City: Biblioteca Apostolica Vaticana, 2006, 105–127.

Nuovo, Angela. "Manuscript writings on politics and current affairs in the collection of Gian Vincenzo Pinelli (1535–1601)." *Italian Studies*, 66.2 (2011), 193–205.

Nussdorfer, Laurie. *Brokers of Public Trust: Notaries in Early Modern Rome*. Baltimore: Johns Hopkins University Press, 2009.

O'Donnell, James. *Avatars of the Word. From Papyrus to Cyberspace*. Cambridge, MA: Harvard University Press, 1998.

Ogborn, Miles. *Indian Ink. Script and Print in the Making of the East India Company*. Chicago: University of Chicago Press, 2007.

Ogilvie, Brian. "Encyclopedism in Renaissance botany: from *historia* to *pinax*." In Peter Binkley, ed. *Pre-modern Encyclopaedic Texts. Proceedings of the Second COMERS Congress, Groningen, 1–4 July 1996*. Leiden: Brill, 1997, 87–97.

Ogilvie, Brian. "The many books of nature: Renaissance naturalists and information overload." *Journal of the History of Ideas*, 64.1 (2003), 29–40.

Ogilvie, Brian. *The Science of Describing: Natural History in Renaissance Europe*. Chicago: University of Chicago Press, 2006.

O'Hara, James. "'A chaos of jottings that I do not have the leisure to arrange and mark with headings': Leibniz's manuscript papers and their repository." In Michael Hunter, ed., *Archives of the Scientific Revolution: the Formation and Exchange of Ideas in Seventeenth-Century Europe*. Woodbridge, UK: Boydell and Brewer, 1998, 159–170.

Olmi, Giuseppe. "'Molti amici in varij luoghi': studio della natura e rapporti epistolari nel secolo XVI." *Nuncius. Annali di Storia della Scienza*, 7.1 (1991), 3–31.

Olson, David. *The World on Paper. The Conceptual and Cognitive Implications of Writing and Reading*. Cambridge: Cambridge University Press, 1994.

Ong, Walter. *Ramus, Method and the Decay of Dialogue*. Chicago: University of Chicago Press, 1958.

Ong, Walter. "From allegory to diagram in the Renaissance mind: a study in the significance of the allegorical tableau." *The Journal of Aesthetics and Art Criticism*, 17 (1959), 423–440.

Ong, Walter. "Ramist method and the commercial mind." *Studies in the Renaissance*, 8 (1961), 155–172.

Ophir, Adi. "A place of knowledge: the library of Michel de Montaigne." *Science in Context*, 4.1 (1991), 163–189.

Pagnin, B. *I formulari di un notaio e cancelliere padovano del sec. XV*. Padua: Istituto di storia medievale e moderna, 1953.

Palatino, Gianbbatista. *Compendio del gran volume de l'arte del bene et leggiadramente scrivere tutte le sorti di lettere et caratteri*. Rome: Heredi di Valerio et Luigi Dorici Fratelli Bresciani, 1566.

Palliser, D. M. *The Age of Elizabeth: England under the Later Tudors*. London: Routledge, 2014.

Park, Katherine and Lorraine Daston. "Introduction: the age of the new." In Katherine Park and Lorraine Daston, eds. *The Cambridge History of Science*, Vol. 3: *Early Modern Science*. Cambridge: Cambridge University Press, 2006.

Parker, Geoffrey. *Emperor. A New Life of Charles V*. New Haven, CT: Yale University Press, 2019.

Parker, Geoffrey. *The Grand Strategy of Philip II*. New Haven, CT: Yale University Press, 1998.

Parker, Geoffrey. *Imprudent King. A New Life of Philip II*. New Haven, CT: Yale University Press, 2014.

Parkes, Malcolm. "The literacy of the laity." In David Daiches and Anthony Thorlby, eds. *Literature and Western Civilization*, Vol. 2: *The Mediaeval World*. London: Aldus, 1973, 555–577.

Parry, J. H. "Transport and trade routes." In Edward Miller, Cynthia Postan, and M. M. Postan, eds. *The Cambridge Economic History of Europe from the Decline of the Roman Empire*, Vol. 2: *Trade and Industry in the Middle Ages*. Cambridge: Cambridge University Press, 1987, 155–219.

Pastine, Onorato. "L'organizzazione postale della Repubblica di Genova." *Atti della Società Ligure di Storia Patria*, 53 (1926), 393–397.

Pattison, Mark. *Isaac Casaubon, 1559–1614*. London: Longmans, 1875.

Pegolotti, Francesco Balducci. *La Pratica della Mercatura (1340)*. Ed. by Allan Evans. Medieval Academy Books, No. 24. Cambridge, MA: Medieval Academy of America, 1936.

Pellegram, Andrea. "The message in paper." In Daniel Miller, ed. *Material Cultures. Why Some Things Matter*. London: UCL Press, 1997, 103–120.

Péquignot, Stéphane. *Au Nom du Roi: Pratique diplomatique et pouvoir durant le règne de Jacques II d'Aragon (1291–1327)*. Madrid: Casa de Velázquez, 2009.

Perez del Barrio Angulo, Gabriel. *Secretario y Consegero de Señores y Ministros: Cargos, Materias, Cuydados, Obligaciones y curioso Agricultor de quanto el Govierno, y la Pluma piden para cumplir con ellas: El indice las toca, y estan ulustradas con sentencias, conceptos, y curiosidades, no tocadas.* Madrid: Francisco Garcia de Arroyo, Impressor del Reyno, 1645.

Peri, Domenico. *Il negotiante di Giovanni Domenico Peri Genovese.* Genoa: Pier Giovanni Calenzano, 1638.

Persico, Panfilo. *Del segretario del signor Panfilo Persico, Libri Quattro etc.* Venice: Damian Zenaro, 1629.

Petitjean, Johan. *L'intelligence des choses: une histoire de l'information entre Italie et Mediterranée (XVIe–XVIIe siècle).* Rome: École française de Rome, 2013.

Petrucci, Armando. "Scrittura, alfabetismo ed educazione grafica nella Roma del primo Cinquecento: da un libretto di conti di Maddalena Pizzicarola in Trastevere." *Scrittura et civiltà*, 2.2 (1978), 163–207.

Petrucci, Armando. "L'écriture dans l'Italie de la Renaissance." *Annales. Histoire, Sciences Sociales*, 43.4 (1988), 823–847.

Petrucci, Armando. "Copisti e libri manoscritti dopo l'avento della stampa." In Emma Conello and Giuseppe de Gregorio, eds. *Scribi e colofoni: le sottoscrizioni di copisti dalle origini all'avento della stampa.* Spoleto: Centro Italiano di Studi sull'Alto Medioevo, 1995, 57–69.

Petrucci, Armando. *Writers and Readers in Medieval Italy. Studies in the History of Written Culture.* Trans. by Charles Radding. New Haven, CT: Yale University Press, 1995.

Pettegree, Andrew. "A provincial news community in sixteenth-century Europe." In Judith Pollmann and Andrew Spicer, eds. *Public Opinion and Changing Identities in the Early Modern Netherlands: Essays in Honour of Alastair Duke.* Leiden: Brill, 2007, 33–48.

Pettegree, Andrew. *The Book in the Renaissance.* New Haven, CT: Yale University Press, 2010.

Pettegree, Andrew. *The Invention of News. How the World Came to Know About Itself.* New Haven: Yale University Press, 2014.

Pettegree, Andrew. *Brand Luther: 1517, Printing and the Making of the Reformation.* New York: Penguin, 2015.

Pettegree, Andrew. "The Renaissance library and the challenge of print." In Alice Crawford, ed. *The Meaning of the Library.* Princeton: Princeton University Press, 2015, 72–90.

Petter, Andreas. "Schriftorganisation, Kulturtransfer und Überformung – drei Gesichtspunke zur Entstehung, Funktion und Struktur städtischer Amtsbuchhüberlieferung aus dem Mittelalter." In Jürgen Sarnowsky, ed. *Verwaltung und Schriftlichkeit in den Hansestädten.* Trier: Porta Alba Verlag, 2006, 17–63.

Petty, William. *Five Essays in Political Arithmetick.* London: Henry Mortlock, 1672.

Piérard, Christiane. "Le Papier dans les documents comptables de la ville de Mons aux XIVe et XVe siècles." In Georges Despy et al., eds. *Hommage au Professeur Paul Bonenfant (1899–1965): Études d'histoire médiévale dédiées à sa mémoire par les anciens élèves de son séminaire à l'Université Libre de Bruxelles* (Brussels: Pro Civitate, 1965), 341–363.

Bibliography

Pigna, Giovan Battista. *Il principe di Giovanni Battista Pigna*. Venice: Francesco Sansovino, 1561.

Pinon, Laurent. *Livres de zoologie de la Renaissance: une anthologie (1450–1700)*. Paris: Klincksieck, 1995.

Pinon, Laurent. "Conrad Gessner and the historical depth of Renaissance natural history." In Gianna Pomata and Nancy Siraisi, eds. *Historia: Empiricism and Erudition in Early Modern Europe*. Cambridge, MA: MIT Press, 2005, 242–267.

Pitton de Tournefort, Joseph. *Relation d'un voyage du levant*. 2 Vols. Lyon: Anisson et Poseul, 1717.

Polastron, Lucien. *Le Papier. 2000 ans d'histoire et de savoir-faire*. Paris: Imprimerie Nationale, 1999.

Polydore, Vergil. *On Discovery*. Trans and ed. by Brian P. Copenhaver. I Tatti Renaissance Library 6. Cambridge, MA: Harvard University Press, 2002.

Pomata, Gianna. "*Praxis Historialis*: the uses of *historia* in early modern medicine." In Pomata and Nancy Siraisi, eds. *Historia: Empiricism and Erudition in Early Modern Europe*. Cambridge, MA: MIT Press, 2005, 105–146

Pomata, Gianna. "Sharing cases: the *observationes* in early modern medicine." *Early Science and Medicine*, 15.3 (2010), 193–236.

Pomata, Gianna. "Observation rising: birth of an epistemic genre, 1500–1650." In Lorraine Daston and Elizabeth Lunbeck, eds. *Histories of Scientific Observation*. Chicago: University of Chicago Press, 2011, 45–80.

Pomata, Gianna, and Nancy Siraisi, eds. *Historia: Empiricism and Erudition in Early Modern Europe*. Cambridge, MA: MIT Press, 2005.

Pomerantz, Kenneth. *The Great Divergence: China, Europe and the Making of the Modern Economy*. Princeton: Princeton University Press, 2000.

Poncet, Olivier. "Les Archives de la papauté (XVIe–milieu XVIIe siècle), la genèse d'un instrument de pouvoir." In Armand Jamme and Poncet, eds. *Offices, écrit et papauté (XIIIe–XVIIe siècle)*. Rome: École française de Rome, 2007, 737–762.

Poole, Stafford. *Juan de Ovando. Governing the Spanish Empire in the Reign of Philip II*. Norman, OK: University of Oklahoma Press, 2004.

Poovey, Mary. *A History of the Modern Fact. Problems of Knowledge in the Sciences of Wealth and Society*. Chicago, University of Chicago Press, 1998.

Popkin, Jeremy. "New perspectives on the early modern European press." In Joop Koopmans, ed. *News and Politics in Early Modern Europe (1500–1800)*. Leuven: Peeters, 2005.

Popper, Nicholas. "Archives and the boundaries of early modern science." *Isis*, 107.1 (2016), 86–94.

Potin, Yann. "Entre trésor sacré et vaisselle du prince: Le roi medieval est-il un collectionneur?" *Hypothèses*, 1 (2003), 45–56.

Pozza, Marco. "La cancelleria." In Girolamo Arnaldi, Giorgio Gracco, and Alberto Tenenti, eds. *Storia di Venezia III. La formazione dello Stato patrizio*. Rome: Istituto della Enciclopedia Italiana, 1997, 365–387.

Presser, Jacob. "Memoires als geschiedbron." In Presser, ed. *Uit het werk van J. Presser*. Amsterdam: Athenaeum – Polak & Van Gennep, 1966, 277–282.

320 Bibliography

Preto, Paolo. "L'ambassadeur vénitien: diplomate et 'honorable espion.'" In Lucien Bély, ed. *L'invention de la diplomatie. Moyen Âge – Temps modernes*. Paris: Presses universitaires de France, 1998, 151–166.

Priscianese, Francesco. *Del governo della corte d'un Signore in Roma. Dove si ragiona di tutto quello, che al Signore, & à suoi Cortigiani si appartiene di fare. Opera non manco bella, che utile, & necessaria*. Rome: Francesco Priscianese, 1543.

Prodi, Paolo. *La diplomazia del Cinquecento: istituzioni e prassi*. Bologna: Casa Editrice Prof. Riccardo Patron, 1963.

Quattrone, Paolo. "Accounting for God: accounting and accountability practices in the Society of Jesus (Italy, XVI–XVII centuries)." *Accounting, Organizations and Society*, 29 (2004), 647–683.

Queller, Donald. "How to succeed as an ambassador: a sixteenth-century Venetian document." *Studia Gratiana*, 15 (1972), 655–671.

Racevskis, Roland. *Time and Ways of Knowing Under Louis XIV: Molière, Sévigné, Lafayette*. Lewisburg, PA: Bucknell University Press, 2003.

Raman, Bhavani. *Document Raj. Writing and Scribes in Early Colonial South India*. Chicago: University of Chicago Press, 2012.

Ramsey, G. D. "Some Tudor merchant accounts." In A. C. Littleton and Basil Yamey, eds. *Studies in the History of Accounting*. London: Sweet and Maxwell, 1956, 185–201.

Raugei, Anna Maria. "Deux collections humanistes: la bibliothèque de Thou et la bibliothèque Dupuy." In Gilles Bertrand, Anne Cayuela, Christian Del Vento, and Raphaële Mouren, eds. *Bibliothèques et lecteurs dans l'Europe moderne (XVIIe–XVIIIe siècles)*. Geneva: Droz, 2016, 225–242.

Raven, James. "Selling books across Europe, c. 1450–1800. An overview." *Publishing History*, 34 (1993), 5–19.

Raymond, Joad. *Pamphlets and Pamphleteering in Early Modern Britain*. Cambridge: Cambridge University Press, 2003.

Raymond, Joad. *The Invention of the Newspaper: English Newsbooks 1641–1649*. Oxford: Clarendon Press, 2005.

Rhodes, Neil and Jonathan Sawday, eds. *The Renaissance Computer: Knowledge Technology in the First Age of Print*. London: Routledge, 2000.

Richardson, Brian. "A scribal publisher of political information: Francesco Marcaldi." *Italian Studies*, 64.2 (2009), 296–313.

Richardson, Malcolm. "The fading influence of the medieval *ars dictaminis* in England after 1400." *Rhetorica*, 19 (2011), 225–247.

Richardson, W. C. *History of the Court of Augmentations, 1536–54*. Baton Rouge, LA: Louisiana State University Press, 1962.

Richmond, Colin. "Hand and mouth: information gathering and use in the later Middle Ages." *Journal of Historical Sociology*, 1.3 (1988), 233–252.

Rio, Alice. *Legal Practice and the Written Word in the Early Middle Ages: Frankish Formulae, c. 500–1000*. Cambridge: Cambridge University Press, 2009.

Ripa, Cesare. *Iconologia di Cesare Ripa Perugino*. Rome: Matteo Florimi, 1613.

Rivers, Kimberly. "Memory, division, and the organisation of knowledge in the Middle Ages." In Peter Binkley, ed., *Pre-modern Encyclopaedic Texts. Proceedings of the Second Comers Congress, Groningen, 1–4 July 1996*. Leiden: Brill, 1997, 147–158.

Rix, Herbert David. "The editions of Erasmus' *De Copia*." *Studies in Philology*, 43 (1946), 595–618.
Rodríguez de Diego, José Luis, ed. *Instrucción para el gobierno del Archivo de Simancas*. Madrid: Ministerio de Educación y Cultura, 1988.
Rodríguez de Diego, José Luis. "La formación del Archivo de Simancas en el siglo XVI. Función y orden interno." In María Luisa López –Vidriero, Pedro M. Cátedra, and María Isabel Hernández González, eds. *El libro antiguo español, IV. Collecionismo y bibliotecas (siglos XV–XVII)*. Salamanca: Universidad de Salamanca, 1998, 519–557.
Rodríguez de Diego, José Luis and Julia T. Rodríguez de Diego. "Un archivo no solo para el rey, significado social del proyecto simanquino en el siglo XVI." In J. Martínez Millán, ed. *Felipe II (1527–1598). Europa y la monarquía católica*. Madrid: Editorial Parteluz, 1998, 463–475.
Rodríguez, Manuel Rivero. *El Consejo de Italia y el gobierno de los dominios italianos de la monarquía hispana durante el reinado de Felipe II (1556–1598)*. Madrid: Universidad Autónoma de Madrid, 1992.
Roest, Bert. "Rhetoric of innovation and recourse to tradition in humanist pedagogical discourse." In Roest and Stephen Gersh, eds. *Medieval and Renaissance Humanism: Rhetoric, Representation and Reform*. Leiden: Brill, 2005, 115–149.
Rosenberg, Daniel. "Early modern information overload." *Journal of the History of Ideas*, 64.1 (2003), 1–9.
Rosenberg, Daniel. "Data before the fact." In Lisa Getelman, ed. *"Raw Data" is an Oxymoron*. Cambridge, MA: MIT Press, 2013, 15–40.
Roseveare, Henry. "Merchant organization and maritime trade in the North Atlantic, 1660–1815. Some reflections." In Olaf Uwe Janzen, ed. *Merchant Organization and Maritime Trade in the North Atlantic, 1660–1815*. St. John's, Canada: International Maritime Economic History Association, 1998, 259–268.
Ross, Alan. *Daum's Boys. Schools and the Republic of Letters in Early Modern Germany*. Manchester: Manchester University Press, 2015.
Rouse, Mary and Richard Rouse. "La naissance des index." In *Histoire de l'édition française*, Vol. I: *Le livre conquérant, du Moyen Âge au milieu du XVIIe siècle*. Paris: Promodis, 1982, 77–86.
Rule, John and Ben Trotter. *A World of Paper. Louis XIV, Colbert de Torcy and the Rise of the Information State*. Montreal: McGill-Queen's University Press, 2014.
Rummel, Erika. "Erasmus' manual of letter-writing: tradition and innovation." *Renaissance and Reformation*, 13 (1989), 299–312.
Ryder, Alan. "Antonio Beccadelli, a humanist in government." In C. H. Clough, ed. *Cultural Aspects of the Italian Renaissance. Essays in Honour of Paul Oskar Kristeller*. Manchester: Manchester University Press, 1976, 123–140.
Safina, Carl. *Beyond Words. What Animals Think and Feel*. New York: Henry Holt, 2015.
Saiber, Arielle. *Measured Words: Computation and Writing In Renaissance Italy*. Toronto: University of Toronto Press, 2017.
Sardella, Pierre. *Nouvelles et spéculations à Venise au début du XVIe siècle*. Paris: A. Colin, 1948.

Savary, Jacques. *Le Parfait Négociant* (1675). Ed. by Édouard Richard. Geneva: Droz, 2011.
Savelli, Rodolfo. "Giuristi francesi, biblioteche italiane. Prime note sul problema della circolazione della letteratura giuridica in età moderna." In Mario Ascheri and Gaetano Colli, eds. *Manoscritti, editoria e biblioteche dal medioevo all'età contemporanea: studi offerti a Domenico Maffei per il suo ottantesimo compleanno.* Rome: Roma del Rinascimento, 2006, 1239–1270.
Scaligero, Julio Caesare. *Aristotelis historia de animalibus; Julio Caesare Scaligero interprete.* Toulouse, 1619.
Scarton, Elisabetta. *Giovanni Lanfredini: uomo d'affari e diplomatico nell'Italia del Quattrocento.* Florence: Olschki, 2007.
Schaffer, Simon. "Newton on the beach: the information order of *Principia Mathematica.*" *History of Science*, 47 (2009), 243–276.
Schiess, Traugott. "Der Briefwechsel Heinrich Bullingers." *Zwingliana*, 5 (1933), 396–408.
Schiess, Traugott. "Ein Jahr aus Bullingers Briefwechsel (1559)." *Zwingliana*, 6 (1934), 16–33.
Schmidt, S. J. *Die Welten der Medien. Grundlagen und Perspektiven der Medienbeobachtung.* Brunswick: Vieweg, 1996.
Schmitt, W. O. "Die Ianua (Donatus): Ein Beitrag zur lateinischen Schulgrammatik des Mittelalters und der Renaissance." *Beiträge zur Inkunabelkunde, dritte Folge*, 4 (1969), 43–80.
Schulte-Albert, H. G. "Gottfried Wilhelm Leibniz and library classification." *The Journal of Library History*, 2 (1971), 133–152.
Schulz-Grobert, Jürgen. *Das Straßburger Eulenspiegelbuch: Studien zu enstehungs-geschictlichen Voraussetzungen der ältesten Drucküberlieferung.* Tübingen: De Gruyter, 1999
Schutte, Ann. "Printing, piety and the people in Italy: the first thirty years." *Archiv für Reformationsgeschichte*, 71 (1980–1), 5–19.
Schweizer, Gottfried. "From Fabriano into the heart of Europe: the transfer of the Italian art of papermaking to Germany and Austria." In Giancarlo Castagnari, ed. *L'impiego della techniche e dell'opera dei cartai Fabrianesi in Italia e in Europa: Atti delle Giornate Europee di Studio.* Fabriano: Cartiere Milani Fabriano, 2007, 379–399.
Scott, Hamish. "The rise of the first minister in eighteenth-century Europe." In Timothy Blanning and David Cannadine, eds. *History and Biography: Essays Presented to Derek Beales.* Cambridge: Cambridge University Press, 1996, 21–52.
Scott, James. *Seeing Like a State: How Certain Schemes to Improve the Human Condition Have Failed.* New Haven, CT: Yale University Press, 1998.
Scott, James. *Against the Grain. A Deep History of the Earliest States.* New Haven, CT: Yale University Press, 2017.
Scott, Tom. *Society and Economy in Germany, 1300–1600.* Basingstoke, UK: Palgrave, 2002.
Seely Brown, John, and Paul Duguid. *The Social Life of Information.* Boston: Harvard Business School Press, 2000.

Bibliography

Seifert, Arno. *Cognitio historica: die Geschichte als Namengeberin der frühneuzeitlichen Empirie*. Berlin: Duncker & Humblot, 1976.

Seneca, Lucius Annaeus. *Moral Epistles to Lucilius*, Vol. 2. Trans. and ed. by Richard Mott Gummere. Cambridge, MA: Harvard University Press, 1920.

Senatore, Francesco, ed. *Dispacci sforzeschi da Napoli*, Vol. I: *1444–2 luglio 1456*. Naples: Istituto italiano per gli studi filosofici, 1997.

Senatore, Francesco. *"Uno mundo di carta": forme e strutture della diplomazia sforzesca*. Naples: Liguori, 1998.

Senn, Matthias. *Johann Jakob Wick (1522–1588) und seine Sammlung von Nachrichten zur Zeitgschichte*. Zurich: Leemann, 1974.

Shapin, Steven. *The Scientific Revolution*. Chicago: University of Chicago Press, 1996.

Shapin Steven, and Simon Schaffer. *Leviathan and the Air Pump: Hobbes, Boyle and the Experimental Life*. Princeton, NJ: Princeton University Press, 1985.

Shapiro, Barbara. *A Culture of Fact. England 1550–1720*. Ithaca, NY: Cornell University Press, 2000.

Shaw, David. "The book trade comes of age: the sixteenth century." In Simon Eliot and Jonathan Rose, eds. *A Companion to the History of the Book*. Oxford: Blackwell, 2003, 220–231.

Sherman, Claire Richter. *Writing on Hands: Memory and Knowledge in Early Modern Europe*. Seattle: University of Washington Press, 2001.

Sherman, William. *Used Books: Marking Readers in Renaissance England*. Philadelphia: University of Pennsylvania Press, 2008.

Sherman, William. "A New World of Books: Hernando Colón and the *Biblioteca Colombina*." In Ann Blair and Anja-Silvia Goeing, eds. *For the Sake of Learning. Essays in Honor of Anthony Grafton*, Vol. I. Leiden: Brill, 2016, 404–414.

Shooner, H. V. "La production du livre per la pecia." In Louis Bataillon, Bertrand Guyot, and Richard Rouse, eds. *La production du livre universitaire au Moyen Âge*. Paris: CNRS, 1988.

Shorter, Alfred. *Paper Mills and Paper Makers in England, 1495–1800*. Hilversum: Paper Publications Society, 1957.

Signorini, Rodolfo. *Opus hoc Tenue: la camera dipinta di Andrea Mantegna: lettura storica iconografica iconologica*. Parma: Artegrafica, 1985.

Silvestri, Alessandro. "Archivi senza archivisti. I Maestri notai e la gestione delle scritture nel Regno di Sicilia (prima metà XV sec.)." In Filippo de Vivo, Andrea Guidi and Silvestri, eds. *Archivi e archivisti in Italia tra medioevo ed età moderna*. Rome: Viella, 2015, 43–69.

Silvestri, Alessandro. "Ruling from afar: government and information management in late medieval Sicily." *Journal of Medieval History*, 42.3 (2016), 357–381.

Simonetta, Marcello. *Rinascimento segreto. Il mondo del segretario da Petrarca a Machiavelli*. Milan: Franco Angeli, 2004.

Siraisi, Nancy. *Medieval and Early Renaissance Medicine. An Introduction to Knowledge and Practice*. Chicago: University of Chicago Press, 1990.

Siraisi, Nancy. *The Clock and the Mirror. Girolamo Cardano and Renaissance Medicine*. Princeton: Princeton University Press, 1997.

Slack, Paul. "Government and information in seventeenth-century England." *Past and Present*, 184 (2004), 33–68.
Slack, Paul. *The Invention of Improvement. Information and Material Progress in Seventeenth-century England*. Oxford: Oxford University Press, 2015.
Smith, Helen. "'A unique instance of art': the proliferating surfaces of early modern paper." *Journal of the Northern Renaissance*, 8 (2017), 1–39.
Smith, Pamela. "Laboratories." In Katherine Park and Lorraine Daston, eds. *The Cambridge History of Science*. Vol 3: *Early Modern Science*. Cambridge: Cambridge University Press, 2006, 291–305.
Smith, Woodruff. "The function of commercial centers in the modernization of European capitalism: Amsterdam as an information exchange in the seventeenth century." *The Journal of Economic History*, 44.4 (1984), 985–1005.
Smyth, Adam. *Autobiography in Early Modern England*. Cambridge: Cambridge University Press, 2010.
Soll, Jacob. "The hand-annotated copy of the *Histoire du gouvernement de Venise*, or how Amelot de la Houssaie wrote his history." *Bulletin du Bibliophile*, 2 (1995), 279–293.
Soll, Jacob. "Healing the body politic: French royal doctors, history and the birth of a nation 1560–1634." *Renaissance Quarterly*, 55 (2002), 1259–1286.
Soll, Jacob. "The uses of historical evidence in early modern Europe." *Journal of the History of Ideas*, 64.2 (2003), 149–157.
Soll, Jacob. "How to manage an information state: Jean-Baptiste Colbert's archives and the education of his son." *Archival Science*, 7 (2007), 331–342.
Soll, Jacob. *The Information Master: Jean Baptiste-Colbert's Secret State Intelligence System*. Ann Arbor, MI: University of Michigan Press, 2009.
Soll, Jacob. "From note-taking to data banks: personal and institutional information management in early modern Europe." *Intellectual History Review*, 20.3 (2010), 355–375.
Soll, Jacob. "Accounting and accountability in Dutch civic life." In Margaret Jacob and Catherine Secretan, eds. *In Praise of Ordinary People. Early Modern Britain and the Dutch Republic*. New York: Palgrave Macmillan, 2013, 123–137.
Soll, Jacob. *The Reckoning. Financial Accountability and the Rise and Fall of Nations*. New York: Basic Books, 2014.
Soll, Jacob. "Jean-Baptiste Colbert, accounting, and the genesis of the state archive in early modern France." In Liesbeth Corens, Kate Peters, and Alexandra Walsham, eds. *Archives and Information in the Early Modern World*. Proceedings of the British Academy 212. Oxford: Oxford University Press, 2018, 87–101.
Sombart, Werner. *Der moderne Kapitalismus*, Vol. II, Part I. Leipzig: Duncker & Humblot, 1916.
Somerville, C. John. *The News Revolution in England: Cultural Dynamics of Daily Information*. Oxford: Oxford University Press, 1996.
Sowards, J. K. "Erasmus and the apologetic textbook: a study of the '*De Duplici Copia Verborum ac Rerum*.'" *Studies in Philology*, 55.2 (1958), 122–135.
Spallanzani, Marco. *Mercanti fiorentini nell'Asia portoghese (1500–1525)*. Florence, Edizioni SPES, 1997.

Sprat, Thomas. *History of the Royal Society* (1667). Ed. by Jackson Cope and Harold Whitmore. St. Louis, MO: Washington University Press, 1956.

Spufford, Peter. "Late medieval merchants' notebooks: a project; their potential for the history of banking." In Markus Denzel, Jean Claude Hicquet, and Harald Witthöft, eds. *Kaufmannsbücher und Handelspraktiken vom Spätmittelalter bis zum beginnenden 20. Jahrhundert*. Stuttgart: Franz Steiner, 2002, 47–62.

Stallybrass, Peter "Books and scrolls: navigating the Bible." In Jennifer Andersen and Elizabeth Sauer, eds. *Books and Readers in Early. Modern England: Material Studies*. Philadelphia: University of Pennsylvania Press, 2002, 42–79.

Stallybrass, Peter. "Little jobs. Broadsides and the printing revolution." In Sabrina Alcorn, Eric Lindquist, and Eleanor Shevlin, eds. *Agent of Change: Print Culture Studies after Elizabeth Eisenstein*. Amherst, MA: University of Massachusetts Press, 2007, 315–341.

Stallybrass, Peter. "Printing and the manuscript revolution." In Barbie Zelizer, ed., *Explorations in Communication and History*. New York: Routledge, 2008, 111–118.

Stallybrass, Peter, Heather Wolfe, Roger Chartier, and J. Franklin Mowery. "Hamlet's tables and the technologies of writing in Renaissance England." *Shakespeare Quarterly*, 55.4 (2004), 379–419.

Steinberg, Justin. *Accounting for Dante: Urban Readers and Writers in Late Medieval Italy*. South Bend, IN: University of Notre Dame Press, 2007.

Steinberg, Sigfrid Henry. *Five Hundred Years of Printing*. New York: Penguin, 1974.

Sternberg, Giora. "Manipulating information in the Ancien Régime: ceremonial records, aristocratic strategies, and the limits of the state perspective." *Journal of Modern History*, 85 (2013), 239–279.

Stevens, Kevin. "Vincenzo Girardone and the popular press in Counter-reformation Milan: a case study (1570)." *Sixteenth-Century Journal*, 26.3 (1995), 639–659.

Stevenson, Allan. "Briquet and the future of paper studies." In E. J. Labarre, ed. *Briquet's Opuscula*. Hilversum, Netherlands: Paper Publications Society, 1955, xv–l.

Stevin, Simon. *Disme: The Art of Tenths, or Decimall Arithmetike*. Trans. by Richard Norton. London, 1608.

Stock, Brian. *The Implication of Literacy: Written Language and Models of Interpretation in the Eleventh and Twelfth Centuries*. Princeton, NJ: Princeton University Press, 1983.

Stolberg, Michael. "John Locke's 'new method of making common-place books': tradition, innovation and epistemic effects." *Science and Medicine*, 19 (2014), 448–470.

Stolzenberg, Daniel. "A spanner and his works: books, letters, and scholarly communications networks in early modern Europe." In Ann Blair and Anja-Silvia Goeing, eds. *For the Sake of Learning. Essays in Honor of Anthony Grafton*, Vol. I. Leiden: Brill, 2016, 157–172.

Strauss, Felix. "The 'Libcrey' of Duke Ernst of Bavaria (1500–1560)." *Studies in the Renaissance*, 8 (1961), 128–143.

Stromer, Wolfgang von. "Das Handelshaus der Stromer von Nürnberg und die Geschichte der ersten deutschen Papiermühle." *Vierteljahrschrift für Sozial und Wirtschaftsgeschichte*, 47 (1960), 81–104.

Stromer, Wolfgang von and Lore Sporhan-Krempel. "Die Papierwirtschaft der Nürnberger Kanzlei und die Geschichte der Papiermacherei im Gebiet der Reichsstadt bis zum Beginn des 30 jährigen Krieges." *Archiv für Geschichte des Buchwesens*, 2 (1958), 161–169.

Struik, Dirk. *The Land of Stevin and Huygens. A Sketch of Science and Technology in the Dutch Republic during the Golden Century.* Dordrecht: D. Reidel, 1981.

Studer, Paul. *Le Mystère d'Adam: An Anglo-Norman Drama of the Twelfth Century.* Manchester: Manchester University Press, 1949.

Studt, Birgit. *Haus- und Familienbücher in der städtischen Gesellschaft des Spätmittelalters und der Frühen Neuzeit.* Cologne: Böhlau, 2007.

Summit, Jennifer. *Memory's Library: Medieval Books in Early Modern England.* Chicago: University of Chicago Press, 2011.

Svenonius, Elaine. *The Intellectual Foundation of Information Organization.* Cambridge, MA: MIT Press, 2000.

Sydserf, Thomas. *Tarugo's Wiles, or the Coffee House. A Comedy. As it was acted in his Highness's The Duke of York's Theatre.* London: Henry Herringman, 1668.

Synghel, Geertrui van. "The use of records in medieval towns: The case of 's-Hertogenbosch (Brabant)." In Marco Mostert and Anna Adamska, eds. *Writing and the Administration of Medieval Towns.* Turnhout: Brepols, 2014, 31–47.

Tavoni, Maria Gioia. *Circumnavigare il testo. Gli indici in età moderna.* Naples: Liguori, 2009.

Taylor, John. "Letters and letter collections in England." *Nottingham Medieval Studies*, 24 (1979), 57–70.

Te Heesen, Anke. "The notebook: a paper technology." In Bruno Latour and Peter Weibel, eds. *Making Things Public: Atmospheres of Democracy.* Cambridge, MA: MIT Press, 2005, 582–589.

Tesauro, Emanuele. *Dell'arte delle lettere missiue del conte, e caualier Gran Croce D. Emanuele Tesauro.* Venice: Paolo Baglioni, 1674.

Thomas, Keith. "The meaning of literacy in early modern England." In Gerd Baumann, ed., *The Written Word: Literacy in Transition.* Oxford: Clarendon, 1986, 97–131.

Thompson, John. *The Coevolutionary Process.* Chicago: University of Chicago Press, 1994.

Thompson, Susan "Paper manufacturing and early books." In Madeleine Pelner Cosman and Bruce Chandler, eds. *Machaut's World: Science and Art in the Fourteenth Century.* Annals of the New York Academy of Sciences, 314. New York: New York Academy of Sciences, 1978, 167–174.

Thomson, Erik. "Swedish variations on Dutch commercial institutions, practices and discourse, 1605–1655." *Scandinavian Studies*, 77.3 (2005), 331–346.

Thomson, Erik. "For a comparative history of early modern diplomacy. Commerce and French and Swedish emissarial cultures during the early 17th century." *Scandinavian Journal of History*, 31.2 (2006), 151–172.

Thomson, Erik. "Axel Oxenstierna and Swedish diplomacy in the seventeenth century." In Paul Dover, ed. *Secretaries and Statecraft in the Early Modern World.* Edinburgh: Edinburgh University Press, 2016, 140–154.

Thornton, Dora. *The Scholar in His Study: Ownership and Experience in Renaissance Italy*. New Haven, CT: Yale University Press, 1997.
Tilly, Charles. *Coercion, Capital, and European States, AD 990–1992*. Cambridge, MA: Blackwell, 1992.
Trapp, Joseph B. *Manuscripts in the Fifty Years after the Invention of Printing*. London: Warburg Institute, 1983.
Tsuen-Hsuin, Tsien. *Paper and Printing*, Vol. 5, Part 2 of *Science and Civilisation in China*, ed. Joseph Needham. Cambridge: Cambridge University Press, 1985.
Tucci, Ugo. "Manuali di mercatura e pratica degli affari del Medioevo." In Carlo Cipolla and Roberto López, eds. *Fatti e idee di storia economica nei secoli XII–XX*. Bologna: Mulino, 1977, 215–231.
Turchi, Laura. "Storia della diplomazia e fonti estensi: note a margine." *Quaderni Estensi. Rivista online degli Istituti culturali estensi*, 6 (2014), 368–395.
Tyson, Gerald and Sylvia Wagonheim, eds. *Print and Culture in the Renaissance: Essays on the Advent of Printing in Europe*. Newark, DE: University of Delaware Press, 1986.
Valenti, Filippo. *Scritti e lezioni di archivistica, diplomatica a storia istituzionale*. Rome: Ministero per i beni e le attività culturali, ufficio centrale per i beni archivistici, 2000.
Valiente, Francisco Tomás. *Los validos en la monarquía española del siglo XVII*. Madrid: Istituto de Estudios Políticos, 1963.
Van Vliet, Rietje. "Print and public in Europe 1600–1800." In Simon Eliot and Jonathan Rose, eds. *A Companion to the History of the Book*. Oxford: Blackwell, 2003, 247–257.
Varanini, Gian Maria. "Public written records." In Andrea Gamberini and Isabella Lazzarini, eds. *The Italian Renaissance State*. Oxford: Oxford University Press, 2012, 385–405.
Velten, Hans-Rudolf. *Das selbst geschriebene Leben. Eine Studie zur deutschen Autobiographie im 16. Jahrhundert*. Heidelberg: Winter, 1995.
Ventura, Comino. *Tesoro politico in cui si contengono Relationi, Istruttioni, Trattati, & varii Discorsi, pertinenti alla perfetta intelligenza della ragion di stato*. Vicenza: Giorgio Greco, 1602.
Ventura, Iolanda. "Changing representations of botany in encyclopaedias from the Middle Ages to the Renaissance." In Anja-Silvia Goeing, Anthony Grafton, and Paul Michel, eds. *Collector's Knowledge: What is Kept, What is Discarded = Aufbewahren oder wegwerfen – Wie Sammler entscheiden*. Leiden: Brill, 2013, 97–143.
Verdon, Jean. *Information et désinformation au Moyen Âge*. Paris: Perrin, 2010.
Vermeij, Geerat. *The Evolutionary World: How Adaptation Explains Everything from Seashells to Civilization*. New York: Thomas Dunne, 2010.
Vickers, Brian, ed. *Francis Bacon: The Major Works*. Oxford: Oxford University Press, 1996.
Villani, Pasquale, ed. *Dispacci di Antonio Giustinian, ambasciatore veneto in Roma dal 1502 al 1505*. Florence: Successori le Monnier, 1876.
Vine, Angus. "Commercial commonplacing: Francis Bacon, the waste-book, and the ledger." In Richard Beadle, Peter Beal, and Colin Burrow, eds. *Manuscript Miscellanies, c. 1450–1700*. London: British Library, 2011, 197–218.

Vismann, Cornelia. *Files: Law and Media Technology*. Trans. by Geoffrey Winthrop-Young. Stanford: Stanford University Press, 2008.
Voet, Léon. *The Golden Compasses: A History and Evaluation of the Printing and Publishing Activities of the* Officina Plantiniana *at Antwerp*, Vol. 1. Amsterdam: Van Gendt, 1969.
Vossius, Gerard. *Gerardi Joan. Vossii et Clarorum Virorum ad Eum Epistolae*. Augsburg: Sumptibus Laurentii Kronigeri, 1691.
Wacquet, Françoise. "Qu'est-ce que la République des Lettres? Essai de semantique historique." *Bibliothèque de l'École de Chartres*, 147 (1989), 473–502.
Wagner, Klaus. *La biblioteca colombina en tiempos de Hernando Colón*. Seville: Universidad de Sevilla, 1992.
Wahrman, Dror. *Mr. Collier's Letter Racks: A Tale of Art and Illusion at the Threshold of the Modern Information Age*. Oxford: Oxford University Press, 2012.
Watkins, Owen. *The Puritan Experience: Studies in Spiritual Experience*. New York: Schocken Books, 1972.
Watson, Thomas. *The Christian Soldier: Or, Heaven Taken by Storm*. London: Thomas Parkhurst, 1669.
Watt, Tessa. *Cheap Print and Popular Piety*. Cambridge: Cambridge University Press, 1991.
Watts, John. *The Making of Polities. Europe 1300–1500*. Cambridge: Cambridge University Press, 2009.
Weber, Johannes. "Strassburg, 1605: The origins of the newspaper in Europe." *German History*, 24.3 (2006), 387–412.
Webster, Tom. "Writing to redundancy: approaches to spiritual journals and early modern spirituality." *The Historical Journal*, 39.1 (1996), 33–46.
Weidhaas, Peter. *A History of the Frankfurt Book Fair*. Trans. and ed. by Carolyn Gossage and W. Aldis Wright. Toronto: Dundurn Press, 2007.
Weinberger, David. *Too Big to Know. Rethinking Knowledge Now That Facts Aren't Facts, Experts are Everywhere, and the Smartest Person in the Room is the Room*. New York: Basic Books, 2011.
Weiss, Wisso. *Zeittafel Zur Papiergeschichte*. Leipzig: Fachbuchverlag, 1983.
Weitenauer, Ignatius. *De modo legendi et excerpendi libri II*. Augsburg: Ignatius Eagner, 1775.
Weld, Kirsten. *Paper Cadavers. The Archives of Dictatorship in Guatemala*. Durham, NC: Duke University Press, 2014.
Wellisch, Hans. "How to make an index – 16th century style: Conrad Gessner on Indexes and Catalogs." *International Classification*, 8.1 (1981), 10–15.
Wennerlind, Carl. *Casualties of Credit: the English Financial Revolution, 1620–1720*. Cambridge, MA: Harvard University Press, 2011.
Wenzel, Horst, Wilfried Seipel and Gotthard Wunberg, eds. *Die Verschriftlichung der Welt: Text und Zahl in der Kultur des Mittelalters und der frühen Neuzeit*. Vienna: Kunsthistorisches Museum/Skira, 2000.
West, William. *Theatres and Encyclopedia in Early Modern Europe*. Cambridge: Cambridge University Press, 2002.

Wheatley, Chloe. "The pocket books of early modern history." In Henry Turner, ed. *The Culture of Capital. Property, Cities and Knowledge in Early Modern England.* London: Routledge, 2002, 183–202.
Wheatley, Henry B. *How to Make an Index.* London: Eliot Stock, 1902.
Whyman, Susan. *Sociability and Power in Late-Stuart England. The Cultural Worlds of the Verneys, 1660–1720.* Oxford: Oxford University Press, 1999.
Wiedenhofer, Siegfried. *Formalstrukturen humanistischer und reformatorischer Theologie bei Philipp Melanchthon*, Vol. 1. Bern: Lang, 1976.
Wijnum, J. O. *The Role of Accounting in the Economic Development of England, 1500–1750.* Urbana, IL: Center for International Education and Research in Accounting, 1972.
Wilding, Nick. "Manuscripts in motion: the diffusion of Galilean Copernicanism." *Italian Studies*, 66.2 (2011), 221–233.
Williams, Megan. "The Apothecary, the Secretary, and the Diplomat: Apothecaries as Purveyors of Paper, Ink, and Information." Paper delivered as part of the panel, "Paper as a Material Artifact of Governance and Trade, 1500–1800," Renaissance Society of America Annual Convention, Berlin, March 26–28, 2015.
Williams, Megan. "Unfolding diplomatic paper and paper practices in early modern chancery archives." In Arndt Brendecke, ed., *Praktiken der Frühen Neuzeit. Aktuere, Handlungen, Artefakte.* Cologne: Böhlau Verlag, 2015, 496–508.
Williams, Megan. "'Zu Notdurff der Scheiberey.' Die Einrichtung der frühneuzeitlichen Kanzlei.'" In Dagmar Freist, ed. *Duskurse – Körper – Artefakte. Historische Prazeologie in der Frühneuzeitforschung.* Bielefeld: Transcript Verlag, 2015, 335–372.
Williams, Megan. "'This continuous writing': the paper chancellery of Bernhard Cles." In Paul Dover, ed. *Secretaries and Statecraft in the Early Modern World.* Edinburgh: Edinburgh University Press, 2016, 63–89.
Wilson-Lee, Edward. *The Catalogue of Shipwrecked Books. Christopher Columbus, His Son, and the Quest to Build the World's Greatest Library.* New York: Scribner, 2019.
Wolfe, Heather and Peter Stallybrass. "The material culture of record-keeping in early modern England." In Liesbeth Corens, Kate Peters, and Alexandra Walsham, eds. *Archives and Information in the Early Modern World.* Proceedings of the British Academy 212. Oxford: Oxford University Press, 2018, 179–208.
Wolfe, Heather and Alan Stewart. *Letterwriting in Renaissance England.* Washington, DC: The Folger Shakespeare Library, 2004.
Woolf, Daniel. "Speech, text and time: the sense of hearing and the sense of the past in Renaissance England." *Albion*, 18.2 (1986), 159–193.
Wootton, David. *The Invention of Science.* London: Allen Lane, 2015.
Wright, Alex. *Glut. Mastering Information through the Ages.* Washington, DC: Joseph Henry Press, 2007.
Wu, Tim. *The Master Switch. The Rise and Fall of Information Empires.* New York: Vintage, 2010.
Xivrey, Berger de, ed. *Collection de documents inédits sur l'histoire de France: Recueil des lettres missives de Henri IV.* 9 Vols. Paris: Imprimerie Royale, 1843–1858.

Yale, Elizabeth. "With slips and scraps: how early modern naturalists invented the archive." *Book History*, 12 (2009), 1–36.
Yale, Elizabeth. "Marginalia, commonplaces, and correspondence: scribal exchange in early modern science." *Studies in History and Philosophy of Biological Biomedical Sciences*, 42 (2011), 193–202.
Yale, Elizabeth. "The history of archives: the state of the discipline." *Book History*, 18 (2015), 332–259.
Yale, Elizabeth. "The book and the archive in the history of science." *Isis*, 107.1 (2016), 106–115.
Yale, Elizabeth. *Sociable Knowledge. Natural History and the Nation in Early Modern Britain*. Philadelphia: University of Pennsylvania Press, 2016.
Yamey, Basil. "The functional development of double-entry bookkeeping." *The Accountant*, 103 (1940), 333–342.
Yamey, Basil. "Notes on the origin of double-entry bookkeeping." *The Accounting Review*, 22.3 (1947), 263–272.
Yamey, Basil. "Oldcastle, Peele and Melis: a case of plagiarism in the sixteenth century." *Accounting and Business Research*, 9.35 (1963), 209–216.
Yax, Maggie. "Arthur Agarde, Elizabethan archivist: his contributions to the evolution of archival practice." *American Archivist*, 61 (1998), 56–69.
Yeo, Richard. "Between memory and paperbooks: Baconianism and natural history in seventeenth-century England." *History of Science*, 45 (2007), 1–46.
Yeo, Richard. *Notebooks, Virtuosi, and Early Modern Science*. Chicago: University of Chicago Press, 2014.
Zaar-Görgens, Maria. *Champagne, Bar, Lothringen. Papierproduktion und Papierabsatz vom 14. bis zum Ende des 16. Jahrhunderts*. Trier: Porta Alba, 2004.
Zawrel, Sandra. "Papierhandel im Europa der Frühen Neuzeit: Ein Forschungsbericht." *Jahrburch für Kommunikationsgeschichte*, 19 (2017), 98–120.
Zedelmaier, Helmut. "Johann Jakob Moser et l'organisation érudite du savoir a l'époque moderne." In Élisabeth Décultot, ed. *Lire, copier, écrire: les bibliothèques et leurs usages au XVIIIe siècle*. Paris: CNRS, 2003, 43–62.
Zedelmaier, Helmut. "Wissensordnungen der Frühen Neuzeit." In Ranier Schützeichel, ed. *Handbuch Wissenssoziologie und Wissensforschung*. Constance: UVK Verlagsgesellschaft, 2007, 835–845.
Zedelmaier, Helmut. "Suchen und Finden vor Google: Zur Metadatenproduktion im 16. Jahrhundert." In Ann Blair and Anja-Silvia Goeing, eds. *For the Sake of Learning. Essays in Honor of Anthony Grafton*, Vol. I. Leiden: Brill, 2016, 423–440.
Zorzi, Marino. "La circolazione del libro a Venezia nel Cinquecento. Biblioteche private e pubbliche." *Ateneo Veneto*, 177 (1990), 155–163.
Zucchi, Bartolomeo. *L'idea del segretario dal signore Bartolomeo Zucchi da Monza. Rappresentata in un Trattato de l'Imitatione, e ne le lettere di Principi, e d'altri Signori*. Venice: Compagnia Minima, 1600.

Index

Abbasid Caliphate, 25, 43–44
Abelard, Peter, 27
Acccademia dei Lincei (Rome), 204
account books, 19, 38, 56, 60–64, 81, 83, 84, 87, 131, 243, 261, 267, 278
accounting, 32, 53, 59, 62, 63, 66, 86, 89, 144, 209, 214, 242, 244
Acosta, José de, 200
Acta eruditorum, 166
Adagia (Erasmus), 161
Admonition to Christendom against the Turks, 157
Adriaensz, Job (painting), 74
adversaria. *See* waste-books
advertising, 74
Aelius Donatus, 157
Agricola, Rudolf, 213
Aix-en-Provence, 253
al Rashid, Harun, 43
Alberti, Leon Batista, 59
Albizzi, Girolamo, 185
Albrecht V, Duke of Bavaria, 171
Alcalá, 124
Aldrovandi, Ulisse, 34, 78, 205, 208, 214–15, 233
Alexander VI, Pope, 182
Alfonso II d'Este, Duke of Ferrara, 102
Alfonso X, King of Castile, 51, 96
Allison, Rayne, 111
almanacs, 26, 161, 185–86, 237, 281
alphabetization, 5, 6, 7, 33–34, 177, 178
Americas, 124–27
amicitia, 227, 231
Amsterdam, 74, 75, 76, 164, 255
  bourse, 74
anatomy, 80, 166
Anatomy of Melancholy (Burton), 27, 244
annotations. *See* marginalia
antiquaries, 224, 234, 242
Antwerp, 52, 70, 71, 73, 163, 164, 205, 247, 275
  bourse, 73

Apian, Peter, 183
Apian, Philipp, 183
apothecaries, 54, 258, 260
Appuhn, Karl, 82
Aquilon, Pierre, 174
archives, 13, 19, 20, 22, 28, 29, 44, 93, 96, 97, 100, 101, 109, 110, 130–41, 145, 146, 208, 209, 210, 222, 226, 242, 244, 249, 276, 280, 281
  access, 139–40
  ambassadorial, 120
  centralization, 140
  finding aids, 139
  means of storage, 137
  Registraturen, 139
  scientific, 222–23
  types of documents, 131, 134
Aristotle, 7, 27, 166, 194, 195, 196, 205, 208, 219
armies, 95
ars dictaminis, 227, 229
ars memoria, 6, 12, 211
Ars Minor (Aelius Donatus), 157
Artifoni, Enrico, 96
Ashmolean Museum, 224
Aston, Margaret, 188
astronomy, 166, 199, 202, 224, 234
Athenian Gazette, 259
Aubrey, John, 223
Augsburg, 65, 70, 157, 175, 276
Aurifodina artium et scientiarum omnium excerpendi sollertia (Drexel), 213
Austrian Court Chancery, 110
Austrian National Library, 70
Avignon, 57, 62, 95
Avisenschreiber, 249
avisi, 71, 72, 172, 245, 249, 250, 258
Ayala, Diego de, 135

Bacon, Francis, 6, 21, 31, 40, 77, 81–82, 123, 192, 193, 195, 198

331

Index

Baghdad, 44, 45
  sack of (1258), 45
Baillet, Adrien, 232
Ball, Philip, 264
Barcelona, 98
Barisoni, Albertino, 138
Bartoli Langeli, Attilio, 99
Basel, 156, 163
Bauhin, Caspar, 205
Bautier, R.H., 131
Beale, Robert, 122
Becker, Peter, 137
Benedetto (Tuscan peasant), 243
Benedictine Order, 153, 156
Berne, 275
Beza, Theodore, 275
Bianchini, Giovanni Battista, 174
Biblioteca Colombina, 176–77
Bibliotheca universalis (Gessner), 33, 172, 177–78
Bibliothèque française (De la Croix du Maine and Du Verdier), 179
Bibliothèque Mazarine, 178–79
Bibliothèque Méjanes (Aix-en-Provence), 253
bills of exchange, 59
Blackwood, Christopher, 4, 42
Blair, Ann, 2, 211, 220
Blarer, Ambrosius, 275
Bloch, Marc, 262
Bloom, Jonathan, 44
Bock, Jerome, 204
Bodin, Jean, 123, 221
Bodleian Library (Oxford), 180
Boerhaave, Herman, 197
Bologna, 53, 78, 208
Bonet, Théophile, 218
Bonifacio, Baldassare, 138
book fairs, 162–63
Book of the Martyrs (Foxe), 33
books of hours, 154, 164, 165
booksellers, 162, 163, 164–65, 176, 185
Borkenau, Franz, 83
Borromeo, Carlo, Archbishop, 239
Boswell, James, 279
botany, 80, 166, 197, 202, 203–5
  New World, 205
Botero, Giovanni, 123
Boutier, Jean, 143, 144
Boyle, Robert, 78, 219, 234, 235
Braudel, Fernand, 142
Brendecke, Arndt, 135, 147
Brescia, 78

Briefe Instruction and Maner How to Keepe Bookes of Accompts after the Order of Debitor and Creditor (Melis), 61, 66
Briefzeitung, 249
British East India Company (EIC), 79, 85, 87–89, 228
broadsides, 155, 161
Brooks, C.W., 187
Brown, John Seely, 281
Brown, Thomas, 75
Bruges, 48, 249
Brussels, 134, 247
Buckingham, Duke of (George Villiers), 105
Budapest, 250
Bullard, Melissa, 116
Bullinger, Heinrich, 182, 273–277, 278
Bullinger-Zeitungen, 276
bureaucracy, 22, 30, 92, 127, 145, 146
Burghley, William, Lord Cecil, 122
Burke, Peter, 91, 120
Burling, Robbins, 269
Burton, Robert, 27
business press, 70–77
business records, 77
Butterfield, Herbert, 10

cabinets of curiosities, 28
Cabrera de Córdoba, Luis, 129
Caizzi, Bruno, 245
Calais, 247
calendars, 156, 237
Calvin, John, 230, 274, 275
Cambridge, 279
Cambridge, University of, 175, 186
Camerarius, Joachim, 276
Camers, Johannes, 182
Camillo, Giulio, 6
Campanella, Tommaso, 191
Capaccio, Giulio Cesare, 103, 120
capitalism and information, 56
Capra, Carlo, 92
Cardano, Girolamo, 217
Carolingian Renaissance, 161
Carpi, Jacopo Berengario da, 197
Carruthers, Mary, 12
Casale, Giambattista, 239
Casaubon, Isaac, 172, 212
Cassini, Giovanni Domenico, 235
Castañeda, Juan de, 204
catasto (Florence), 121, 240
Catologi triennales (Society of Jesus), 86
Causabon, Meric, 267
Cavalli, Marino, 110, 120
Cecil, Robert, Earl of Salisbury, 130

Index

censorship, 165, 188
censuses, 26, 106, 120, 121, 123, 281
Certeau, Michel de, 266
Cerutti, Angelo, 258
Cesalpino, Andrea, 205
chanceries, 19, 30, 46, 95, 96, 97, 98, 99, 101, 107, 109, 110, 112, 114, 116, 119, 120, 134
chapbooks, 154
Chappe, Paulinus, 156
Charles II, King of England, 259
Charles V, Holy Roman Emperor, 105, 117, 124, 129, 134, 135, 143, 176, 246
Chartier, Roger, 1, 108, 154, 180
China
 Sui Dynasty, 43
 Tang Dynasty, 43
Chur, 275
Cicero, Marcus Tullius, 161, 201, 229
Cistercian Order, 174
Clanchy, Michael, 13, 94
Clark, William, 137
Clavius, Christoph, 85
Clerselier, Claude, 233
Cles, Bernhard, 110
Cluniac Order, 153
Clusius, Carolus, 200, 204–5
codex Orient 298 (Leiden), 46
Codogno, Ottavio, 23
coevolution of paper and people, 4
coffee houses, 76, 194, 259–60
Colbert de Torcy, Jean-Baptiste, 145
Colbert, Jean-Baptiste, 83, 140, 144–45
 Mélanges Colbert, 144
Colbert, Jean-Baptiste the Younger, Marquis of Torcy, 118
Cologne, 70, 156, 242, 247, 250, 254
Colón, Hernando, 176–77
Colón, Luis, 176
Columbus, Christopher, 176
commercial information centers, 77
commodity price lists, 60, 71, 73, 74, 76, 82, 83, 88, 190, 259
Common Core standards, 269
commonplacing, 19, 22, 29, 30, 34, 37, 81, 177, 178, 198, 199, 209, 212, 214, 215–19, 220, 222, 229, 237, 238, 252, 267
Communications Revolution, 2, 245
Compagni, Dino, 59
Compton Census (1676), 123
Conservatoria (Sicily), 98
Consiglio Segreto (Milan), 119
Constance, 275
consultas (Philip II), 128, 129

contracts, 57
Contradicentium medicorum (Cardano), 217
Conversations on the Plurality of Worlds (Fontenelle), 226, 264
Cook, Harold, 80
Copernicus, Nicolaus, 183, 199
copia, 29–30, 31, 37, 205, 208, 226, 265, 277, 278, 280, 281, 283
Coronelli, Vincenzo, 185
corrantoes, 155, 245
Correspondence Revolution, 2
Coryatt, Thomas, 163
Cotrugli, Benedetto, 65
Council of State (Spain), 105
Council of the Indies (Spain), 126, 130
Council of War (Spain), 130
Courante uyt italien, duytsland, etc., 255
Court documents, 16–17
Cowley, Abraham, 195
Cranach, Lucas, 166
crisis of classification, 31
Croissy, Marquis de (Charles Colbert), 145
Cromwell, Thomas, 122, 135
culture of collection, 27–28, 29, 30, 80
curiosity, 219, 263–65
Czaja, Karin, 240

Daily Courant, 256
Darnton, Robert, 7
Daston, Lorraine, 195, 219
data, 192, 193, 194, 196, 202, 209, 211, 213, 219–20, 221, 222, 226, 233, 264
Datini, Francesco, 57, 62, 64
Daum, Christian, 236–37
Davidson, Cathy, 281
Davies, Joan, 176
De archivis (Bonifacio), 138
De archivis commentarius (Barisoni), 138
De arte excerpendi (Placcius), 213
De augmentis (Bacon), 198
De Biasi, Pierre-Marc, 39
De Caix, Honoré, 117
De copia verborum (Erasmus), 15, 29, 281
De dissectione partium corporis humani (Estienne), 201
De humani corporis fabrica (Galen), 199
De la Croix Du Maine, François, 179
De magnete (Gilbert), 192
De modo legendi et excerpendi (Weitenauer), 280
De ratione libros cum profectu legendi libellus (Sacchini), 213
De remediis utriusque fortunae (Petrarch), 272
De revolutionibus orbium coelestium (Copernicus), 183, 199

De Roover, Raymond, 64
De Sallo, Denis, 165
De Thou, Jacque-Auguste, 173
De Vera, Juan Antonio (Spanish ambassador in Venice), 72
De Vives, Juan, 213
De Vivo, Filippo, 14, 131, 258
De Vries, Jan, 75
Decades (Bullinger), 275
Defoe, Daniel, 72
Dei difetti della giurisprudenza (Muratori), 174
Del secretario (Sansovino), 102
Del segretario (Persico), 118
Dell'arte delle lettere missive (Tesauro), 142
Della famiglia (Alberti), 59
Derrida, Jacques, 132
Dery, David, 93
Descartes, René, 77, 198, 232, 233
description, 106, 192, 196, 202–8, 217, 219, 225, 231, 235, 241
Dewerpe, Alain, 144
diaries, 214, 218, 237, 261, 278
dichotomous classification, 221
Diderot, Denis, 6
dietaris, 239
Digges, Leonard, 185
digital information, 6, 7, 36, 154, 190, 263
Digital Revolution, 267–71, 282
Dioscorides, Pedanius, 203, 204, 205
diplomacy, 95, 97, 98, 99, 104, 111, 112–20, 249
 correspondence, 114
 resident, 118
diplomats, 77, 91, 93, 104, 111, 112–20, 176, 235, 245, 249
Discourse Touching the Office of the Principal Secretary of Estate (Walsingham), 138
Dissolution of the monasteries (England), 135
Divine Comedy (Dante), 182
doctors, 171, 175, 197, 201–2, 209, 213, 217, 234
Document Raj (EIC), 89
Donne, John, 184
Dooley, Brian, 257
double-entry bookkeeping, 59, 62, 63, 64–67, 79, 82, 83, 86
Dover, 247
Down Survey of Ireland, 123
Drexel, Jeremias, 42, 211, 213
Du Verdier, Antoine, 179
Dufay, Charles François de Cisternay, 219
Duguid, Paul, 281
Dunhuang hoard, 43

Dunton, John, 259
Dutch East India Company (VOC), 67, 74, 75, 76, 77, 81, 85, 228
Dutch Revolt, 253

ebooks, 270
Eco, Umberto, 269
ego-documents, 20, 237–44, 261, 278
 spiritual, 239
Einkommende Zeitungen, 256
Eisenstein, Elizabeth, 24, 26, 152, 161, 189
Elizabeth I, Queen of England, 111, 122, 130, 136, 138
empiricism, 79–82, 124, 147, 194, 195, 197, 198, 199, 201, 202, 219, 222, 231
encyclopedias, 28, 34, 207, 208, 214, 232, 267, 281
Encyclopédie (Diderot), 6
Engelsing, Rolf, 166
England's View in the Unmasking of Two Paradoxes (Malynes), 123
English Civil War, 165, 253, 255
English medieval government, 13, 94, 95
Epicurean Philosophy (Hill), 185
Erasmus, Desiderius, 15, 29, 151, 161, 163, 181, 215, 229, 230, 281
Erfurt, 156
Escorial, 142
Esquivel, Pedro de, 124
Este family, 249
Estienne, Charles, 201
Estienne, Henri, 33, 150, 163
Estienne, Robert, 32
Euclid, 79
Evelyn, John, 195
experience, 194, 195, 196–97, 199–202, 264
experiment, 31, 192, 193, 194, 197, 198, 202, 209, 212, 217, 219, 222, 225

Fabriano, 48
facts, 7, 9–10, 194, 217, 218–20, 226, 234, 265
Fajardo, Diego de Saavedra, 87
family books, 20, 239–42, 244
Faunt, Nicholas, 138
Favorites, royal, 105
Febvre, Lucien, 12, 174
Ferdinand I, Archduke of Austria, King of Bohemia, Holy Roman Emperor, 110
Ferdinand I, King of Aragon, 98
Ferdinand II, Archduke of Tyrol, 139
Ferdinand II, King of Aragon and Castile, 117
Ferrara, 98, 119

Index

Ferrara, University of, 175
financial manuals, 61–62
Findlen, Paula, 207
Florence, 98, 115, 117, 121, 136, 240
Flori, Ludovico, 86
florilegia, 27
Flugschriften, 159, 160, 275
Foisil, Madeleine, 237
Fontenelle, Bernard le Bovier de, 226, 264
Foucault, Michel, 132
Foxe, Matthew, 33
Francis I, King of France, 117
Frankfurt, 74, 151, 247, 254, 255
Frankfurt Book Fair, 27, 150, 163, 172, 177
Franzesi, Matteo, 260
Frederick II, Holy Roman Emperor, 51
Freising, 156
French foreign ministry, 145
French Wars of Religion, 117, 248
Friedrich, Markus, 3
Frigo, Daniela, 118
Froben, Johann, 163
Fronde, 179, 256
Froschauer, Christoph, 163, 177
Fuchs, Leonhard, 166
Fuenteovejuna (Lope de Vega), 168
Fugger bank, 59, 65
Fugger, Ernst, 171
Fugger, Johann Jakob, 171
Fugger-Zeitungen, 276
Fuller, Thomas, 33

Galen (Aelius Galenus), 166, 197, 199
Galilei, Galileo, 78, 151, 166, 172, 188, 200
gardens, 28, 80, 205
Garzoni, Tommaso, 41, 149
Gassendi, Pierre, 210
Gasser, Achilles Pirmin, 175
Gavard, Claude, 96
Gazette de France, 255
Geisecke, Michael, 156
Generaltabellen (Prussia), 127
Geneva, 218, 275
Geneva Bible (1560), 33
Geniza documents, 45
Genoa, 47, 59, 64, 117
Gessner, Conrad, 33, 166, 172, 177–78, 200, 215, 232
gift-giving, 235
Gilbert, William, 192
Gingerich, Owen, 183
Giornale dei letterati, 165
Girardone, Vincenzo, 162
Giunti publisher, 164
Giustinian, Antonio, 116

Glorious Revolution (England), 165
Goldgar, Anne, 232
Gonzaga family (Mantua), 100
Goody, Jack, 94
Google, 7, 263
Grafton, Anthony, 189, 200
Gramigna, Vincenzo, 102
Granada, 247
Graz, 250
Gresham College (London), 208
Grew, Nehemiah, 208
Grotius, Hugo, 230
Gründlicherelationen, 275
Grüninger, Johann, 160
Guarini, Battista, 101
Guarino da Verona, 169
Guicciardini, Francesco, 17, 174, 246
Guidi, Andrea, 97
Gutenberg, Johannes, 7, 8, 24, 25, 35, 149, 150, 156, 157, 189
Gwalther, Rudolf, 275

Habermas, Jürgen, 260
Hagenau, 153
Hague, the, 238
Hakewill, George, 169
Haller, Johannes, 275
Haller, Wolfgang, 275
Hamburg, 211, 254
Harrington, James, 259
Harris, Steven, 80, 203
Hartlib, Samuel, 223
Hatton, Ragnhild, 37
Head, Randolph, 132, 139, 140
Helmstedt, University of, 211
Henri II, King of France, 111
Henri IV, King of France, 111, 248
Henry VIII, King of England, 122, 136
herbalists, 234
herbals, 184
Hernández, Francisco, 204
Herold, Jürgen, 107
Herzog August Bibliothek, 180
Hevelius, Johannes, 235
Hill, Nicholas, 184
Hippocrates, 218
historia, 194, 199–202, 209, 264
Historia animalium (Gessner), 200
Historia general y natural de las Indias (Oviedo), 203
Historia Natural y Moral de las Indias (Acosta), 200
Historische Tabellen (Prussia), 127
Hobart, Michael, 5, 31
Hobbes, Thomas, 219, 234

Hofregistratur (Innsbruck), 139
Hooke, Robert, 214, 225
Hortus Indicus Malabaricus (Van Rheede), 81
Hotman, Jean, Marquis of Villiers-Saint Paul, 120
House of Commons (England), 135
House of Knowledge (Baghdad), 44
House of Lords (England), 52, 135
Howell, James, 74
Hull, Matthew, 87
humanism, 11, 98, 99, 100, 144, 160, 161, 169, 171, 173, 178, 181, 199, 200, 201, 209, 213, 229, 276
Huygens, Christiaan, 224, 235
Hyde, Thomas, 180

Iconius, Tobias Egli, 275
Iconografia (Ripa), 264
Idea de un principe político christiano en cien empresas (Saavedra Fajardo), 87
Idea del segretario (Zuchi), 108
illustrations, 160, 166–67, 198, 235
incunabula, 152, 158, 159
Index of Prohibited Books, 177
indexes, 33, 97, 136, 138, 177, 198
indulgences, 26, 27, 155–57, 165, 183
information
  Early modern understandings of, 8–10
information ages, 5–7
Ingegneri, Angelo, 23
Innsbruck, 50, 139, 246, 247
Instagram, 263
Institutes of the Christian Religion (Calvin), 275
Instructions concerning Erecting a Library (Naudé), 178
intelligence gathering, 114–17
intendants, 91, 99, 106, 121, 131, 144, 147
Internet, 7, 8, 10, 264, 265, 267, 268, 271, 279
Invention du quotidien (Certeau), 266
Isagoge Breves Prelucide ac Uberine in Anatomiam Humani Corporis (Carpi), 197
Isselt, Michael ab, 254
Istanbul, 256
Italian League (1455), 114
Italian Wars (1494-1559), 117

Jacob, Louis, 178
James I, King of England, 136
Jaume I, King of Aragon, 96
Jaume II, King of Aragon, 96
jobbing (printing), 157, 160
Johns, Adrian, 150, 259
Jonson, Ben, 185
Journal des savants, 165

Kafka, Ben, 91
Kanzlei (Austria), 137
Keene, Derek, 67
Kepler, Johannes, 199, 230
Khaldûn, Ibn, 44
Kircher, Athanasius, 85, 233
Knight, Jeffrey Todd, 265
Koninklijke Bibliotheek (the Hague), 238
Kräuterbuch (Bock), 204
Kreß (merchant house in Nuremberg), 65

l'Homme, Jean (publisher), 253
laboratories, 197
Laertius, Diogenes, 37
Lagarde, Antoine, 176
Lamarck, Jean-Baptiste Chevalier de, 207
Landi, Dandro, 143
Latour, Bruno, 18, 21
Lauber, Diebolt, 153
Lawes or Standing Orders of the East India Company, 87
lawyers, 171, 173–74, 209, 213, 220, 238, 241
Le Nain, Jean, 138
Leibniz, Gottfried, 180, 230, 235, 277–79
Leiden, University of, 188, 205, 224
Leipzig, 247, 256, 276
Leipzig, University of, 278
Leonardo da Vinci, 79
Leoniceno, Nicolò, 175
Lesenrevolution, 166
letrados, 99
Lettera a Madama Cristina (Galileo), 188
'letterocracy', 107, 109, 131, 229
letters, 20, 107–20, 141–44, 227–37
  familiar, 228
  littera clausa, 109
  modalities, 108–9, 228–29
Leuven, 142
Levant Company, 78
Leverotti, Franca, 104
Liber chronicarum (Schedel), 49
libraries, 28, 29, 80, 167–81, 236
  ecclesiastical, 152
  Islamic world, 44
  private, 162, 168, 177

Index

library catalogs, 28, 33, 172, 176, 177, 178, 179, 180, 181, 188, 236, 281
Il libro dell'arte di mercatura (Cotrugli), 65
Life of Samuel Johnson (Boswell), 279
Linnaeus, Carl, 31, 221
Linz, 50
Lipsius, Justus, 173, 230
Lisbon, 117
literacy, 5, 14, 96, 162, 168, 243, 244
Litschel, Andrea, 16
Livre de compte de prince à la manière d'Italie (Stevin), 82
livres de raison, 239, 241
Lloyds Coffee House, 259
loci communes, 214
Loci communes rerum theologicarum (Melanchthon), 215
Locke, John, 197, 218
London, 75, 76, 88, 89, 151, 165, 188, 247, 250, 255, 256, 259
London News-Letter, 256
Lorkyn, Thomas, 175
Los Cobos, Francisco de, 105
Lost or Intercepted Letter from the Prince of Orange, 253
Louis XI, King of France, 248
Louis XIII, King of France, 178, 255
Louis XIV, King of France, 83, 118, 140, 144, 145, 178, 248
Love, Harold, 41
Lowood, Henry, 204
Loyola, Ignatius, 54, 86, 141
Lübeck, 156
Lucca, 119
Ludolf of Saxony, 160
Lundin, Matthew, 240
Lüneberg, 16
Luschner, Johann, 156
Luther, Martin, 151, 159, 166, 215, 230, 274
Lyons, 33, 158, 162
Lyons, Martyn, 5

Machiavelli, Niccolò, 98
Mackenzie, D.F., 25
Madrid, 129, 130, 135, 247
Maestlin, Michael, 183
Magdeburg, Siege of (1631), 253
Mainz, 156
Malabar, 81
Malpighi, Marcello, 235
Malynes, Gerald, 123
Mamluk Empire, 45
Man and Nature (Marsh), 37

Mandeville, Bernard, 197
Mantua, 98, 100
manuscript copying, 187
manuscript publishing, 187–88
Manutius, Aldus, 182, 197
Marcaldi, Francesco, 253
marchant libraire (merchant-bookseller), 164
marginalia, 183, 198, 199, 275
Margócsy, Dániel, 80
Marks, Steven, 56
Marsh, George Perkins, 37
Martin, Henri-Jean, 31, 170
Mascranni banking firm, 144
Matthias Corvinus, King of Hungary, 170
Mattioli, Pietro, 204
Maurice of Nassau, Stadtholder, 82
Mazarin, Cardinal (Giulio Raimondo Mazzarino), 105, 140, 178
McKitterick, David, 186
McKitterick, Rosamond, 14
McLuhan, Marshall, 12, 18, 24, 40, 154, 189
Mechelen, 48
Medici, Lorenzo de', 117
medicine, 167, 196, 197, 201–2, 217–18
medieval government, 94–100
Melanchthon, Philip, 215, 276
Melis, Federigo, 246
Melis, John, 61, 65
memoirs, 237
memory, 6, 12, 13, 22, 51, 62, 120, 133, 182, 198, 209, 212, 213, 218, 237, 244, 266, 280
Mendel (merchant house in Nuremberg), 65
Merchant's Remembrance, 76
merchants, 50, 51, 56–84
  Islamic, 45
  Italy, 48, 82
Merchants Mappe of Commerce (Roberts), 78
merciers (street vendors), 185
Mercuriale, Girolamo, 217
Mercurii Ordinari Zeitung, 254
Mercurius gallobelgicus, 254
Mermet, Claude, 241
Mersenne, Marin, 232
metadata, 177, 280
Milan, 98, 100, 112, 115, 116, 117, 119, 130, 161, 174, 239, 246, 250
Miles' Coffee House (Westminster), 259
Military Revolution, 2
Miller, Peter, 240
Mizolio, Mario, 201

Index

Modena, 249
Moissac, 153
Mons, 48
Montaigne, Michel de, 21, 37, 171, 233
Montanus, Johannes Fabricius, 275
Montefeltro, Federico da, Duke of Urbino, 170
Montserrat, 156
Moore, R.I., 14
Moral Epistles to Lucilius (Seneca), 212
More, Thomas, 74
Morelli, Giovanni di Francesco, 60
Muffet, Thomas, 197
Muir, Edward, 243
Müller, Lothar, 52, 271
Munich, 254
Muqaddimah (Ibn Khaldun), 44
Muratori, Ludovico, 174
Murphy, Hannah, 199
museums, 28, 80, 207–8

Naples, 121, 247
Naudé, Gabriel, 178–79
Navagero, Bernardo, 105, 112, 114
Nelles, Paul, 151
Neue Zeitungen, 252
New Atlantis (Bacon), 41
New Spain, 124, 126, 141, 247
news, 69, 244–61, 266, 274, 275–77
 and public opinion, 257
 commercial, 70–75
 timeliness, 257–59
newsletters, 250, 251, 252, 275, 276
newspapers, 165, 190, 228, 245, 254–58, 259, 281
 Germany, 254–55
newssheets, 27, 71, 72, 161, 245, 250, 252, 256, 259, 275
Nicolucci, Giovanni Battista, 102
Nieuwe Tijdinghen, 255
Niewe Instructie ende bewwijs der looffelijcker consten des rekenboeks (Ympyn de Christoffels), 65
Nördlingen, 157
Nordman, Daniel, 144
notaries, 20, 51, 99, 101–6, 118, 136, 243, 280
notebooks, 213–15
 notebooks, blank, 64
note-taking, 51, 53, 74, 85, 172, 181, 182, 196, 198, 199, 208–21, 225, 278
Novum Organum (Bacon), 31, 40, 192, 195

numeracy, 6, 58, 63, 82, 121, 123, 128, 226, 244
Nuremberg, 49, 65, 70, 157, 175, 240, 247, 276
Nuremberg Chronicle, 157

observation, 144, 167, 192, 193, 194–99, 200, 201, 202, 203, 208, 209, 210, 212, 214, 219, 221, 222, 225, 226, 229, 231, 234, 235, 237, 241, 252, 264, 265
observationes (medicine), 201–2, 218
Observationes et curationes chirurgicae (von Hilden), 202
Observationes in Marcum Tullium Ciceronem (Mizolio), 201
Observationum et curationum chirurgicarum (van Foreest), 202
occasionnels, 252
Offray de la Mettrie, Julien, 197
Ogborn, Miles, 87, 88
Ogilvie, Brian, 203
Oldcastle, Hugh, 65
Oldenburg, Henry, 235
Oliva, Gianpaolo, 141
Olivares, Count-Duke of (Gaspar Guzmán y Pimentel), 105
On Discovery (Polydore Vergil), 149
Ong, Walter, 12, 18, 24, 217
oral communication, 11–13, 17, 18, 267
Ordinari-Boten, 247
Ornithologia (Aldrovandi), 207
Osborne, Thomas, Lord Danby, 123
Ottoman Empire, 252
Ovando, Juan de, 126
Ovid, 153
Oviedo, Gonzalo Fernández, 203
Owen, Richard, 279
Oxenstierna, Axel, 83, 118
Oxford, University of, 180, 244

Pacioli, Luca, 64, 65, 79
Padua, University of, 172
pagination, 32
Pagnini, Santi, 32
Palma, Georg, 175
pamphlets, 16, 26, 27, 154, 155, 159, 160, 161, 172, 183, 187, 188, 190, 245, 252, 253, 274
Pandechion Epistemonicon (Aldrovandi), 214
papal curia, 95
Paper
 cost, 50, 52, 53, 54
 invention, 43
 material features, 38–39, 40, 41

Index

paradoxes, 39, 42
rag, 46
varieties, 40, 53–54
Paper Memory (Lundin), 240
papermaking
  Arab, 43, 45
  English, 49
  European, 46–50
  French, 49
  Italian, 48
paperwork, 2, 20, 22, 30, 55, 61, 92, 98, 103–4, 106, 128, 145, 146, 201, 271
paratexts, 33–34, 160
parchment, 26, 43, 47, 50, 51, 52, 53, 152
Parfait Negociant (Savary), 61
Paris, 72, 74, 158, 164, 175, 247, 250
Paris, University of, 51, 153, 176
parish registers, 122
Park, Katherine, 195
Parker, Geoffrey, 128
Parlement de Paris, 95, 138, 179
Parliament (England), 122
Parma, 151
Pascal, Blaise, 226
Passau, 48
Paston family, 228
pecia system, 51, 153, 167, 176
Peiresc, Nicolas, 210–11, 223, 232
Pellegram, Andrea, 270
Pelli, Giovanni di Andrea, 239
Pepys, Samuel, 123, 180
Péquignot, Stephane, 95
Peraudi, Cardinal Raymund, 156
Pere, King of Aragon, 96
Perez del Barrio Angulo, Gabriel, 103
Peri, Giovanni Domenico, 38, 58, 67
periodical publications, 165, 190, 226, 228, 245, 249, 254, 259
Persico, Panfilo, 118
Petit, Jean (publisher), 164
Petrarch, Francesco, 271–72
Pettegree, Andrew, 159, 253, 260, 263
Petty, William, 83, 123
Pflanzmann, Jodocus, 157
Phaedrus (Plato), 266
Philip II, King of Spain, 17, 111, 117, 124–27, 128–30, 135, 142, 148, 177, 204, 247
Philip IV, King of Spain, 106
Philip VI, King of France, 51
philology, 199, 209
Philosophical Transactions (Royal Society), 225

Piazza Universale di Tutte le Professioni del Mondo, e Nobili et Ignobili (Garzoni), 149
La Piazza Universale di Tutte le Professioni del Mondo, e Nobili et Ignobili (Garzoni), 41
Il Negotiante (Peri), 38
Pinax theatrici botanici (Bauhin), 205
Pinelli, Gian Vincenzo, 172–73
Pinon, Laurent, 177
Pisa, 205
Pius V, Pope, 136
Placcius, Vincent, 213
Plantin press, 52
Plantin, Christophe, 164, 204
Plato, 33, 266
Pliny the Elder, 166, 196, 203, 204
Plutarch, 33, 181
political arithmetic, 123, 128
politics of inscription, 92, 130
Polydore Vergil, 149
Polyhistor (Solinus), 182
Pomeranz, Kenneth, 57
Poovey, Mary, 82
Pope, Alexander, 169
Populationlisten (Prussia), 127
postal services, 23, 69–70, 122, 227, 245, 250
  England, 248
  France, 248
  Germany, 247
  Italy, 245–47
  private, 247
  Spain, 247
  Tasso family, 246–47
posters, 154, 161, 190
pragmatic literacy (*pragmatische Schriftlichkeit*), 19, 58, 227
Pratique de l'orthographe françoise (Mermet), 241
Prato, 57
prayer books, 159, 165
preaching, 15
Precepts for Advancing the Sciences and Arts (Leibniz), 277
Presser, Jacob, 237
price currents, 71, 76
Principe (Nicolucci), 102
Printing Act (England), 165
printing press, 2, 6, 7, 12, 24, 25, 26, 51, 52, 122, 149–67, 192–93, 263, 272
Priscianese, Francesco, 102
Priuli, Girolamo, 116
privy councils, 105–6
  England, 105, 122
  Spain, 105

Index

Profitable Treatyse (Oldcastle), 65
Progostication Everlasting, A (Digges), 185
Proteus, 103
Ptolemy, Claudius, 196
public opinion, 260

quaternetti, 249
questionnaires, 26, 120, 190
Quintilian (Marcus Fabius Quintilianus), 29
Quorli, Giovanni, 250

Raburin-Chantal, Marie de, Marquise de Sévigné, 248
Raman, Bhavani, 89
Ramism, 84, 170, 215
Ramus, Petrus, 12, 84, 170, 215, 221
Rariorum plantorum historia (Clusius), 200
Ray, John, 205
Recchi, Nardo Antonio, 204
record-keeping, 59, 62, 64, 84, 90, 187, 201
  scientific, 133, 222–25
reference books, 32
Reformation, 29, 160, 163, 230, 238, 252, 253, 275, 276
Regensburg, 156
Relaciones geograficas, 126–27
relazioni, 112, 119, 250, 267
religious publishing, 156, 160, 165
Renaudot, Théophraste, 255, 256
reportisti (Venice), 72, 250
Republic of Letters, 36, 144, 171, 173, 181, 198, 229, 231–37, 266, 275
requêtes du palais (France), 95
Reynolds, Joshua, 279
Richelieu, Cardinal (Armand Jean de Plessis), 105, 140, 255
ricordanze (family account books), 239–40
ricordanze (list of transactions), 60
Ricordi (Guicciardini), 17
Rieter family (Nuremberg), 240
Rieter, Peter, 240
Ripa, Cesare, 264
Ritzsch, Timotheaus, 256
Roberts, Lewes, 78
Roger II, King of Sicily, 47
Rogers, Kenny, 37
Rome, 72, 85, 87, 98, 112, 115, 116, 117, 121, 141, 182, 204, 246, 247, 249, 250, 260, 269, 275
Rosa, Maria, 93
Ross, Alan, 236
Rostock, University of, 211, 236
Rouchon, Olivier, 143
Royal Exchange (London), 75

Royal Society, 208, 224–25, 234–35
  Correspondence Committee, 234
rubricari (Venice), 119
Rudolf II, Holy Roman Emperor, 247
Ruiz, Simon, 60

Sacchini, Francesco, 213
Saladin, 44
Salamanca, University of, 168
Salmuth, Heinrich, 214
Sánchez, Francisco, 272
Sánchez, Luis, 126
Sansovino, Francesco, 102
Sardella, Pierre, 246
Savary, Jacques, 60, 61
Scaliger, Joseph, 173, 212
scarselle, 246
Schaffer, Simon, 234
Schedel, Hartmann, 49, 157
Scheurl, Christoph, 276
Schiffman, Zachary, 5, 31
Scientific Revolution, 2, 10, 191–94, 226, 234
Scott, James, 109
scribes, medieval, 153
scriptoria, 152, 153
scriptural economy (Michel de Certeau), 21
scripture, 18, 32
  organization, 32
secretaries, 19, 20, 23, 30, 32, 44, 93, 101–6, 111, 137, 143, 280
  ambassadorial, 120
  treatises, 101–3
secretaries of state, 104–6
Secretario qualificato, il (Parnell), 103
Secretario y Consegero de Señores y Ministros (Barrio Angulo), 103
Secretario, il (Capaccio), 103, 120
Secretario, il (Guarini), 101
'secular scriptorium', 18–24, 53, 172
Seifert, Arno, 200
Seignelay, Marquis de (Jean-Baptiste Antoine de Colbert), 140, 145
Seneca, Lucius Annaeus, 179, 212
Sepulchretum sive Anatomica practica (Bonet), 218
Settling the Postage for England, Scotland and Ireland Act (1657), 248
Seville, 177, 204, 247, 252
Sforza dukes of Milan, 246
Sforza, Francesco, Duke of Milan, 98, 100, 115, 117
Shaffer, Simon, 84
Shapin, Steven, 191, 234

Index

Shirky, Clay, 266
Shorter, Alfred, 50
Sic et Non (Abelard), 27
Silvestri, Alessandro, 97
Simancas (Spanish royal archive), 135
Simonetta, Cicco, 112
simultaneity, 257
Slack, Paul, 123
Small Catechism (Luther), 159
Smith, Woodruff, 76
societies, scientific, 193
Society of Jesus, 54, 85–87, 120, 141–42, 144, 228, 233
Solinus, Caius Iulius, 182
Soll, Jacob, 145, 211
Sombart, Werner, 79
sommari, 119
Sopra le nuove (Franzesi), 260–61
speciation, 221
Speculum vitae Christi (Ludolf of Saxony), 160
Spiritual Exercises (Loyola), 86
Sprat, Thomas, 224
St. Gallen, 275
Stallybrass, Peter, 26, 154, 183
State Paper Office (England), 130, 136, 140
stationers, 162, 185, 188
Stationers' Company (England), 185, 188
statistics, 128
Stelluti, Francesco, 204
Sternberg, Giora, 146
Stevin, Simon, 82
Stieler, Kaspar, 254
Stock, Brian, 13
Stolzenberg, Daniel, 233
Strasbourg, 156, 160, 254, 276
Stromer, Ulman, 49
strong ties, 234
Sturm, Jacob, 276
Sturm, Johannes, 84, 276
Sully, Duke of, Maximilien de Béthune, 140
Summa de arithmetica (Pacioli), 64, 65, 79
Summit, Jennifer, 28
Superintendent General of the Posts (France), 248
Sybilline Prophecies, 157
Sylva Sylvarum (Bacon), 41
Systema naturae (Linnaeus), 31

Table books, 70
Tafelen van Interest (Stevin), 82
Tägebücher, 239
Tantalus, 282
Tasso, Gabriele, 246

Tasso, Torquato, 149
Tate, John, 49
taverns, 260
taxation, 94, 95, 106, 121, 131
taxonomy, 6, 27, 30–34, 84, 145, 196, 198, 203, 205, 208, 221, 266
Terence (Publius Terentius Afer), 161
Tesoro Messicano, 204
Tesoro politico (Ventura attr.), 122
textbooks, 178
That the Goods of Mankind May Be Much Increased by the Naturalists' Insight into the Trades (Boyle), 78
Theophrastus, 196, 203, 205
Thirty Years' War, 118, 252, 253, 254
Thomas, Keith, 17
Thomson, Erik, 82
Thurzo family, 250
Tilly, Charles, 91
Tilly, Count of (Johann Tserclaes), 253
Toledo, 46, 247
Toulouse, University of, 176
Tournefort, Joseph de, 205
Traicté des plus belles bibliothèques publiques et particulieres (Jacob), 178
Trattato del modo di tenere il libro doppio domestico col suo essemplare (Flori), 86
Trebon, Jean, 33
Trent, Council of, 165
Trumbull, William, 256
Tudor Revolution in Government, 123, 135
Twain, Mark, 270
Twelfth-Century Renaissance, 161

Ummayad dynasty, 46
universities, 51, 152, 167, 171, 175, 193
university students, 175–76
Urbino, 170
Ussher, Archbishop James, 229
Utopia (More), 74

Vadian, Joachim, 171, 275
Valencia, 170
Valladolid, 60
Valor Eclesiasticus (Cromwell), 122
Van Aitzema, Lieuwe (Dutch diplomat and spy), 74
Van der Woude, Ad, 75
Van Foreest, Pieter, 202
Van Goens, Rijklof Michael, 238
Van Hamme, Petrus Thomas, 141
Van Rheede, Jan Hendrick Adriaan, 81
Vatican Archive, 136
Vázquez de Leca, Mateo, 129
Vega, Lope de, 168, 229

vellum, 26, 50, 51
Venice, 47, 65, 70, 72, 98, 112, 115, 116, 117, 119, 121, 151, 158, 175, 182, 185, 250, 258
Ventura, Comino, 122
Verhoeven, Abraham, 255
Verney family (Buckinghamshire), 242
Verschriftlichung (textualization), 241
Vesalius, Andreas, 166, 199
Vienna, 70, 134, 171, 250
Virgil (Publius Vergilius Maro), 161
Vismann, Cornelia, 139
Vitruvian Man (Leonardo), 79
Vittorino da Feltre, 169
VOC. *See* Dutch East India Company
Voet, Léon, 52
Von Grimm, Melchior, 146
Von Hilden, Wilhelm Fabry, 202
Vossius, Gerardus, 229
Vostre, Simon, 164

Walsingham, Francis, 138
Ward, John (pastor), 16
Waser, Johann Heinrich, 136
waste-books, 41, 81, 199, 214
Watermarks, 54
Watson, Thomas (Puritan preacher), 86
Watts, John, 94
weak ties, 234, 235
Weber, Max, 92
Weinsberg, Hermann, 240–41, 242
Weitenauer, Ignatius, 280
Welser family (Augsburg), 65
Westminster, 259
Wharman, Dror, 165

Whitehall Palace, 136
Whitson, James, 76
Wick, Hans Jacob, 250
Wickiana, 250
Wilding, Nick, 188
Williams, Megan, 110
wills, 237
Wilson, Thomas, 136, 140
Wisselbank (Amsterdam), 74
Wittenberg, 159, 276
Woolf, Daniel, 15
Woolgar, Steve, 18
Wright, Alex, 6
Wunderkammern, 28, 208
Württemberg, 180

Xátiva, 46

Yates, Frances, 6
Yax, Maggie, 136
Ympyn de Christoffels, Yan, 65
YouTube, 268

Zaar-Görgens, Maria, 51
Zedelmaier, Helmut, 177
Zeitungs Lust und Nutz, 254
Zentralbibliothek Zurich, 275
zibaldoni, 64
zoology, 166, 205
Zorzi, Marino, 175
Zucchi, Bartolomeo, 108
Zurich, 136, 163, 177, 182, 250, 273, 274, 275, 276, 277
  archive, 136
Zwingli, Huldrych, 163, 230, 273, 274